ESSENTIAL
U.S. HISTORY

Paul M. Roberts
Paula A. Franklin

AMSCO SCHOOL PUBLICATIONS, INC.

315 Hudson Street, New York, N.Y. 10013

Contributing Authors: Gerard J. Pelisson, Lillian Forman

REVIEWERS:
Jason Brown, History Instructor, Saint Andrew's School, Boca Raton, Florida

Paul Tremel, Director, Adult High School, Seminole Community College, Sanford, Florida

Lisa Valentine, U.S. History Teacher, Harding University High School, Charlotte, North Carolina

Lisa Yamasaki, Teacher of High School Subjects, Davis Adult School, Davis, California

Composition: **Northeastern Graphic, Inc.**

Cover design: **Meghan J. Shupe**

Art: **Hadel Studio**

Please visit our Web site at:
www.amscopub.com

When ordering this book, please specify:
R 39 P or ESSENTIAL U.S. HISTORY, PAPERBACK
or
R 39 H or ESSENTIAL U.S. HISTORY, HARDBOUND

ISBN: 978-1-56765-643-5
       NYC Item 56765-643-4 (Paperback edition)
ISBN: 978-1-56765-644-2
       NYC Item 56765-644-1 (Hardbound edition)

Printed in the United States of America

1 2 3 4 5 6 7 8 9 10   13 12 11 10 09 08 07

PREFACE

You know that the United States is one of the great nations of the modern world. But you may not know all the reasons for its greatness. To understand our nation, you need to be aware of events that influenced its development 10 years ago, 50 years ago, 200 years ago, and more. The main purpose of *Essential U.S. History* is to acquaint you with America's past so that you can better understand the American present and be better equipped to play a part in our nation's future.

In this text you will learn:

- how democratic institutions have developed since colonial times
- how a nation of only 13 states on the Atlantic coast expanded westward to the Pacific in less than 75 years
- what contributions were made to American life by groups from many parts of the world
- what policies our government has adopted to maintain U.S. leadership in world affairs
- how new technologies have transformed American society.

There is more. But the above list suggests why knowledge of history is vitally important to all Americans.

This text tells the story of our nation's past in clear, simple language organized around a chronological framework. A number of features will make your study easier. *Essential U.S. History* contains the following features:

- **Content richness.** The text underlines the contributions of regional cultures and various ethnic groups to the American way of life. U.S. leaders and other key figures are presented in their historical contexts. Contemporary issues and problems are traced from their historical origins.
- **Standards based.** The text has been developed in conformity to the curricular and assessment requirements common to several states.
- **Test preparation.** To assist you in developing the skills necessary for standardized and nonstandardized exams, a wide range of exercises appear within and at the end of each

chapter. To help you remember what you have read, there are helpful *section-review questions* at the end of every section. Among them are *identification exercises* and thought-provoking *discussion questions*. Included within the chapter are series of skills questions relating to the maps, graphs, and tables that accompany them. The Chapter Review section at the end of every chapter contains matching exercises, multiple-choice questions, essay questions, and document-based questions (DBQs). Some Chapter Review sections also contain chronology or map exercises.

- **Illustrations.** The text contains many *photographs* and *historical prints* to give you a better understanding of the issues and events of the past. Many *maps* are provided to help you locate the events you are reading about. Numerous *tables* and *charts* offer a bird's-eye view of developments that were affecting the nation at different times. *Political cartoons* illustrate some of the key issues that concerned various groups of Americans.

- **Reference section.** You can also acquire a useful social studies vocabulary by regularly turning to the *glossary* in the back of the book. The items listed and defined there provide an A-to-Z summary of all the important terms you will encounter in your study of American history. *Internet links* and an *index* will provide you help in understanding the material in the rest of the book.

America's greatness is built on a remarkable history of struggle and achievement. As the authors of this text, we feel privileged to present that history to you.

Paul M. Roberts
Paula A. Franklin

CONTENTS

Preface *iii*

List of Maps, Diagrams, and Graphs *vi*

Unit I   **The Peopling of the Americas**

Chapter 1   The Development of Early Cultures in North America *1*

Chapter 2   Europeans in North America *18*

Unit II   **An Independent Nation**

Chapter 3   Seeds of Independence *41*

Chapter 4   Difficulties With England Lead to Revolution *61*

Chapter 5   Forming a New Government *85*

Unit III   **Growth of the Republic**

Chapter 6   Federalists and Democratic-Republicans in Power *99*

Chapter 7   Expansion and Progress *123*

Chapter 8   The Age of Jackson *142*

Unit IV   **Division and Reunion**

Chapter 9   Expansionism and Sectionalism *161*

Chapter 10   The Civil War and Reconstruction *181*

Unit V   **The Nation Transformed**

Chapter 11   The Age of Industrialization *203*

Chapter 12   The Last Frontier, Farmers, and Politics *223*

Chapter 13   The Progressive Era *248*

Chapter 14   Overseas Expansion and World War I *263*

Unit VI   **Trials and Hope**

Chapter 15   The Twenties and Thirties *287*

Chapter 16   World War II *312*

Unit VII   **Postwar Concerns**

Chapter 17   The Cold War *333*

Chapter 18   Prosperity, Idealism, and Commitment *352*

Unit VIII   **Challenges of the Modern Era**

Chapter 19   Political Concerns in a Troubled Period *377*

Chapter 20   Political Partisanship and the War on Terrorism *397*

Glossary *419*

Internet Sources in U.S. History *427*

Index *431*

Photo Acknowledgments *441*

MAPS, DIAGRAMS, AND GRAPHS

Routes to the Americas During the Ice Age   *2*

Native-American Culture Areas of North America   *6*

Early European Explorers   *20*

European Settlements in North America, 1640   *23*

The Regions of English North America   *34*

Important Events in European Exploration of North America   *37*

English Colonial Population, by Race, 1660–1780   *42*

Patterns of Triangular Trade   *47*

The French and Indian War, 1754–1763   *63*

North America After the Treaty of Paris, 1763   *64*

New York Campaigns, June–October 1777   *76*

The Revolutionary War in the South, 1778–1781   *78*

North America After the Treaty of Paris, 1783   *79*

Four Ways to Amend the U.S. Constitution   *92*

The Louisiana Purchase and the Lewis and Clark Expedition   *110*

The War of 1812   *114*

Acquisition of Florida   *116*

Settling the Old Southwest   *124*

A Typical Township, Land Ordinance of 1785   *125*

Percent Distribution of U.S. White Population, by Nationality, 1790   *133*

The Republic of Texas, 1836–1845   *135*

Routes to the Far West   *136*

U.S. War With Mexico, 1846–1848   *164*

Territorial Growth to 1853   *165*

The Free-Slave Balance, 1854   *172*

The Secession of States and Territories From the Union   *182*

The Civil War in the East   *184*

Western and Southern Theaters of War   *189*

Military Reconstruction of Former Confederate States   *195*

Immigration to the United States, 1840–1919   *213*

The West and the Railroads   *227*

New States and Native-American Reservations, 1864–1890   *231*

Urban and Rural Populations, 1870–1920   *240*

The Structure of the Federal Reserve System   *256*

U.S. Possessions in the Pacific, 1899   *264*

U.S. Involvement in the Caribbean Region   *271*

Allies and Central Powers, 1915   *274*

Western Front and Allied Drives to Victory, 1918   *277*

Europe After World War I   *280*

Gross Domestic Product, 1929–1945   *299*

Unemployment, 1929–1945   *299*

The Dust Bowl   *304*

Axis Aggression in Europe, 1935–1939   *317*

Allied Campaigns in Europe and North Africa, 1942–1945   *322*

World War II in the Pacific, 1942–1945   *326*

European Military Alliances, 1982   *339*

The Korean War   *343*

War in Southeast Asia, 1964–1976   *370*

Gross Domestic Product Since 1940   *410*

UNIT I

THE PEOPLING OF THE AMERICAS

CHAPTER 1

The Development of Early Cultures in North America

The year 1776 marks the birth of the United States as an independent nation. But that date does not represent the starting point of America's history. In fact, the American past is rooted in events that took place long before the United States existed.

HUNTERS OF THE ICE AGE

Many thousands of years ago, the continents of North and South America had no human inhabitants. The Western Hemisphere was an immense wilderness. It was the home of mammoths, mastodons, saber-toothed tigers, and other animals that are now extinct. The Earth was experiencing an *Ice Age,* an era when a gigantic glacier covered much of North America and Europe. The last major Ice Age lasted from about 25,000 to about 10,000 years ago.

1. Migration From Asia.   During this Ice Age, there were several major waves of people migrating in different ways from Asia to North America.

   a. By land.   The level of the oceans fell because so much water froze into ice. As ocean waters receded, they exposed a piece of land between East Asia and western Alaska that formed a kind of bridge linking Asia and North America. Bands of Asians wandered east across this land bridge. These *nomadic* Asian hunters and their families were probably tracking herds of wild animals.

1

b. By sea.   Asians could have ventured around the northern rim of the Pacific Ocean to North America in small, skin-covered boats. They could have survived by fishing and hunting seals and other sea mammals.

READING A MAP

Routes to the Americas During the Ice Age

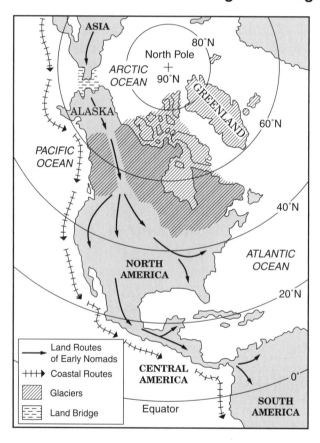

1. In what general direction did nomads from Asia travel after they passed through Alaska?

2. Why do you suppose that glaciers did not cover the lower part of North America?

3. The coastal routes of the Asian nomads were along which body of water?

4. According to the map, the nomads reached South America first at about what degree of latitude? (*a*) 80°N (*b*) 45°N (*c*) 20°N (*d*) 10°N.

After reaching ice-free parts of lower North America, the early migrants continued south and east. New generations of American-born *hunter-gatherers* spread out until they occupied most of North, Central, and South America and the Caribbean islands.

2. Earliest Americans. The early people of the Americas lived in many different groups and spoke many different languages. Each group had a name for itself—in most cases, one that meant simply "the people."

Later settlers of the Western Hemisphere called the first Americans "Indians"—a name given them by the Italian explorer Christopher Columbus on his arrival in America in 1492. He so gave them that name because he thought he had landed in a part of Asia known as the Indies. The term continued in use even after people realized Columbus's mistake. Today, descendants of North America's first settlers are frequently identified as Native Americans.

In American history, the era before the arrival of Columbus is called the *Pre-Columbian Period.* It covers the huge span of years going back to the first Ice-Age hunters. Our knowledge of pre-Columbian times is limited because early Native Americans had no form of writing and thus left no written records.

The first Americans had a very simple *culture* (way of life). Since spear points have been found in various places, we know that the people used stone-tipped spears to hunt animals. They may also have *domesticated* (tamed) dogs to help them in the hunt. They wore clothing made of animal skins, and they probably knew how to make fire.

DEFINE OR IDENTIFY: Ice Age, nomadic, hunter-gatherer, culture, domesticated.

CRITICAL THINKING: Do you think Asians could have come to America before the Ice Age?

AGRICULTURE AND OTHER ADVANCES

As time passed, Native Americans slowly developed a more complex culture. They invented the bow and arrow and learned how to make a wide variety of stone tools. Some groups fished as well as hunted. Most became expert at gathering wild plants, seeds, and fruit.

Their most important advance was the discovery of agriculture. More than 5,000 years ago, some Native-American peoples discovered that food could be grown and harvested, not simply gathered from wild plants. We do not know exactly where farming began in North America. It may have started in Mexico and spread from there. Perhaps it started in several different places in North America at roughly the same time.

One of the first important plants grown by Native Americans was *maize* (corn). This plant, native to the Western Hemisphere, was developed from wild types into several different varieties. Other important Native American crops were beans, potatoes, peppers, pumpkins, cotton, and tobacco.

1. Changes in Native-American Life.   Farming brought about fundamental changes in the way Native Americans lived. It led to the following: (*1*) a more dependable food supply; (*2*) settlement in permanent locations instead of movement from place to place in search of food; (*3*) the banding together of families to form small farming villages; (*4*) the development of such crafts as pottery, basketry, and weaving; (*5*) the expansion of some villages into cities; and (*6*) in cities, the organization of formal government, the emergence of different social classes, and the growth of trade and commerce. Few cities developed in the lands we now call the United States.

2. Contrasts With Other Cultures.   Unlike the peoples of other continents, pre-Columbian Native Americans had no horses, cattle, oxen, sheep, goats, or pigs. This meant that the Native Americans' supply of food was limited. More important, there were no *draft animals,* such as horses and oxen, to plow fields and carry heavy loads.

Mining and metalworking were also slower to develop in the Americas than in other parts of the world. Several Native-American peoples used gold, silver, and copper to make jewelry and small ceremonial objects. But there was no large-scale mining of iron for tools or weapons.

3. Population.   In pre-Columbian times, North and South America were not densely populated. Scholars disagree on the total population. Many believe that there were only about 20 million people in the Americas, while other scholars say the number might be 50 million, or more. Of this number, the area that is now the United States was inhabited by some 2 to 10 million people.

4. Varied Languages and Cultures.   The landforms, resources, and climates of the Western Hemisphere are extremely varied. Native Americans adapted to this variety as they migrated from region to region. Gradually, they developed different cultures suited to their surroundings.

At the same time, a great number of languages developed as one group separated from another. Altogether, more than 1,500 languages were spoken in the pre-Columbian Americas. About 200 of this total were spoken in the region north of Mexico.

Scholars classify languages into large groupings called *language families*. (All the languages within a given family have similar grammar and word origins.) In North America, for example, the Algonquian language family consisted of more than 25 languages. These included Pequot and Narragansett on the Atlantic coast, Shawnee and Ojibwa in the Midwest, and Cheyenne and Blackfoot on the Great Plains.

NATIVE CULTURES OF NORTH AMERICA

In the part of the Americas that eventually became the United States and Canada, pre-Columbian culture was quite varied. This book discusses seven culture areas in North America. A *culture area* is a large region inhabited by people who share a similar way of life. (As used in this chapter, "North America" refers to the part of the continent north of Mexico. Locations of culture areas are given in terms of their present-day names.)

1. The Southwest.   The Southwest culture area included most of Arizona and New Mexico, plus parts of neighboring states and northernmost Mexico. The Southwest is a warm, dry, generally flat land. There are also some mountains and valleys, and large, flat-topped rock formations. The area supported a fairly large population of Native Americans from earliest times.

a. The Pueblo.   *Pueblo* is the Spanish word for "village." This name is applied to one group of Native Americans because they were living in villages when Spaniards arrived. They had a long history of settled community life.

Ruins of ancient settlements have been found in many parts of the Southwest. Some of the buildings were made of earth and logs, others of stone or *adobe* (sun-dried brick). Many were constructed at ground level, while some stood on ledges in steep cliffs. Several were like apartment houses, with many levels. The earliest "apartment house" ruins date back to A.D. 700. For a combination of reasons (climate

READING A MAP

Native-American Culture Areas of North America

1. In which culture area did the Nez Percé live?

2. Which Native Americans were more dependent on the sea for their food, the Chinook or the Pawnee?

3. Locate and name a Native-American culture area that includes the Great Lakes.

4. Which culture area bordered both the Gulf of Mexico and the Atlantic Ocean?

5. Name a Native-American group of the Southwest culture area.

change, droughts, overpopulation, deforestation, wars), the inhabitants abandoned their cliff houses by the late 13th century.

The descendants of these people, the Pueblo, moved elsewhere and built simpler multifamily dwellings, usually at ground level. These complexes were from one to five stories high. About 30 of them still exist, mostly in northern New Mexico.

The Pueblo were excellent craftsworkers and peaceful farmers. They developed special methods for growing crops on their dry land, including large *irrigation* systems. The Pueblo grew mainly corn, beans, and squash. Surpluses were stored, to be used when crops failed. After the Spaniards brought sheep to the New World, raising livestock became an important part of Pueblo life. The Pueblo made beautifully decorated pottery, baskets, blankets, and jewelry.

Pueblo life was regulated by an elaborate series of religious ceremonies. Each season had its own spirits and rituals, and every village formed organizations devoted to carrying out the proper observances. The Pueblo believed in *kachinas,* ancestral spirits that acted as messengers between gods and humans.

b. Navajo and Apache.   Two other groups of Native Americans in the Southwest, the Navajo and Apache, were latecomers to

The Pueblo were known for multistoried structures such as these in Canyon de Chelly, Arizona.

the region. They arrived sometime after A.D. 1200, probably from the north.

The Navajo built *hogans* (eight-sided houses of earth and wood) near Pueblo settlements. From the Pueblo, the Navajo learned how to weave and make pottery. With the introduction of sheep, Navajos took up sheepherding and blanket weaving. They also became fine silversmiths.

Unlike the Navajo, the Apache had little interest in settling down in permanent villages. Most of them were nomadic hunters. They were also fierce fighters who preyed on the farms and livestock of their neighbors.

DEFINE OR IDENTIFY: draft animal, language family, culture area, adobe, irrigation.

CRITICAL THINKING: How did the Pueblo manage to grow crops on land that is now arid?

---

2. The Southeast.   The Southeastern culture area extended from the Gulf of Mexico northward to Kentucky and from eastern Texas eastward to the Atlantic Ocean. The people of the Southeast had a long history. Beginning about 700 B.C., large earth mounds were built in many parts of the Mississippi River Valley. (They were located in the Eastern Woodlands culture area as well as in the Southeast.) Some of the mounds contained burials. Others had temples on top. The most unusual mounds were built in the shape of animals, such as birds and turtles. The mounds have yielded beautiful carvings and jewelry made of copper, stone, and mica. Many of these arts and crafts are decorated with designs like those found on objects in Mexico. It seems clear that there was trade with people in Mexico.

When European settlers arrived, Native Americans in the area knew nothing about the origins of the mounds. For a long time, people thought that a mysterious race of "Mound Builders" had once existed and then died out. We now know that an earlier group of Native Americans built the mounds.

At the time Europeans came to the Southeast, Native Americans were living in simple villages surrounded by log fences. Since the climate was mild, the people preferred light, airy houses—sometimes just a roof supported by poles. Clothing was simple, too. Southeastern peoples hunted, fished, and farmed. Their main crop was corn. They also grew potatoes, melons, tobacco, and sunflowers. For travel along the many streams, rivers, and swamps of the region, Southeasterners used cane rafts and dugout canoes.

Groups of this region included the Creek, Choctaw, Chickasaw, Cherokee, and Seminole. It was common for groups and villages to form alliances. One of the most important of these alliances was the Creek Confederacy, which linked more than 50 settlements in Alabama and Georgia.

3. The Eastern Woodlands. Extending from Kentucky into Canada and from the Atlantic coast to beyond the Mississippi River was the Eastern Woodlands culture area. Many of its groups—from the Penobscot in the east to the Ojibwa in the west—spoke languages in the Algonquian language family. Most others spoke Iroquoian languages.

a. Woodlands culture. Eastern Woodlands peoples were hunters and farmers. For much of their food, they depended on deer, bear, wild fowl, and fish. They also raised corn, beans, squash, and tobacco. From the sap of maple trees, Eastern Woodlands peoples made syrup and sugar. Those in the upper Great Lakes region harvested wild rice.

Nearly all Eastern Woodlands tribes lived in villages. The most common kind of dwelling was the dome-shaped *wigwam* covered with bark. Iroquois lived in big, rectangular *longhouses,* often covered with bark. Each one could house many families.

b. Political organization. Most Eastern Woodlands peoples had a simple, democratic political organization. There were no hereditary rulers. People chose a good military leader or someone in close touch with the spirit world as chief. Usually a group of such chiefs made the major decisions for a tribe.

A notable political achievement was the Iroquois Confederacy, or Five Nations, formed around 1570. Its members were the Mohawk, Oneida, Onondaga, Cayuga, and Seneca of central New York. They were later joined by the Tuscarora of North Carolina to form the Six Nations. Although each group was independent in local affairs, a central governing body of *sachems* decided matters of common interest. Older women chose the sachems to represent their nation. (Iroquois women played an important role, for society was organized around the "fireside"—a woman and her children.) The Iroquois Confederacy dominated much of the Eastern Woodlands region for 200 years.

c. Religion. All Native-American groups believed in a supernatural force inhabiting all living things, human and nonhuman. The Native Americans tried to communicate with this power through visions and dreams. The Eastern Woodlands peoples, like Native Americans elsewhere, practiced many rituals and ceremonies. Some had to

Iroquois longhouses.

do with planting, growing, and harvesting crops. Others marked important events in a person's life, such as birth, puberty, marriage, and death. There were also rituals for driving out evil spirits, for victory in war, and for a successful hunt.

d. The Woodlands legacy.   Inhabitants of the Eastern Woodlands were the first Native Americans whom English settlers met. Thus, many Eastern Woodlands words for distinctively American plants and animals entered the English language. Examples are hickory, tamarack, chipmunk, moose, opossum, raccoon, and skunk. English settlers also learned about many customs common to most North American peoples. Such traditions included ceremonial smoking (passing the peace pipe) and burying a hatchet (tomahawk) to signal peace, holding councils of elders (powwows), and carrying babies (papooses) in cradleboards.

4. The Plains.   The Native Americans that many cowboy movies have made familiar are those of the Great Plains. Their distinctive feather headdresses, their skill on horseback, and their bravery as fighters made them famous all over the world. Plains peoples inhabited a large territory between the Mississippi River and the Rocky Mountains. Much of this region was dry and relatively treeless and was covered with tall grass.

Centuries ago, the Plains peoples, like those of the Southeast and Eastern Woodlands, depended on both hunting and farming. Unlike these other groups, however, Plains peoples were nomadic. Most of the year, they lived in solid *earth lodges,* built partly underground along riverbanks in the eastern plains. Nearby, the community grew corn, beans, squash, and other crops. But in the summer, they moved westward into the area called the High Plains, where they hunted buffalo. There they lived in cone-shaped *tepees* made of animal skin.

Vast herds of buffalo once lived on the plains. (As late as 1850, there were more than 20 million of them.) From buffalo, the Plains peoples obtained meat, fur (for robes), hides (for clothing, tepees, and shields), and bones (for tools). Buffalo sinews were used as bowstrings, their hooves and horns were heated to make glue, and their droppings were burned as fuel.

a. The coming of the horse. Hunting buffalo on foot required special skills. One method Native Americans used was to disguise themselves in buffalo robes and sneak up on a herd. Another was to stampede the animals into pens or over a cliff. But days or weeks might go by before scouts could track down a herd.

Then about 1700, things changed. By this time, Spaniards had settled in Mexico and the Southwest, bringing horses with them. Some of the horses escaped, and others were traded. Early in the 18th century, Plains peoples started to acquire horses in large numbers. Now buffalo hunting became much easier. Many Native Americans gave up their farming life and stayed permanently on the High Plains as nomadic hunters. Those who did so include the best-known Plains tribes: the Cheyenne, Blackfoot, Crow, Comanche, and Arapaho. Other tribes, including the Mandan, Pawnee, and Omaha, kept to the old ways. The Sioux (or Dakota) split up; some lived as part-time farmers in Minnesota, while others moved westward onto the plains.

b. Life on the plains. Plains peoples moved about in groups of a few families, settling here and there within a large tribal territory. (Like most Native Americans, Plains people did not believe in individual land ownership. They did, however, regard certain regions as tribal homelands.) Several bands might assemble once or twice a year for a council or special celebration. As in most other culture areas, chiefs who had proved themselves as hunters, fighters, or spiritual leaders made the important decisions.

Fighting was important to Plains peoples. They often conducted raids to steal horses. But the most important reason for fighting was to gain honor. As a measure of honor, individuals *counted coup:* They received credit for certain brave deeds such as touching an enemy in combat without being hurt or downing a buffalo with one shot.

Seeking spiritual help, Plains people might go alone to a special place and fast for several days, hoping that a spirit would appear and predict the future. The spirit could also advise the vision-seeker to get help from a special animal or sacred object. Some people were noted for their ability to get in touch with the spirit world. They were called upon to heal illnesses or cast spells on enemies. Europeans called such gifted Native Americans medicine men (although women might also perform these functions).

5. The Great Basin. Small nomadic bands of Ute, Paiute, and Shoshone lived in the Great Basin, the partly barren region between the Rockies and the Sierra Nevada. This area included Utah, Nevada, and Colorado. Here, large game was scarce, and the land was too dry for farming.

Great Basin peoples gathered the nuts of the piñon tree and ground them into meal. They also caught grasshoppers, hunted small animals, collected wild seeds, and dug for edible roots. Shelter was provided by caves or by brush huts called *wickiups*. Basketry developed into a distinctive art form. Women wove reeds and plant fibers so tightly together that their baskets could hold water. They cooked in the baskets by dropping in heated stones until the contents simmered.

6. California. Many small tribes—among them the Hupa, Modoc, and Pomo—inhabited the coastal section and interior valleys of California. California tribes lived apart from one another and spoke a variety of related languages. A mild climate, abundant food, and favorable environment enabled them to live simply and peaceably. They made brush huts or tepee-like bark shelters.

Native Americans of California made the finest baskets in America. Women wove colored grasses, fibers, and feathers to form artistic containers with intricate designs.

Since California Native Americans did not farm, they relied largely on acorns for nutrition. Acorns were shelled, ground, and soaked with water to remove the bitter, poisonous tannic acid. After being dried, roasted, and ground again, acorn meal was cooked as porridge or baked as bread. The Californians also fished, hunted deer and other game, and gathered fruits and seeds.

7. The Northwest Coast. Along the northern Pacific stretched a narrow region with a very special culture. Here, in western Oregon, Washington, and British Columbia, the forests were full of game and the waters teemed with fish. The Northwest Coast groups, from the Tlingits in the north to the Chinooks in the south, had no need to grow their own food.

Depending on their location, Northwest Coast peoples relied on various staples. Those living along the rivers could catch enough salmon during the spawning season to last them the rest of the year. (The fish were dried or preserved in oil.) Those close to the ocean caught halibut, cod, herring, and shellfish. Group hunts for sea lions, otters, porpoises, and whales were organized as well. Northwest Coast peoples also gathered berries and hunted game in nearby woods.

Most Native Americans of the Northwest Coast lived in villages of wooden houses with slanting roofs. Built of posts, beams, and planks, each house was generally large enough for dozens of people. In front of each house stood the family totem pole. This tall, wooden post was carved with animal, bird, and human figures sacred to the family.

Skilled woodworkers, the Northwest Coast peoples could make from one tree a boat up to 60 feet long. They carved handsome, watertight storage boxes and richly ornamented masks. Other Northwest crafts included hammering copper into thin, shield-shaped ornaments and weaving decorative blankets from bark and animal hair.

Most of the gods of the Northwest Coast peoples were associated with animals of the region. In many of their ceremonies, these Native Americans acted out roles as animal spirits. Wearing fantastic costumes and giant masks, dancers flew through the air (suspended by

Totem poles in Kitoanga, British Columbia. They are representative of the totem poles of all Northwest Coast Native Americans.

cords) or appeared from the floor (out of trapdoors). By speaking through hidden reeds, some of the actors even made their voices seem to come from flames.

Wealth and social position were extremely important to the Northwest peoples. Society was divided into nobles, common people, and slaves. (Slaves were taken during raids on other tribes.) Nobles competed keenly to improve their social standing. This competition gave rise to the *potlatch*. The main purpose of this celebration was to show off wealth by giving away or destroying valuable possessions. Guests and rivals would then have to hold even more costly potlatches, or else be publicly disgraced.

DEFINE OR IDENTIFY: wigwam, longhouse, sachem, tepee, earth lodge, wickiup.

CRITICAL THINKING: The first group of Europeans that the Eastern Woodlands people along the Atlantic Coast in Massachusetts saw were probably fishermen. What do you think the two groups thought of each other?

Chapter Review

MATCHING TEST

Column A
1. maize
2. totem pole
3. counting coup
4. kachina
5. potlatch

Column B
a. a spirit; a doll that represents a spirit
b. an item that honors one's ancestors
c. ceremony to display and give away wealth
d. a food grown by many Native Americans
e. an act of bravery among Plains braves

MULTIPLE-CHOICE TEST

1. The ancestors of today's Native Americans probably came from (*a*) East Asia (*b*) Europe (*c*) Africa (*d*) India.

2. A land bridge connected Asia and North America until about (*a*) 8000 B.C. (*b*) 200 B.C. (*c*) the time of the birth of Christ (*d*) A.D. 1500.

3. One of the most important crops native to the Western Hemisphere was (*a*) wheat (*b*) corn (*c*) barley (*d*) rye.

4. The "apartment house" dwellings of the ancient Southwest were built by (*a*) ancestors of the Pueblos (*b*) the Navajos (*c*) the Apaches (*d*) the Spaniards.

5. Native-American groups in the Southeast (*a*) lived in pueblos (*b*) caught salmon (*c*) built large ceremonial mounds (*d*) never farmed.

6. The culture area that contributed such Native-American words as *chipmunk, hickory, moose,* and *raccoon* to the English language was the (*a*) Eastern Woodlands (*b*) Southwest (*c*) Northwest Coast (*d*) Plains.

7. The buffalo was a mainstay of the Native Americans of the (*a*) Great Basin (*b*) Eastern Woodlands (*c*) Southwest (*d*) Plains.

8. California Native Americans were known best for making especially fine (*a*) baskets (*b*) pottery (*c*) boats (*d*) jewelry.

9. Northwest Coast peoples made (*a*) earth mounds (*b*) totem poles (*c*) tepees (*d*) hogans.

10. Native Americans of the Northwest Coast (*a*) were among the poorest in America (*b*) grew vast fields of corn (*c*) competed by giving away property (*d*) lived in tepees made of hides.

 ESSAY QUESTIONS

1. Describe the culture of the earliest inhabitants of America at the time of their arrival in North America.

2. What improvements in living conditions did the introduction of agriculture in North America make possible?

3. Compare and contrast any *two* culture areas described in this chapter.

4. Describe some of the ways Native Americans made use of animal skins and fur.

5. From what you have read of Native-American cultures in North America, which aspects of the cultures might have made it

difficult for Native Americans and Europeans to live together in peace? Explain your answer.

DOCUMENT-BASED QUESTION

This question is based on the accompanying documents (1–4). It will improve your ability to work with historical documents.

Historical Context:

Our knowledge of prehistoric America is based on archaeological evidence and oral history.

Task:

Using information from the documents and your knowledge of United States history, read each document and answer the question or questions that follow it. Your answers to the questions will help you write the document-based essay.

Document 1.   Study the map on page 2. It depicts the latest scientific research on how Asians came to North America thousands of years ago.

According to the map, what routes did Asians take to come to North America?

Document 2.   The Paiute, a Native-American people, settled in what is today the western United States. Some of their legends tell the story of how they first came to North America. When the following legend was first told is unknown, but it describes a challenge many people faced thousands of years ago as they moved through the northwestern areas of North America.

> Ice had formed ahead of them, and it reached all the way to the sky. The people could not cross it. . . . A raven flew up and struck the ice and cracked it. Coyote said, "These small people can't get across the ice." Another raven flew up again and cracked the ice again. Coyote said, "Try again, try again." Raven flew up again and broke the ice. The people ran across.
>
> **Source:** Parfit, Michael, "The Dawn of Humans," *National Geographic*, Vol. 198, No. 6, December 2000, p. 43.

a.   What do you think the Paiute legend meant by the description of the ice that "reached all the way to the sky"?

b. Describe what you think the place was where "the people ran across."

Document 3. A creation story from the Cheyenne, a Native-American people who once lived in the Great Lakes region but eventually settled in the Great Plains:

> Now where they came in the south, the land was barren, and food and water were not plentiful. So the Great Power taught the red people to hunt and to make clothes to cover themselves against the cold, and they had a pretty good life.
>
> **Source:** Parfit, *ibid.*, p. 61.

Describe one advantage and one disadvantage of hunting on "barren" land.

Document 4. The words of a Hopi man in the 16th century. (The Hopi are part of the Pueblo peoples. Find the Pueblo on the map on page 6.)

> We perform the Snake Dance for rain to fall to water the earth, so that planted things may ripen and grow large.
>
> **Source:** Maynard, Jill (ed.) *Through Indian Eyes: The Untold Story of Native American Peoples.* NY: Readers Digest Books, 1955, p. 87.

How do the Hopi man's words show that he believed he could influence the workings of nature?

DOCUMENT-BASED ESSAY

Using information from the above documents and your knowledge of United States history, write an essay in which you:

- Explain how geography affected the development of early cultures in North America.
- Explain how climate affected the development of early cultures in North America.

CHAPTER 2
Europeans in North America

During the 9th and 10th centuries, Scandinavians (Vikings) journeyed across the North Atlantic to settle Iceland and Greenland. From there, a few adventurers sailed to the mainland of North America.

Icelandic legends describe the Scandinavian voyages to America, which took place around the year 1000. On one of these journeys, Leif Ericson, a Norseman from Greenland, probably visited Newfoundland or Nova Scotia. Because he saw many wild grapes, he called the area Vinland (land of vines). Scandinavian settlements in America were short-lived and news of them did not reach many people in Europe.

EUROPEANS SAIL TO AMERICA

In the 15th century, Europeans were interested in finding a water route to East or South Asia. These Asian areas were rich in such goods as silk, spices, and jewels. Land routes existed, but they were long, dangerous, and expensive. European merchants knew that a safe and easy route to eastern trading centers would make their fortunes. European rulers knew that helping their merchants to trade with the East would enrich and empower their countries.

1. Portuguese Explorers. Since Italian traders controlled the Mediterranean, Portuguese explorers began to look for water routes to the East that went around the coast of southern Africa. In 1498, Vasco da Gama was the first to use this route to sail to India. He returned to Portugal with a ship full of spices and jewels. His voyage proved that an all-water route to the East existed.

2. Columbus. Christopher Columbus, a seaman from the Italian city of Genoa, had a different idea for simplifying European trade with the East. Instead of sailing eastward to reach East Asia, he wanted to sail west. Like most educated people of his day, he knew that the world is round. Columbus convinced King Ferdinand and Queen Isabella of Spain of his theories. He persuaded them to help fund a voyage that would bring wealth, power, and prestige to their country.

In August 1492, Columbus left Spain with three ships. On October 12, Columbus's crew sighted land, probably Watlings Island in the Bahamas. Columbus thought that he had reached an island off the coast of Asia. While searching for the Asian mainland, he landed on the islands of Cuba and Hispaniola. In the spring of 1493, Columbus returned to Spain.

Columbus made three more voyages across the Atlantic. He explored other Caribbean islands, part of the coastline of present-day Honduras and Panama in Central America, and the mouth of the Orinoco River in South America. When he died in 1506, Columbus still did not know that he had not made it to Asia.

3. Exploration After Columbus. With both Portugal and Spain sending out expeditions, the two nations sometimes claimed the same lands. To prevent disputes, the pope divided the world into two parts. The so-called Line of Demarcation, drawn in 1493, ran from the North Pole to the South Pole, through a point about 300 miles west of the Azores in the Atlantic Ocean. (In 1494, the line was moved 1,000 miles farther west.) The pope said that Portugal could claim all newly found lands east of the line, while Spain could claim those west of the line. Because of the pope's rulings, Spain would gain control over much of the Americas. Portugal had a free hand in Africa and Asia.

a. Cabral. In 1500, the Portuguese navigator Pedro Cabral sailed south along the African coast on his way to India. But then he swung so far west that he sighted the coast of Brazil. After landing, he claimed the area for Portugal. The Portuguese soon began colonizing Brazil.

b. Vespucci. Italian navigator Amerigo Vespucci made three voyages to South America—one in 1499 sponsored by Spain, the others in the early 1500s sponsored by Portugal. He then wrote letters claiming that he had discovered a new continent. The southern part of the Western Hemisphere became known as "America" in honor of Vespucci's first name. The word was later applied to the whole hemisphere.

c. Magellan. Ferdinand Magellan succeeded in reaching the East by sailing west. A Portuguese in the service of Spain, Magellan crossed the Atlantic in 1519 with five ships. Then, he sailed along the coast of South America to the southern tip. He passed through the Strait of Magellan (named after him) and entered the Pacific Ocean.

After many hardships, the small fleet reached the Philippines, where Magellan was killed by natives. One of his ships finally made it back to Spain in 1522. It thus became the first ship to *circumnavigate* (go completely around) the world.

Early European Explorers

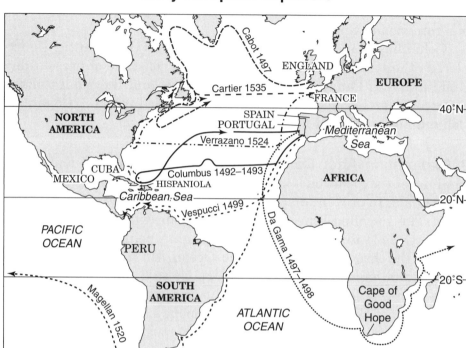

4. Spanish Explorers North of Mexico.
Spanish explorers also traveled into what is now the United States. Their findings gave Spain claims to Florida, the Southwest, and California.

a. Juan Ponce de León.   In 1513, Ponce de León traveled into Florida. Unlike other Spanish explorers, he was not searching for precious metals but for the Fountain of Youth, a legendary spring that made anyone who drank from it young again. Spain claimed Florida.

b. Álvar Núñez Cabeza de Vaca.   He was the first European to explore southern Texas, New Mexico, and Arizona (1528–1536).

c. Francisco Vásquez de Coronado.   He led an expedition through the Southwest (1540–1542). A member of his expedition reached the Grand Canyon.

d. Hernando de Soto.   After exploring Florida, de Soto traveled westward into the southern United States, crossing the Mississippi River in 1540. Citing de Soto's explorations, Spain claimed the entire Gulf Coast region of North America.

e. Juan Rodriguez Cabrillo.   A Portuguese sailor, Cabrillo explored the California coast for Spain (1542).

DEFINE OR IDENTIFY: Vinland, Watlings, Coronado, de Soto, Ponce de León, Cabrillo.

CRITICAL THINKING: Why is the New World named "America" after Amerigo Vespucci rather than "Columbia" after Christopher Columbus?

SPANISH COLONIES IN AMERICA

Spain's rulers quickly realized that the Americas offered land, wealth, and power. Ambitious Spaniards saw a chance to win fame and fortune in the new lands. Others were motivated by the desire to spread Christianity. These goals of Spanish expansion are sometimes summarized as "glory, God, and gold."

Beginning in the late 15th century, the Spaniards created a vast empire in North and South America. In time, Spanish control extended from southern Chile as far north as Florida and California. The empire also included most of the islands of the Caribbean.

1. Exploitation of the Colonies.   Spain strictly supervised the economic life of its colonies in America. It forbade colonists to produce any goods that might compete with Spanish ones. It also banned the colonists from trading with any country other than Spain. It did, however, encourage agriculture and mining in the colonies. Huge quantities of gold and silver were shipped to the home country. This wealth made Spain, for a time, the richest and most powerful nation in Europe.

The Spanish empire had many harmful effects, too. One of the most devastating was the introduction of new diseases such as smallpox, measles, and diphtheria. Because Native Americans had no immunity to these diseases, epidemics swept across the Americas and killed millions. As early as 1510, for example, it was reported that few Indians remained alive in the Bahamas and Hispaniola. According to another estimate, some 90 percent of those in the former Aztec empire of present-day Mexico died within 50 years of the arrival of the Spanish conqueror Hernando Cortés.

Another harmful effect of the Spanish (and other European) empires was the transatlantic slave trade. Slaves were wanted to work in the gold and silver mines. In the 1500s, Portugal dominated the slave trade. In the 1600s, though, the Dutch became the major players in shipping slaves from Africa to the Americas. By the mid-1600s, the French and English also became major players in the slave trade. The height of the slave trade was the 1700s, when as many as 70,000 slaves a year crossed the ocean. The experiences of the Africans enslaved and herded onto ships were horrible. The Africans were chained to the deck, or (more likely) in the dark, dank hold. Some were whipped into submission. Many died of diseases or hunger.

2. Spanish Settlements in the United States.   As a result of its explorations north of Mexico, Spain gained entry into what is now the United States. Spaniards began to settle Florida, the Southwest, and California.

a. Florida.   In 1565, Pedro Menendez founded St. Augustine—the first European settlement in the United States. To convert the Native Americans of that region, the Spanish established missions in northern Florida, Georgia, and the Carolinas. They then built a fort at Pensacola on the Gulf Coast to protect their holdings against invaders from other countries.

b. The Southwest.   Spaniards, looking for more gold, moved north from Mexico into what is now the United States. This region (which they named New Mexico) included Texas, New Mexico, and Arizona. They founded Santa Fe as its capital in 1609. Abandoning their hopes of finding gold, Spanish settlers set up large cattle ranches in the region.

c. California.   In the 1700s, the Spanish began to settle California. Some of their earliest settlements were Monterey, San Francisco, Santa Barbara, San Jose, and Los Angeles. The settlements usually began as Catholic missions where priests converted Native Americans to Christianity and taught them European skills and culture.

OTHER COLONIAL POWERS

Since Spain and Portugal dominated the central and southern regions of America, the other European powers sent explorers farther north. They wanted to find a *northwest passage*—a route through or around North America leading directly to Asia.

1. France.   The first explorer sent out by France was Giovanni da Verrazano, an Italian navigator. In 1524, he sailed along the North

American coast from North Carolina to Nova Scotia. He was probably the first European to enter New York Bay. Not long afterward, in
1534, Jacques Cartier explored the eastern part of Canada along the
Gulf of St. Lawrence. The following year, he made a second voyage,
sailing up the St. Lawrence River to the present site of Montreal.

a. French territories.   Years later, in 1608, another great
French explorer, Samuel de Champlain, founded the settlement of
Quebec on a height overlooking the St. Lawrence River. This was the
beginning of the first permanent French colony in North America.
Champlain also explored parts of New England and New York.

The French explored the forested lands to the south and west of
Quebec and Montreal. Robert Cavelier de La Salle traveled through
the Great Lakes and the Ohio River Valley. Sailing down the Mississippi River to the Gulf of Mexico in 1682, he claimed the entire
river valley for France. He called it Louisiana in honor of King Louis
XIV of France.

b. French settlers.   The French established few large settlements in New France. They wanted mainly to develop a profitable

---

European Settlements in North America, 1640

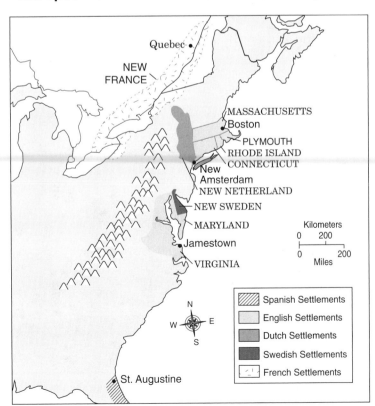

fur trade with Native Americans. Thus, the newcomers built trading posts and forts at strategic points. These helped control the waterways and served as centers for the trade.

The system of landholding in New France was similar to that in France. Large estates were granted to *seigneurs* (lords). In turn, they rented small farms to *habitants* (settlers). This system tended to discourage the immigration of French families who wanted to own farms. After 150 years of French control, New France had only 80,000 European settlers.

French missionaries followed the fur traders into the wilderness to convert natives to Christianity. Many of the missionaries explored the central parts of North America, along the upper Mississippi River and the central Mississippi Valley. As a result, Catholicism became firmly established in the Mississippi Valley and in eastern Canada.

c. French policy toward Native Americans.   Perhaps because there were few French settlers in North America, the French had better relations with Native Americans than did the Spanish or British. The French depended on them to supply the French with furs for trade.

2. The Netherlands.   The people of the Netherlands, the Dutch, also wanted to share the rich trade with Asia. A group of Dutch merchants hired Henry Hudson, an English navigator, to find a new water route to the Indies. In 1609, Hudson sailed his ship the *Half*

The southern tip of Manhattan Island looked like this in 1656. Note the windmill and the Dutch architecture of New Amsterdam.

Moon along the North American coast from Maine to the Carolinas searching for a northwest passage. He entered Delaware Bay and, later, New York Bay. From there, he sailed up the Hudson River as far as present-day Albany.

As a result of this voyage, the Dutch claimed the area from the Hudson River Valley south to Delaware Bay. They called this region New Netherland. In 1624, a trading company called the Dutch West India Company sent 30 families to be the first European settlers of New Netherland. Most of the settlers went up the Hudson River to the area now called Albany. Within the next two years, more colonists arrived. Many of them settled around New York Bay and on the lower Delaware River. A large settlement, New Amsterdam, was made on Manhattan Island. It soon became the seat of government, chief port, and main trading center of New Netherland.

ENGLAND'S RISE TO POWER

Like other European nations, England wanted to trade with the East. In 1497 and again in 1498, King Henry VII sent an Italian navigator, John Cabot, to search for a northwest passage to Asia. During his explorations, Cabot claimed for England the area that now stretches from Newfoundland to Chesapeake Bay. At this time, however, England lacked the sea power to compete with Spain in the Americas.

1. English Pirates. In the 1560s and 1570s, during the reign of Queen Elizabeth I, English pirates called "sea dogs" began to challenge Spain's control of the seas. One of the best known of these sea dogs, Sir Francis Drake, preyed on Spanish treasure ships and Spanish settlements in the Americas.

On one of his voyages (1577–1580), Drake circumnavigated the globe. On a quest to find a northwest passage, he explored the coastline north of California. Failing to find it, he returned south, landing near present-day San Francisco and claiming the region for England. From there, he sailed west around the globe back to England.

In the summer of 1588, King Philip II of Spain, angered by the English pirates' attacks on Spanish ships and colonies, sent the Spanish Armada (a fleet of 130 ships) to conquer England. The smaller English fleet defeated the Armada. After this defeat, Spain declined as a naval power.

2. More Searches for a Northwest Passage. Despite Cabot's failure to find a northwest passage (which did not exist), English mariners continued to search for it. The map on page 20 traces Cabot's route.

3. Reasons for Colonization. England's rise as a major naval power led to the development of trade abroad and to the establishment of colonies overseas. People were attracted to these colonies for two main reasons:

a. Economic reasons.   Poor and landless people hoped to obtain farms in America. England's leaders thought that colonies would enrich the nation's economy. *Mercantilism,* an economic theory of the time, held that nations should be self-sufficient and own large stores of gold and silver. If a country did not have sufficient natural resources, it should obtain colonies that could supply raw materials, provide a market for manufactured goods, and yield gold and silver.

b. Religious reasons.   In 1534, the Church of England (the Anglican church) split from the Roman Catholic Church. The English monarch became the head of this new religion. English law required everyone to attend an Anglican church and pay taxes for its support. Many opposed the law. Many Catholics wanted to remain Catholics. One group of Protestants—the Puritans—wanted to "purify" the Anglican church by simplifying its rituals. Another Protestant group—the Separatists—broke away from it completely. America promised to be a refuge where people could worship as they pleased.

DEFINE OR IDENTIFY: Verrazano, mercantilism, sea dog, *seigneur, habitant,* La Salle.

CRITICAL THINKING: Why did the French enjoy better relations with the Native Americans than did the British and Spanish?

THE FIRST FOOTHOLDS

Promoters of a colonizing venture had to seek a grant of land from the monarch, as well as the right to govern the area and to control its trade. The crown granted such privileges in the form of a *charter* (royal patent) to wealthy and influential people.

During the late 1500s, two men—Sir Humphrey Gilbert and Sir Walter Raleigh—made separate, unsuccessful attempts to plant

The settlement at Jamestown did not thrive until women arrived from England.

colonies in North America. It soon became clear that a single individual could not easily bear the expense of setting up a colony. Therefore, groups of wealthy merchants and investors banded together to sponsor colonial projects. Some organized large enterprises called *joint-stock companies*. Investors who purchased stock in such a company became shareholders and were entitled to a proportionate share of any profits earned.

1. Jamestown.   A group of merchants and investors called the London Company made the first permanent English settlement in America at Jamestown, in Virginia. The company hoped to earn a profit by mining precious metals, exporting American products to Europe, and trading with Native Americans.

a. Early hardships.   Jamestown's first settlers landed at the mouth of the James River in the spring of 1607. Chiefly interested in finding gold, they did not plant crops or build shelters. The area around the settlement was swampy and unhealthful. During the first seven months, more than half the settlers died of starvation and disease. Frequent attacks by Native Americans also threatened Jamestown's survival.

Captain John Smith took command and ordered all able-bodied settlers to build houses and plant crops. Smith also obtained food from the native peoples. After Smith returned to England in the fall of 1609, the colony almost failed again.

b. A turn for the better.   The arrival of fresh supplies and more settlers kept Jamestown alive. But the colony remained on the edge of failure until several important changes took place:

1. *Land Ownership.* Originally, the Jamestown colonists were merely employees of the London Company, which owned all property. Later, individual settlers were given their own land. This change encouraged them to work harder.

2. *Family Life.* The first few women came to Jamestown in 1608. Starting in 1620, many more began to come. Family life made the community more stable.

3. *Tobacco Cultivation.* The use of tobacco, a plant grown by Native Americans, became popular in England during the 16th century. One colonist, John Rolfe, made a successful business of cultivating tobacco. Soon, the colonists were raising it on a large scale. As settlements spread beyond Jamestown, the colony became known as Virginia.

4. *Increased Labor Supply.* At first, *indentured servants* worked the tobacco fields. These men and women wanted to settle in America but did not have enough money to pay for their passage. They agreed to work for a certain period without wages for anyone who paid their way. During the time of the indenture agreement—usually four to seven years—the servants received food and clothing. In 1619, the first Africans arrived as prisoners aboard a Dutch ship. The settlers bought them as indentured servants. Merchants later sold other captive Africans to the colonists as slaves.

5. *Relations With Native Americans.* Initially, the leader of the Powhatans (Native Americans who lived in the area) tried to drive out the Jamestown colonists. Later, however, relations between the two groups improved. In 1614, the leader's daughter Pocahontas married John Rolfe, the tobacco planter. Their marriage brought a period of peace. In 1622, however, the Powhatans broke the peace by killing nearly 350 settlers. The colonists drove them out of the area.

c. Representative government.   The London Company appointed a governor and council—a group of men who advised the governor—to rule the colony. Then in 1619, the Virginia Company (as the London Company was now called) allowed the colonists to form a representative assembly called the *House of Burgesses.* It was made up of two delegates, or burgesses, from each settlement in Virginia. The House of Burgesses was the first elective legislature in America.

2. Plymouth.   The second permanent English colony in North America was at Plymouth, Massachusetts.

a. Beginnings.   Separatists established the Plymouth colony. A group of English merchants financed the venture. In return, the Separatists promised the merchants all the profits earned by the colony in its first seven years. They set sail on the *Mayflower* in September 1620 and arrived at Plymouth in December.

The Pilgrims, as these settlers came to be known, drew up the *Mayflower Compact* before they landed. In this document, they agreed to make and obey just and equal laws for the common good. This agreement is one of the earliest expressions of self-government in America.

b. The first years.   During the first winter at Plymouth, shelter was poor, disease widespread, and food scarce. Fortunately, some Native Americans helped the Pilgrims obtain food. One chief, Massasoit, made a peace treaty with the Pilgrims. The contact between the English colonists and the Native Americans was not as fortunate for the Native Americans as it was for the colonists. The Native Americans had no resistance to germs carried by the Europeans, and many died from the diseases they caused.

Governor William Bradford governed Plymouth colony wisely. Under his leadership, two important changes took place: (*1*) Each adult male acquired land for himself. At first, all the land had belonged to the community and was worked in common. (*2*) The Pilgrims became financially independent by repaying the merchants who had sponsored the new colony.

3. Massachusetts Bay.   The Puritans also came to North America in search of religious freedom. In 1630, some 1,000 Puritans, sponsored by a joint-stock company formed by leading English Puritans, sailed to Massachusetts Bay and settled around Boston. John Winthrop was the first governor of this Massachusetts Bay Colony.

At this time in England, the conflict between the king (an Anglican) and religious dissenters resulted in the "Great Migration" of the 1630s. More than 60,000 people came to the Americas then. Of this number, about 20,000 settled in New England. The Massachusetts Bay Colony expanded into the Maine–New Hampshire region and later took over Plymouth Colony.

Everyone who lived in Massachusetts Bay was forced to support the Puritan church. Only church members could vote and hold public office. The clergy acted as governmental advisers and made sure that people lived according to Puritan values. Critics of the regime were threatened with banishment from the colony.

DEFINE OR IDENTIFY: charter, joint-stock company, House of Burgesses, John Rolfe.

CRITICAL THINKING: Why was life difficult for the early settlers in Jamestown?

OTHER NEW ENGLAND COLONIES

The number of New England settlements grew steadily. Some were set up by colonists who moved north and south from Massachusetts. Newcomers from England founded other colonies.

1. Connecticut.   Thomas Hooker, a Puritan minister, disapproved of the harsh rule of the Bay Colony's leaders. In 1636, he led a number of followers west to settle Hartford in the Connecticut River Valley. Other colonists from Massachusetts founded the nearby river towns of Wethersfield and Windsor. Farther south, Puritans from England settled in and around New Haven.

In 1639, Hartford, Wethersfield, and Windsor joined to form a government. They drew up a constitution with provisions for (*1*) electing deputies from each town to a legislature, (*2*) choosing a governor, (*3*) limiting the terms of office of public officials, and (*4*) assuring fair taxation. This document, the *Fundamental Orders of Connecticut,* was the first written constitution in America. In 1662, King Charles II of England united the towns of Connecticut into one colony.

2. Rhode Island.   Roger Williams was another Massachusetts clergyman opposed to Puritan rule. When Massachusetts officials ordered him back to England for demanding religious freedom, he took shelter among Native Americans. Other colonists from the Bay Colony joined him. Williams then bought land from Native Americans and, in 1636, founded Providence.

Anne Hutchinson was also driven out of Massachusetts for religious reasons. With her followers, she moved to Portsmouth, Rhode Island. Other Massachusetts colonists founded Newport and Warwick. In time, England gave Providence, Portsmouth, Newport, and Warwick a charter allowing them to set up a government. The four settlements formed Rhode Island.

Under Roger Williams, Rhode Island adopted the principle of *separation of church and state*. This meant that the government could not pass laws restricting religious liberty or set religious standards for voting or holding office. Rhode Island was the first Amer-

Anne Hutchinson was tried by the General Court of Massachusetts Bay Colony for challenging the authority of the Puritan clergy. After being banished from Massachusetts, she helped found Rhode Island.

ican colony to guarantee religious freedom to everyone who lived there.

3. New Hampshire and Maine. The principal towns of New Hampshire were established between 1623 and 1640. Anglicans from England founded Dover and Portsmouth. Followers of John Wheelwright, a Puritan minister who had been banished from Bay Colony, founded Exeter. In the 1640s, Massachusetts annexed all these settlements. It retained control of the area until 1679, when New Hampshire was granted a charter making it a separate royal colony.

Settlement in Maine began in the 1620s. Augusta, the present capital, was founded as a fur-trading post on the Kennebec River in 1628. Massachusetts Bay Colony took over the region in the 1650s. Massachusetts held Maine until 1820.

THE MIDDLE COLONIES

South of New England lay a region that became known as the Middle Colonies. As we learned earlier, the Dutch had established the colony of New Netherland along the Hudson River.

1. New York. The English decided to take over New Netherland for the following reasons: (*1*) They claimed that Cabot's explorations had given them a right to the area. (*2*) New Netherland separated the English colonies in New England from those farther south. (*3*) The

Dutch violated English trade laws by carrying on extensive trade with the English colonies. (4) The English coveted the Dutch fur trade with Native Americans. (5) England wanted to control New Amsterdam's harbor.

a. Overthrow of the Dutch. King Charles II gave New Netherland (which he regarded as English territory) to his brother James, the Duke of York. In 1664, an English fleet sailed to New Amsterdam and took New Netherland from the Dutch. In honor of the Duke of York, the colony and its main town were named New York.

b. Government. As *proprietor* (owner) of the colony, the Duke of York ruled New York through an appointed governor and council. This arrangement denied the people representation in government. After the colonists protested, the Duke appointed Thomas Dongan as governor and authorized him to hold elections to a representative assembly. In 1683, the assembly drew up a *Charter of Liberties and Privileges*. It provided for an elective assembly, freedom of worship, and trial by jury. When the Duke of York became King James II in 1685, though, he abolished the charter and assembly. Representative government was not restored until 1691.

2. New Jersey. New Netherland had included the area between the Hudson and Delaware rivers. When the Duke of York took over New Netherland, he gave this area to friends. The new proprietors named their colony New Jersey. They encouraged colonization by promising settlers large grants of land, representative government, and freedom of religion.

3. Pennsylvania. Quakers, who also lacked religious freedom in England, needed a refuge where they could worship as they pleased.

a. William Penn's Quaker principles. King Charles II gave William Penn land in North America. The area was called Pennsylvania ("Penn's woods"). Penn, a devout Quaker, envisioned a colony where people of all beliefs and nationalities could live together in peace. They would also be equal before the law and enjoy freedom of speech and religion. The first settlers arrived in 1682.

b. Growth and prosperity. Pennsylvania became large and successful for several reasons:

1. *Many Settlers.* Penn's belief in self-government, in making land available on good terms, and in freedom of religion attracted many Europeans. Philadelphia became the largest city in the colonies.

2. *Good Government.* Penn drew up a constitution that became known as the *Frame of Government.* It provided for a deputy governor to be appointed by the proprietor and for a council and an assembly to be elected by the people. At its first meeting, held in 1682, the legislature adopted a code of laws for the colony called the *Great Law.* It granted freedom of religion to all people in Pennsylvania. (But only Christian men could vote or hold office.) It provided for the care of the poor, protection against unfair trials, and humane treatment of wrongdoers.

3. *Friendly Relations With Native Americans.* Penn paid Native Americans fair prices for their lands and negotiated a peace treaty between them and European settlers.

4. Delaware. The Middle Colonies were also colonized by Swedes. One group settled Fort Christina (present-day Wilmington) in 1638. Other groups built forts along the Delaware River and named the region New Sweden. The Dutch seized New Sweden in 1655. When New Netherland fell to the English in 1664, New Sweden also became English property. The new owner, the Duke of York, renamed it Delaware. To provide Pennsylvania with access to the sea, the Duke gave Delaware to Penn. In 1703, Delaware became a separate colony with a legislature of its own.

THE SOUTH

The Virginia colony grew steadily as restless pioneers began to leave the coast for inland regions.

1. Maryland. Cecilius Calvert (Lord Baltimore), a prominent Catholic noble, founded Maryland in the land just north of Virginia as a haven for Catholics. As proprietor, Lord Baltimore could assign, sell, or rent the land as he saw fit. He also had the power to levy taxes, set up courts, and control church matters. But he could not make laws without the advice and consent of the free, white men of the colony. In 1634, a settlement was started at St. Mary's, near the mouth of the Potomac River. The colony did well from the start. Growing tobacco soon became an important source of income.

Although Maryland was founded as a refuge for Catholics, Christians of all denominations flocked to the colony. Soon Protestants outnumbered Catholics. Lord Baltimore wanted to prevent religious

The Regions of English North America

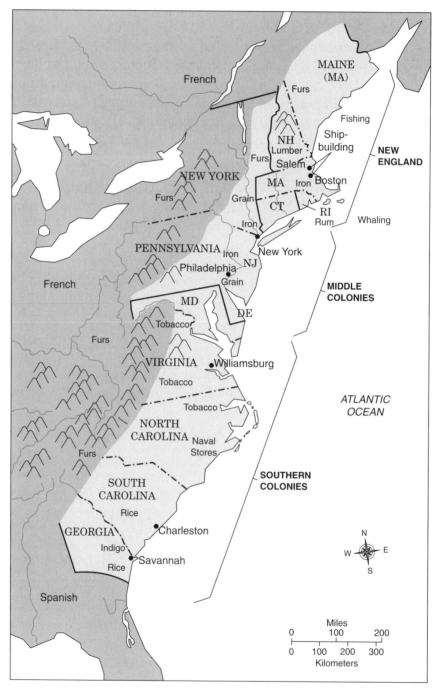

French

MAINE
(MA)

Furs

Fishing

French

NEW YORK

NH
Lumber

Furs

Ship-
building

**NEW
ENGLAND**

Salem

MA   Iron   Boston

Furs

Grain

CT

Iron

RI
Rum

Whaling

PENNSYLVANIA   Iron

Philadelphia

NJ

New York

Grain

French

MD

DE

Tobacco

**MIDDLE
COLONIES**

Furs

VIRGINIA   •Williamsburg

Tobacco

*ATLANTIC
OCEAN*

Tobacco

NORTH
CAROLINA   Naval
Stores

Furs

**SOUTHERN
COLONIES**

SOUTH
CAROLINA

Rice

GEORGIA

•Charleston

Indigo

N

Savannah

Rice

W   E

Spanish

S

Miles
0   100   200

0   100   200   300
Kilometers

disputes and protect Catholics against discrimination. Accordingly, the Maryland Assembly passed the *Toleration Act* in 1649. It provided that all Christians were free to worship as they pleased. Although the law did not protect non-Christians, it was an important step toward full religious liberty.

2. The Carolinas.   In 1663, Charles II issued a charter to eight noblemen allowing them to develop Carolina, the region south of Virginia. The proprietors offered liberal land terms, freedom of religion, and representation of landowners in an assembly. In 1670, the first group of settlers founded Charles Town (Charleston), which soon became a thriving seaport and main center of the colony.

From the beginning, Carolina seemed to divide itself naturally into a northern and southern section. In the north, the colonists raised tobacco and produced forest products. In the south, the settlers grew rice and indigo. (*Indigo* is a plant from which a blue dye is made.) Carolinians in the north traded mainly with New England, while those in the south dealt directly with England.

The Carolinians began to rebel against proprietary rule. Unable to maintain law and order, the proprietors surrendered their charter to the king. In 1729, North Carolina and South Carolina became separate royal colonies.

3. Georgia.   Georgia was the last of the 13 original colonies to be established. Its founder, James Oglethorpe, was a member of the British legislative body, *Parliament.* He wanted to provide a place where imprisoned debtors could make a fresh start in the New World. (At that time, people who could not pay their debts were sent to jail.) Oglethorpe with a small band of settlers founded Savannah in 1733.

A board of trustees, made up of Oglethorpe and his associates, governed the colony. Aiming to make Georgia a region of small, independent farms, the trustees limited landholding and forbade the use of slaves. The colonists opposed these policies, so they were soon abandoned. In 1752, the trustees surrendered their rights to the king, and Georgia became a royal colony.

DEFINE OR IDENTIFY: Fundamental Orders of Connecticut, William Penn, indigo, Parliament.

CRITICAL THINKING: How did the British acquire the areas that became the colonies of New York, New Jersey, and Delaware?

Chapter Review

MATCHING TEST

Column A	Column B
1. Powhatan	*a.* Pennsylvania
2. Anne Hutchinson	*b.* Rhode Island
3. William Penn	*c.* Connecticut
4. James Oglethorpe	*d.* Georgia
5. Thomas Hooker	*e.* Jamestown

MULTIPLE-CHOICE TEST

1. About how many years before Columbus's voyages did the Vikings explore a part of North America? (*a*) 100 years (*b*) 300 years (*c*) 500 years (*d*) 1,000 years.

2. The first Portuguese explorer to sail around Africa to India was (*a*) Vasco da Gama (*b*) Dias (*c*) Vespucci (*d*) Magellan.

3. In 1492, Columbus wanted to (*a*) reach Asia by sailing east (*b*) prove that the Earth is round (*c*) discover America (*d*) reach Asia by sailing west.

4. The main reason that the Dutch settled in North America was to gain (*a*) trade (*b*) political freedom from Spain (*c*) religious liberty (*d*) converts for Christianity.

5. The first man to explore North America for the English was (*a*) Sir Francis Drake (*b*) Sir Walter Raleigh (*c*) John Cabot (*d*) Henry Hudson.

6. Plymouth Colony was organized by (*a*) Separatists (*b*) Catholics (*c*) Quakers (*d*) Anglicans.

7. The first American colony to guarantee all its people religious freedom was (*a*) Massachusetts Bay (*b*) Maryland (*c*) Pennsylvania (*d*) Rhode Island.

8. The first European settlers in the Middle Colonies were the (*a*) Swedes (*b*) Dutch (*c*) English (*d*) French.

9. The English colony settled at first mainly by debtors was (*a*) Maryland (*b*) Georgia (*c*) Rhode Island (*d*) New Hampshire.

10. North Carolina and South Carolina (*a*) were at first part of Georgia (*b*) were founded as one colony (*c*) began as homes for jailed debtors (*d*) attracted few settlers at first.

UNDERSTANDING A TIMELINE

Important Events in European Exploration of North America

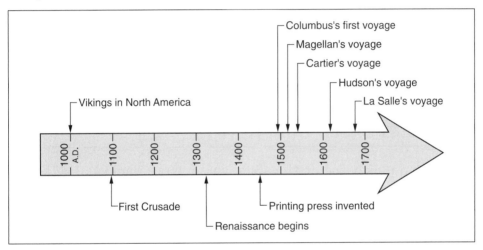

1. The event on the timeline that took place first was (*a*) the first voyage of Columbus to America (*b*) Cartier's voyage (*c*) Vikings in North America (*d*) Hudson's voyage.

2. An event that took place in the same century as Cartier's voyage was (*a*) Magellan's voyage (*b*) Columbus's first voyage (*c*) Hudson's voyage (*d*) Champlain's voyage.

3. The date of Henry Hudson's exploration of the Hudson River is (*a*) 1580 (*b*) 1609 (*c*) 1677 (*d*) 1710.

4. No event is listed on the timeline for the (*a*) 11th century (*b*) 12th century (*c*) 14th century (*d*) 15th century.

5. Which of the following could *not* be considered a reason why Columbus made a successful voyage to America in 1492? (*a*) Magellan's voyage (*b*) the Crusades (*c*) the Renaissance (*d*) the invention of the printing press.

ESSAY QUESTIONS

1. Describe the voyages of da Gama, Columbus, and Magellan. Which of these voyages do you think was most important? Why?

2. What were the main effects of Spanish rule in the Americas?

3. Why did the English want to colonize the New World in the 1600s?

4. Describe the system of indentured servitude. Why was it introduced? What system eventually replaced it? Why?

5. What was the role of religion in the founding of Pennsylvania? Massachusetts Bay? Rhode Island? Plymouth? Maryland? Which of these colonies was the most tolerant? The least tolerant?

DOCUMENT-BASED QUESTION

This question is based on the accompanying documents (1–4). It will improve your ability to work with historical documents.

Historical Context:

Most of Central America, South America, and the Caribbean was colonized by the Spanish. They helped shape the course of American civilization in many ways.

Task:

Using information from the documents and your knowledge of history, read each document and answer the question that follows it. Your answers to the questions will help you write the document-based essay.

Document 1. In late 1492, Christopher Columbus made the following entries in his journal about the first Native Americans whom he encountered:

> **A.** I knew that they were a people who could be more easily freed and converted to our holy faith by love than by force. . . . [They] appeared to me to be a race of people very poor in everything.

B. If your Highnesses [King Ferdinand and Queen Isabella] order either to bring all of them to Castile or to hold them as *captivos* [captives] on their own island, it could easily be done, because with about fifty men, you could control and subjugate them, making them do whatever you want.

> **Sources:** Jameson, J. Franklin (ed.) *Original Narratives of Early American History.* NY: Charles Scribner's Sons, 1909, p. 110.

Did Columbus plan to treat the Native Americans the same way in both entries, A and B? Explain your answer.

Document 2.   In 1519, Spanish explorer Hernando Cortés arrived in Mexico. In the following letter to King Charles V of Spain, Cortés described his experience:

> Before dawn, I came upon two villages in which I killed many people. . . . I fell upon another town, so large that more than twenty thousand houses were found there. . . . As I caught them by surprise, they came out unarmed, and the women and children went naked in the streets; and I opened fire. . . . Since we were . . . fighting for our faith and in the service of your Holy Majesty. . . , God gave us so great a victory that we killed many people without suffering any losses.

> **Source:** Letters to Charles V, quoted in *Americas* (August 1972), p. S-10.

What mood do you think Cortés was in as he wrote the letter to Charles V? Explain.

Document 3.   Bartolomé de las Casas was a Spanish priest who worked to prevent the enslavement of Native Americans. In the mid-1500s, he expressed the following view of Native Americans, whom he called "savage people":

> For all the peoples of the world are . . . formed in the image and likeness of God. . . . [But] no one is born enlightened. . . . All of us must be guided . . . by those who were born before us. And the savage peoples of the earth may be compared to uncultivated soil that readily brings forth weeds and useless thorns, but has within itself such natural virtue that by labor and cultivation it may be made to yield sound and healthful fruits.

> **Source:** www.oregonstate.edu/dept/philosophy/ideas/papers/keen.html

How does Las Casas see Native Americans as both equal and unequal to Europeans?

Document 4. Study the illustration below.

Why do you think the Spanish destroyed Native-American religious art in Mexico?

DOCUMENT-BASED ESSAY

Using information from the above documents and your knowledge of United States history, write an essay in which you:

- Explain why many Spanish of the 15th and 16th centuries believed that the Spanish conquest of the Americas was justified.
- Explain why many people of that time, especially Native Americans, believed that Spanish rule was *not* justified.

UNIT II

AN INDEPENDENT NATION

CHAPTER 3
Seeds of Independence

The English colonies in North America attracted more and more immigrants. At first, the newcomers kept the customs they had known in their native lands. As the years went by, however, the colonists began to create a distinctly American culture.

THE PEOPLE

Population in colonial America grew steadily. In 1630, there were fewer than 6,000 newcomers scattered along the coast. By 1775, the number of settlers and their descendants had risen to 2.5 million. Most of this growth was due to natural population increase—more births than deaths. But immigration and the importation of enslaved people also added to the total.

Settlers of English origin made up the largest single group in the colonies. There were also sizable numbers of Africans, Dutch, Irish, and Germans. Other, smaller groups included Belgians, French Huguenots, Scots, Scotch-Irish, Spaniards, Swedes, and Welsh.

1. Social Classes. Class differences in colonial America did not depend as much on family background as they had in Europe. A person's ancestry did make a difference, but so did occupation, property, and income. The population was divided into three broad classes:

a. Upper class. The upper class controlled the economic, political, and social life of the colonies. This group was made up of (1) plantation owners in the South and large landholders in the Middle Colonies, (2) wealthy merchants in the cities of New England and the Middle Colonies, (3) Puritan clergy in New England, and (4) government officials, lawyers, and doctors.

INTERPRETING A GRAPH

English Colonial Population, by Race, 1660–1780

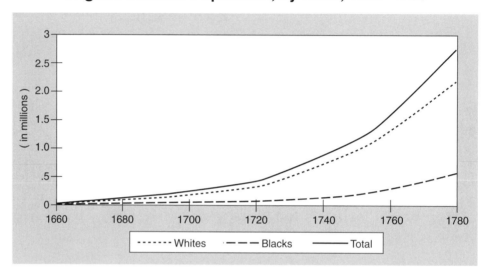

1. What general trend is shown on the graph for the total population?

2. In what year did the colonial population reach 2,500,000?

3. How many white colonists were there in 1730?

4. In what year did the African-American population reach 500,000?

5. Which *one* of the following time spans shows the greatest overall growth? (*a*) 1660–1680 (*b*) 1680–1700 (*c*) 1700–1720 (*d*) 1760–1780

---

b. Middle class. The middle class made up the largest part of the colonial population. This group consisted of (1) independent farmers with small plots of land, (2) skilled workers, and (3) shopkeepers and other tradespeople.

c. Lower class. The lower class included mainly indentured servants and enslaved people.

2. African Americans. In the mid-1700s, people from Africa and their descendants made up about 20 percent of the population of the colonies. By then, almost all Africans in America were enslaved. Slavery existed in all the colonies but was most widespread in the South. Southern tobacco and rice plantations were large and required many workers. Slaves provided a constant supply of labor.

The slave trade brought to America thousands of Africans taken mostly on the west coast of Africa. Harsh conditions on slave ships killed many of the Africans on the way to America. Once brought to America, African-American families were commonly split up: Children were separated from their parents; husbands were separated from wives. Unlike enslaved people in Africa, children of slaves were considered enslaved for life.

3. Native Americans. The earliest European settlements could not have survived without Native-American help. But friendly feelings between whites and Native Americans soon changed to mistrust. The settlers took thousands of acres of Native-American land. Many of the takeovers were arranged through treaties that were meaningless because the idea of land transfer through sale was foreign to Native Americans. Without understanding what the transaction involved, Native Americans would exchange vast tracts of land for items of small worth. Moreover, many settlers did not honor the treaties that they had made.

Some Native Americans fought back, such as in King Philip's War. In the 1670s, they destroyed many New England towns. But after "King" Philip (a Wampanoag leader) was killed, the Native Americans were scattered. The colonists, with their superior weapons and numbers, then easily defeated them.

The Wampanoag suffered great mortality from diseases brought by European colonists.

ECONOMIC DEVELOPMENTS

The area in which the 13 original colonies were located contained thick forests, fertile land, broad rivers, and a favorable climate. These resources enabled the hardworking colonists to create a healthy economy.

1. Farming. About 90 percent of the colonists made their living by farming. Most of the farms were small, family-operated, and self-supporting. Because farms were widely scattered and travel was difficult, a colonial farm family had to supply most of its own needs.

   a. New England. This area was hilly and had rocky soil. The growing seasons were short; the winters, severe. The average farm was small. It produced food primarily for the family, with little left over for sale. The main crops were corn, barley, rye, *flax* (used for making linen), vegetables, and fruits. Farmers raised chickens, pigs, cows, and sheep. A farm family usually owned one or two horses and a pair of oxen.

   b. The Middle Colonies. This area had broad, fertile plains and a moderate climate. Its land yielded large crops of corn and wheat. Farmers also planted orchards, grew vegetables and flax, and raised livestock. Much of the farm produce was sold. The average farm was of medium size.

   c. The South. The South had good soil, a warm climate, and a long growing season. Besides planting crops and raising livestock for their own needs, Southern farmers produced three major *cash crops*—those grown for sale rather than for home use. These were tobacco, rice, and indigo. Most Southern farms were small, family-operated holdings. But the South also had large plantations, which produced most of the cash crops.

2. Industry. Local industries served the needs of their communities. Blacksmiths shod horses and made tools and ironware. Coopers made barrels. Leatherworkers turned out shoes and animal

READING AN ENCYCLOPEDIA ARTICLE

Read carefully the following *World Book Online* article on Elizabeth Lucas Pinckney. You will be asked questions about this reading.

Pinckney, Eliza Lucas (1722?–1793), a colonial planter of South Carolina, did much to promote the economic growth of South Carolina in the 1700's. She successfully developed and grew indigo plants on her father's plantations. The blue dye produced from the plant was in great demand in Europe. Pinckney shared her knowledge with other South Carolina farmers and helped indigo become a leading export for the colony.

Pinckney was probably born on Dec. 28, 1722, in Antigua, then a British colony in the West Indies. Her father, George Lucas, served as the lieutenant governor there. In 1738, Lucas brought his family to South Carolina, where he had inherited three plantations near Charleston. The next year, he returned to Antigua, leaving Elizabeth, then 16 years old, in charge of the plantations. In 1744, Elizabeth married Charles Pinckney, a planter and lawyer. Among their children were two future statesmen, Charles Cotesworth Pinckney and Thomas Pinckney. After Eliza's husband died in 1758, she successfully managed the Carolina plantations for the next 35 years. She died in Philadelphia on May 26, 1793. President George Washington, who had met her on a tour of the South in 1791, served as a pallbearer at his own request.   *W. Calvin Smith*

From *The World Book Encyclopedia,* © 2006 World Book, Inc. By permission of the publisher. www.worldbook.com

1. According to the article, when was Elizabeth Lucas born?

2. Where did her family live before they moved to South Carolina?

3. Who was her husband?

4. Who were two of her children and in what manner did they become famous?

5. What was Elizabeth Pinckney's major contribution to the colony of South Carolina?

harnesses. Cabinetmakers built furniture. Millers operated gristmills to grind grain into flour.

Local businesses were usually small in scale, run by the owner and a few boys who served as apprentices. *Apprentices* lived and worked with a master craftsman for a number of years—until they learned the trade.

Some colonial industries produced goods on a large scale, for sale to other localities and to England. Such businesses had to abide by laws set up by England to enforce mercantilist policies (discussed on pages 21 and 26).

a. Fishing and whaling. The waters off New England teemed with cod, halibut, mackerel, haddock, and herring. Tons of fish were salted, dried, and shipped to Europe and the West Indies. Whale oil, widely used as fuel for lamps, brought high prices. Whaling became an important New England industry.

b. Shipbuilding. Boston and Salem were the main centers of New England's shipbuilding industry. Shipbuilders used wood from nearby forests and imported iron, canvas, and rope from England. New England vessels became world-famous for their speed and easy handling.

c. Lumber and naval stores. New England's forests provided lumber for general building purposes. So did the forests in the Hudson Valley, southeastern Pennsylvania, and North Carolina. The pine trees of North Carolina yielded pitch, tar, resin, and turpentine. Because these products were used mainly in shipbuilding, they were called *naval stores*.

d. Fur trading. In New England, the Middle Colonies, and the Southern Colonies, Native Americans and colonial traders engaged in the trading of skins and furs. Native Americans exchanged their animal skins for axes, knives, beads, cloth, guns, ammunition, and rum.

e. Distilling. Molasses imported from the West Indies was used to make rum. By 1750, distilleries in New England were producing several million gallons a year. Rum was sold in the colonies and used as an item of exchange in the fur trade and the African slave trade.

f. Ironworking. The discovery of iron ore in southern New England, the Hudson Valley, and southeastern Pennsylvania led to the establishment of an ironworking industry. Colonists in these areas produced unfinished bar and pig iron for export to England.

3. Commerce. In accordance with England's mercantilist policies, the American colonies exported raw materials to England and imported finished products mainly from that country. They also traded with other European countries, with the West Indies, and among themselves.

a. New England. Merchants from New England carried on a busy trade with Europe, the West Indies, and other colonies. The colonists exported fish, whale oil, furs, lumber, ships, leather goods, and iron bars and imported manufactured items. Boston was the region's trading center.

b. The Middle Colonies. Philadelphia and New York were the chief ports of the Middle Colonies. From these cities, ships carried furs, iron, and lumber to England, in exchange for manufactured

INTERPRETING A DIAGRAM

Patterns of Triangular Trade

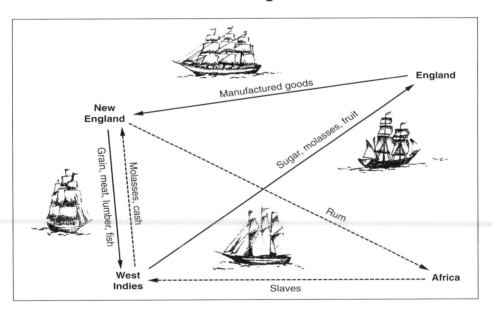

1. According to the diagram, England was a source of what?

2. Enslaved African Americans were transported to the West Indies. What were they exchanged for?

3. Molasses and cash were shipped to New England. What was the molasses made into?

4. What did England import from the West Indies?

goods. To the West Indies went wheat, beef, lumber, and horses, in return for sugar, molasses, and wine.

c. The South. The South traded mainly with England. Southern exports included tobacco, rice, indigo, naval stores, and hides. In return, the South imported tools and fine finished items. Charleston, Savannah, and Baltimore were the main trading centers.

d. Triangular trade. Much colonial commerce formed a triangular pattern. *Triangular trade* worked like the diagram on page 47.

IDENTIFY OR DEFINE: King Philip's War, apprentice, naval stores, triangular trade.

CRITICAL THINKING: Why do you think triangular trade routes developed?

RELIGION

In the early days, many colonies set up an *established religion*—an official church supported by taxes. The Episcopal Church (the Anglican Church) was the official religion of Virginia, Maryland, Georgia, the Carolinas, and New York. Puritanism (later called Congregationalism) was the official church in Massachusetts, Connecticut, and New Hampshire.

1. The Growth of Toleration. Before long, many other religious denominations took root in America. Most of the Scots and Scotch-Irish were Presbyterians. Americans of Dutch descent belonged to the Dutch Reformed Church. Many Germans were Lutherans, while others belonged to smaller groups such as the Mennonites. Quakers and Baptists were fairly numerous. There were also some Roman Catholics and a few Jews.

Religious freedom increased in America chiefly because people practiced so many different forms of worship. By the 1700s, the strict rules of earlier times had been largely relaxed. Most people found a place where they could worship as they pleased.

Some people, however, remained intolerant of religions not their own. Fearing the pope, many settlers distrusted Roman Catholics. Maryland—noted for its early toleration—passed anti-Catholic laws after 1691 (when it became a royal colony). Catholics lost the right to vote and to hold public religious services. Although some colonies permitted Jews to worship in public, most denied them the right to vote or hold public office.

2. The Great Awakening. As time passed, many colonists lost their intense zeal for religion. In the 1730s and 1740s, however, a new religious movement, the *Great Awakening*, revived their fervor. Traveling clergy preached fiery sermons. The Great Awakening stimulated church attendance, the founding of new sects, and an increased concern for the poor and oppressed.

POLITICAL AFFAIRS

England was separated from its colonies in America by 3,000 miles of ocean. The English were busy acquiring territory in and expanding trade with other parts of the world. They made little attempt, therefore, to supervise their North American settlements closely during the early colonial period. The settlers learned to manage their own political affairs.

1. Colonial Government. As new colonies emerged and settlement spread, many political changes took place. By 1775, there were three different kinds of colonies. Rhode Island and Connecticut were self-governing. Maryland, Pennsylvania, and Delaware were proprietary. The remaining eight were royal, that is, supervised directly by the English crown.

Despite these differences, the structure of government in all the colonies was similar. Each had (*1*) a governor, (*2*) a council that served both as adviser to the governor and as the upper house of the legislature, and (*3*) a representative assembly, or lower house. In the self-governing colonies, qualified voters elected the governor and members of both houses of the legislature. In the proprietary and royal colonies, the proprietor or king appointed the governor. The governor usually selected the council. Voters elected only members of the assembly.

a. Representative assemblies. For centuries, the people of England had gained many important political and civil rights. Some were guaranteed by such documents as the *Magna Carta* and the English *Bill of Rights*. Others were part of English common law— laws based on court decisions rather than a code of rules.

When English settlers came to North America, they brought with them "the rights of Englishmen." These included (*1*) trial by jury,

(2) protection against unreasonable imprisonment, (3) the right to petition the government to correct abuses, and (4) the right to a voice in government. The latter guarantee was the basis for setting up representative assemblies in the colonies.

Like the British Parliament, the colonial assemblies had the right to levy taxes and decide how public funds should be spent. This "power of the purse" was used to curb the authority of the governors and protect the interests of the people represented by assemblies. By threatening to withhold money needed to pay salaries, for instance, an assembly could force a governor to approve laws it had passed.

The right to vote was granted only to white, male property owners. In some colonies, voters also had to meet certain religious qualifications. African Americans (both enslaved and free), women, and Native Americans were denied *suffrage* (the right to vote). Despite these restrictions, colonial government was more democratic than governments in England or continental Europe.

b. Town meetings. A special form of local government was the *town meeting*, which was common in New England. People in this region settled close to one another in small villages. The center of village political activity was the town hall, where town meetings were held. In open discussions, the colonists passed laws and levied taxes

A New England town meeting.

to support the local church and schools. Colonists also selected local officials and representatives to the colonial legislature. The town meeting was (and is) a good example of *direct democracy*. In this form of government, people vote on matters directly rather than relying on elected representatives.

c. The militia. Every colony had its *militia*, a local group of armed citizens. Since communication and travel were slow, the colonists could not count on the help of British troops in emergencies. They relied on militia members to protect them from immediate danger. Serving in the militia gave colonists valuable experience. Members learned to work together as a fighting unit. Militia officers gained leadership skills. Like the town meeting, the militia provided colonists with training in self-government.

2. Stresses and Strains. Political life in England's colonies did not always run smoothly. Sometimes, conflicts broke out between the colonists and the royally appointed governors.

a. Bacon's Rebellion. In the 1670s, there was conflict between some colonists and Native Americans in the frontier areas of Virginia. A group of colonists, feeling that the current governor (William Berkeley) did not do enough to protect them, decided to act on their own. Led by Nathaniel Bacon, they destroyed a band of Susquehannock in 1676. When Berkeley proclaimed Bacon a traitor, Bacon and

Governor Berkeley faced angry colonists during Bacon's Rebellion in Jamestown, 1676.

500 supporters marched to Jamestown, Virginia's capital. They forced the governor to agree to a military campaign against Native Americans. After Bacon's men had left the capital, Berkeley ordered their arrest as rebels. Upon hearing this, Bacon attacked Jamestown and took control of the government. The governor fled. Shortly afterward, Bacon died. Berkeley returned, put down the revolt, and hanged 23 rebels. King Charles II, angered by the governor's harsh actions, removed him from office.

b. The Dominion of New England. In 1686, King James II united New York, New Jersey, and New England into a single royal province. He called it the Dominion of New England and appointed Sir Edmund Andros as its governor. All forms of the colonies' self-government were abolished. Aided by a council appointed by the king, Andros made the laws, imposed taxes, and set up his own courts. He also put a stop to colonial trade with countries other than England.

Late in 1688, King James II was overthrown. When the news reached America, a Boston mob captured Andros and sent him back to England. The new king broke up the Dominion of New England and restored the colonies' charters. But Massachusetts, largely self-governing before 1686, became a royal colony.

c. Leisler's Rebellion. While New York was part of the Dominion of New England, Andros appointed Francis Nicholson as deputy governor there. Nicholson's harsh rule aroused much anger.

After Andros was forced out, Jacob Leisler, a German-born merchant and a captain in the militia, led New Yorkers to revolt. When Leisler took control of the colony, Nicholson fled to England. Leisler headed the government from 1689 to 1691. He was popular with the common people but angered the upper classes by trying to curb their influence. Leisler lost power when a new governor was appointed to replace him. His enemies convinced the new governor that Leisler was guilty of treason. He was then arrested, sentenced to death, and hanged.

IDENTIFY OR DEFINE: established religion, suffrage, town meeting.

CRITICAL THINKING: How did the Great Awakening contribute to religious tolerance?

EDUCATION

Educational facilities in the colonies were quite limited. Wealthy families had tutors for their children or sent them to private academies or to schools in England. In most towns and cities, schooling of some sort was available to local residents. But in many remote areas, there were no schools at all. And in most colonies, it was forbidden to teach enslaved children to read or write.

1. Schools. Massachusetts Puritans set up the first public school system in the colonies. In 1647, they passed a law requiring each town of 50 families to have a primary school. These taught the basics—reading, writing, and arithmetic. Each town of 100 families also had to have a Latin grammar school (a sort of high school) that prepared qualified boys for college. Similar laws were later enacted in Connecticut and New Hampshire.

In the Middle Colonies, schools were generally church-sponsored or privately owned. The Dutch Reformed Church opened the first primary school in New Amsterdam in 1638 and the first Latin school about 20 years later. William Penn set up the first private schools in Pennsylvania in 1683. They were supported by the students' families. In the South, private academies were the rule.

2. Colleges. In 1636, Massachusetts Puritans created Harvard, the first college in the English colonies, to train young men for the

The tradition of free public education began in New England. A Massachusetts law of 1647 called on every town of at least 50 households to hire someone to teach reading and writing.

ministry. Almost all other colonial colleges were started by various religious groups for the same purpose, including William and Mary (1693), Yale (1701), and Princeton (1748).

3. Subjects Taught. Most schoolchildren did not advance beyond the "three R's" (reading, 'riting, 'rithmetic). Pupils often learned their letters by using a *hornbook*. This was a sheet of paper mounted on a board and protected with a thin covering of transparent animal horn. The hornbook displayed the alphabet, the Lord's Prayer, and the Roman numbers.

The most widely used textbook in colonial days was the *New England Primer*. It taught the alphabet, reading, and religion by means of rhymed sayings, such as the following:

In *Adam's* Fall
We Sinned all.

Thy Life to Mend
This *Book* Attend.

The *Cat* doth play
And after slay.

COLONIAL CULTURE

The literature of the colonial period dealt mainly with religion and history. Members of the New England clergy wrote and published sermons and religious tracts. A noted historical work was William Bradford's *History of Plymouth Plantation 1620–47*. Benjamin Franklin published *Poor Richard's Almanac* every year from 1732 to 1757. It presented useful information, proverbs, and rules of conduct in a witty style. Anne Bradstreet, a devout Puritan and mother of eight, wrote poetry. Two volumes of her verse were published.

1. Newspapers. The *Boston News-Letter*, started in 1704, was the first colonial newspaper to last more than a short time. By 1750, weekly newspapers were being published in almost every colony. Newspapers did much to shape American public opinion.

One occurrence strengthened freedom of the press in the colonies. John Peter Zenger, a German immigrant, was a printer and publisher in New York City in the 1720s. His newspaper, the *Weekly Journal*, carried articles criticizing the royal governor, William

Cosby. Cosby ordered Zenger's arrest. At his trial in 1735, Zenger's lawyer, Andrew Hamilton, argued that a paper had the right to publish anything that was true. The jury found Zenger not guilty. Newspapers could now openly criticize colonial authorities and their policies.

2. Libraries. During the early colonial period, people had little time for reading. Moreover, not everyone knew how to read. Imported from Europe, books were expensive and thus were bought mainly by members of the upper class. Most people owned only a Bible and an almanac.

In time, leisure and literacy increased. In 1731, Benjamin Franklin helped to found the colonies' first lending library, in Philadelphia. It was a *subscription library*, which meant that only its supporting members could use it. By the 1770s, every large town had a subscription library.

EVERYDAY LIFE

Life for the first settlers was harsh and often cheerless. But by the end of the colonial period, the standard of living in America had improved greatly. There was also a good deal of variety in everyday customs. Social position made a difference in how Americans lived. So did the region in which they settled.

1. Homes. The shelters of the earliest settlers were of two main types, either bark-covered huts or log cabins. Later, when more attention could be paid to comfort and beauty, the colonists built better homes.

In New England, the typical colonial house was a low wood cottage with a sloping roof. It was simple, with little outside decoration. (This style is known as a salt box.) In New York, the Dutch influence could be seen in the brick houses with steeply slanted roofs. Many houses in Pennsylvania were made of local stone. In the South, wealthy planters built roomy mansions with wide porches, large halls, and graceful stairways. The main house was usually surrounded by a number of separate buildings. These included a kitchen, barn, carriage house, and laundry. Slaves' cabins formed a separate community nearby.

In the average colonial home, furniture was simple and practical. Whether homemade or by the village carpenter, colonial furniture was built for long life and hard wear. Its beauty and simplicity are still admired and copied. A necessary feature in a colonial house was the fireplace. It was used not only for heating but also for cooking. Whale-oil lamps and candles supplied light.

Wealthy merchants and planters imported furnishings from England. Upper-class homes contained fine mahogany furniture and expensive linens, silverware, and china.

2. Food. Colonial food was plentiful but plain. Women did most cooking in iron pots hung over a fire in the fireplace. Meats were roasted on rotating spits, and bread and cakes were baked in ovens built into the fireplace. There was no refrigeration. Meats were salted, dried, or smoked. Vegetables and fruits were pickled or dried.

3. Recreation. The colonists worked hard, but they also found time to have fun. They fished and hunted all year round. In the winter, they enjoyed ice skating and sleigh riding. Dancing, card playing, cricket, and cockfighting contests were other popular pastimes. People also got together at house-raisings, corn huskings, elections, fairs, church services, and weddings. Wealthy Southern planters enjoyed horse racing, fox hunting, and elaborate balls.

The Puritans in New England disapproved of "idle amusements." The Sabbath was to be a day of rest and worship. To make sure of this, the Puritans passed strict *blue laws* banning all forms of entertainment on Sundays.

4. Travel and Communication. The earliest colonial roads followed narrow Native-American trails. By the middle 1700s, the main seacoast cities were connected by *post roads*—routes for the transport of mail. Travelers journeying over these roads on horseback or by stagecoach faced many hazards. They bounced over deep ruts and tree stumps, and got wet crossing streams that had no bridges. They traveled through mud in the spring, dust in the summer, and snow in the winter.

Inland travel was even more difficult because the country was covered with dense forests. Travelers followed trails or paddled boats along the many rivers. Because of the lack of good roads, few colonists journeyed far from home.

IDENTIFY OR DEFINE: hornbook, subscription library, blue law, post road.

CRITICAL THINKING: In what ways was living in colonial America different from living in the United States today?

Chapter Review

MATCHING TEST

Column A
1. Bacon's Rebellion
2. flax
3. militia
4. Leisler's Rebellion
5. direct democracy

Column B
a. allowing all citizens the right to vote on all matters before a local council
b. a crop used for making linen
c. a revolt by western Virginian farmers against their governor
d. a revolt by a New York militia against colonial authority
e. a group of armed citizens who come together during emergencies

MULTIPLE-CHOICE TEST

1. By 1750, the percentage of African Americans in the British colonies was about (*a*) 5 percent (*b*) 10 percent (*c*) 20 percent (*d*) 50 percent.

2. All of the following were important colonial economic activities *except* (*a*) fishing (*b*) coal mining (*c*) shipbuilding (*d*) lumbering.

3. Puritans were the forerunners of today's (*a*) Presbyterians (*b*) Baptists (*c*) Quakers (*d*) Congregationalists.

4. During the colonial period, representative assemblies exercised control over their governors by (*a*) using the power of the purse (*b*) vetoing royal orders (*c*) refusing to meet (*d*) forming alliances with the French.

5. The region noted for town meetings was (*a*) Chesapeake Bay (*b*) the Middle Colonies (*c*) New England (*d*) the South.

6. Bacon's Rebellion was an armed uprising against the royal governor of (*a*) Georgia (*b*) South Carolina (*c*) Virginia (*d*) Maine.

7. The first public schools in the colonies were organized in (*a*) Massachusetts (*b*) Rhode Island (*c*) Connecticut (*d*) New York.

8. The first college founded in the 13 original colonies was (*a*) Harvard (*b*) Yale (*c*) William and Mary (*d*) Columbia.

9. The Zenger trial was important because it (*a*) increased religious toleration (*b*) led to the founding of the first colonial newspaper (*c*) freed New York from royal control (*d*) strengthened colonial freedom of the press.

10. The first lending library in the colonies was founded by (*a*) Anne Bradstreet (*b*) John Peter Zenger (*c*) Ben Franklin (*d*) William Penn.

 ESSAY QUESTIONS

1. What were the *three* main classes in colonial society? Describe the kinds of people in each one.

2. Explain *three* present-day practices or institutions that we have inherited from the colonial period.

3. What is the meaning of the term "triangular trade"? Describe the operation of one such form of trade.

4. What basic features of government did all 13 colonies have in common in the early 1770s? How did their governmental structures differ?

5. Describe life in either colonial New England or colonial Virginia. Include in your answer the following: economic activities, religion, education, government, amusements.

DOCUMENT-BASED QUESTION

This question is based on the accompanying documents (1–4). It will improve your ability to work with historical documents.

Historical Context:

In the United States today, most people welcome cultural diversity. This means that they are tolerant of people who are from different backgrounds. Back in colonial America, however, things were different.

Task:

Using information from the documents and your knowledge of United States history, read each document and answer the question that follows it. Your answers to the questions will help you write the document-based essay.

Document 1. Excerpt from a resolution passed in 1688 by Mennonites, a Protestant religious group that was opposed to slavery in the colonies:

> There is a saying that we should do to all men as we will be done ourselves, making no difference of what generation, descent or color they are. And those who steal or rob men, and those who buy or purchase them, are they not all alike?

> **Source:** Green, Robert P., Jr., Becker, Laura L. & Coviello, Robert E. *The American Tradition: A History of the United States.* Columbus, OH: Charles E. Merrill, 1984.

Why do you think the Mennonites condemned people who bought slaves as much as they condemned people who dealt in the slave trade?

Document 2. Comments made by Benjamin Franklin in 1751:

> Why should the [Germans] be suffered to swarm into our Settlements, and, by herding together, establish their language and manners to the exclusion of ours? Why should Pennsylvania, founded by the English, become a colony of aliens, who will shortly be so numerous as to Germanize us instead of our Anglifying them?

> **Source:** Franklin, Benjamin. "Observations Concerning the Increase of Mankind," http://bc.bernard.columbia.edu/~lgordis/earlyAC/documents/observations.html

What did Franklin mean by wanting to "Anglify" the Germans?

Document 3. Comments made by John Adams in 1759:

> Who can study in Boston streets? I am unable to observe the various objects that I meet with sufficient precision. My eyes are so diverted with Chimney Sweeps, Carriers of Wood, Merchants, Ladies, Priests, Carts, Horses, Oxen, Coaches, Market men and Women, Soldiers, Sailors, and my Ears with the Rattle Gabble of them all that I can't think long enough in the street upon any one thing to start and pursue a thought.

> **Source:** Adams, John. *The Diary and Autobiography of John Adams.* Cambridge, MA: Belknap Press, 1961.

From John Adams's comments, what can you say about colonial Boston other than it was crowded and noisy? Explain your answer.

Document 4. Excerpt from a 1782 letter written by J. Hector St. John de Crèvecoeur:

> What then is the American, this new man? . . . I could point out to you a family whose grandfather was an Englishman, whose wife was Dutch, whose sons married a French woman, and whose present four sons have now four wives of different nations. . . . Here individuals of all nations are melted into a new race of men whose labors and posterity will one day cause great changes in the world.
>
> **Source:** de Crèvecoeur, J. Hector St. John. *Letters From an American Farmer*. NY: E.P. Dutton, 1912.

Why might a person be different if he or she had parents from two different ethnic backgrounds than from the same ethnic background? Explain your answer.

DOCUMENT-BASED ESSAY

Using information from the above documents and your knowledge of United States history, write an essay in which you:

- Explain to what extent you think that colonial Americans welcomed cultural diversity.
- Explain what advantages colonial America gained from its cultural diversity.

CHAPTER 4

Difficulties With England Lead to Revolution

For many years, there was only occasional friction between England and its North American colonies. Then in the 1760s, relations began to worsen. A major reason for this change was war between Great Britain* and France.

THE END OF THE FRENCH THREAT

Beginning in the 17th century, England and France contended for leadership in Europe. They also competed for control of the seas and for territory and influence in India and North America. During the 17th and 18th centuries, the two nations waged several wars against each other. In North America, the underlying causes of Anglo-French rivalry were (*1*) overlapping territorial claims and (*2*) competition over the fur trade. Between 1689 and 1748, three wars that started in Europe spread to the colonies. In the course of these struggles, the French and their Native-American allies raided English frontier settlements. The British tried unsuccessfully to seize Canada.

The fourth and final struggle was the French and Indian War (1754–1763). Unlike the other three conflicts, it broke out in North America and spread to Europe, India, and the Caribbean, where it was known as the Seven Years' War (1756–1763).

1. The French and Indian War: Early Years. The immediate cause of the French and Indian War was a dispute between France and England over land west of the Appalachians, especially the Ohio River Valley. In the 1740s, American fur traders began to extend their operations into that area and American farmers began to settle there.

a. Outbreak of the war. In 1753, the French began to build a chain of forts from Lake Erie south to the Ohio River. George

---

*When England and Scotland became one country in 1707, the resulting union was known as *Great Britain*. The people were called *British*. The terms *England* and *English*, however, continued in use.

Washington, a 21-year-old surveyor from Virginia, was sent to warn the French that they were trespassing on English territory and to demand that they leave. The French rejected the demand.

In 1754, the French built Fort Duquesne where the Allegheny and Monongahela rivers join to form the Ohio River. This site was the key to the Ohio Valley. This time Washington led a militia to take Fort Duquesne. His troops defeated a small group of French soldiers and quickly built Fort Necessity. But French reinforcements drove them out. This encounter marked the beginning of the French and Indian War.

b. The Albany Plan of Union. In 1754, the British set up a meeting to organize the colonies against the French. This Albany Congress had two main purposes: (*1*) to gain the help of the Iroquois Confederacy and (*2*) to unite the colonies for purposes of defense. Benjamin Franklin of Pennsylvania proposed the Albany Plan of Union. It provided for a council of delegates representing all the colonies. It would have the power to maintain an army, levy taxes, deal with Native Americans, and control westward expansion.

Both Britain and the colonial legislatures rejected Franklin's plan. Britain felt that a union of the colonies would make them too strong. The individual colonies were unwilling to give up any of their powers to such a council. Although defeated, the Albany Plan indicated that at least some colonists were thinking about union.

c. French victories. The French did well in the early years of the French and Indian War. With strong support from some Native-American groups, they defended their own positions and took key British outposts. Nevertheless, George Washington got valuable military experience as a colonial officer fighting the French.

2. Later Years of the War. The tide began to turn for the British after William Pitt became prime minister in 1757. He sent more sol-

This famous cartoon appeared in Benjamin Franklin's *Pennsylvania Gazette* shortly before the Albany Congress convened in 1754.

diers and supplies to America and appointed able officers. Pitt's actions encouraged colonial legislatures to support the war effort more actively. As a result, the British and colonial forces began to dislodge the French from such strategic positions as Fort Duquesne.

READING A MAP

The French and Indian War, 1754–1763

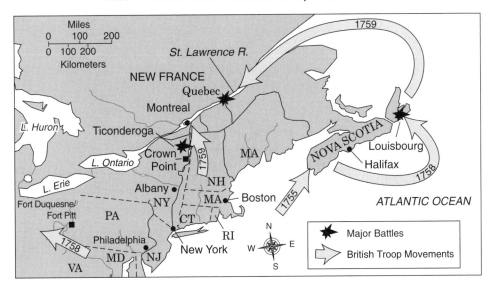

Locate the following places on the map above. Then explain why each place was important during the French and Indian War.

1. Louisbourg

2. Fort Duquesne/Fort Pitt

3. Quebec

4. St. Lawrence River

5. Ticonderoga

a. The English conquest of Canada. The most powerful French stronghold in North America was Quebec. In 1759, British troops under the command of James Wolfe defeated the French and captured the city. The following year, the British took Montreal, thus breaking France's power in North America.

b. The Peace Treaty. France and England continued to fight in other parts of the world for another three years. Therefore, the French and Indian War did not end officially until 1763, when the

Treaty of Paris was signed. The map below shows how the treaty divided the Americas among the European powers. Note that the western border of British territory was now the Mississippi River. England gained Canada. Also, Spain ceded Florida to England.

North America After the Treaty of Paris, 1763

INCREASED BRITISH CONTROL

In line with mercantilist aims, England as early as 1650 had started to pass Navigation Acts. They expanded English shipping and manufacturing by banning foreign vessels from trading with the colonies. The acts also banned the export of colonial raw materials except to England.

Nonetheless, colonial merchants continued to deal in banned goods and traded with foreign ports that were supposed to be off-limits. The English seldom enforced trade laws strictly. Their attitude was known as *salutary neglect*, a policy of letting well enough alone.

After the French and Indian War, British leaders felt it was reasonable to ask the colonists to help pay for the war and share the cost of keeping troops on the colonial frontiers. Therefore, they decided to enforce the existing trade laws and to introduce new revenue measures as well. They also took steps to increase the author-ity of British officials in America.

1. Writs of Assistance. In 1761, before the French and Indian War had ended, officials began to use *writs of assistance* to stop colonial merchants from illegally trading with foreign nations. The writs were search warrants that allowed customs officers to enter any ship, home, or warehouse and search for smuggled goods. Boston lawyer James Otis argued that the writs of assistance violated the English right to be free from unreasonable searches and seizures. The courts ruled that the use of writs was legal, but the colonists continued their protests.

2. The Proclamation of 1763. After the French were defeated, colonists began to pour into the Ohio Valley. Native peoples there be-came alarmed. In the spring of 1763, they rose up under a leader named Pontiac. Before Pontiac's Rebellion was put down, they de-stroyed most of the British frontier forts in the area and killed many white settlers. To avoid further trouble, Britain issued the Procla-mation of 1763. Among other things, this act (*1*) ordered all settlers in the Ohio Valley to move back east, (*2*) forbade new settlements west of the Appalachians, and (*3*) banned traders from entering the region without government approval.

American colonists, especially those on the frontier, resented the Proclamation of 1763. They had helped win the Ohio Valley from the French. Therefore, they felt that they had a right to develop it. Many pioneers continued to settle in the forbidden area.

3. The Sugar Act. Another British law—the Sugar Act of 1764—was designed to raise money from the American colonies. It in-creased duties on refined sugar, textiles, and other goods imported from non-British sources. (*Duties* are taxes on imports.) To discour-age smuggling, the act lowered the duty on colonial imports of for-eign molasses. The Sugar Act added more products to the list of *enumerated articles*—colonial items that could be sold only to Britain or its colonies.

Merchants of New England and the Middle Colonies complained that the higher import duties and the stricter enforcement of old trade laws would ruin them. These merchants continued to smuggle goods into the country and to carry on trade with foreign nations.

4. The Quartering Act. The colonials also resented the Quartering Act of 1765. It required colonial legislatures to *quarter* (provide funds, living quarters, and supplies to troops) to help meet the costs of keeping British troops in America. Since the colonists objected to England's policy of keeping a peacetime army in America, they certainly did not want to pay for its support. When New York's Assembly refused to comply with the act, Parliament suspended the Assembly.

5. The Stamp Act. No other British law of the 1760s stirred up such protest as the Stamp Act of 1765. It taxed newspapers, almanacs, pamphlets, playing cards, and legal documents. A government stamp had to be placed on each of these articles to show that the tax had been paid.

    a. Colonial protest. Unlike the trade laws, the Stamp Act affected all colonists. Some formed secret patriotic groups, known as the Sons of Liberty, to resist the tax. Others attacked stamp-tax collectors. Merchants canceled imports from Britain. Colonists vowed to *boycott* (stop buying) English products until the tax was repealed. At the urging of Patrick Henry, the Virginia House of Burgesses passed a resolution asserting that it had the sole power to tax Virginians. "No taxation without representation" was the slogan of the day.

    In the fall of 1765, delegates from nine colonies met in New York City as the Stamp Act Congress. They drew up a declaration explaining why they wanted the Stamp Act repealed: (*1*) Colonists were entitled to the rights of Englishmen. (*2*) Taxation without the consent of representatives elected by the people violated these rights. (*3*) Since colonists were not represented in the English Parliament, it could not tax them.

    b. British reaction. Disturbed by the strong colonial reaction to the stamp tax, some British officials, including William Pitt, spoke out against the tax. English merchants suffered badly from the colonial boycott. Therefore, Parliament repealed the Stamp Act in 1766. At the same time, though, it passed the Declaratory Act, which reaffirmed Parliament's authority over the colonies.

6. The Townshend Acts. To obtain more revenue from the colonies, Parliament in 1767 passed a group of measures known as the Townshend Acts. They levied duties on colonial imports of glass, lead, paint, paper, and tea. Income from these duties was to be used to pay the salaries of such colonial officials as governors and judges. (Previously, their salaries had been controlled by the colonial legislatures.) The Townshend Acts also restated the right of officials to use writs of assistance in searching for smugglers.

The BLOODY MASSACRE perpetrated in King——Street BOSTON on March 5th 1770 by a party of the 29th REGT

On March 5, 1770, tension in the colonies led to this confrontation between colonists and British troops in Boston. Angered by a mob, soldiers fired into the crowd and killed five colonists, including an African American—Crispus Attucks. Engraving by Paul Revere.

Led by Samuel Adams, the Massachusetts legislature urged the colonies to cooperate in resisting English taxation. Colonists responded with a boycott of many English products. It was so effective that it led to the *repeal*, in 1770, of all the Townshend taxes except the one on tea. This duty, though slight, was kept to show that Parliament still had the right to tax the colonies.

7. The Boston Massacre. The ill feelings of the 1760s erupted into violence. One March evening in 1770, a crowd of Bostonians shouted insults and threw snowballs at some British soldiers. The soldiers fired into the crowd, killing five people and wounding six. Angry citizens called the event the Boston Massacre. Prominent Bostonians urged the British to remove their troops from the city. When the British did so, further violence was avoided.

IDENTIFY OR DEFINE: Albany Plan of Union, Proclamation of 1763, Sugar Act, Quartering Act, Stamp Act.

CRITICAL THINKING: Why did more British soldiers come to the colonies after the French and Indian War? Why did some colonists object to their coming?

A WORSENING CRISIS

For a time after the Boston Massacre, tensions lessened. But it was the calm before the storm.

1. Committees of Correspondence. People like Samuel Adams were determined to keep anti-British feeling alive. In 1772, he and other Sons of Liberty in Boston formed a local Committee of Correspondence to publicize complaints against the British. The idea soon spread throughout most of colonial America. This communications network enabled various towns and colonies to keep one another informed of new developments. The committees helped shape public opinion and encouraged a feeling of unity among the colonies.

2. Trouble Over Tea. Colonial anger erupted once again when Parliament passed the *Tea Act* of 1773 to aid the financially troubled British East India Company. It allowed the company to ship tea to America without paying the heavy duty required in England. This made it possible for the company to undersell colonial importers of English tea, as well as smugglers of foreign tea. Although the Tea Act lowered the cost of tea in America, colonists had good reasons for objecting to it: (*1*) Colonial tea merchants could not match the company's low prices. (*2*) It enabled the British East India Company to gain exclusive control of the American tea trade. (*3*) If Parliament granted similar rights to other English companies, all colonial merchants would be ruined.

Bostonians refused to allow the unloading of three tea ships. Then one night, the Sons of Liberty, dressed as Native Americans, boarded the ships and dumped its cargo into the harbor. The Boston Tea Party of 1773 inspired similar "parties" elsewhere in the colonies.

3. Punishing the Colonies. To punish Massachusetts for the Boston Tea Party, the British Parliament passed four Coercive

Bostonians pay the tax collector—
not with money but with tar and
feathers and steaming hot tea.

Acts in 1774: (*1*) The port of Boston was closed to all commerce until the colonists paid for the destroyed tea. (*2*) The people of Massachusetts were deprived of the right to elect certain officials, select jurors, and hold town meetings, except by permission. Thomas Gage was appointed military governor of the colony. (*3*) British soldiers and officials accused of certain crimes in Massachusetts were to be tried in England, not in the colony. (*4*) People in all the colonies were required to quarter British soldiers.

The Quebec Act, a fifth law enacted at this time, extended the boundary of the Canadian province of Quebec southward to the Ohio River. This law was not passed to punish colonists. But Americans regarded it as a punishment, because it gave the Ohio Valley to Canada. The act also subjected the area to French-Canadian law (with its emphasis on centralized, royal authority) and to settlement by Roman Catholics. The colonists called this entire group of five laws the "Intolerable Acts."

4. The First Continental Congress. With Boston Harbor closed to commerce, the people of Boston faced economic ruin. Some colonial leaders warned that the British punishment of Massachusetts endangered the liberties of all the colonies.

Colonial leaders convened an intercolonial congress. Delegates from all the colonies except Georgia met in Philadelphia in September 1774. This First Continental Congress took three major steps: (*1*)

It issued the Declaration of Rights, stating that colonists were entitled to all the rights of Englishmen. The colonial legislatures alone had the right to tax colonists (subject only to veto by the king). The declaration called the Coercive Acts unconstitutional and asked colonists not to obey these laws. (2) The delegates organized themselves into the Continental Association. As members, they agreed not to trade with Britain or to use English goods until the Coercive Acts were repealed. (3) The delegates decided to meet again the following spring if their grievances were not settled by then.

IDENTIFY OR DEFINE: Committees of Correspondence, Tea Act, Coercive Acts, Quebec Act, First Continental Congress.

CRITICAL THINKING: The Coercive Acts were so named by colonists. Why do you suppose they gave these four acts that name?

THE REVOLUTIONARY WAR

About six months after the First Continental Congress met, the American colonies went to war with England. The conflict (1775–1783) resulted in American independence. At the time of the Revolutionary War, about 2.5 million people lived in the 13 American colonies. Approximately one-third, known as *Patriots*, actively opposed British rule. Another third, called *Loyalists* or *Tories*, remained loyal to Britain. The rest were neutral, favoring neither side. As the war went on, most of the neutral colonists became Patriots.

The Patriots believed that colonists were entitled to the "rights of Englishmen." One of these was the right not to be taxed without the people's consent: "no taxation without representation." The Patriots insisted that only the colonial assemblies had the authority to tax colonists.

The English felt that Parliament represented the interests of the entire British Empire. They claimed that Americans were indirectly represented by Parliament and should therefore pay the taxes required of them. But some prominent leaders—including William Pitt and Edmund Burke—urged compromise instead of war.

In the fall of 1774, the men of Massachusetts began to organize into a militia and to stockpile weapons. They called themselves *Minutemen* because they could fight at a minute's notice.

The Battle of Concord. Note the women participating in the action on the side of the Patriots.

1. Lexington and Concord. In defiance of Governor Thomas Gage, the Massachusetts assembly secretly prepared for war. Gage found out about this, however. In April 1775, he sent soldiers to Lexington to capture John Hancock and Samuel Adams and to seize the gunpowder stored at Concord. Learning of Gage's plans, Patriots Paul Revere and William Dawes rode through the countryside, warning the colonists that the British were coming.

When British troops arrived at Lexington on April 19, 70 local Minutemen fired on them. Minutemen also attacked the British solders in Concord. As Gage's troops marched back to Boston, angry colonists fired into their ranks.

2. The Second Continental Congress. In May 1775, the Second Continental Congress met in Philadelphia with John Hancock as president. The delegates faced the choice of complying with the home country or resisting until colonial grievances were satisfied. They decided to resist.

To provide for the defense of the colonies, Congress (*1*) created the Continental Army, which included the Minutemen in the Boston area; (*2*) appointed George Washington commander in chief; and (*3*) asked each colony to raise troops and help pay for the war effort. In spite of these proceedings, the delegates reaffirmed their loyalty to the King George III.

The Colonies vs. Great Britain: Relative Strengths and Weaknesses

	Strengths	*Weaknesses*
Colonies	A great leader, George Washington	Continuous turnover because of short-term enlistments; soldiers unused to military discipline
	Fighting for freedom on familiar ground	Practically no navy
	Soldiers skilled in hit-and-run warfare	Unity hindered by local jealousies
	Foreign military and financial aid	Chronic shortage of money and supplies
Britain	Experienced generals	Fighting in hostile lands
	Well-equipped and disciplined troops	Hampered by traditional strategies
	Good navy	Long supply lines

3. Ticonderoga and Crown Point. Years before the war started, Ethan Allen in Vermont had organized a militia called the Green Mountain Boys. In May 1775, as the Second Continental Congress was meeting, Allen's militia secretly crossed Lake Champlain and attacked the British forts at Ticonderoga and Crown Point in northeastern New York. The Americans captured the forts, seized cannon and ammunition, and sent them to the Boston area to aid colonists.

4. Fighting Around Boston. After the fighting at Lexington and Concord, about 10,000 militia members camped around Boston. As they gained more recruits, the American forces decided they were ready to drive the British from the city.

   a. Bunker Hill. To obtain a commanding position over Boston and its harbor, the Americans secretly fortified Breed's Hill, near Bunker Hill. On June 17, the British attacked the Americans. Although the Americans lost this battle (mistakenly called "Battle of Bunker Hill"), they inflicted far more casualties than they suffered. They also proved their fighting ability.

   b. Boston is freed. Soon after the Battle of Bunker Hill, George Washington arrived in Boston to assume command of the Continental Army. The following spring, troops under Washington's command forced the British commander in chief, William Howe, to withdraw his troops.

5. Fighting in the South. Early in 1776, militiamen crushed a Loyalist force at Moore's Creek Bridge, in North Carolina. Later that year, American troops drove off a British attack on Charleston, South Carolina.

6. Moving Toward Independence. Proclaiming the colonists to be in a state of rebellion, King George III approved an act of Parliament closing the colonies to all commerce. He also hired thousands of soldiers from Germany to strengthen the British forces in America. (Since many of these Germans were from Hesse-Cassel, they are known as *Hessians*.)

More and more Americans began to feel that the colonies had to break away from England. Thomas Paine, an immigrant from England, sparked the spirit of independence by writing a pamphlet called *Common Sense* (January 1776). He argued that it was foolish for a whole continent to be controlled by a small island 3,000 miles away. He called upon America to break its ties with Britain.

Meanwhile, the Second Continental Congress began to function as a central government. It sent delegates abroad to seek foreign aid. The Congress also organized a navy, authorized American ships to attack English ships, and proclaimed the opening of colonial ports to trade with all countries except Britain.

7. Declaring Independence. In June 1776, Richard Henry Lee of Virginia introduced a resolution in Congress declaring that "these United Colonies are, and of right ought to be, free and independent states." Congress then chose a committee to draw up a Declaration of Independence. It was written chiefly by Thomas Jefferson.

The Declaration first stated that "all men are created equal." They are endowed by God with the rights to "life, liberty, and the pursuit of happiness." If a government threatens these rights, the people are entitled "to alter or to abolish it, and to institute new government." The document then listed 27 injustices that King George III and Parliament had committed against the colonists. It pointed out that the colonists had repeatedly petitioned the king to correct these injustices but that he had ignored the appeals. For these reasons, the 13 colonies were dissolving their connection with Britain and creating free and independent states. Congress adopted the Declaration of Independence on July 4, 1776, and cut ties with Great Britain. The United States of America was born.

Some Americans tore down a statue of George III of England in 1776 to celebrate their independence.

IDENTIFY OR DEFINE: Minutemen, Paul Revere, John Hancock, Second Continental Congress, Bunker Hill, Hessians.

CRITICAL THINKING: What danger were the signers of the Declaration of Independence putting themselves into just by signing their name?

THE MIDDLE YEARS

After the British left Boston, the war shifted from New England to the Middle Colonies. In 1776–1777, both sides won important victories.

1. Retreat From New York. Recognizing the strategic value of New York City, Washington moved his army south to defend it. In the fall of 1776, Howe, supported by a strong fleet, took New York City, forcing the Americans to withdraw into New Jersey.

2. Trenton and Princeton. The Continental Army then left New Jersey and crossed the Delaware River into Pennsylvania. On Christmas night in 1776, Washington led his troops back across the Delaware. He surprised a force of Hessians camped at Trenton, New Jersey, and took a large store of supplies. Howe sent a force under Lord Cornwallis to capture Washington. Eluding Cornwallis's army, Washington went on to defeat two British regiments at Princeton and set up winter quarters in New Jersey. The bold strokes at Trenton and Princeton encouraged the Continentals.

3. Failure of the British Plan. The main British plan in 1777 was to divide the colonies by splitting off New England. To do so, the British planned a three-pronged drive that would enable them to occupy all of New York State: (*1*) Barry St. Leger was to march one force east from Lake Ontario through the Mohawk Valley. (*2*) Howe was to lead another army northward up the Hudson River Valley from New York City. (*3*) John Burgoyne was to lead a third army south from Canada along Lake Champlain. The three forces were to meet at Albany. (See the map on page 76.)

The British strategy was unsuccessful. St. Leger encountered fierce resistance in the Mohawk Valley and was forced to retreat to Canada. Howe and Burgoyne also failed to carry out their parts of the plan.

a. The Philadelphia Campaign. Instead of proceeding up the Hudson, Howe sailed from New York City to Chesapeake Bay. He then marched on the American capital, Philadelphia. Washington tried to stop the British but was beaten at Brandywine on September 11, 1777. Howe occupied Philadelphia later that month. The Americans tried unsuccessfully to drive him out.

Washington then set up winter quarters at nearby Valley Forge. During that winter (1777–1778), supplies were scarce, and pay was irregular. Although the Americans endured almost unbearable hardships, Washington kept the army together.

b. The Battle of Saratoga. Burgoyne, meanwhile, did march south from Canada according to plan. He won an early victory at Fort Ticonderoga. But his soldiers became exhausted, supplies ran short, and settlers fought him every step of the way. Attempts to capture American supplies failed. Finally, Continentals defeated Burgoyne near Saratoga on October 17, 1777. This American victory wrecked the British plan to divide the colonies, boosted Patriot morale, and convinced France to aid openly the American cause.

New York Campaigns, June–October 1777

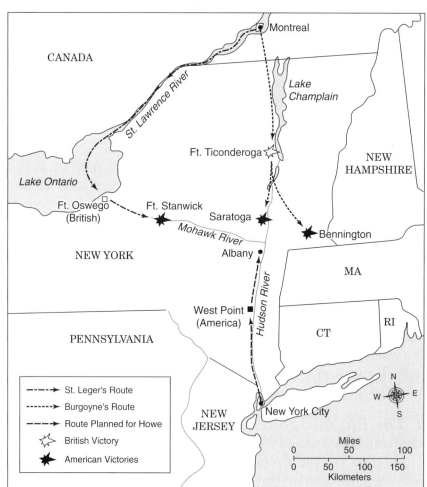

4. Foreign Aid. Hoping to weaken England, France, Spain, and the Netherlands had been secretly giving the Americans supplies, weapons, and credit ever since 1776. After Saratoga, which showed that an American victory was possible, France formed an open alliance with the United States. Early in 1778, France and the United States signed military and trade agreements. Under their terms, France sent money, supplies, a small army, and a fleet of ships to aid the Americans. The Netherlands also signed a treaty of alliance.

A number of foreign volunteers served with the Continental Army. The Marquis de Lafayette, a wealthy French noble, served as an aide to Washington. Baron de Kalb, a German-born officer in the French army, fought bravely for the Americans. Another German, Baron von Steuben, reorganized and trained the Continentals at

Valley Forge. Two Poles also aided the Americans—Thaddeus Kosciusko, who planned the fortifications of West Point, in New York, and Casimir Pulaski, who led a cavalry corps.

IDENTIFY OR DEFINE: Battle of Princeton, Battle of Brandywine, Valley Forge, Thaddeus Kosciusko, Baron von Steuben.

CRITICAL THINKING: Why is the Battle of Saratoga considered a turning point in the war?

THE END OF THE WAR

In the spring of 1778, Sir Henry Clinton replaced Howe as British commander in chief. Clinton abandoned Philadelphia and concentrated British strength in New York City. Washington prevented Clinton's army from leaving the New York area until almost the end of the war.

1. Clark in the Midwest. Meanwhile, the British were stirring up Native Americans to attack American settlements in the Northwest Territory. To end these raids, George Rogers Clark led a band of American frontier fighters into the area in the summer of 1778. In February 1779, Clark and his troops forced the main garrison of British soldiers to surrender. The Americans thus gained control of the Northwest Territory.

2. The War at Sea. Before the French fleet came to their aid, the Americans had only a few small warships and a number of privateers. (*Privateers* are privately owned vessels fitted with guns and authorized to attack enemy ships.) These ships brought supplies and munitions from Europe and seized military equipment that was on its way to British forces in America. American vessels also attacked British ships and raided English coastal towns. By 1781, Americans had captured or destroyed nearly 600 enemy vessels.

3. The British Attempt to Win the South. Failing to make headway in New England and the Middle Colonies, the British turned their attention to the South. They captured Savannah in December 1778 and Charleston in May 1780. In August of that year, British forces defeated an American army at Camden, South Carolina. American

The Revolutionary War in the South, 1778–1781

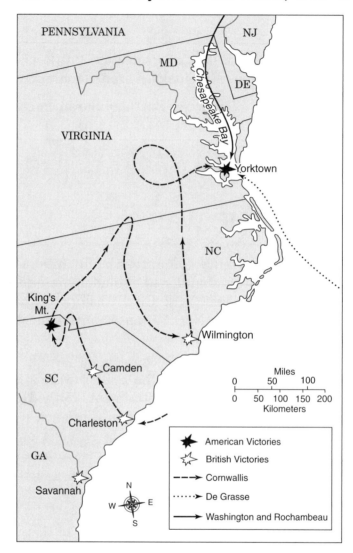

sharpshooters at King's Mountain, however, foiled one British attempt to invade North Carolina.

In 1780, Nathanael Greene took charge of Continental troops in
the South. Though Greene lost many early battles, he so weakened
British troops in North Carolina that they had to withdraw to the
coast. Greene then turned south and recaptured most of the inland
positions held by the British. By the summer of 1781, the British in
the South occupied only the seacoast cities of Savannah, Charleston,
and Wilmington. In May 1781, Cornwallis invaded Virginia and set up
a base at Yorktown, near the mouth of Chesapeake Bay.

North America After the Treaty of Paris, 1783

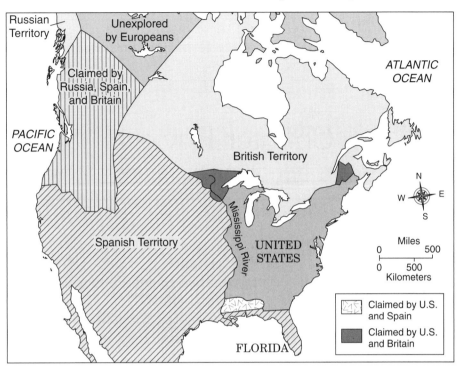

Working with the French, Washington struck a surprise blow at the British. A French fleet under Count de Grasse sealed off the entrance to Chesapeake Bay. Washington, reinforced by 5,000 French soldiers under Count Rochambeau, marched his forces from New York to Virginia. The combined army then laid siege to Yorktown. Cornwallis fought hard. Nonetheless, trapped by the American and French troops on land and by de Grasse's fleet offshore, on October 19, 1781, he surrendered. This was the last major battle of the war.

4. The Peace Treaty. Although the British still occupied New York City and Southern seaports, their hopes for victory were shattered. Early in 1782, Parliament voted to begin peace talks. In the Treaty of Paris, signed in September 1783, Britain acknowledged the independence of the 13 colonies. The boundaries of the new nation were to be the Atlantic Ocean on the east, the Mississippi River on the west, Canada on the north, and Florida on the south. Britain granted Americans full fishing rights in the Newfoundland area. It also returned Florida to Spain.

IDENTIFY OR DEFINE: privateer, George Rogers Clark, Nathaniel Greene, Yorktown, Treaty of Paris (1783).

CRITICAL THINKING: Could the United States have gained independence without the help of the French and other European nations? Explain your answer.

Chapter Review

 MATCHING TEST

Column A	Column B
1. Navigation Acts	*a.* restated right to use writs of assistance
2. Sugar Act	*b.* confined colonial imports to British ships
3. Stamp Act	*c.* lowered tax on molasses
4. Declaratory Act	*d.* taxed printed matter and legal documents
5. Townshend Acts	*e.* stated Parliament's authority over colonies

▶ **MULTIPLE-CHOICE TEST**

1. The causes of the French and Indian War included all of the following *except* (*a*) conflicting territorial claims by England and France (*b*) competition over the fur trade (*c*) the discovery of gold in the Appalachian Mountains (*d*) the movement of Americans into the Ohio Valley.

2. The Albany Plan of Union was proposed by (*a*) Samuel Adams (*b*) Benjamin Franklin (*c*) George Washington (*d*) Edward Braddock.

3. The decisive event of the French and Indian War was the (*a*) French capture of Fort Oswego (*b*) British seizure of Fort Niagara (*c*) capture of Quebec (*d*) fall of Montreal.

4. As a result of the French and Indian War, the western boundary of British territory in North America was fixed at (*a*) the Appalachian Mountains (*b*) the Mississippi River (*c*) the Allegheny and Monongahela rivers (*d*) Lake Erie.

5. After the French and Indian War, Britain (*a*) became a second-rate power in Europe (*b*) began a policy of salutary neglect

(*c*) loosened its hold on its American colonies (*d*) decided to enforce its trade laws more strictly.

6. The Stamp Act aroused heated opposition because it (*a*) taxed articles that most colonists used (*b*) slowed down mail deliveries (*c*) was passed by the colonial assemblies (*d*) provided that British soldiers were to be quartered in American towns in peacetime.

7. The British responded to the Stamp Act crisis by (*a*) sending more troops to America (*b*) closing the port of Boston (*c*) stopping colonial exports (*d*) repealing the law.

8. The colonists forced the British to repeal most of the Townshend taxes by (*a*) killing troops in Boston (*b*) boycotting English goods (*c*) destroying English imports (*d*) refusing to unload British ships.

9. Colonists objected to the Tea Act of 1773 because it (*a*) raised the price of tea (*b*) gave colonial merchants an unfair advantage (*c*) cut off colonial supplies of tea (*d*) threatened to put colonial tea merchants out of business.

10. The main reason for the First Continental Congress was to (*a*) protect colonial liberties (*b*) declare independence from Britain (*c*) plan an attack on Quebec (*d*) organize the Boston Tea Party.

▶ INTERPRETING A CARTOON

The Goose That Laid Golden Eggs

This cartoon is based on one that appeared in a London publication in 1776. Already political cartoonists were using their craft to criticize government policies.

1. Who or what does the man with the sword represent?

2. Who or what does the goose represent?

3. What do the eggs in the basket represent?

4. What relationship between the sword and the eggs does the cartoonist suggest?

5. What viewpoint is the cartoonist trying to express in the cartoon? Do you think that he or she was successful? Why or why not?

 ESSAY QUESTIONS

1. What effect did the French and Indian War have on the size of Britain's empire in North America? On Britain's relations with its 13 American colonies?

2. How did American colonists fight the Stamp Act? Were their actions effective?

3. What were the major strengths and weaknesses of the Americans and the British in fighting the Revolutionary War?

4. What was the meaning of the Patriot slogan "no taxation without representation"?

5. Name *three* Europeans who volunteered their services to the Continental Army. How did these volunteers help?

DOCUMENT-BASED QUESTION

This question is based on the accompanying documents (1–4). It will improve your ability to work with historical documents.

Historical Context:

The American Patriots in the Continental Army won the Revolutionary War only with great sacrifice. The British army was better trained and better equipped. It had a good navy and a number of experienced generals. Nevertheless, the Patriots were able to beat the British for a number of reasons.

Task:

Using information from the documents and your knowledge of United States history, read each document and answer the question or questions that follow it. Your answers to the questions will help you write the document-based essay.

Document 1.   Excerpts from a recruiting poster issued by the Continental Army's 11th Regiment at the beginning of the American Revolution:

> TO ALL BRAVE, HEALTHY, ABLE BODIED, AND WELL DIS-POSED YOUNG MEN . . . who have any inclination to join the troops, now being raised under GENERAL WASHINGTON . . . for the defence of the liberties and independence of the united states . . . TAKE NOTICE. . . . The encouragement, at this time, to enlist, is . . . a bounty of twelve dollars . . . clothing . . . provisions, together with sixty dollars a year. . . .
>
> **Source:** www.ushistory.org/valleyforge/youasked/047.htm

a.   What did "encouragement" mean?

b.   Why do you think it was necessary to offer "encouragement" to get young men to enlist?

Document 2.   Excerpt from a letter written by General Washington to the president of Congress, in which he described the condition of his army at Valley Forge, December 23, 1777:

> The soap, vinegar, and other articles allowed by Congress, we see none of. . . . The first, indeed, we have now little occasion for; few men having more than one shirt, . . . we have . . . no less than two-thousand eight hundred and ninety-eight men in camp unfit for duty, because they are barefoot and otherwise [unclothed]. . . .
>
> **Source:** Ford, Worthington Chauncey (ed.) *The Writings of George Washington*. NY: G.P. Putnam's Sons, 1889, VI, p. 260.

Describe one fear that General Washington may have had about the condition of his army at Valley Forge.

Document 3.   Excerpt from a letter written by Hessian Captain Johann Ewald in 1782, while serving as a soldier in the Continental Army:

> With what soldiers in the world could one do what was done by these men, who go about nearly naked and in the greatest privation? Deny the best-disciplined soldiers of Europe what is due

them and they will run away in the droves, and the general will soon be alone. But from this, one can perceive what an enthusiasm—which these poor fellows call "Liberty"—can do!

> **Source:** Ewald, Captain Johann. *Diary of the American War: A Hessian Journal*. New Haven: Yale University Press, 1979. Reprinted with permission of Yale University Press.

What reason did Captain Ewald give for why the American soldiers were willing to sacrifice so much? Explain your answer.

Document 4.   Excerpt from the journals of Major Samuel Shaw, describing how most of the soldiers in the Pennsylvania company under the command of General Anthony Wayne reacted when they did not receive their pay, January 1781:

> The accumulated distresses of the army have . . . produced most dreadful effects. The noncommissioned officers and privates . . . have mutinied, broken up . . . and in a body are marching to Philadelphia to demand redress of their grievances from Congress. . . .
>
> On General Wayne's cocking his pistol there were a hundred bayonets at his breast. "We love you, we respect you," said they, "but you're a dead man if you fire," and added; "Do not mistake us; we are not going to the enemy; on the contrary, were they now to come out, you should see us fight under your orders with as much resolution and alacrity [energy] as ever." They began their march that night, and the next day General Wayne forwarded after them provisions, to prevent the otherwise inevitable deprecation [destructive search for food] which would be made on private property.

> **Source:** Shaw, Samuel. *The Journals of Major Samuel Shaw*. Boston: William Crosby and H.P. Nichols, 1847.

Why did the mutinying soldiers believe they were also loyal soldiers?

DOCUMENT-BASED ESSAY

Using information from the above documents and your knowledge of United States history, write an essay in which you:

- Evaluate the bravery of the American Patriots.
- Discuss why in the end the Patriots beat the British forces.

CHAPTER 5
Forming a New Government

The newly independent United States faced political and economic difficulties. The first government the Americans set up was unable to deal with these difficulties. The second not only met the needs of the times, but it also still survives.

THE CONFEDERATION PERIOD

During the Revolution, the Continental Congress had written a constitution called the Articles of Confederation. Adopted in 1781, the Articles provided a government that would last only eight years— the so-called Confederation period. The Articles gave more power to the states than they gave to Congress. As a result, the central government was unable to operate effectively.

1. Postwar Problems. Under the Articles of Confederation, the government could not solve the nation's economic problems.

   a. Trade problems. The old British trade regulations had provided guaranteed markets in the British Empire for colonial goods. Now, Americans had to compete with everyone else. Other nations refused to make trade agreements with the United States because Congress lacked the power to enforce such agreements.

   b. Debts. In addition, the government was unable to pay its debts. To carry on the war, Congress had borrowed money from Americans. The United States also owed a great deal of money to other countries. Since Congress could not levy taxes, it had to depend on the states for funds. But the states refused to give more than a sixth of what Congress requested. Foreigners had little faith that the United States could pay its debts.

   c. Territorial disputes. There were conflicts over control of the American frontier. Contrary to the terms of the 1783 peace treaty, Britain kept military posts in the Northwest Territory. Spain claimed land in what the United States considered its own territory west of Georgia. Spain refused to allow Americans to navigate the lower Mississippi River.

Government Under the Articles of Confederation

Provision	Weakness
States were organized into loose confederation, with single branch of government: Congress.	There was no executive to enforce laws and no judiciary to settle disputes.
Congress could request funds from states.	Congress lacked power to tax.
Congress could request troops from states.	Congress had no power to raise an army on its own.
Congress could issue money and regulate weights and measures.	States could also issue money. Congress could not regulate states' domestic and foreign trade.
Each state had one vote in Congress.	Heavily populated states were not represented proportionately.
Any measure required 9 of 13 votes for passage; amending Articles required unanimous vote.	Legislation was difficult to pass; amendment was virtually impossible.

d. State vs. state. During the Confederation period, the individual states quarreled with one another. Many states claimed western boundaries that extended to the Mississippi River or even the Pacific Ocean. The land claims of some states overlapped one another. States also disagreed over navigation rights on rivers that served as boundaries between states. The states taxed one another's products and set up their own systems of duties on foreign imports.

2. Accomplishments of the Confederation. In spite of its limitations, the government of the Confederation led the American people through the last years of the Revolution. It negotiated the 1783 Treaty of Paris. It also kept the 13 states together until they were able to work out a stronger government.

One of the Confederation Congress's most important accomplishments was passage of two laws that lay the foundation for America's expansion: (1) The Ordinance of 1785 provided for the sale of public land to settlers. (2) The Northwest Ordinance (1787) drew up a plan for governing the Northwest Territory. (Both of these measures are discussed at greater length on pages 124–126.)

3. Growing Dissatisfaction. Many Americans liked the weak government. After all, they had just fought a revolution to be rid of

In 1786, Shays's forces temporarily occupied the State Supreme Courthouse in Springfield, Massachusetts.

strong central authority. But others wanted a stronger national government and began to work for change.

An event in Massachusetts made the situation more urgent. Because of the weak economy, farmers had trouble making their mortgage payments to banks. When the farmers fell behind, the banks *foreclosed* (seized) their property. In western Massachusetts, Daniel Shays, a former captain in the Continental Army, organized farmers who feared foreclosure. In the fall of 1786, these farmers forced the closing of a number of state courts that were prosecuting debtors. They also organized a march on Springfield to seize federal arms stored there. Massachusetts raised a large state militia, which succeeded in ending the disturbance in February 1787. Shays's Rebellion was a minor uprising, but it shocked such prominent citizens as George Washington. Support for a stronger national government increased.

THE CONSTITUTIONAL CONVENTION

Early in 1787, Congress called on the states to send delegates to a meeting to revise the Articles of Confederation. This conference, later known as the Constitutional Convention, met at Independence Hall in Philadelphia in May 1787.

1. The Delegates. All the states except Rhode Island sent delegates to the Constitutional Convention. Its 55 members—often called the *Founders*—shared a conservative outlook. About half of them were lawyers. Many of the others were planters and merchants.

The delegates elected George Washington president of the convention. Another delegate, James Madison, took detailed notes of the debate; he also played a key role in the debates and formulated compromises. Other important members included Benjamin Franklin, John Rutledge, and Alexander Hamilton. No women, African Americans, or Native Americans were delegates. Some prominent men, such as Patrick Henry, refused to attend because they liked the looseness of the Confederacy.

2. Constitutional Compromises. The delegates soon abandoned their original purpose of revising the Articles of Confederation. Instead, they began to work out a new constitution for a new government. Serious differences arose but were resolved by compromises.

a. State representation. One compromise dealt with the question: Should all states be represented equally, or should states with larger populations have more representatives? Large states favored the Virginia Plan, which called for representation based on population. Small states supported the New Jersey Plan, which gave each state equal representation. The so-called Great Compromise settled this dispute. Congress would consist of two houses. In the upper house, the *Senate*, each state would have two senators. In

American artist Junius Brutus Stearns made this oil painting in 1856. It is titled *Washington Addressing the Constitutional Convention.*

the lower house, the *House of Representatives*, each state would be represented on the basis of population.

b. Determining population. The Great Compromise led to another issue. How should enslaved people be counted in each state's population? The Southern states wanted the number of their representatives in the House of Representatives to be based on their total populations, including slaves. But they did not want slaves to be counted for the purpose of direct taxation. The Northern states did not want to count enslaved people for representation, but they did want to include them for taxation. This difficulty was resolved by the Three-Fifths Compromise. It stated that three-fifths of the enslaved population would be counted for both representation and taxation.

c. Regulating commerce. Manufacturers and shippers in the North wanted Congress to have the power to regulate interstate and foreign commerce. But farmers in the South were worried that Congress might use this power to tax agricultural exports. Southerners were afraid that Congress might ban the importation of enslaved people. Compromises gave Congress the power to regulate both interstate and foreign commerce. It could levy tariffs on imports, but it could not tax exports. Congress would be unable to restrict the importing of slaves until 1808.

IDENTIFY OR DEFINE: Articles of Confederation, foreclose, Virginia Plan, New Jersey Plan, Great Compromise, Three-Fifths Compromise.

CRITICAL THINKING: Do you think that the U.S. Constitution could have been adopted by the Constitutional Convention without the use of compromises? Explain your answer.

FEATURES OF THE CONSTITUTION

The introduction to the Constitution of the United States is known as the Preamble. It says that the purposes of the new government are "to form a more perfect union, establish justice, insure domestic tranquility, provide for the common defense, promote the general welfare, and secure the blessings of liberty."

1. Separation of Powers. The Founders set up three branches of government: legislative, executive, and judicial. This division of governmental authority and duties is called *separation of powers*.

a. Legislative branch. The chief duty of the legislative branch is to make laws. The legislature, Congress, has two houses. The upper one, the Senate, consists of two members from each state. The present membership is 100, since there are now 50 states. In the lower house, the House of Representatives, each state is represented according to its population. Current law fixes its membership at 435.

b. Executive branch. The executive branch enforces the laws. The president, or chief executive, is aided by a vice president and executive assistants. At present, there are 15 executive departments and many administrative agencies. The heads of the executive departments serve in the president's *Cabinet*.

c. Judicial branch. The judicial branch interprets the laws. The federal court system consists of a Supreme Court and lower federal courts. At present, the Supreme Court has nine justices, one of whom serves as chief justice. The lower courts consist of 12 circuit courts of appeals, 94 district courts, and several special courts.

2. Checks and Balances. The Founders devised the system of *checks and balances* to give each branch of the federal government some control over the others.

a. Legislative checks. Congress can check the president by refusing to allot money to the executive branch. The legislature can also block the creation of new executive agencies and do away with existing ones. The Senate can reject a treaty made by the president. (A two-thirds vote of the Senate is required to ratify a treaty.) It can reject presidential appointments by a majority vote. The House of Representatives has the power to impeach the president—that is, to bring charges of wrongdoing against him or her. If it does so, the Senate tries the president.

Congress can check the judiciary by creating or abolishing lower federal courts. It can also impeach federal judges. In addition, the Senate must approve the appointment of all federal judges. The Senate and House can check each other. Both houses must pass a bill before it becomes law.

b. Executive checks. The president can check Congress through the *veto*, a refusal to sign a bill into law. (But Congress can override a veto by a two-thirds vote of both houses.) The president can check the courts by his or her powers to appoint federal judges and to pardon convicted persons.

c. Judicial checks. The judiciary can declare acts of Congress and actions of the president *unconstitutional* (contrary to the Constitution) and therefore void. The Court's power to make this kind of judgment is called *judicial review*. (Judicial review is discussed further on page 109.)

d. Checks on the people. The Founders had little confidence in people's ability to choose officials wisely. Therefore, they called for the president to be elected indirectly by an *electoral college*. (At first, state legislatures voted for members of the electoral college. After a few decades, citizens voted directly for members of the electoral college.) Judges were to be appointed, instead of elected. Until the passage of the Seventeenth Amendment in 1913, senators were chosen by the legislatures of their states rather than elected by citizens. The delegates also wanted to keep voters from upsetting the machinery of government at any one election. To avoid this, the terms of officeholders were varied. U.S. representatives serve two-year terms; presidents, four-year terms; and senators, six-year terms. Members of the federal judiciary can hold office for life.

3. Federalism. To give the states adequate authority to function effectively, the delegates set up a system called federalism, in which power is shared by a national government and states. In the United States, powers assigned to the national government are known as delegated powers. Those retained by the states are reserved powers. Powers shared by both levels of government are concurrent powers.

In the *elastic clause*, the Constitution grants the national government the right to make all laws "necessary and proper" for carrying out its delegated powers. Powers derived from the elastic clause, called *implied powers*, are implied from those stated in the Constitution.

4. Amending the Constitution. Changing the provisions of the Articles of Confederation required the consent of every state. The Founders made the Constitution more flexible.

The Constitution can be amended in four ways. The most common of these is to have an amendment proposed by a two-thirds vote of both houses of Congress. Then the legislatures of three-fourths of the states must ratify it. The chart on the next page explains the four ways to amend the Constitution.

INTERPRETING A DIAGRAM

Four Ways to Amend the U.S. Constitution

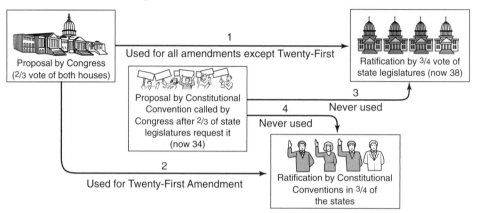

1. Although there are four legal methods to amend the Constitution, all amendments to the Constitution have started with the same action. What is that?

2. What has been the most common method for ratifying the Constitution?

3. What method of ratification has been used successfully only once?

4. Name *one* method never used successfully to amend the Constitution.

RATIFYING THE CONSTITUTION

Before the Constitution could be put into effect, at least 9 of the 13 states had to *ratify* (officially approve) it. This was to be done by a special convention in each state, not by the people directly.

1. The Struggle for Adoption. The issue of ratification divided the politically active into two groups: (*1*) *Federalists* (those who favored the Constitution) were mainly businesspeople, large landowners, and professionals. They wanted a strong central government that could regulate commerce, maintain law and order, and improve the nation's finances. (*2*) *Anti-Federalists* opposed ratifying the Constitution. People such as Patrick Henry of Virginia argued that the Constitution failed to protect fundamental rights. Federalist leaders promised them that a bill of rights would be added to the Constitution after its adoption.

Each side argued its case in articles and pamphlets. Alexander Hamilton, James Madison, and John Jay presented pro-Federalist arguments in newspaper articles that were later collected in a book called *The Federalist*. After heated debates, the Constitution was approved.

2. The Bill of Rights. The first ten amendments that make up the *Bill of Rights* were ratified and added to the Constitution in 1791. They restrict the central government and assure individual freedoms.

The First Amendment guarantees a number of basic personal rights, including freedom of religion, speech, and press. It also guarantees people the right to hold peaceful meetings and to ask the government to correct wrongs. Amendments Two, Three, and Four guarantee citizens the right to bear arms, prohibit the quartering of troops in private homes, and protect people against unreasonable searches of their property. The next four amendments provide legal safeguards (trial by jury, for example). Amendments Nine and Ten are general guarantees of individual rights and state powers.

IDENTIFY OR DEFINE: separation of powers, unconstitutional, federalism, ratify, Federalist, Anti-Federalist.

CRITICAL THINKING: To what extent is the Bill of Rights the product of the process to ratify the Constitution? Explain your answer.

Chapter Review

 MATCHING TEST

Column A	**Column B**
1. Daniel Shays	*a.* leader of rebellion of Massachusetts farmers
2. George Washington	
3. delegated powers	*b.* powers assumed under elastic clause
4. reserved powers	*c.* president of Constitutional Convention
5. implied powers	*d.* powers given to the federal government alone by the Constitution
	e. powers to be used by states

▶ **MULTIPLE-CHOICE TEST**

1. The United States was governed by the Articles of Confederation during (*a*) 1776–1783 (*b*) 1776–1789 (*c*) 1781–1789 (*d*) 1775–1781.

2. Under the Articles of Confederation, Congress (*a*) had the power to tax (*b*) could raise an army (*c*) had one representative from each state (*d*) could amend the Articles by a 9-to-4 vote.

3. All of the following were problems for the United States after the Revolutionary War *except* (*a*) failure to negotiate a peace treaty with Britain (*b*) lack of unity among Americans (*c*) a large debt (*d*) British forts in the Northwest Territory.

4. The only state *not* represented at the Constitutional Convention was (*a*) Georgia (*b*) New York (*c*) Virginia (*d*) Rhode Island.

5. The Virginia Plan and New Jersey Plan offered different methods of (*a*) counting slaves (*b*) allotting representation in the national legislature (*c*) regulating foreign trade (*d*) taxing imports.

6. Under the Constitution, enforcing laws is the main task of (*a*) the legislative branch (*b*) the executive branch (*c*) the judicial branch (*d*) all of the above.

7. The power of the courts to declare an act of Congress unconstitutional is called (*a*) judicial review (*b*) separation of powers (*c*) impeachment (*d*) federalism.

8. In order to limit the power of the people, the Founders provided for all of the following *except* (*a*) the appointment of judges (*b*) indirect election of the president (*c*) indirect election of senators (*d*) election of members of the House of Representatives by state legislatures.

9. The Constitution gives the power to declare war to (*a*) the states only (*b*) both the federal government and the states (*c*) the people only (*d*) the federal government only.

10. Anti-Federalists opposed the Constitution because they felt that it (*a*) did not give the president enough power (*b*) did not safeguard the people's fundamental rights (*c*) gave the states too much authority (*d*) did not allow for regulating commerce.

| **ESSAY QUESTIONS**

1. What were *three* weaknesses of the Articles of Confederation? How were these weaknesses corrected by the Constitution?

2. Describe *two* important compromises that were worked out by the delegates during the Constitutional Convention.

3. Explain the operation of the system of checks and balances, using examples from each branch of government.

4. Why did the Founders set up a federal system? Give *two* examples to show how the system divides governmental power.

5. List *three* rights guaranteed by the Bill of Rights and tell why you think each is important.

DOCUMENT-BASED QUESTION

This question is based on the accompanying documents (1–5). It will improve your ability to work with historical documents.

Historical Context:

The Articles of Confederation, the country's constitution since 1781, could not solve the many problems the United States had. In part, this was because Congress had no power to tax and the government lacked an executive branch. In 1787, the Constitutional Convention drafted and sent to the states a new Constitution. Since many Americans opposed this Constitution, it was not ratified by all 13 states until 1790.

Task:

Using information from the documents and your knowledge of United States history, read each document and answer the question or questions that follow it. Your answers to the questions will help you write the document-based essay.

Document 1. Excerpt from a letter by Abigail Adams to her husband, John Adams, written in 1776 when the Second Continental Congress was beginning to draft the Articles of Confederation:

In the new Code of Laws which I suppose it will be necessary for you to make I desire you would Remember the Ladies, and be more generous and favourable to them than your ancestors. Do not put such unlimited power into the hands of the Husbands. Remember all Men would be tyrants if they could.

Source: Adams, Charles Francis (ed.) *Familiar Letters of John Adams and His Wife Abigail Adams.* Boston: Houghton Mifflin, 1876.

What did Abigail Adams think that men could do with "unlimited power"?

Document 2. Excerpts from the Articles of Confederation, agreed to by Congress November 15, 1777, and in force after ratification by Maryland, March 1, 1781:

> **X.** The Committee of the States, or any nine of them, shall be authorized to execute . . . such of the powers of Congress as the United States in Congress assembled, by the consent of the nine States, shall from time to time think expedient. . . .

> **XIII.** Every State shall abide by the . . . Articles of this Confederation . . . ; nor shall any alteration at any time hereafter be made in any of them; unless such alteration be agreed to in a Congress of the United States, and be afterwards confirmed by the legislatures of every State.

Source: www.constitution.org/cons/usa-conf.htm

a. How many states had to approve giving the Committee of the States the authority to execute the powers of Congress?

b. How many states had to approve altering the Articles of Confederation?

Document 3. Excerpt from James Madison's notes during the Philadelphia convention that drew up the U.S. Constitution, June 11, 1787:

> Mr. GERRY [of Massachusetts] thought property not the rule of representation. Why then should the blacks, who were property in the South, be in the rule of representation more than the Cattle & horses of the North.

Source: www.teachingamericanhistory.org/convention/debates/0911.html

Slave owners in the South did not want slaves to be considered persons. Why did they want the slaves to count for the purpose of deciding representation in Congress?

Document 4. Excerpt from remarks by Amos Singletree during the debate in the Massachusetts Ratifying Convention, January 25, 1788:

> We contended with Great Britain . . . [over the] right to tax us and bind us in all cases whatever. And does not this constitution do the same? . . . Does it not lay all taxes, duties, imports and excises? . . . These lawyers and men of learning, and monied men [who wrote this constitution] . . . expect to get into Congress themselves . . . and get all the power and all the money into their own hands, and then they will swallow up all us little folks.
>
> **Source:** Elliot, Jonathan. *The Debates in the Several State Conventions on the Adoption of the Federal Constitution*, 2nd ed. Philadelphia: J.B. Lippincott, 1881, II, pp. 101–102.

Why did Amos Singletree feel that the U.S. Constitution was not going to be able to protect the little folks' money?

Document 5. Excerpt from Patrick Henry's remarks during the debate in the Virginia Ratifying Convention, June 5, 1788:

> This constitution . . . squints towards monarchy. . . . Your president may easily become king. . . . If your American chief be a man of ambition and abilities, how easy it is for him to render himself absolute. . . . Away with your president, we shall have a king: the army will salute him monarch.
>
> **Source:** *ibid.*, III, pp. 58–60.

Did Henry believe that the proposed U.S. Constitution contained sufficient "checks and balances" over the three branches of government? Explain your answer.

DOCUMENT-BASED ESSAY

Using information from the above documents and your knowledge of United States history, write an essay in which you:

- Explain how the issues raised in the documents and elsewhere in the chapter divided Americans in the 1770s and 1780s and made it difficult to write and ratify a new constitution for the country.
- Discuss whether it was inevitable that a new constitution would be drawn up and ratified.

UNIT III

GROWTH OF THE REPUBLIC

CHAPTER 6
Federalists and Democratic-Republicans in Power

In April 1789, the members of the electoral college unanimously elected Washington president. John Adams, with the second highest number of votes, became vice president.

DOMESTIC DEVELOPMENTS UNDER WASHINGTON

New York City was the first capital of the United States under the Constitution. At Federal Hall, on April 30, 1789, Washington was inaugurated as the nation's first president.

1. Organizing the Government. The first Congress created three executive departments—State, Treasury, and War. For secretary of the treasury, the most important post at the time, Washington selected Alexander Hamilton. He made Thomas Jefferson secretary of state and Henry Knox secretary of war. The three secretaries and Attorney General Edmund Randolph formed the nation's first Cabinet.

Congress set up a court system. The Judiciary Act of 1789 provided that the Supreme Court would have six judges: a chief justice and five associate justices. Washington appointed John Jay, a lawyer from New York, as the first chief justice. The first federal court system also consisted of 13 district courts and 3 circuit courts.

The first presidential Cabinet included (from left to right after Washington): Henry Knox, secretary of war; Alexander Hamilton, secretary of the treasury; Thomas Jefferson, secretary of state; and Edmund Randolph, attorney general.

2. Hamilton's Financial Program. The most serious problem facing the new government was finances. The Second Continental Congress and the Confederation had not repaid most of the money that it had borrowed from both foreign sources and U.S. citizens. The individual states had large debts, too. The federal treasury did not hold enough money to operate the government. Secretary of the Treasury Hamilton proposed a number of bills to place the nation on a solid financial footing.

a. Restoring credit. Hamilton believed that the U.S. government had to pay its debts in full, both abroad and at home. Few objected to funding the $12 million owed to foreign investors. But his proposal to fully repay the debts owed to people at home met with resistance.

The federal government owed about $44 million to Americans. During the war, the Continental Congress had raised money by selling *bonds*, and had paid soldiers with IOUs called *pay certificates*. Many of those who held bonds and certificates, doubting that the government would ever redeem them, sold their holdings to speculators for considerably less than their face value. At first, Congress objected to enriching speculators by funding the national debt at full value. But it finally passed the required laws.

There was even greater resistance to a proposal called *assumption of debt*. Under this plan, the federal government would assume (take over) some $25 million in debts owed by the states. Northern states owed more money than Southern states, and Southerners objected to paying off Northern debts. Hamilton overcame the Southerners' opposition by granting their demand that the nation's permanent capital be located in the South. (While Washington, D.C., was being built, Philadelphia served as the temporary capital.)

b. Establishing a National Bank. Hamilton proposed that a National Bank be organized. He gave three main arguments for a

National Bank: (*1*) It would provide a safe place for federal funds. (*2*) It would make it easier for the government and private individuals to borrow. (*3*) It would create a uniform and dependable currency by issuing sound paper money. The bank would be chartered for 20 years. Its headquarters would be in Philadelphia, with branches elsewhere. The bank would be privately owned and managed. But the government would own a fifth of the stock.

Many people were afraid that such a bank would dominate the banking business. Jefferson and others thought that the plan was unconstitutional since the Constitution did not specifically grant Congress the power to create banks. (This view, called *strict construction*, maintains that the government cannot do anything that is not clearly specified in the Constitution.)

Hamilton held that the bank bill was constitutional because Congress had the right to coin money, collect taxes, and borrow money. And the elastic clause of the Constitution enabled Congress to do what is "necessary and proper" to carry out its specified tasks. In this case, said Hamilton, a bank was needed to handle finances. (Hamilton's view, called *loose construction*, argues that the government has powers that are implied in the Constitution.) Hamilton's view prevailed, and in 1791, Congress set up the first National Bank.

c. Creating a coinage system. The many different foreign coins in circulation had to be replaced with a uniform metal currency. Hamilton proposed a *decimal system* of coinage (one based on units of 10). Congress set up a mint to produce a new series of gold, silver, and copper coins.

d. Raising money. A 1789 tariff act had placed duties on certain imports. But the levies did not bring in enough money to run the government. Therefore, in 1791 Congress approved Hamilton's idea for a tax on making whiskey. Frontier farmers, who distilled whiskey from their surplus grain, complained that this tax cut deeply into their profits. Farmers in western Pennsylvania refused to pay the tax and threatened federal tax collectors with violence. As a result, President Washington sent a force of 13,000 troops to put down the Whiskey Rebellion of 1794. Order was quickly restored. By this action, the government showed that it was able to enforce the laws.

e. Encouraging industry. Hamilton believed that the United States should encourage manufacturing. One way to do so was to adopt *protective tariffs* (high taxes on imported goods in order to protect domestic manufacturers from foreign competition). Congress did not approve this measure, mainly because of Southern opposition. The South had fewer factories and imported more foreign goods than the North.

After violence erupted in western Pennsylvania in 1794, George Washington and Alexander Hamilton led a militia from four states to put down this Whiskey Rebellion.

3. The First Political Parties. Hamilton's financial program created a strong financial foundation for the United States. But since it helped the well-to-do more than average Americans, it aroused opposition as well as support. This division of opinion led to the formation of the nation's first political parties. One group called themselves Federalists. The other group was known as Democratic-Republicans, or simply Republicans. (The Democratic-Republican party was a forerunner of the present-day Democratic party. Today's Republican party was not founded until 1854.)

The Federalist party, which backed Hamilton's policies, was especially strong in the Northeast. Its members, mainly merchants, bankers, and manufacturers, favored a strong national government and loose construction of the Constitution. They wanted to encourage commerce and industry, as well as farming. The Federalists distrusted democracy, preferring government to be in the hands of the educated and wealthy.

Thomas Jefferson and James Madison led the Democratic-Republicans. The party's chief strength was in the South and West. Most of its members were small farmers and laborers. Fearing that a strong federal government might hamper individual freedom, Democratic-Republicans supported strict construction of the Constitution as a way of limiting the government's power.

The Federalists controlled the government during the presidencies of Washington and his successor, John Adams. The years 1789–1801 are therefore known as the Federalist period. Washington is considered a Federalist, but he did not side officially with either party. In fact, in his Farewell Address he pointed out that political parties would lead to "riot and insurrection."

IDENTIFY OR DEFINE: bond, pay certificate, assumption of debt, protective tariff, strict construction, loose construction.

CRITICAL THINKING: Do you think that setting up the National Bank was constitutional? Why or why not?

FOREIGN AFFAIRS

The French Revolution took place about the same time that Washington was in office. This uprising, which broke out in 1789, led to a series of wars that involved most of Europe. In the conflicts between France and Britain, Democratic-Republicans generally favored France, while Federalists usually supported Britain.

1. France and the Genêt Affair. Early in 1793, the French king was executed. France then found itself at war with Britain, Spain, and the Netherlands. The French expected the United States to help them because the two nations had signed a treaty of alliance during the American Revolution. But Washington, Jefferson, and Hamilton felt that the United States was too weak to go to war. Washington issued a Proclamation of Neutrality in April 1793. It declared that the United States would remain at peace with both sides. The president warned U.S. citizens to avoid unfriendly acts against any nation at war.

Meanwhile, the French government sent a diplomat, Edmond Genêt, to obtain help from the United States. In the spring of 1793, "Citizen" Genêt began to organize military expeditions against Spanish-held Florida and Louisiana. He provided Americans with commissions in the French army. He also arranged for privateers to sail from U.S. ports to attack British merchant ships. After Genêt ignored warnings to stop these activities, Washington asked the French government to recall him. As it turned out, a new regime had come to power in France that wanted Genêt brought home under arrest. Fearing for his life, Genêt requested and received permission to remain in the United States.

2. Britain and the Jay Treaty. In violation of the 1783 Treaty of Paris, the British continued to occupy the Northwest Territory, where they carried on a far-reaching fur trade. They also sold guns to Native Americans and incited them to attack frontier settlements. Britain justified its occupation of U.S. territory by claiming that the United States had not honored several provisions of the peace treaty. These included (*1*) failure to pay prerevolutionary debts owed by Americans to British merchants and (*2*) failure to pay Loyalists for property taken by the states.

As a neutral nation, the United States traded with both France and Britain. To keep supplies from reaching the French, the British navy in 1793 began seizing neutral ships bound for France or its colonies. The British also took American seamen from U.S. ships and forced them to serve in the British navy. This practice was known as *impressment.*

Washington sent John Jay to Britain to negotiate an end to the U.S.-British conflict. The resulting 1794 Jay Treaty provided for (*1*) withdrawal of British troops from the Northwest Territory, (*2*) payment of debts owned to British creditors by Americans, and (*3*) compensation to American shippers for ships and cargoes seized by the British.

This treaty was widely criticized in the United States. Britain made no promises to stop seizing U.S. ships bound for French territory. Nor did it agree to halt the impressment of Americans. Washington himself did not like the treaty. But he felt that it would help keep peace at a time when the United States was not prepared to fight a war. At his urging, the U.S. Senate ratified the Jay Treaty.

3. Spain and the Pinckney Treaty. Americans wanted the right to ship goods down the Mississippi. They also wanted to deposit the goods in New Orleans and then transfer them to oceangoing vessels without paying duties to Spain. This so-called *right of deposit* was important to Western farmers because New Orleans was their only outlet to Eastern and European markets. A third concern was the disputed boundary between Georgia and Spanish Florida. Thomas Pinckney negotiated a settlement of these concerns. The Pinckney Treaty (1795) guaranteed Americans navigation rights on the lower Mississippi and the right of deposit at New Orleans. It also fixed the boundary between Spanish and U.S. territories east of the Mississippi at the 31st parallel.

IDENTIFY OR DEFINE: French Revolution, Edmond Genêt, Jay Treaty, Pinckney Treaty.

CRITICAL THINKING: Identify *two* problems the Washington administration had with Great Britain. Tell how or whether these problems were resolved by 1797.

ADAMS AS PRESIDENT

Washington decided not to run for a third term in 1796. The Federalist candidate, John Adams, won by a narrow margin over his Democratic-Republican opponent, Thomas Jefferson. Jefferson became vice president.

1. More Trouble With France. Relations with France grew worse after the signing of the Jay Treaty. The French felt that the United States was ignoring its mutual-aid agreement with them and moving closer to Britain. French vessels began to seize merchant ships bound for British ports. The French government refused to receive the U.S. minister, Charles Pinckney.

a. XYZ Affair. In 1797, Adams sent a delegation to France to try to settle the difficulties. It met with three French agents, who demanded a large bribe and the promise of a U.S. loan to France before

THE GRANGER COLLECTION, NEW YORK.

French Monster in the XYZ Affair: "Money, Money, Money!" U.S. Commissioners: "Cease bawling, Monster! We will not give you six pence."

negotiations could begin. These demands were rejected. Early the next year, American newspapers reported the demands made by the French agents, who were identified simply as X, Y, and Z. The XYZ Affair, as it was called, aroused a storm of anti-French protest in the United States. In preparation for war, Congress passed defense measures and created the Department of the Navy.

b. Undeclared naval war. From 1798 through 1800, the United States and France fought an undeclared naval war. The tiny U.S. Navy took more than 80 French ships while losing only one of its own. Not wanting a full-scale war, the French negotiated an agreement with the United States that ended the hostilities.

2. The Alien and Sedition Acts. At the height of the French crisis, in 1798, the Federalist-dominated Congress passed four laws known as the Alien and Sedition Acts. (An *alien* is a resident noncitizen; *sedition* means treason.) (*1*) One act raised the residency requirement for citizenship from 5 to 14 years. (*2*) Another gave the president power to deport any alien considered dangerous to the nation. (*3*) The third act gave the president authority to arrest or deport enemy aliens in time of war. (*4*) The fourth made it a crime to publish "false, scandalous, and malicious writing" about the U.S. government or its officials. Federalists defended the Alien and Sedition Acts as necessary war measures. The real purpose of the acts, though, was to check the growing power of the Democratic-Republicans. Since most immigrants tended to be anti-Federalist in their outlook, delaying citizenship for newcomers prevented them from voting for Democratic-Republican candidates. The only people to be arrested for "seditious" writings were Democratic-Republicans.

3. The Kentucky and Virginia Resolutions. In 1798 and 1799, the state legislatures of Kentucky and Virginia passed resolutions declaring the Alien and Sedition Acts unconstitutional. Both sets of statements claimed that since the states had created the national government, they could ignore acts of Congress that they regarded as illegal. The resolutions formed the basis of the nullification doctrine. This is the belief that states have the power to *nullify* (declare invalid) any federal action that they consider unconstitutional. Other states, however, did not support the resolutions and the issue of nullification died down for the time being.

THE ELECTION OF 1800

In the presidential election of 1800, the Federalists nominated John Adams for a second term. Opposing him as the Democratic-Republican candidate was Thomas Jefferson.

1. Jefferson Chosen. The Democratic-Republicans won a sweeping victory in 1800. But an unusual problem then arose. According to the Constitution, members of the electoral college were to vote for two candidates, without indicating which office each was to fill. The person receiving the most votes was to become president; the runner-up, vice president. The Democratic-Republicans had nominated Jefferson for president and Aaron Burr for vice president. Since each elector cast two votes for his party's candidates, Jefferson and Burr tied.

The Constitution provides that when two candidates are tied in the electoral college, the House of Representatives must choose between them. Federalist congressmen tried to swing the election to Burr because his political views were closer to those of the Federalists. The deadlock was finally broken by Hamilton. Although a Federalist, Hamilton did not trust Burr and influenced the House to choose Jefferson. To prevent such a mixup in the future, the Twelfth Amendment was adopted in 1804. It provided that electors were to cast separate ballots for president and vice president.

2. Decline of the Federalists. The Federalists never won a presidential election again and disappeared from the political scene some 15 years after their defeat in 1800. While Federalist policies had done much to get the United States off to a good start, they favored business groups over the majority of the population. Moreover, Federalist sponsorship of the Alien and Sedition Acts aroused people's fears that a Federalist administration would destroy civil liberties.

IDENTIFY OR DEFINE: XYZ Affair, alien, sedition, nullify, Aaron Burr.

CRITICAL THINKING: How was the presidential election of 1800 unusual? How did it lead to a change in the U.S. Constitution?

DEMOCRATIC-REPUBLICANS IN POWER

The election of Thomas Jefferson as president in 1800 ended 12 years of Federalist domination of the government. It also marked a shift in political power from wealthy merchants and landowners to small farmers and property holders. Jefferson's election is often called "the revolution of 1800," but this is an exaggeration. Although his administration did reverse some Federalist policies, the changes were fewer than expected.

Jefferson was one of the best educated and most versatile of U.S. presidents. He had written the Declaration of Independence and served as governor of Virginia, foreign diplomat, secretary of state, and vice president. In addition, he was an inventor, a musician, a scientific farmer, and an architect. On the negative side, he was a slaveholder.

1. Undoing Federalist Measures. The Democratic-Republicans repealed some of the Alien and Sedition Acts and allowed others to expire. Jefferson pardoned people who had been imprisoned

The surveyor Benjamin Banneker (*inset*) helped lay out the boundaries of the new capital—Washington, D.C. Jefferson's inauguration was the first to be held in the city.

under the acts. Congress lowered the residence requirement for citizenship from 14 to 5 years. The Democratic-Republicans also repealed the tax on whiskey and cut federal expenses.

2. Marshall and the Judiciary. Shortly before the Federalists left office, Congress passed the Judiciary Act of 1801, which authorized an increase in the number of federal judges. By filling these positions with their supporters, the Federalists hoped to keep control of the judiciary. The newly appointed officials were called "midnight judges."

When the Democratic-Republicans came into office, they repealed the Judiciary Act and removed most of the last-minute appointees. But the episode led to another judicial development that was contrary to Jefferson's principles. This was the Supreme Court decision in a case called *Marbury* v. *Madison* (1803).

One of the "midnight judges," William Marbury, asked the Supreme Court to issue an order forcing Secretary of State James Madison to deliver his appointment. An earlier Judiciary Act, passed in 1789, had given the Supreme Court the right to rule in certain cases involving federal officials. The Supreme Court, however, pointed out that the *Marbury* v. *Madison* case was not one of the types of cases that the Constitution had specified could go directly to the Supreme Court. Therefore, part of the Judiciary Act of 1789 was unconstitutional. This decision helped establish the principle of judicial review (discussed first on page 91).

The decision in *Marbury* v. *Madison* was a brilliant move on the part of Chief Justice John Marshall—himself a Federalist appointed by Adams. Although the decision gave the Democratic-Republicans the power to deny a job to a Federalist judge, it limited the kinds of cases that the Supreme Court could hear. But the underlying idea— that the Supreme Court could judge a law or action unconstitutional—conflicted with the Democratic-Republican belief in strict construction. Supporters of this view felt that the Supreme Court was taking on powers not granted by the Constitution. Marshall dominated the Supreme Court from 1801 to 1835. His views angered Jefferson and his followers. But Marshall's influence helped make the Court a strong arm of the government.

THE LOUISIANA PURCHASE

The most significant event of Jefferson's presidency was the purchase of Louisiana. At this time, the term referred to vast lands lying between the Mississippi River and the Rocky Mountains.

1. Background. France, which had originally claimed Louisiana, ceded it to Spain at the end of the French and Indian War (1763). But the French ruler Napoleon wanted to restore France's empire in America. In 1800, he forced Spain to return Louisiana to France. Two years later, the French canceled the American right of deposit at New Orleans.

Western farmers were worried about shipping their goods. Americans in general did not want Napoleon's troops at the nation's back door. Therefore, Jefferson decided to buy New Orleans from the French. Early in 1803, he delegated James Monroe and Robert Livingston to offer France $10 million for New Orleans.

2. A Surprise Package. By this time, Napoleon had given up his dream of an empire in America. He had lost thousands of French troops in trying to crush a slave rebellion led by Toussaint L'Ouverture on the island of Hispaniola. In addition, France was again on the verge of war with England and needed money. Napoleon offered to sell the United States all of Louisiana, including New Orleans, for only $15 million.

This bargain doubled the size of the United States. But it troubled Jefferson. A believer in strict construction, Jefferson knew that the Constitution did not clearly authorize the government to buy foreign territory. But he was convinced that Louisiana was essential to the development of the United States. In spite of his misgivings, Jefferson persuaded the Senate to ratify the treaty.

The Louisiana Purchase and the Lewis and Clark Expedition

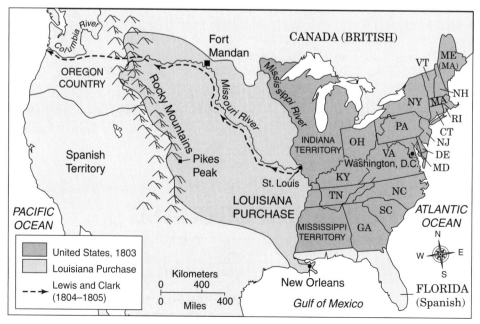

3. Explorations of the Territory. Few Americans of Jefferson's time knew anything about the region that was now called the Louisiana Purchase.

a. Lewis and Clark. Jefferson sent Meriwether Lewis and William Clark to explore the northern part of the Louisiana Purchase. Their two-year expedition started in 1804 from St. Louis and followed the Missouri River to its source. The group then crossed the Rocky Mountains into Oregon Country, where they followed the Columbia River to the Pacific Ocean. A Shoshone woman, Sacagawea, and other Native Americans aided the explorers. The reports of Lewis and Clark informed Americans about the climate, geography, animals, and peoples of the West. The exploration of the Oregon Country also laid the basis for U.S. claims to that area.

b. Pike. Jefferson sent Zebulon Pike to find the source of the Mississippi River. Pike explored the northeastern part of the Louisiana Purchase in 1805 and 1806. Later in 1806, Pike made a second trip, to the southwestern region of the territory and into Spanish territory. His account of his travels aroused much interest in the new U.S. territory.

IDENTIFY OR DEFINE: *Marbury* v. *Madison*, Louisiana Purchase, Toussaint L'Ouverture, Lewis and Clark Expedition, Sacagawea.

Sacagawea with Lewis and Clark. Sacagawea's knowledge of the country and its people proved invaluable. She helped guide the explorers to and through the Shoshone lands.

CRITICAL THINKING: Why was President Jefferson troubled about buying Louisiana?

APPROACHING CONFLICT

Jefferson was re-elected president in 1804. His second term (1805–1809) was beset with problems that arose from another war in Europe. Although U.S. interests were seriously threatened, Jefferson managed to keep the nation at peace.

1. Interference With American Shipping. Britain and France, briefly at peace, renewed their war in 1803. Their conflict again endangered the neutrality of the United States. Neither nation recognized the right of neutral countries to trade with its enemy. The British navy seized hundreds of American ships, confiscated their cargoes, and impressed their sailors.

2. Economic Pressure. Jefferson urged Congress to pass the Embargo Act of 1807. It set up an *embargo* (an official ban) on all U.S. trade with foreign countries. But it failed to bring about any change in British or French policies. Worse, it was a disaster for the U.S. economy. Merchants and shippers, faced with ruin, turned to smuggling. American shipbuilding came to a halt. Sailors, dock workers, and clerks were idled. The loss of foreign markets for crops hurt American farmers.

Opposition to the embargo was so great that it was repealed. A substitute, the Non-Intercourse Act of 1809, reopened trade with all nations except Britain and France. But since the new law failed to change British and French war policies, it was allowed to lapse after a year.

3. The War Hawks. The War Hawks, a group of legislators from the West and South, dominated Congress at this time. They wanted the United States to expand. Henry Clay of Kentucky, John C. Calhoun of South Carolina, and other War Hawks called for a war with Britain. They hoped that it would enable the United States to take over British-held Canada and Spanish-held Florida. (Spain was Britain's ally at the time.)

4. Native Americans and the Frontier. American migration to the West had increased after 1794. In that year, troops under Anthony

Wayne had defeated a Native-American force at the Battle of Fallen Timbers (near present-day Toledo, Ohio). Wayne's victory ended organized Native-American resistance to settlement in Ohio.

Western migration then spread into Indiana and Illinois, where native groups became increasingly hostile. Two Shawnee chiefs, Tecumseh and his brother, "the Prophet," aimed to prevent settlement of their lands by uniting all the tribes east of the Mississippi into a powerful confederacy. During the summer of 1811, Native Americans attacked many pioneer settlements. Settlers blamed the British for stirring up the Native Americans. U.S. troops defeated Native Americans in the Battle of Tippecanoe (in northwestern Indiana) on November 7, 1811. British arms were found on the Native Americans. Using this evidence, the War Hawks called for an invasion of Canada.

THE WAR OF 1812

James Madison succeeded Jefferson as president in 1809. For the next three years, he tried to protect U.S. neutrality by using economic pressure against Britain. But the British continued to interfere with U.S. ships and otherwise violate the United States' rights as a neutral country. In June 1812, Congress, at Madison's request, declared war against Britain. Though the war lasted more than two years, it is known as the War of 1812.

1. America Holds Its Own. The United States was not prepared for war. Its army was small, poorly equipped, and lacked competent leaders. Its navy was tiny and, though it performed well, proved to be no match for the British navy.

The war seriously damaged the U.S. economy. It halted foreign trade and brought about a decline in tariffs. To add to the United States' difficulties, its citizens were not united in support of the war. Many merchants and shipowners in the U.S. Northeast were against it because it cut off trade with England. Therefore, they refused to buy government bonds to help pay for the war. The war also caused political dissension. A group of Federalists met in 1814 in Hartford, Connecticut (the so-called Hartford Convention), to pass resolutions condemning the war. Some called for *secession* (withdrawal) from the union.

In spite of these problems, Americans fought bravely and well. Although they never managed to achieve their aim of taking Canada from the British, they achieved some major victories. (See the map on page 114.)

In August 1814, a British squadron entered Chesapeake Bay and landed troops in Maryland. They marched into Washington, D.C., almost unopposed. Retaliating for the destruction of York (in Canada) by American raiders the year before, the British set fire to many U.S. government buildings. Among them were the Capitol and the White House. Shortly thereafter, the British withdrew from the city.

In September the British sailed north to attack Baltimore but found it better prepared to resist invasion. Their landing party was stopped at the city's outskirts. British ships tried to destroy Fort McHenry at the entrance to the Baltimore's harbor. Despite an all-night bombardment, they failed. This unsuccessful attack ended the British offensive in Chesapeake Bay. One American who watched the attack was Francis Scott Key. The sight of the U.S. flag still flying the next morning inspired him to write the words to "The Star-Spangled Banner."

The War of 1812

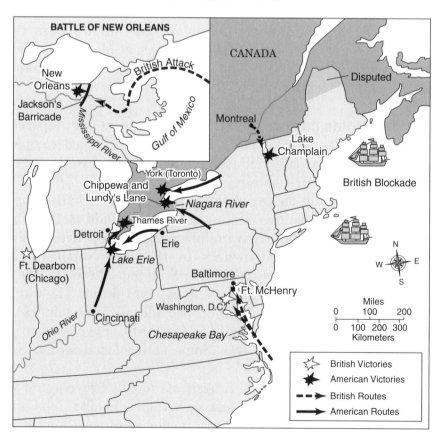

Andrew Jackson led American forces to a major victory over British forces near New Orleans, 1815. Later, Americans heard that a treaty of peace had been signed in Europe two weeks earlier.

2. The End of the War. Britain and the United States signed a treaty of peace in Ghent, Belgium, late in 1814. The treaty restored the boundaries as they had been before. The Treaty of Ghent did not mention two major causes of the war: the impressment of U.S. sailors and the violation of U.S. rights at sea. But since the wars with Napoleon were over, these issues had less urgency.

Neither side won the War of 1812, but it had important effects on the United States: (*1*) It inspired a feeling of nationalism among Americans. (*2*) It encouraged the growth of industry in the United States. Since Americans were unable to buy foreign manufactured goods during the war, their factories expanded their facilities and increased their output. (*3*) It stimulated westward expansion by ending Native-American resistance in a huge area between the Appalachians and the Mississippi. (*4*) It demonstrated to the world that the United States was capable of defending its rights.

After the war, Britain and the United States settled several problems. The Rush-Bagot Agreement of 1817 provided that neither nation would keep warships on the Great Lakes. The Convention of 1818 fixed the disputed boundary between Canada and the United States from Minnesota to the Rockies along the 49th parallel. This agreement also reaffirmed U.S. fishing rights off the coasts of Labrador and Newfoundland, and opened the Oregon Country to settlers from both nations.

TWO IMPORTANT MOVES UNDER MONROE

In the presidential election of 1816, the Federalists ran their last candidate, Rufus King. The party, already weakened, had been further damaged by its opposition to the War of 1812. James Monroe of Virginia soundly defeated King. The period of Monroe's presidency (1817–1825) is sometimes called the Era of Good Feelings. Since the only party was that of the Democratic-Republicans, it was a time of political harmony. The period is noted for two developments in foreign relations—the acquisition of Florida and the Monroe Doctrine.

1. Adding Florida. In the early 19th century, Spain controlled an important area south of the United States. One part of it, East Florida, was the long peninsula jutting into the Atlantic. The other part, West Florida, was a narrow stretch of land extending west along the Gulf of Mexico to the Mississippi River. The United States claimed that a large portion of West Florida was included in the Louisiana Purchase. When American colonists north of New Orleans declared their independence from Spanish rule in 1810, the United States annexed this section. Three years later, during the War of 1812, U.S. troops captured the Spanish fort at Mobile. The United States kept this part of West Florida, too, despite Spain's protests.

Acquisition of Florida

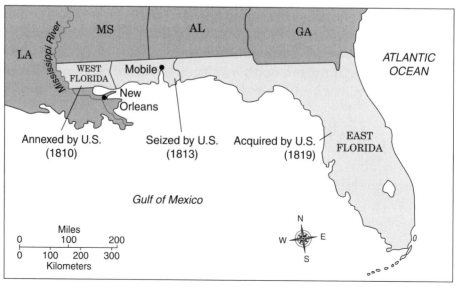

Americans had long resented Spanish control of East Florida. Native Americans escaped to the area after attacking Southern settlements. Runaway slaves fled there, too. Pirates and smugglers used it as a base of operations. In 1818, Andrew Jackson pursued some Seminoles into East Florida who had been raiding settlements in Alabama and Georgia. He not only defeated them, he also captured several Spanish forts. His expedition made it clear that the United States could take *all* of East Florida by force if it wanted to. In 1819, Spain agreed to give up the region. In exchange, the United States agreed to cancel Spain's $5 million debt to U.S. citizens. The Spaniards also surrendered their rights to West Florida. The United States, in turn, gave up its claim to Texas (which Americans considered part of the Louisiana Purchase).

2. The Monroe Doctrine. One reason why Spain was unable to defend Florida was that Spanish colonies in Latin America were in rebellion. The revolts, which began in Venezuela in 1810, soon spread to the other South American countries. In 1824, a Spanish army was decisively beaten in Peru. This defeat signaled the end of Spanish control of Latin America. Only the islands of Cuba and Puerto Rico remained under Spanish rule.

The United States quickly recognized the newly independent nations of Latin America, but Europe lagged behind. Spain was planning to recover its colonies with the aid of France. Russia, starting from its base in Alaska, was expanding southward. In 1821, the Russians claimed the Pacific coast as far south as the 51st parallel, within Oregon Country.

In 1823, President Monroe issued a strong warning to Europe to keep out of the Western Hemisphere. This proclamation, later called the Monroe Doctrine, became a cornerstone of U.S. foreign policy. It made three major points: (*1*) The American continents were closed to further colonization by European nations. (*2*) Any attempt by European powers to interfere with existing governments in America would be regarded as an unfriendly act against the United States. (*3*) The United States would not interfere in European affairs or with existing European colonies in the Western Hemisphere.

The British backed the Monroe Doctrine. They feared that Spanish or French occupation of Latin America would cut off British trade with the newly independent countries. Britain also opposed Russian expansion in the Oregon Country, where it had claims of its own. Faced with the opposition of Britain and the United States, the European powers dropped plans to retake Spain's former colonies. Russia, too, decided to pull back. In 1824, it agreed to set the boundary between the Oregon Country and Alaska at 54°40′ north latitude.

IDENTIFY OR DEFINE: embargo, War Hawk, Hartford Convention, Battle of New Orleans, Treaty of Ghent.

CRITICAL THINKING: Do you think that the Monroe Doctrine was justified? Why or why not?

Chapter Review

 MATCHING TEST

Column A	**Column B**
1. James Madison	*a.* guide to Lewis and Clark in their explorations
2. Tecumseh	
3. Sacagawea	*b.* American who explored the Southwest
4. Zebulon Pike	
5. James Monroe	*c.* U.S. president during the War of 1812
	d. U.S. president who warned Europe to stay out of the Western Hemisphere
	e. Native-American chief who tried to unite Northwest Territory tribes

▶ **MULTIPLE-CHOICE TEST**

1. The first chief justice of the United States was a lawyer named (*a*) Alexander Hamilton (*b*) George Clinton (*c*) John Jay (*d*) Henry Knox.

2. The first secretary of the treasury of the United States was (*a*) Alexander Hamilton (*b*) George Clinton (*c*) John Jay (*d*) Henry Knox.

3. The site of Washington, D.C., was chosen for the nation's capital as a result of a controversy over (*a*) assumption of debt (*b*) a national bank (*c*) a protective tariff (*d*) the Florida boundary.

4. Foreign affairs during the 1790s were complicated by (*a*) a civil war in England (*b*) wars between Britain and France (*c*) a revolution in Spain (*d*) the American Revolution.

5. U.S. grievances against the British in the 1790s included all of the following *except* (*a*) British trading posts in the Northwest Territory (*b*) Native-American attacks on frontier settlements (*c*) impressment of seamen (*d*) assumption of debts.

6. One accomplishment of the Pinckney Treaty was to (*a*) settle U.S. claims against Spanish smugglers (*b*) fix the boundary between the Northwest Territory and Louisiana (*c*) secure the right of deposit for Americans at New Orleans (*d*) buy Florida from Spain.

7. The XYZ Affair involved the United States and (*a*) France (*b*) Spain (*c*) Britain (*d*) the Netherlands.

8. The Kentucky and Virginia Resolutions were reactions against (*a*) the XYZ Affair (*b*) the Jay Treaty (*c*) an undeclared naval war with France (*d*) the Alien and Sedition Acts.

9. The Federalist candidate for president in 1800 was (*a*) Washington (*b*) Adams (*c*) Burr (*d*) Hamilton.

10. The election of 1800 was settled by the (*a*) Senate (*b*) Supreme Court (*c*) House of Representatives (*d*) electoral college.

 ESSAY QUESTIONS

1. Describe at least *three* major provisions of Alexander Hamilton's financial program. Explain what happened to each provision in Congress.

2. Why did America's first two political parties form? What was President Washington's attitude toward them?

3. Explain how the power of the federal government was challenged by the Whiskey Rebellion and the Kentucky and Virginia Resolutions.

4. Why did many Americans want to go to war in 1812?

5. Describe *two* changes that the War of 1812 helped bring about in the United States.

DOCUMENT-BASED QUESTION

This question is based on the accompanying documents (1–5). It will improve your ability to work with historical documents.

Historical Context:

Since war is the word, let us strain every nerve
To save our America, her glory increase;
So, shoulder your firelock, your country preserve,
For the hotter the war, boys, the quicker the peace.

These lyrics were printed on a poster put up by Republicans in Boston to gather support for a war with England. But New England was the main region of the country opposed to the war. Being divided, one wonders whether the young nation was ready for another war with its former home country.

Task:

Using information from the documents and your knowledge of United States history, read each document and answer the question that follows it. Your answers to the questions will help you write the document-based essay.

Document 1. Excerpt from a speech made by Representative Henry Clay of Kentucky, February 22, 1810:

It is said . . . that no object is attainable by war with Great Britain. . . . [But] the conquest of Canada is in your power. . . . It is nothing to the British nation. . . . Is it nothing for us to extinguish the torch that lights up savage warfare? Is it nothing to acquire the entire fur trade connected with the county?

Source: *Annals of Congress*, 11th Congress, 1st Session (1810), pp. 580–581.

To what was Clay referring when he spoke of "the torch that lights up savage warfare"?

Document 2. Excerpts from remarks made by Representative John Randolph of Virginia, 1811:

It is our own thirst for territory, our own want of moderation, that had driven these sons of nature [Native Americans] to desperation, of which we felt the effects. . . .

Sir, if you go to war it will not be for the protection of, or defence of your maritime rights. . . . It is to acquire a preponderating Northern influence that you are to launch into war.

Source: *Annals of Congress*, 12th Congress, 1st Session (1811), I, pp. 446, 533.

What reason did Randolph give for why Native Americans were driven to desperation?

Document 3. Excerpt from President James Madison's war message to Congress, June 1, 1812, which resulted in Congress declaring war on Great Britain:

> British cruisers have been in the continued practice of violating the American flag on the great highway of nations, and of seizing and carrying off persons sailing under it. . . . Thousands of American citizens . . . have been dragged on board ships of war of a foreign nation. . . . British cruisers have been in the practice also of violating the rights and the peace of our coasts. They hover over and harass our entering and departing commerce. . . . [O]ur attention is necessarily drawn to the warfare just renewed by the savages on one of our extensive frontiers. . . . It is difficult to account for the activity . . . without connecting their hostility with . . . [British] influence.

> **Source:** Richardson, James D. (ed.) *Messages and Papers of the Presidents.* Bureau of National Literature, 1897, II, p. 485ff.

What were the two basic reasons Madison gave for why Congress should declare war on Great Britain?

Document 4. Excerpt from an 1812 statement signed by 34 Federalist members of Congress who did not support war against Britain:

> . . . how will war upon the land protect commerce upon the ocean? . . . But it is said that war is demanded by honor. . . . If honor demands a war with England, what . . . [about] the wrong done to us by France? On land, robberies, seizures, imprisonments by French authority; at sea, pillage, sinkings, burning under French orders.

> **Source:** *Annals of Congress,* 12th Congress, 1st Session (1812), II, p. 2219ff.

What reasons did these members of Congress give in protest against a war with Britain?

Document 5. Excerpt from the Treaty of Ghent (1814), which officially ended the War of 1812:

> All hostilities, both by sea and land, shall cease as soon as this treaty shall have been ratified by both parties, as hereinafter mentioned. All territory, places, and possessions whatsoever, taken by either party from the other, during the war, or which may be taken after the signing of this treaty, excepting only the islands hereinafter mentioned, shall be restored without delay, and without causing any destruction, or carrying away any of the

artillery or other public property originally captured in the said forts or places, and which shall remain therein upon the exchange of the ratifications of this treaty, or any slaves or other private property.

Source: http://www.historycentral.com/documents/Ghent.html. Also, Miller, Hunter (ed.) *Treaties and Other International Acts of the United States of America.* Washington: Government Printing Office, 1931, II.

Why might a War Hawk in Congress have not supported the Treaty of Ghent? Explain your answer.

DOCUMENT-BASED ESSAY

Using information from the above documents and your knowledge of United States history, write an essay in which you:

- Explain why some historians call the War of 1812 the "Second American War for Independence" and others call it the "First American War of Conquest."
- Explain why it can be said that the War of 1812 brought no changes and many changes at the same time.

CHAPTER 7
Expansion and Progress

During the early 19th century, the size of the United States doubled, and its population increased four times. Although the country remained predominantly agricultural, industrialization began to reshape the nation's economy.

THE WESTWARD MOVEMENT

The unsettled regions of the United States lay in the West. These regions attracted people looking for a better life—adventurers, farmers who had exhausted their land, unemployed workers, and new immigrants. When the first census was taken in 1790, only about 5 percent of the population lived west of the Appalachians. In 1840, the sixth census showed that more than 42 percent of Americans lived there.

1. The Old Southwest. One of the first trans-Appalachian regions to be settled was the area south of the Ohio River. It is called the Old Southwest to differentiate it from the "newer" Southwest west of the Mississippi.

   a. Kentucky and Tennessee. Some years before the Revolution, pioneers from North Carolina and Virginia settled in northeastern Tennessee. Other Americans soon followed and settled in the rich valleys of the Cumberland, Tennessee, and Kentucky rivers and their tributaries.
   The most famous pioneer in this region was Daniel Boone, who found a pathway across the Appalachians through the Cumberland Gap. It became the Wilderness Road, a main route for migration into the territory.

   b. Mississippi and Alabama. The Mississippi Territory, which was farther south, was opened to settlement in 1798. Thousands of Southerners in the Carolinas and Georgia then gave up their worn-out farms and headed southwest. Southern planters moved there with their slaves and developed large cotton plantations in the fertile lowlands. Native Americans fought the settlers until Andrew Jackson defeated them at Horseshoe Bend in 1814.

Settling the Old Southwest

2. The Northwest Territory. The Old Northwest, or the Northwest Territory, had also attracted settlers before the Revolution. During the Confederation period, Congress passed two laws that affected not only the Northwest Territory but other parts of the West as well.

a. The Ordinance of 1785. This law provided that the land was to be surveyed and divided into *townships* six miles square. The planners divided the townships into uniform sections, setting regular boundaries to prevent boundary disputes among the settlers. Each township was to contain 36 *sections*, each one mile square (640 acres). One section in each township was set aside for the support of public schools. The rest of the land was then sold for $1 an acre. A purchaser had to buy a full section of land. Since most settlers could not afford to buy 640 acres, land companies bought up much of the region. They subdivided the sections and sold the smaller lots to settlers at a profit.

b. The Ordinance of 1787. This law, often called the Northwest Ordinance, organized the Old Northwest into the Northwest Territory. It included six important provisions:

- Congress would appoint a temporary governor and three temporary judges.
- When the territory had 5,000 free adult males, a representative legislature would be set up.
- When a part of the territory had a population of 60,000 free settlers, that region would be eligible for admission into the Union as a state. No fewer than three and no more than five states were to be created from the Northwest Territory.
- Personal rights, such as freedom of religion, freedom of speech, and trial by jury, were guaranteed.
- Slavery was banned.
- Public schools were encouraged.

The Northwest Ordinance is generally considered to be Congress's outstanding achievement under the Articles of Confederation. This law set a pattern for dealing with America's public lands.

READING A DIAGRAM

A Typical Township, Land Ordinance of 1785

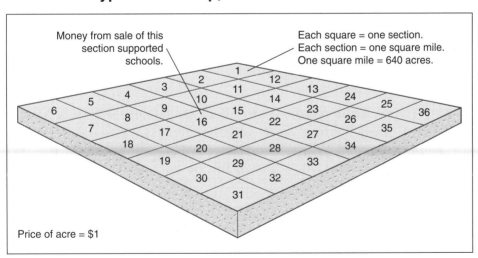

Money from sale of this section supported schools.

Each square = one section.
Each section = one square mile.
One square mile = 640 acres.

Price of acre = $1

1. What does each small box in the diagram represent?

2. In each township, how were schools supported?

3. How many acres are there in a section?

4. If you walked one length of a township, how many miles would you have walked?

5. How much did it cost to purchase a section?

It made sure that new states would be the equals of the original 13. And it guaranteed civil liberties, democratic government, and public education to Americans in new territories.

c. Settlement. The rich, level land of much of the Northwest Territory drew many New Englanders away from their rocky farms. It also attracted pioneers from New York and Pennsylvania. After their defeats at Fallen Timbers in 1794 and Tippecanoe in 1811, most Native-American groups in the eastern Northwest Territory were relocated. American settlers then flocked to the area.

3. Conditions on the Frontier. Many Americans who moved west prided themselves on their self-sufficiency and democratic spirit.

a. Pioneers develop communities. The first farm families in the West lived much as the earliest settlers had along the Atlantic coast. The men hacked clearings out of the wilderness, built log cabins, and raised food for their families. The women preserved food, made clothes, and used home remedies to treat sicknesses. As more settlers arrived, they set up churches, schools, and local businesses for their communities. A few professionals also settled in the towns to provide medical, legal, financial, and other services.

b. Outlook of the Westerners. Frontier people generally regarded each other as social and political equals. Common problems and dangers drew pioneer families together. Westerners had a strong sense of loyalty toward the national government and supported greater political democracy.

c. Native Americans. The American settlers felt that Native Americans were holding back progress by their resistance to the spread of farms and towns. The Native Americans saw that the settlers were destroying their way of life by cutting down forests and killing wild game.

The federal government arranged treaties for the purchase of Native-American lands, setting up smaller tracts for the Native Americans to live on. Many of these sales took territories from the Native Americans that earlier had been promised to them for "as long as the grass shall grow." When Native Americans refused to sign new agreements, U.S. troops forced them to move.

Thousands of Native Americans chose to move west of the Mississippi, where few American settlers lived. Others were forced to go. During the 1830s, the U.S. government removed most Native Americans of the Southeast. The Cherokees, Chickasaws, Choctaws, Creeks, and Seminoles—known as the "Five Civilized Tribes"—had

Thousands died on the Trail of Tears, a forced migration of Cherokees and others from Georgia, Alabama, and Tennessee to Indian Territory in the West. Painting by Robert Lindueux.

taken up farming and had otherwise adapted to the culture of their white neighbors. Nonetheless, U.S. troops drove many into what is now Oklahoma. So many died on the way that the journey is called the "Trail of Tears."

IDENTIFY OR DEFINE: Old Southwest, Old Northwest, township, section, Northwest Ordinance, Trail of Tears.

CRITICAL THINKING: How was U.S. democracy extended into the Northwest Territory?

THE BEGINNINGS OF INDUSTRIALIZATION

Around the mid-1700s, England began to experience the *Industrial Revolution*. Hand methods of production gave way to machine methods, and manufacturing shifted from homes to factories (the *factory system*).

The Industrial Revolution started in England's textile industry. The invention of spinning and weaving machines, operated by waterpower, made possible the large-scale manufacture of thread and cloth. (Steam replaced falling water as a source of power later in the century.) As the factory system spread to other industries, Britain became the world's leading manufacturing country.

1. Factors Favoring New England. Americans were slow to industrialize at first because they imported British manufactured goods. But then, during the Napoleonic Wars and the War of 1812, U.S. trade with England almost stopped. Enterprising New Englanders began to build factories and manufacture goods for the U.S. market.

Several conditions favored New England as a manufacturing region: (*1*) Its many swift rivers and streams provided sources of waterpower to run factories. (*2*) It had an adequate supply of laborers. (*3*) New Englanders had a tradition of craftsmanship. (*4*) The interruption of trade with Europe left merchants and shippers with idle capital to invest in factories.

2. The Textile Business. Trying to keep their industrial methods secret, the English forbade skilled workers to emigrate and banned the export of machines (or models and sketches of them). But one experienced textile worker, Samuel Slater, managed to get to the United States. Aided only by his memory, he made there the machinery necessary to spin cotton yarn. In 1790, Slater built the first successful cotton mill in America, at Pawtucket, Rhode Island.

In 1813, Francis Lowell set up the first textile factory in which all the processes for turning raw cotton into cloth took place under one roof. Similar factories were then built throughout New England. By 1840, more than 1,300 cotton mills employed 75,000 people and produced $46 million worth of cotton goods a year. Machines produced more cloth at a lower cost than people could make by hand. In 1815, a yard of cloth cost 40 cents. By 1830, it cost only $4\frac{1}{4}$ cents.

3. Stimulating Industry. The industrial growth of the United States was aided by the ingenuity of the American people and the encouragement of the federal government.

a. Interchangeable parts. Before the 1800s, single workers produced all the parts of guns and then assembled them. In the late 1790s, an inventor named Eli Whitney had the idea of assigning each part to a different worker, who would produce large quantities of that unit on a machine. These standard parts—triggers, barrels, stocks, and so on—could then be assembled into finished products.

Whitney's experiments with the new method fell short of success. It was John Hall who, in the 1820s, demonstrated that firearms made entirely of *interchangeable parts* could be produced quickly and cheaply.

The system of interchangeable parts soon spread to the production of pistols, clocks, and watches. In time, this "American system of manufacturing" was used in all industrial production—both in the United States and abroad.

b. Government help. After the War of 1812, English manufacturers tried to win back American markets by flooding the United States with cheap goods. To prevent the ruin of the nation's "infant industries," Congress in 1816 passed the first U.S. protective tariff. It raised duties on imports so that U.S. manufacturers could undersell foreign competitors. That same year, Congress chartered the Second Bank of the United States. This move enlarged the banking system and provided better credit facilities for U.S. manufacturers.

4. Growth of Cities. Before the Industrial Revolution, most Americans lived in rural areas. Industrialization changed this. Factories were built in or near cities, or cities grew up around new factories. As more Americans got factory jobs, they became city dwellers. Between 1800 and 1840, the number of U.S. cities with a population of 10,000 or more rose from 6 to 37.

The invention of the cotton gin by Eli Whitney in 1793 made the growing of cotton more profitable than ever before. Cotton production dominated the Southern economy and increased the demand for slave labor.

5. Improvements in Agriculture. In the early 1800s, machines began to replace the hand tools customarily used by farmers. The most important invention in this period was probably the *cotton gin*, invented by Eli Whitney and introduced in 1793. This machine separated seeds from cotton fibers 50 times faster than the process could be done by hand. Because of the cotton gin, the South greatly increased its cotton production—from 73,000 bales in 1800 to 732,000 bales in 1830. Thus, there was a steady supply of raw cotton for the North's growing textile industry.

Other improved farm implements appeared early in the 19th century. The *reaper* replaced the sickle for cutting grain. The *thresher* replaced the flail for separating grain from stalks. Metal plows took the place of wooden ones. Mowing and haying machines, seed drills, and cultivators also enabled farmers to increase their productivity and meet the nation's rising demand for food.

PROGRESS IN TRANSPORTATION

As the United States increased in size, it needed improved networks of transportation. Industries wanted better and faster ways to get raw materials and to ship finished products to market.

1. Vehicles and Roads. In the early 19th century, the chief means of carrying passengers and mail across land was the stagecoach. For transporting freight, Americans developed the Conestoga wagon. It was canvas-covered, with a high body, broad-rimmed wheels, and a watertight bottom for crossing streams.

a. Turnpikes. The first development in land transportation after the Revolutionary War was the building of *turnpikes* (toll roads constructed by private companies for profit). Turnpikes got their name from a pike (pole) across the road that was pushed aside after a traveler paid the toll.

The first turnpike, the Philadelphia-Lancaster Turnpike, was opened in Pennsylvania in the 1790s. Thousands of miles of toll roads were built during the next 25 years, especially in New England and the Middle Atlantic states. The network of turnpikes linking the East with frontier settlements carried farm produce to market. Turnpikes also stimulated the flow of manufactured goods to the West and South. But tolls made the cost of traveling and of shipping freight quite high. And private companies lacked the resources to build roads in difficult areas, such as in mountains.

Erie Canal at West Troy, New York. Notice that the barges were pulled by horses.

b. The National Road. In 1811, the federal government began building the National Road, or Cumberland Road, to link the East with the Northwest Territory. The first section, opened in 1818, led from Cumberland, Maryland, to Wheeling, Virginia (now West Virginia). Later extensions reached to Columbus, Ohio, and finally to Vandalia, Illinois.

2. Canals. It was cheaper to travel and transport goods by rivers and lakes than by roads. To connect bodies of water, Americans built a network of canals.

The Erie Canal was started in 1817 under the leadership of Governor De Witt Clinton of New York. This 363-mile waterway linked Lake Erie at Buffalo with the Hudson River at Albany. A series of locks raised or lowered boats from one level to another. Goods could now be shipped all the way from the Great Lakes to New York City. Dug by manual labor, the canal took eight years to complete and cost the lives of thousands of laborers.

The Erie Canal reduced freight costs between the East and the West by a tenth. It stimulated the settlement and economic development of upstate New York. It also helped make New York City the greatest shipping and trading center in the country. Its success set off an era of canal building that lasted for 20 years. By 1837, Americans had dug some 3,000 miles of canals.

3. Better Ships. After the War of 1812, the United States developed a merchant navy second in size only to that of Britain. American-built *packet boats* carried passengers, mail, and cargo across the Atlantic to European ports. In the 1840s, American ship-builders introduced the *clipper ships*, which were faster than any-thing else afloat. Long and graceful, with high masts and a great spread of sails, American clipper ships dominated the world's sea-lanes for 20 years.

Meanwhile, inventors were looking for ways to use steam power in ships. In the late 18th century, John Fitch had succeeded in pro-pelling boats with steam engines. But the first commercially suc-cessful *steamboat* was built by Robert Fulton. In 1807, his *Clermont* steamed up the Hudson River from New York City to Albany. Within a few years, steamboats were carrying passengers and freight on every navigable waterway. Now, goods could be shipped both up- and downstream. The steamboat thus shortened travel time and lowered shipping costs. They were especially useful in the West, where roads were few. Many thriving ports sprang up along rivers.

4. Railroads. The British pioneered in developing a practical steam locomotive. They also built the world's first railroad, in the 1820s. The first railroads in the United States were opened to the public in the 1830s. By 1840, nearly 3,000 miles of track were in use here.

In the 1840s, Samuel F.B. Morse perfected the telegraph, an invention that aided railroad growth. This instrument sent elec-trical sounds over wires. Morse devised a code of short and long sounds to represent letters. Using *Morse code*, a telegraph opera-tor could tap out messages and send them almost instantly to dis-tant points. In addition to speeding communication, the telegraph proved to be a valuable tool for routing railroad traffic. By 1860, a network of telegraph lines crisscrossed the United States east of the Mississippi.

IDENTIFY OR DEFINE: Industrial Revolution, interchangeable parts, infant industry, Erie Canal, Morse code.

CRITICAL THINKING: How did the Industrial Revolution change where many Americans lived?

INCREASED IMMIGRATION

By 1840, the United States had four times as many people as in 1790. Immigration played a big role in this increase. In the 1820s,

READING A PIE GRAPH

Percent Distribution of U.S. White Population, by Nationality, 1790

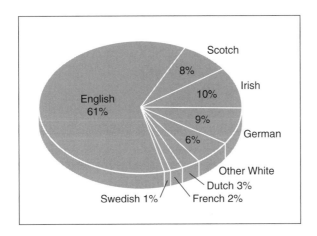

1. This graph shows the distribution of white Americans in what year?

2. Which group of people shown is most numerous?

3. Which group of people shown is least numerous?

4. What percentage does the German population have among white Americans?

5. Assume that overall there were 1,615,434 white Americans in the year depicted. How many Irish Americans would there have been?

---

the average number of newcomers admitted annually to the country was about 13,000. In the 1840s, the annual average jumped to nearly 143,000.

1. More Germans and Irish. Two events in Europe stimulated immigration in the 1840s. One was the failure of the potato crop in Ireland. Deprived of their main food, thousands of Irish starved to death. Thousands more fled to the United States. The second event was a series of unsuccessful uprisings by Germans against their rulers in 1848. Fearing punishment, many Germans came to the United States.

2. Nativist Reaction. Longer-established Americans did not always welcome immigrants. The Germans were generally treated better than the Irish. While many Germans had money and could buy a farm or go into business, most of the Irish were poor. They tended to cluster in slums in the cities where their ships docked. They took whatever manual labor they could find, often at lower wages than many others would accept. Then, too, most Irish people were Roman Catholic. In the mainly Protestant United States, distrust of Catholicism had been strong since the 1600s.

Anti-immigrant feeling gave rise to *nativism*—a movement to enact policies that favored established citizens over newcomers. In the 1840s, nativists worked to secure passage of stricter naturalization laws and to keep Catholics out of public office. In 1849, several of these groups formed the secret Order of the Star-Spangled Banner. Members were sometimes called Know-Nothings because they answered "I know nothing" when asked about the organization. The Know-Nothings strongly influenced American politics in the 1850s.

EXPANSION TO THE PACIFIC

In the 1830s and 1840s, American pioneers pushed west beyond the Mississippi. Most bypassed the Great Plains and traveled to the Rockies, the Far West, or the Southwest. In doing so, many of them settled in areas claimed by foreign nations. Some of the conflicts that arose were resolved peaceably. Others led to war.

1. Trappers and Traders. Beginning about 1820, fur trappers known as *mountain men* explored much of the Rocky Mountain region. Mountain men spent months setting traps, collecting furs, and trading with Native Americans. Many of them married Native-American women and adopted their customs.

Some frontier adventurers headed toward the Southwest into Mexican territory. Mexico, which had won its independence from Spain in 1821, was eager to increase its contacts with Americans. The Mexican town of Santa Fe attracted many traders. To get there, caravans started at Independence, Missouri, and traveled more than 700 miles along the Santa Fe Trail. Traders carried manufactured goods to exchange for silver, wool, and mules. Kit Carson was a famous Western scout who traveled this route.

2. The Republic of Texas. The Mexican government encouraged American immigration to Texas by offering liberal land grants.

The Republic of Texas, 1836–1845

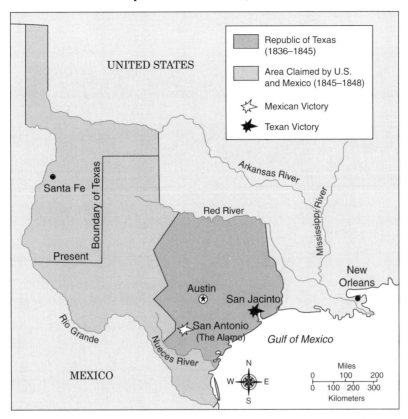

Stephen Austin founded the earliest American settlements there, in the 1820s. The area was well suited to growing cotton. Many Southern planters moved there, taking their slaves with them. By 1835, there were about 30,000 Americans in Texas.

Before long, the Americans and the Mexicans quarreled over taxation and political representation. When the Mexican government tried to stop the importation of slaves and to halt further immigration, some Texans rebelled. Early in 1836, they declared their independence from Mexico, setting up the Republic of Texas.

In an attempt to win Texas back, President Antonio de Santa Anna of Mexico led troops northward. In February, Santa Anna's forces surrounded a small band of Americans stationed in the Alamo, an old Spanish mission in San Antonio. Commanded by William Travis, the Americans also included Davy Crockett and Jim Bowie. They fought to the last man but were finally overwhelmed after 12 days.

"Remember the Alamo!" became the rallying cry of Americans in Texas. Led by Sam Houston, they defeated Mexicans at the Battle of San Jacinto and captured Santa Anna. Mexico then agreed to

Routes to the Far West

recognize the independence of the Republic of Texas. Sam Houston became its first president. Texas sought admission to the Union as a new state but was rejected. Northerners feared it would mean the extension of slavery and an increase in Southern strength in Congress. Many Americans also feared that annexing Texas would involve the United States in a war with Mexico.

3. Settling Oregon. Americans were also attracted to Oregon Country. It was bounded by the Rocky Mountains on the east and the Pacific Ocean on the west. To the south was Mexican territory; to the north were lands belonging to Russia and Britain. Its northern boundary had been set at 54°40′ north latitude in 1824 when Russia withdrew its claim to territory south of that line. Both the United States and Britain claimed Oregon, but in 1818 they had agreed to a joint occupation of the region.

Among the first Americans in the region were missionaries, who arrived in the 1830s to convert native peoples. These early settlers wrote to families and friends about the fertile soil and pleasant climate beyond the Rockies. Many Easterners decided to see for themselves. A Great Migration to Oregon began in 1843. Caravans left from Independence, Missouri, and crossed the Great Plains. Mountain men often guided travelers through the Rockies along a route known as the Oregon Trail. By 1845, about 5,000 Americans had settled in Oregon.

IDENTIFY OR DEFINE: mountain man, Stephen Austin, Republic of Texas, Alamo, Oregon Country.

CRITICAL THINKING: Why did Texas break away from Mexico in 1836?

Chapter Review

 MATCHING TEST

Column A	**Column B**
1. Ordinance of 1785	*a.* replaced the sickle for cutting grain
2. thresher	*b.* machine production of goods outside the home
3. factory system	*c.* separated grain from stalks
4. reaper	*d.* linked the East to the Northwest Territory
5. National Road	*e.* provided that land should be surveyed and divided into townships

▶ **MULTIPLE-CHOICE TEST**

1. Who found a pathway across the Appalachians through the Cumberland Gap? (*a*) Davy Crockett (*b*) Daniel Boone (*c*) Zebulon Pike (*d*) Lewis and Clark.

2. According to the Ordinance of 1787, a region in the Northwest Territory would be eligible for admission into the Union when

(*a*) it had a population of 60,000 free settlers (*b*) its total population of settlers, slaves, and Native Americans reached 60,000 (*c*) it set up public schools, courts, and a legislature (*d*) it outlawed slavery.

3. The forced migration of Native Americans from the Southeast during the 1830s is called (*a*) the Western Migration (*b*) New Frontier (*c*) Trail of Tears (*d*) Southeast Push.

4. The area of the United States that began industrializing the most after the War of 1812 was (*a*) New England (*b*) the Mid-Atlantic states (*c*) the South (*d*) the West.

5. Eli Whitney invented the (*a*) reaper (*b*) cotton gin (*c*) thresher (*d*) seed drill.

6. The state that opened the first turnpike was (*a*) North Carolina (*b*) New York (*c*) Pennsylvania (*d*) Massachusetts.

7. The Erie Canal affected commerce by (*a*) reducing freight costs (*b*) destroying the fledging railroad industry (*c*) increasing business costs (*d*) reducing taxes.

8. The first invention that made long-range communication possible was the (*a*) telephone (*b*) radio (*c*) telegraph (*d*) television.

9. The main reason that 1.5 million Irish migrated to America in the 1840s was (*a*) Parliament's Catholic Emancipation Act (*b*) the British Corn Laws (*c*) the invitation of the U.S. government (*d*) the failure of Ireland's potato crops.

10. Anti-immigrant feeling in the United States during the 1840s was known as (*a*) patriotism (*b*) nativism (*c*) federalism (*d*) regionalism.

 ESSAY QUESTIONS

1. What were the chief provisions of the Ordinance of 1787? For what region was it intended? Why was it important there and elsewhere?

2. How did conditions on the frontier affect the outlook of settlers there?

3. Describe *three* improvements in transportation in early 19th-century America. How did each benefit farms and factories?

4. Why was New England a good location for industry in the early 19th century? How did Francis Lowell contribute to New England's industrial development?

5. Describe immigration in the 1840s. Why did nativists oppose some groups of immigrants?

DOCUMENT-BASED QUESTION

This question is based on the accompanying documents (1–4). It will improve your ability to work with historical documents.

Historical Context:

In the first half of the 19th century, the economic development of the United States benefited many people, but sometimes at the expense of many others.

Task:

Using information from the documents and your knowledge of United States history, read each document and answer the question or questions that follow it. Your answers to the questions will help you write the document-based essay.

Document 1. Comments made by Samuel Young, a New York State political leader, at the groundbreaking ceremony for the Erie Canal, July 4, 1817:

> We have assembled here to commence [begin] the excavation [digging] of the Erie Canal. This work when accomplished will connect our western inland seas [Great Lakes] with the Atlantic Ocean. . . . By this great highway, unborn millions will easily transport their surplus productions to the shores of the Atlantic, procure their supplies, and hold a useful and profitable intercourse with all the maritime [sea trading] nations of the earth. Let us proceed then to work . . . cheered with the anticipated benedictions of a grateful posterity.

> **Source**: Shaw, Ronald E. *Erie Water West: A History of the Erie Canal, 1792–1834*. Lexington, KY: Univ. Press of Kentucky, 1990.

The words "benedictions of a grateful posterity" mean the "approval and thanks of people in the future." Why did Young believe that posterity would be grateful for the Erie Canal?

Document 2. Excerpt from the observations of American life made by Patrick Shirreff, a native of Scotland, upon his arrival in Chicago, 1833:

> Chicago consists of about 150 wood houses, placed irregularly on both sides of the river, over which there is a bridge. This is already a place of considerable trade, supplying salt, tea, coffee, sugar, and clothing to a large tract of country to the south and west. . . . Almost every person I met regarded Chicago as the germ of an immense city, and speculators have already bought up . . . all the building-ground in the neighborhood. Chicago will, in all probability, attain considerable size.
>
> **Source**: www.usgennet.org/usa/topic/preservation/epochs/vol6/pg130.htm

According to Shirreff, what may be the reason why Chicago will grow into a large city?

Document 3. Excerpt from a description by Evan Jones, a Baptist minister, on the forced evacuation of many Cherokee from Georgia, during which 4,000 Cherokee people died from cold, hunger, and disease, 1838:

> The Cherokee are nearly all prisoners. They have been dragged from their houses, and encamped at the forts and military posts, all over the nation. In Georgia, especially, multitudes were allowed no time to take anything with them, except the clothes they had on. Well-furnished houses were left a prey to plunders, who, like hungry wolves, follow in the train of the captors.
>
> **Source**: Jones, Evan, "The Trail of Tears," *Baptist Missionary Magazine* (1838).

Why do you think the forced evacuation of Cherokees and others to Indian Territory has come to be known as the "Trail of Tears"?

Document 4. Excerpt from a letter from teenager Mary S. Paul describing wages at a factory in Lowell, Massachusetts, November 5, 1848:

> . . . the wages are to be reduced on the 20th of this month. . . . The companies pretend they are losing immense sums every day and therefore they are obliged to lessen the wages. . . . It is very difficult for any one to get into the mill. . . . All seem to be very full of help. I expect to be paid about two dollars a week but it will be dearly earned.
>
> **Source**: www.albany.edu/history/history316/MaryPaulLetters.html (quoted from Mary Paul Letters, Vermont Historical Society)

a. What reason, according to Paul, did the companies give for lowering salaries?

b. How could the fact that all the factories are "very full of help" help to explain why the companies lowered salaries?

DOCUMENT-BASED ESSAY

Using information from the above documents and your knowledge of United States history, write an essay in which you:

- Agree or disagree with the view that in the first half of the 19th century, the economic development of the United States benefited many people, but sometimes at the expense of many others.
- State which groups benefited and which did not from the economic development of the 1800–1850 period.

CHAPTER 8

The Age of Jackson

Andrew Jackson's military exploits during the War of 1812 and his military campaign in Florida made him a national hero. Later, he served as governor of the territory of Florida and then as a U.S. senator. He ran for the presidency unsuccessfully in 1824 but won in 1828 and again in 1832. The period of his presidency (and some years before and after) is often called the Age of Jackson, or the Jacksonian era.

CHANGES IN POLITICAL LIFE

The Age of Jackson is noted for a number of changes that left the United States more democratic than it had been before.

1. Reforms at the State Level. In the original 13 states, only adult male citizens who owned land or paid taxes could vote or hold office. Women and slaves could not vote, nor, in most states, could free African Americans.

A trend toward wider suffrage had begun before Jackson became president. Most of the new states that joined the Union after 1789 allowed all adult white males to vote and hold a political office. The states in the East, seeking to keep discontented residents from moving west, gradually did away with property qualifications for voting and for holding office.

More state officials, previously appointed, were now elected by voters. The terms of elected officials were shortened so that voters could replace unpopular officeholders sooner. One state reform that affected national politics was the method of electing the president and vice president. At first, each state legislature had selected members of the electoral college. These electors, in turn, cast their ballots in presidential contests. By 1828, nearly all the 24 states allowed the general public to choose the electors.

2. National Parties. As the number of voters and elective offices increased, political parties became more important and more democratic. Before the Jacksonian era, congressional leaders from each party held a *caucus* (political meeting) to choose their candidates for president and vice president. In the 1830s, by contrast, each party held a national *nominating convention*. There party delegates representing the entire membership selected the presidential and vice presidential nominees.

FROM ADAMS TO JACKSON

In the election of 1824, all four presidential candidates were Democratic-Republicans—Henry Clay from Kentucky, Andrew Jackson from Tennessee, John Quincy Adams (the son of John Adams) from Massachusetts, and William H. Crawford from Georgia. Jackson led the other candidates in electoral votes. But since no one had a majority, the House of Representatives chose the president. Clay, who was very influential in Congress, gave his support to Adams and made him the winner.

1. A "Corrupt Bargain"? Jackson's supporters were upset because his electoral vote total had exceeded Adams's. And they were enraged when Adams appointed Clay as secretary of state. In the past, this office had often been a stepping-stone to the presidency. Jacksonians charged that Clay had entered into a "corrupt bargain" to support Adams in exchange for a high Cabinet post.

Embittered over the election, Jackson's supporters blocked President Adams at every turn. This caused a split in the Democratic-Republican party. The group supporting Adams and Clay took the name National Republicans. The Jacksonians called themselves Democrats.

2. Jackson Elected. In the election of 1828, the National Republicans nominated John Quincy Adams for a second term. Jackson, the Democrats' candidate, was elected by a large majority.

A STRONG PRESIDENT

Jackson was the first Westerner to become president. He had earlier earned the nickname "Old Hickory" for his toughness and endurance. These qualities, combined with courage, honesty, and independence, won him many admirers. But his quick temper and strong will created enemies, who called him "King Andrew the First."

Opponents of Jackson accused him of trampling on the U.S. Constitution and wielding the power of a monarch. This caricature appeared in an 1832 anti-Jackson pamphlet.

1. Spoils System. Jackson believed that every male citizen had an equal right to hold a government job. He also felt that federal positions should be held by those who had supported the winning candidate. Because of Jackson's beliefs, two practices came into wide use during his administration. One was the *spoils system*, which rewarded loyal party members with government jobs. The other was *rotation in office*. This meant regularly replacing government employees so that no one held the same job for very long.

2. Nullification Issue. One important conflict of Jackson's administration had its roots in Adams's presidency. In 1828, Congress passed a tariff act that imposed very high duties on imports. Southerners protested because the tariff increased the cost of the manufactured goods they imported. The Tariff Act of 1828, they argued, was passed to protect the interests of Northern manufacturers at the expense of Southern farmers.

a. Calhoun's protest. John C. Calhoun of South Carolina wrote a pamphlet called *The South Carolina Exposition and Protest*

(1830). In it, he argued that the tariff law was unconstitutional and, therefore, could be nullified at the state level. He also described the steps that a dissatisfied state should take.

Meanwhile, Jackson had been elected president, with Calhoun as his vice president. The new president's views on *states' rights* were unclear. In 1830, two senators, Daniel Webster of Massachusetts and Robert Hayne of South Carolina, debated the issue. Webster argued that the federal government was supreme. Hayne said that the states could overrule it. Jackson supported Webster's view, while Calhoun agreed with Hayne.

b. Crisis of 1832. In 1831, Calhoun made his nullification views public. He split with Jackson over this issue, as well as others. A new tariff of 1832 lowered some duties but kept the principle of protectionism. In reaction, the South Carolina legislature called for a state convention. At this meeting, an Ordinance of Nullification was adopted. It declared the tariffs of 1828 and 1832 null and void, and banned federal officials from collecting duties in the state.

Jackson was furious and persuaded Congress to pass the Force Bill in 1833. It authorized the use of the military, if necessary, to enforce the tariff laws. A compromise proposed by Henry Clay was worked out. It provided for a gradual reduction of import duties over the next ten years. As a result, South Carolina repealed its Ordinance of Nullification, and the crisis died down.

3. Jackson's Policy Toward Native Americans. During Jackson's presidency, several states in the South forced many Native Americans to move off tribal lands and go farther west. Jackson approved these actions. In the Supreme Court case *Worcester* v. *Georgia* (1832), Chief Justice Marshall ruled that only the federal government had the constitutional right to control Native Americans in the states. In other words, the federal government could prevent a state from seizing Native-American lands. Georgia ignored the Court's ruling, and Jackson did nothing to enforce it. His refusal to protect Native Americans led to the removal of many of them from Georgia and other states to what is now the state of Oklahoma.

4. The Bank War. The Second Bank of the United States, authorized in 1816, was due to have its charter renewed in 1836. Jackson felt that this bank was undemocratic because it concentrated power in the hands of merchants, manufacturers, and bankers. In 1832, four years before the bank's charter was due to run out, Jackson vetoed Congress's bill to renew it.

THE GRANGER COLLECTION, NEW YORK

In the early 1800s, Sequoia developed a system of writing for his people—the Cherokee. It combined letters from the English, Hebrew, and Greek alphabets, enabling the Cherokee to publish books and newspapers in their own language. The Cherokee were one of the tribes forced to follow the Trail of Tears to Oklahoma.

The Second Bank of the United States became the main issue in the election of 1832. Henry Clay, who ran for president against Jackson, favored the bank. Jackson spoke out against it. After winning re-election by a landslide, Jackson withdrew government funds from the bank and deposited the money in several dozen state banks. His enemies charged that these "pet banks" were selected because they supported Jackson.

IDENTIFY OR DEFINE: caucus, nominating convention, rotation in office, states' rights.

CRITICAL THINKING: Why do you think Jackson supported the relocation of Native Americans from the Southeast to Indian Territory, west of the Mississippi?

AFTER JACKSON

In the early 1830s, the National Republicans joined with other anti-Jackson groups to form a new party, the Whigs. Led by Henry Clay and Daniel Webster, the Whigs were supported by commercial and manufacturing people in the Northeast. Most Whigs favored such measures as rechartering a national bank, high protective tariffs, and a strong federal government.

1. Van Buren as President. Near the end of his second term, Jackson persuaded the Democrats to nominate Martin Van Buren of New York. Van Buren easily won the election of 1836.

a. Panic and depression. Jackson's "pet banks" had granted loans freely and issued paper money not backed by gold and silver. The result was a flood of paper money and widespread speculation in public lands. To stop these practices, Jackson had issued the Specie Circular in 1836. It provided that buyers had to pay for government land with gold or silver coins, not with paper money.

By early 1837, the country was in a financial *panic*. Land prices fell sharply because money was hard to borrow and land purchases had to be made in gold or silver. Speculators were ruined. People rushed to their banks to exchange paper money for coins. Lacking enough gold and silver to satisfy the demand, hundreds of banks failed. The panic led to a *depression* (a period of slow business activity and high unemployment). Factories closed, canal and railroad building all but stopped, and unemployment spread. Wage earners in the Northeast were especially hard hit. The depression lasted for about five years.

b. The Independent Treasury System. The federal government could not stop the depression. But in 1840, Van Buren established the Independent Treasury System. The new system set up so-called "subtreasuries" in several key cities, where federal funds were kept safe. By managing its own funds, the government became independent of the nation's private banks. The Independent Treasury System lasted until the early 20th century.

2. A Whig Victory. In 1840, the Democrats nominated Van Buren for a second term, but many people blamed him for the country's hard times. The Whigs' candidate, William Henry Harrison, had won popularity by defeating Native Americans at the Battle of Tippecanoe in 1811. He ran with John Tyler of Virginia.

The campaign of 1840 was the first to use the techniques of showmanship that became common in later elections. Huge meetings and torchlight parades attracted thousands. The campaign resulted in a Whig victory. A month after the inauguration, Harrison died of pneumonia. Tyler, who succeeded him, was a former Democrat who had broken with Jackson over the nullification issue. As a believer in states' rights, he did not agree with the Whig policy of a strong central government. Tyler vetoed many bills passed by the Whig-controlled Congress. He finally broke with the Whigs completely.

AN ERA OF REFORM

The democratic spirit of the Age of Jackson was reflected not only in political changes but also in efforts to reform social abuses. Many of these efforts began before the 1820s and continued after the 1840s. But they were influenced by the Jacksonian era and are, therefore, linked with that era in U.S. history. During the Jacksonian era, Americans were proud of the ways their society had developed. But many realized that society could be further improved.

1. Humanitarian Movements. Several reforms of the early 1800s were *humanitarian* in nature—that is, concerned with easing human distress.

a. Treatment of criminals. For centuries, authorities had punished wrongdoers with long jail terms, flogging, mutilation, or public execution. Reformers believed that prisoners should be taught how to lead useful lives once they were released from prison. Instead of mistreating prisoners, the reformers contended, penal authorities should put them in solitary confinement where they could reflect on their misdeeds and repent. People began to call prisons *penitentiaries* (places for penitence) and *reformatories* (places for reform).

b. Care of the mentally ill. At this time, many mentally ill people were treated badly. Dorothea Dix was a Boston schoolteacher who was interested in prison reform. In 1841, she visited a Massachusetts prison and was shocked to see mentally ill people in chains. She appealed to the Massachusetts legislature to provide better facilities and treatment for the insane. She later carried her message to other states. During the next few years, 15 states built mental hospitals where patients could be properly treated.

c. Training for the disabled. Humanitarian reformers felt that the disabled should be taught basic skills so they could be independent. Thomas H. Gallaudet founded the first school for the deaf at Hartford, Connecticut, in 1817. In 1832, Samuel Gridley Howe started the Perkins School for the Blind in Boston.

2. Temperance. Many people of the early 1800s felt, with much justification, that excessive drinking was a basic cause of problems in American society.

The first U.S. antidrinking organizations urged *temperance* (drinking in moderation). By the 1830s, however, antialcohol societies were proposing *abstinence* (no alcohol at all). Temperance reformers began to form lobbies at the local and national levels of government. (*Lobbies* are special-interest groups that try to influence government to act in their favor.) Temperance lobbyists wanted *prohibition*—a ban against the making and selling of all alcoholic beverages. Maine was the first state to adopt prohibition, in 1846. In the next ten years, several other states followed this example.

3. Religion. Several new or expanding religious groups attracted members in the early 1800s. One new denomination was the Disciples of Christ (known today as the Christian Church), which split from the Presbyterians. Another new group was the Church of Jesus Christ of Latter-Day Saints, or Mormons. Joseph Smith founded the denomination in upstate New York in 1830. The new religion gained thousands of followers but also made many enemies (discussed on page 166).

THE GRANGER COLLECTION, NEW YORK

Women were ardent crusaders in the temperance cause from its beginnings. They achieved a milestone with the founding of the Woman's Christian Temperance Union in 1874, the year in which this Currier and Ives print was first published.

A group called the Unitarians appealed to many New England intellectuals, including Ralph Waldo Emerson. The name of the sect was derived from the belief that God exists as a single Being, not as a Trinity. Unitarians stressed that people are basically good, and that moral living and good works are the road to salvation.

Two churches that dated from the colonial period grew rapidly in the early 1800s. Baptists traced their beginnings to Roger Williams in the 1630s, while the Methodists began arriving in the colonies in the 1760s. Both denominations attracted many new members in the South and West. African Americans, drawn to these churches in large numbers, formed separate Baptist and Methodist congregations. One reason for the success of the Methodists was their use of *circuit riders* (traveling preachers who carried the faith to widely scattered communities in rural areas). The camp meetings that these traveling preachers conducted were the backbone of the religious revival movement that flourished in the late 1700s and early 1800s. Farm and frontier families in particular flocked to these meetings, where they could pray and sing hymns together.

With the surge of Irish immigration in the 1840s and 1850s, the Roman Catholic Church grew rapidly, especially in such large cities as Boston, New York, and Philadelphia. At first, immigrant Catholics ran into strong opposition from Protestants. In time, however, anti-Catholic feelings died down.

4. Early Unions. The factory system gave rise to an American *laboring class*—people who depended on wages for a living. Men,

The Shakers got their name from a worship experience that included dancing, trembling, and shouting. This Shaker meetinghouse is in New Lebanon, New York.

women, and children usually worked long hours, six days a week. Workplaces were often uncomfortable, unsanitary, and even dangerous. The average pay for men was about $5 a week. Women earned less than half as much. Children were paid only $1 a week.

Since workers could not change these conditions as individuals, they organized into groups to negotiate with employers. In the late 1700s, printers and shoemakers formed the nation's first labor unions. The democratic spirit of the Age of Jackson helped this movement grow. In the early 1830s, citywide unions appeared in Philadelphia, New York, and Boston. The National Trades Union, formed in 1834, was the first U.S. labor organization to represent workers in more than one city. An important gain won by organized labor in this period was the ten-hour workday.

These early labor unions, however, faced challenges in the courts. And the depression of the late 1830s threw many people out of work. As a result, most early unions disappeared. Organized labor did not recover from this setback until after the Civil War.

IDENTIFY OR DEFINE: panic, depression, penitentiary, temperance, abstinence, prohibition, circuit rider.

CRITICAL THINKING: When and why did the Whig party come into existence?

IMPROVEMENTS IN EDUCATION

Before the 1830s, public schools in the United States were few and varied in quality.

1. Public Schooling. Horace Mann, a Massachusetts lawyer, supervised the state's public education system from 1837 to 1848. He persuaded Massachusetts to set aside more money for schools and teachers' salaries and to increase the number of subjects taught. The school year was extended from a few weeks to six months. Fifty new high schools were opened. Under Mann's guidance, the first American school for the training of teachers was set up in Lexington, Massachusetts, in 1839. Several other states, particularly in the Northeast, followed this example.

2. Private Institutions. By 1860, there were some 6,000 private academies and only 300 public high schools. Secondary schools and colleges were generally open to boys only. One exception was the Troy (New York) Female Seminary, founded in 1821 by Emma Willard. It taught girls philosophy, mathematics, and other subjects that many educators considered too difficult for women. In 1837, Mary Lyon set up the Mount Holyoke Female Seminary. Lyon's curriculum included physical education, music, and the sciences.

Most colleges of this period were associated with churches. There was no coeducational college until 1833, when Oberlin (in Ohio) opened its doors to both women and men.

WOMEN'S RIGHTS

In the early 19th century, the position of women in U.S. society was far inferior to that of men. Free black women had few rights, and female slaves had none at all. The rights of white women were also very limited. They could not vote, nor, in most cases, own or bequeath property. What little money women earned legally belonged to their father or husband. In case of divorce, the husband almost always won custody of the children. Women were discouraged from getting an advanced education, learning a profession, or speaking in public. Reformers such as Dorothea Dix and Mary Lyon had to present their ideas through men.

Women's roles changed as society changed. As the need for machine operators rose, women began to work in factories. More and more women taught in public schools. But wherever women worked, they were always paid less than men for doing the same job. A few brave women—and men—felt that the time had come to press for greater equality for women. This was the goal of *feminism*, as the movement came to be called.

1. Individual Achievements. Women began to invade fields dominated by men. Maria Mitchell, who discovered a comet in 1847, learned astronomy from her father. She later taught astronomy at Vassar College, which opened in 1861. In 1849, Elizabeth Blackwell became the first woman in the world to receive a medical degree. Blackwell ran into strong opposition when she tried to practice medicine in New York City. She finally had to open a hospital staffed entirely by women.

2. Beginnings of Organized Efforts. The active campaign for women's rights did not begin until the 1840s. Its start was linked to women's participation in another reform movement—*abolition*. (Abolition means doing away with something; in the early 1800s, the term meant doing away with slavery.)

Many women, especially in the Northeast, wrote against slavery, signed petitions against it, and pressured politicians to take a stand against it. When these women spoke out in public, they were often ridiculed for being "unfeminine." This situation outraged women like the Grimké sisters, Angelina and Sarah. The latter pointed out that "Whatsoever it is morally right for a man to do, is morally right for a woman to do."

In 1840, male leaders of the abolitionist movement forbade Lucretia Mott and Elizabeth Cady Stanton to act as delegates at an international meeting against slavery. Mott and Stanton were outraged that men who were working to free African Americans denied them freedom because they were women. Over the next few years, Mott and Stanton talked and wrote about the issue of equality for women. In 1848, they organized a meeting at Seneca Falls, New York. This first Women's Rights Convention adopted a number of resolutions. It also issued a *Declaration of Sentiments*, written by Stanton and based on the Declaration of Independence. It stated that "all men and women are created equal." The declaration demanded that women must "have immediate admission to all the rights and privileges which belong to them as citizens of the United States."

The Seneca Falls meeting was the beginning of an organized feminist movement in the United States. But the struggle for women's rights made little progress until after the Civil War.

THE CRUSADE AGAINST SLAVERY

No reform movement of the early 19th century stirred up stronger feelings than the crusade against slavery. Antislavery crusaders often disagreed about how to end slavery. But their common belief that slavery was evil and had to end helped shape public opinion on the issue.

1. Early Opposition. Although they themselves owned slaves, George Washington and Thomas Jefferson knew that slavery was contrary to the principles of freedom and equality. The Northwest

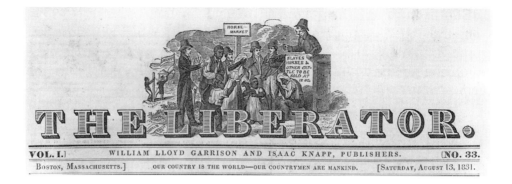

Ordinance banned slavery in the Northwest Territory. The Constitution gave Congress the right to end the importation of slaves after 1808. By that date, too, every Northern state had taken steps to abolish slavery within its borders.

In the Southern states, however, slave labor largely supported the economy. The population of these states included about 900,000 slaves in 1800 (and more than 3 million in 1850). In consideration of these facts, early opponents of slavery believed that it should be ended gradually. They hoped that slave owners would *emancipate* (free) their slaves voluntarily.

One group thought that the best solution would be to send freed slaves to Africa. The American Colonization Society, founded in 1817, sponsored the colony of Liberia in West Africa. But the society was not very successful, mainly because most African Americans had been born in the United States and considered it their homeland.

2. The Abolition Movement. Beginning about 1830, antislavery forces began to call for a quick end to slavery. One of the most famous fighters in the cause of abolition was William Lloyd Garrison, who in 1831 began publishing the antislavery paper *The Liberator*. Two years later, he helped found the American Antislavery Society. Garrison urged immediate abolition. He refused to work within the existing political system, which he regarded as corrupt. Garrison, the Grimké sisters, and former slaves Sojourner Truth and Frederick Douglass wrote at length and lectured widely about the evil of slavery.

More moderate abolitionists formed the Liberty party, which ran presidential candidates in 1840 and again in 1844. The party's main goal was to keep slavery out of new territories, rather than to abolish it entirely.

3. The Underground Railroad. Some abolitionists organized the *Underground Railroad*, a network to help slaves escape north. Men and women acted as "conductors" to guide enslaved African Americans to safe houses called "stations." The "end of the line" was usually Canada, where slavery was illegal and African Americans could live in peace. Two leaders of the Underground Railroad were Levi Coffin, a Quaker, and Harriet Tubman, a former slave.

IDENTIFY OR DEFINE: feminism, Mary Lyon, Elizabeth Blackwell, abolition, Harriet Tubman.

CRITICAL THINKING: What was the most important change in education between 1800 and 1850?

Chapter Review

MATCHING TEST

Column A	Column B
1. Dorothea Dix	*a.* reformer who worked for better public education
2. Joseph Smith	
3. Horace Mann	*b.* author of Seneca Falls declaration
4. Elizabeth Cady Stanton	*c.* reformer who helped improve treatment of the mentally ill
5. Frederick Douglass	*d.* former slave who called for immediate abolition
	e. organizer of the Mormon church

▶ MULTIPLE-CHOICE TEST

1. John Quincy Adams was unable to do much as president because of (*a*) a war with France (*b*) a border dispute with England (*c*) bitterness over his appointment of Clay (*d*) opposition from National Republicans.

2. All the following trends characterized the Age of Jackson *except* (*a*) broadening of voting rights (*b*) an increase in the number of elective offices (*c*) a shift toward popular election of presidential electors (*d*) replacement of national nominating conventions by caucuses.

3. Andrew Jackson was the first president who (*a*) came from the West (*b*) was a military hero (*c*) favored the rights of Native Americans (*d*) was inaugurated in Washington.

4. The practice of rewarding loyal party members with government jobs is known as (*a*) the specie system (*b*) the spoils system (*c*) rotation in office (*d*) speculation.

5. Southerners called the 1828 tariff the tariff of abominations because they felt that it (*a*) would not raise enough revenue (*b*) should have been adopted sooner (*c*) was harmful to manufacturers (*d*) increased the cost of goods they had to buy.

6. An important critic of the tariff of 1828 was (*a*) Henry Clay (*b*) Martin Van Buren (*c*) John C. Calhoun (*d*) Daniel Webster.

7. The major issue in the presidential campaign of 1832 was (*a*) nullification (*b*) the Second Bank of the United States (*c*) policy toward Native Americans (*d*) the Force Bill.

8. A new political party formed in the 1830s was the (*a*) Whigs (*b*) Democrats (*c*) National Republicans (*d*) Know-Nothings.

9. The Panic of 1837 led to (*a*) the election of Van Buren to the presidency (*b*) the establishment of pet banks (*c*) a severe depression (*d*) increased land speculation.

10. The 1840 presidential campaign was the first to (*a*) pit Democrats against National Republicans (*b*) be decided in the House of Representatives (*c*) result in a tie (*d*) feature showmanship as a campaign technique.

TIME TEST

Following are five groups of three related items. In each group, rearrange the items in the order in which they happened.

1. "corrupt bargain"
election of 1824
choice of John Quincy Adams by House of Representatives

2. *The South Carolina Exposition and Protest*
Tariff Act of 1828
South Carolina Ordinance of Nullification

3. founding of Second Bank of the United States
establishment of pet banks
campaign of 1832

4. Panic of 1837
Specie Circular
Independent Treasury System

5. presidency of Tyler
presidency of Van Buren
presidency of Harrison

 ESSAY QUESTIONS

1. In what ways did political life become more democratic in the Age of Jackson?

2. Explain the causes and outcome of the nullification crisis of 1832.

3. Describe *four* ways social reformers tried to improve American society in the Age of Jackson.

4. How was women's freedom limited in the early 19th century? Why did feminists become active in the 1840s?

5. What was Garrison's position on abolition and how it should be achieved? In what ways did moderate abolitionists disagree with him?

DOCUMENT-BASED QUESTION

This question is based on the accompanying documents (1–4). It will improve your ability to work with historical documents.

Historical Context:

Andrew Jackson owed his landslide victory in the election of 1828 to the fact that many states had by that time removed property requirements for voting. Almost all white American men over the age of 21 could now vote, regardless of their financial standing. Many members of the new population of voters were small farmers and frontiersmen. They were not inclined to vote for candidates who had been born into cultured, wealthy families. Instead, they wanted to vote for someone who had a background similar to their own. Thus, Andrew Jackson became known as the "People's President."

Task:

Using information from the documents and your knowledge of United States history, read each document and answer the question that follows it. Your answers to the questions will help you write the document-based essay.

Document 1. Excerpt from a letter written by Margaret Bayard Smith, dated March 11, 1829, in which she describes the scene at the White House following the inauguration of President Andrew Jackson:

> The President, after having been *literally* nearly pressed to death and almost suffocated and torn to pieces by the people in their eagerness to shake hands with Old Hickory [Jackson], had retreated through the back way . . . to his lodgings. . . . Cut glass and china to the amount of several thousand dollars had been broken in the struggle to get the refreshments. . . . Ladies fainted, men were seen with bloody noses, and . . . those who got in could not get out by the door again but had to scramble out of windows.

> **Source**: Smith, Margaret Bayard. *The First Forty Years of Washington Society*. NY: Charles Scribner's Sons, 1906. Also at www.whitehousehistory.org/04/subs/1828_html

How might this letter support the claim that Jackson was the first U.S. president of the "common man"?

Document 2. Comments by a friend of President Andrew Jackson:

> I have seen the President, and have dined with him, but have had no free . . . conversation with him. The reign of this administration . . . seems to have had an unhappy effect on the free thoughts, and unrestrained speech, which has heretofore prevailed. I question whether . . . the correction of abuses are sufficient to compensate for the reign of terror which appears to have commenced [begun]. . . . A stranger is warned by his friend on his first arrival to be careful how he expresses himself in relation to anyone or any thing which touches the administration. . . . Our republic, henceforth, will be governed by factions.

> **Source**: Parton, James. *Life of Andrew Jackson*. James R. Osgood & Co., 1859. III, pp. 213–214.

What did Jackson's friend accuse the president of doing or allowing to happen?

Document 3. Excerpt from President Andrew Jackson's message on vetoing the renewal of the charter of the Second Bank of the United States, 1832:

Every man is equally entitled to protection by law; but when the laws . . . grant exclusive privileges, to make the rich richer and the potent more powerful, the humble members of society . . . have a right to complain of the injustice of their Government. . . . If it [Government] would confine itself to equal protection, and . . . shower its favors alike on the high and the low, the rich and the poor, it would be an unqualified blessing. In the act [to recharter the bank] before me, there seems to be a wide and unnecessary departure from these just principles.

> **Source**: Richardson, James D. (ed.) *A Compilation of the Messages and Papers of the Presidents, 1789–1902*. IndyPublish.com, 2004.

What reason does President Jackson give for vetoing the renewal of the Second Bank's charter?

Document 4. Study the cartoon of Andrew Jackson on page 144.

Why did the cartoonist depict Andrew Jackson as a king?

DOCUMENT-BASED ESSAY

Using information from the above documents and your knowledge of United States history, write an essay in which you:

- Explain how Andrew Jackson could be described as both a president for the common man and a king.

UNIT IV

DIVISION AND REUNION

CHAPTER 9
Expansionism and Sectionalism

In the 1840s, U.S. expansion westward came to be thought of as the *manifest destiny* of the nation. This phrase expressed the belief that Americans had a God-given right to take over new territories all the way to the Pacific Ocean.

EXPANSIONISM

Expansionism (the policy of continually increasing the size of a country) was the major issue in the election campaign of 1844. The Whigs nominated Henry Clay. The Democrats ran a little-known Tennessee politician, James K. Polk.

Clay argued that the United States should not annex Texas without the consent of Mexico. Polk came out strongly in favor of the "re-occupation of Oregon" and the "re-annexation of Texas." (These terms suggested that the two regions had once belonged to the United States.) Since antislavery forces still opposed adding Texas to the Union as a slave state, the Democrats focused on the Oregon issue. Their slogan "Fifty-four forty or fight!" meant that the United States would use force if Britain objected to its taking over the entire Oregon Country. A majority of American voters opted for Polk and expansionism.

1. Annexation of Texas. Even before Polk took office, the Democrats, who had a majority in Congress, acted to acquire Texas. In December 1844, President Tyler recommended that Congress pass a joint resolution authorizing *annexation*. (A joint resolution, requiring only a simple majority in both houses, is easier to pass than ratifying a treaty, which needs a two-thirds majority in the Senate.) The resolution was adopted, and Tyler signed it just before leaving office. Texans later voted in favor of annexation, and the new state joined the Union in December 1845.

Meanwhile, Mexico had broken off diplomatic relations with the United States. The break resulted not only from the annexation but also from a dispute over the size of the Lone Star Republic. The United States claimed that the southern and western boundaries of Texas lay along the Rio Grande. Mexico contended that Texas comprised the area north and east of the Nueces River, a region about half as big as the U.S. claim.

2. Dividing Oregon Country. As trouble with Mexico loomed, Polk's new administration backed down on its claim to Oregon Country. The British suggested that the territory be divided along the 49th parallel. The northern part (including Vancouver Island) would go to Canada, and the southern part to the United States. The Senate approved the British proposal and ratified the resulting treaty in 1846.

In 1848, a territorial government was set up in the Oregon Territory. In 1859, the southern part of the area was admitted to the Union as the state of Oregon. In the late 1800s, Washington and Idaho and parts of Montana and Wyoming were formed from this territory.

3. Troubles in California. Until the 18th century, the main residents of California were a relatively small number of Native Americans. In the late 1760s, however, settlers from Mexico arrived. Franciscan priests (notably Father Junípero Serra) founded a chain of Roman Catholic missions, from San Diego in the south to Sonoma in the north. Here they taught farming and other skills to their Native-American converts.

When Mexico became independent in 1821, the new nation included California and the intervening territory in the Southwest. Mexican control meant few changes for the Spanish-speaking Californians. But for Native Americans it was a disaster. Mexico transferred the Catholic missions to private owners. No longer protected by missionaries, the Native Americans were victimized by white settlers.

Americans began to travel to California in the early 1840s. Explorer John C. Frémont, guided by Kit Carson, traveled throughout the region and wrote glowing reports about it. At various times, the U.S. government tried unsuccessfully to buy California from Mexico.

Families in covered wagons crossing the plains.

Then, in June 1846, dissatisfied American settlers at Sonoma declared California independent of Mexico. This "Bear Flag Revolt" soon became part of a larger struggle between Mexico and the United States.

4. U.S. War With Mexico. President Polk wanted southern and western Texas. He also wanted the rest of the Southwest and California as well. Polk sent John Slidell to Mexico City to negotiate, but the Mexican government refused to see him. Polk then ordered troops under General Zachary Taylor into the disputed area of Texas. He also ordered U.S. warships into the Gulf of Mexico and along the Pacific coast. In April 1846, using a skirmish between Mexican and U.S. troops near the Rio Grande as an excuse, Polk asked Congress for a declaration of war, which it passed on May 13.

The war with Mexico lasted until the spring of 1847, when the Americans won a decisive victory over the Mexicans and occupied Mexico City. The two countries signed a peace treaty—the Treaty of Guadalupe Hidalgo—in 1848. Mexico recognized the Rio Grande as the boundary of Texas and ceded New Mexico and California to the United States. In exchange, the United States paid Mexico $15 million in cash and agreed to pay all claims made by U.S. citizens against Mexico. The territory known as the Mexican Cession was eventually carved into the states of California, Nevada, Utah, and parts of Arizona, New Mexico, Colorado, and Wyoming.

U.S. War With Mexico, 1846–1848

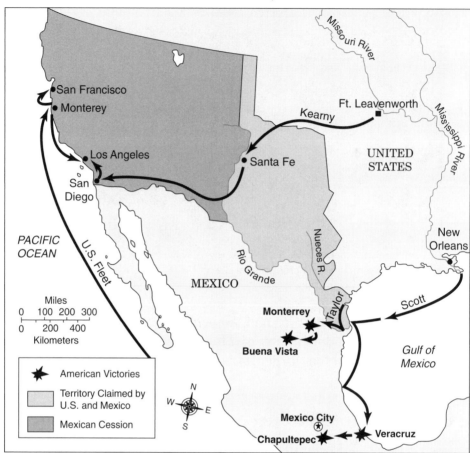

SURGES OF SETTLEMENT

Even as war with Mexico was bringing new lands under U.S. control, waves of new settlers were moving into them.

1. The Gold Rush. Early in 1848, gold was discovered at the sawmill of John Sutter in Sacramento Valley, California. The news traveled quickly, not only to the eastern United States but also to Europe and Asia. People from all walks of life raced to California in what became known as the *gold rush*. An estimated 100,000 people flocked to California in 1849, thereby earning the nickname *forty-niners*. A few forty-niners quickly struck it rich in the gold-fields. Others made fortunes by selling the miners food, supplies, and services at high prices. Those who failed to get rich quickly (the majority) turned to raising cattle, growing fruit, or moving elsewhere.

READING A MAP

Territorial Growth to 1853

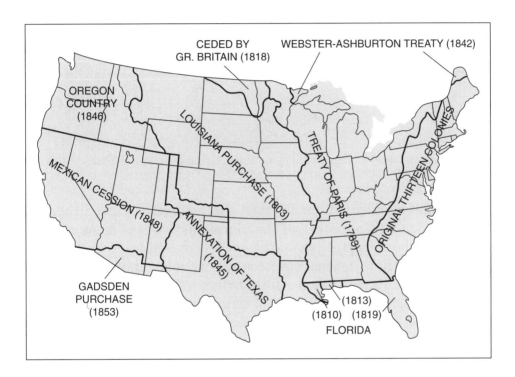

1. How many states were ultimately created, in whole or in part, from Oregon Country? Can you name them?

2. Of the territories that were to become the 48 adjoining states, which territory did the United States acquire last?

3. From which territorial acquisition after 1783 was the largest number of states formed? How many states, in whole or in part, were created from this acquisition?

2. The Mormons in Utah. The Mormon Church gained many new members in the 1830s and 1840s. Led by Joseph Smith, Mormons left New York and migrated first to Ohio and then to Missouri and

Mormon leader Brigham Young arrived at the Great Salt Lake in Utah in 1847.

Illinois. The hostility of non-Mormons in each place forced them to move on. Some disapproved of the Mormon system of owning property in common. Opposition to the sect increased after 1843, when Smith stated that Mormon men could have more than one wife. In 1844, a mob in Illinois killed Smith. Brigham Young, the new leader, led the Mormons west in search of a refuge. In 1847, Young and his followers reached the valley of the Great Salt Lake in Utah. There they founded Salt Lake City. The settlers that followed transformed the wasteland into a land of plenty. In 1850, Utah was organized as a territory, with Young as its governor.

3. The Gadsden Purchase. The United States was enlarged in 1853 with the addition of land along the southern boundary of New Mexico and Arizona. The United States wanted the area for a proposed railroad to the Pacific. Mexico agreed to sell it for $10 million. James Gadsden, the U.S. representative to Mexico, arranged the agreement. The acquisition thus became known as the Gadsden Purchase.

IDENTIFY OR DEFINE: manifest destiny, expansionism, Mexican Cession, Joseph Smith, Gadsden Purchase, forty-niners.

CRITICAL THINKING: What led President Polk to reach a compromise with Great Britain and back down from his earlier pledge to seize Oregon Country?

THE SYSTEM OF SLAVERY

During the mid-1800s, the differences between the North and South regions of the United States increased sharply. The North had many cities and industries and a large working class. Northerners came from many different ethnic and religious backgrounds. The South depended heavily on farming. Most of its inhabitants were Protestants whose ancestors had come from the British Isles. But the chief difference between Northerners and Southerners was their attitude toward slavery.

The practice of slavery goes back to ancient times. Slavery in the United States, however, differed from other slave systems in at least two ways. Enslaved people in the United States had no legal rights. In various African kingdoms, by contrast, they could own property and had protection from abuse. Second, American slaves were racially distinct. By contrast, in ancient Greece and Rome most slaves were white, like their owners.

1. Slave Ownership. The first Africans came to the North American colonies early in the 17th century. Their numbers increased steadily, and by 1800 there were about a million African Americans. Sixty years later, there were about 4.5 million. Nearly 90 percent of them were enslaved.

Slavery existed at one time or another in all the colonies. After the Revolutionary War, however, Northerners gradually eliminated slavery. Some Southern areas, such as Appalachia, had few or no slaves. The majority of slaves lived in the band of states stretching from South Carolina to Texas. In the mid-19th century, three states—South Carolina, Louisiana, and Mississippi—had more African Americans than whites. In 1860, only about a fourth of all Southern white families owned slaves. Less than 1 percent of these families owned 100 or more slaves. But this minority dominated the South.

The slave system was profitable for owners. Although they had to feed, clothe, and house their workers, they could count on them as a steady supply of labor. This supply grew with the birth of enslaved people's children. After the overseas slave trade ended in 1808, the price of slaves rose steadily. By 1860, a strong, young male cost more than $1,500.

2. How Enslaved People Lived. The majority of enslaved people did backbreaking field work. A smaller number were house servants and skilled laborers, such as masons, blacksmiths, cooks, and seamstresses. Enslaved people generally lived in family groups in small, dirt-floor cabins. Not recognizing their marriages, the owner split up their families when it suited him or her. It was illegal to teach slaves to read. Nonetheless, slaves led a rich cultural life centered on music, religion, and storytelling.

READING A TABLE

Slaveholding Families, By Number of Slaves Held, 1850

Number of Families Owning ...	United States	Maryland & Wash., D.C.	Virginia	North Carolina	South Carolina
1 slave	68,998	5,585	11,385	1,204	3,492
2–4 slaves	105,703	5,870	15,550	9,668	6,164
5–9 slaves	80,767	3,463	13,030	8,129	6,311
10–19 slaves	54,595	1,861	9,456	5,898	4,955
20–49 slaves	29,733	657	4,880	2,828	3,200
50–99 slaves	6,196	73	646	485	990
100–199 slaves	1,479	7	107	76	382
200–299 slaves	187	—	8	12	69
300 slaves or over	67	1	1	3	33
Total number slaveholding families	347,725	17,517	55,063	28,303	25,596

1. Of the states listed, which one had the most slaveholding families? How many slaveholding families did that state have?

2. In 1850, how many families in the country owned 100 or more slaves?

3. In Maryland and the District of Columbia in 1850, is it true or false to say that over half of all slaveholding families held four or fewer slaves?

4. Which state listed had the most slaveholding families with 300 or more slaves?

Slavery was harmful to both owners and owned. Having total control over other human beings tended to make the owners callous. And lack of freedom demoralized the Africans.

THE POLITICS OF SLAVERY

At one point during the late 18th century, the decline in tobacco production had reduced the need for large numbers of field-workers. Then, in the 1790s, Eli Whitney invented the cotton gin. By speeding up cotton processing, this device encouraged Southern planters to raise larger crops. The planters had a good market for their output in the factories of England and New England. Since cotton growing required many laborers, slavery became more important to the Southern economy.

Increasing cotton production wore out the soil. Therefore, cotton planters in the Southern colonies along the Atlantic coast welcomed the opening of the Old Southwest. When that region filled up, Southerners began to move to the territories made available by the annexation of Texas and the Mexican Cession in the 1840s.

As slavery spread, so did opposition to it. Some abolitionists wanted to end slavery immediately. Others favored gradual emancipation. Many people in the South favored abolition. The number of Southern abolitionists decreased sharply, however, after Nat Turner's uprising in 1831. Turner, an enslaved preacher in Virginia, led some 70 followers in an attack on whites, killing nearly 60 men, women, and children. The rebellion frightened Southern whites. Soon, abolitionist literature was no longer allowed to go through the mail in the South.

Many Southerners defended slavery as the economic mainstay of their region. They also argued that it offered protection for a race that could not provide for itself. One advocate of slavery wrote: "What a glorious thing to man is slavery, when want, misfortune, old age, debility [weakness], and sickness overtake him." Calhoun defended slavery as "a positive good." As the years passed, positions hardened. Many Northerners believed that there was a "slave power conspiracy" aimed at extending slavery to the whole United States. Many Southerners feared that radicals would seize their property and destroy their way of life.

By the early 19th century, Northern states had either abolished slavery or provided for its gradual elimination. States south of the Mason-Dixon line allowed slavery. Of the original 13 states, 7 prohibited slavery and 6 permitted it. Between 1791 and 1819, 9 new states joined the Union. Of these, 4 were free and 5 slave, thus equalizing the number of free and slave states at 11 each. Keeping this balance became a key issue for both North and South. Neither section wanted the other to gain control of the Senate, where each state had two votes. Equality in the Senate was especially important to the South. It was losing voting strength in the House of Representatives, where the number of votes that each state had depended on its population. The South's population was not growing as fast as that of the North.

1. The Missouri Compromise. In 1819, Missouri (a slaveholding territory) applied for statehood. Northern politicians opposed this request for two reasons: (*1*) It would upset the balance between free and slave states. (*2*) It would officially establish slavery in the northern part of the Louisiana Purchase. If slavery were allowed there, additional states made from the Louisiana territory might also allow slavery.

The problem was resolved when Maine requested admission as a free state. Congress then enacted the Missouri Compromise of 1820. It provided that (*1*) Maine would be admitted as a free state, (*2*) Missouri would be admitted as a slave state, and (*3*) slavery would be prohibited in the Louisiana Purchase north of latitude 36°30′. (This line of latitude formed the southern boundary of Missouri.)

2. The Compromise of 1850. Between 1836 and 1848, six more states were added to the Union—Michigan, Iowa, Wisconsin, Arkansas, Florida, and Texas. The first three were free states; the other three, slave states. The balance was thus kept at 15 states each.

The territory gained in the Mexican Cession revived the dispute about slavery. Southern leaders demanded that slavery be permitted in the region. Northern leaders insisted that it be kept out. When California, a part of the Mexican Cession, asked for admission as a free state in 1850, bitter sectional quarreling broke out. Henry Clay suggested admitting California as a free state, but allowing slavery in the rest of the Mexican Cession. By contrast, Senator William H. Seward of New York argued against admitting any new slave states.

Finally, Congress passed what came to be called the Compromise of 1850 as five separate bills:

- California was admitted as a free state.
- Texas gave up its claim to eastern New Mexico in return for $10 million.
- The territories of New Mexico and Utah were organized on the principle of *popular sovereignty*. That is, the people of each region would decide whether they wanted slavery.

- A new, more severe *Fugitive Slave* Law imposed heavy fines on people who helped slaves to escape. (An earlier law, passed in 1793, had not been strictly enforced.)
- The slave trade (but not slavery) was abolished in the District of Columbia.

IDENTIFY OR DEFINE: Missouri Compromise, Henry Clay, popular sovereignty, fugitive slave.

CRITICAL THINKING: How did Congress in 1850 resolve the dispute over admitting states to the Union?

SECTIONAL STRAINS

The Compromise of 1850 briefly eased relations between North and South. But tensions remained. The publication in 1852 of Harriet Beecher Stowe's *Uncle Tom's Cabin*, an antislavery novel, aroused strong feelings. So did the new Fugitive Slave Law, which was widely disobeyed.

1. The Kansas-Nebraska Act. The West's growing population needed a railroad. Some Americans wanted a northern route to the West, starting at Chicago. This route would pass through territory that had not been politically organized. To address this problem, Senator Stephen A. Douglas, a Democrat from Illinois, sponsored the Kansas-Nebraska Act. This bill organized the region into two territories: Nebraska (in the north) and Kansas (in the south). To gain Southern support, the Kansas-Nebraska Bill provided that popular sovereignty would decide the slavery question in each territory. This bill repealed the part of the Missouri Compromise that had banning slavery north of 36° 30′. The Kansas-Nebraska Act, passed in May 1854, resulted in the formation of a new political party and an outbreak of violence in Kansas.

    a. The Republican party. Many antislavery Northerners were angered by the Kansas-Nebraska Act. They were also unhappy with the Democratic and Whig parties for not taking a strong stand against the law. The discontented Northerners deserted these older parties and formed the Republican party.

    The Republican party began to take shape early in 1854. It called for repeal of the Kansas-Nebraska Act and the Fugitive

Slave Law, and the abolition of slavery in the District of Columbia. The party soon added other aims, including a high protective tariff, construction of a railroad across the continent, and free land for Western settlers.

The Free-Slave Balance, 1854

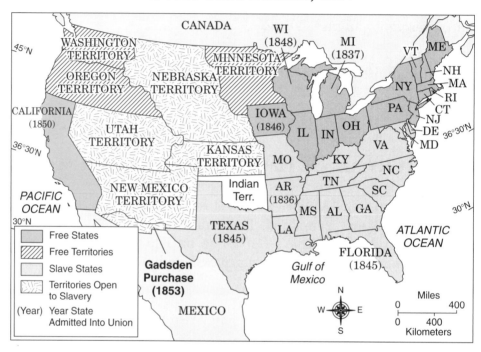

In 1856, the Republicans nominated John C. Frémont of California for president. He ran against James Buchanan, a Democrat from Pennsylvania, and Millard Fillmore of New York, the Whig candidate. Buchanan won the election, but the Republicans showed surprising strength. Frémont received a large popular vote and won the electoral votes of about two-thirds of the free states. After this election, the Whigs ceased to be a force in U.S. politics. There were now two sectional parties: The Republicans dominated the North; the Democrats, the South.

b. "Bleeding Kansas." Meanwhile, proslavery and antislavery forces in Kansas vied for control of the territorial legislature, which was to vote on whether Kansas would allow slavery. Violence broke out in 1855, and some 200 people were killed. John Brown led a group in Kansas in murdering five proslavery settlers at Pottawatomie Creek. "Bleeding Kansas" became a symbol of the sectionalism that threatened the whole nation. (Kansas eventually joined the Union as a free state in 1861.)

2. The Dred Scott Decision. Early in 1857, a Supreme Court decision aroused further sectional feeling. An enslaved person named Dred Scott had traveled with his master from the slave state of Missouri into free territory. After a few years, his master took him back to Missouri. He then sued for his freedom, arguing that since he had lived in free territory, he was no longer enslaved. In *Dred Scott* v. *Sanford*, the Supreme Court ruled that since Scott was not a citizen, he had no right to sue in a federal court. The Court further declared that the Missouri Compromise was unconstitutional because it banned slavery in the northern part of the Louisiana Purchase. Slaves were property, said the Court, and Congress had no right to deprive citizens of their property. The Dred Scott decision, in effect, made it legal to extend slavery into all U.S. territories.

3. The Lincoln-Douglas Debates. In 1858, Republican Abraham Lincoln opposed Democrat Stephen A. Douglas in the Illinois senatorial campaign. Douglas was a powerful speaker and a nationally known U.S. senator. Lincoln challenged him to a series of public debates on the issues of the day. Among these was slavery.

In this scene of one of the Lincoln-Douglas debates, Lincoln spoke while Douglas (behind Lincoln) waited his turn.

In one debate, held at Freeport, Illinois, Lincoln led Douglas into expressing a view that made him unpopular with Southern voters. The principle of popular sovereignty permitted a territory to exclude slavery. The Dred Scott decision held that slavery could *not* be excluded from a territory. Which of these two positions, Lincoln asked, did Douglas favor? Douglas answered that a territorial legislature could keep out slavery by not passing laws to protect it. Douglas won re-election to the Senate, but his "Freeport Doctrine" cost him the support of Southern Democrats when he later made a bid for the presidency. The debates made Lincoln nationally famous.

4. John Brown's Raid. John Brown, who had killed slavery supporters in Kansas, conceived a plan to stir up a slave uprising in the South. In October 1859, he and 18 men seized the government arsenal at Harpers Ferry, Virginia (now West Virginia). His purpose was to obtain weapons for the enslaved people who he hoped would join his force. But no mass uprising took place, and Brown and his men were soon killed or captured. Brown was tried for treason, found guilty, and hanged. Abolitionists regarded Brown as a hero who had given his life for the antislavery cause. He confirmed the fears of many Southerners that Northerners were plotting to destroy their way of life.

THE ELECTION OF 1860

Democrats split into two groups over the choice of a candidate for the 1860 presidential election. The Northern delegates chose Douglas as their presidential candidate, while the Southerners selected John C. Breckinridge of Kentucky. The Republicans nominated Lincoln. Aided by the split among Democrats, Lincoln won the election. His victory was clearly sectional. He won the electoral votes of every free state and not a single slave state.

1. Secession and the Confederacy. Early in 1860, Southern leaders had warned that they would *secede* (leave the Union) if a Republican president were elected. After Lincoln's victory, delegates to a South Carolina state convention declared in favor of secession. By February 1861, six other states had joined South Carolina: Mississippi, Florida, Alabama, Georgia, Louisiana, and Texas.

On February 4, delegates from the seceding states met at Montgomery, Alabama, and formed the Confederate States of America.

In this anti-Buchanan cartoon, the eagle, symbol of the United States, is thriving when Buchanan takes office in 1857 and a sorry specimen four years later.

The constitution the delegates drew up was like the U.S. Constitution in many ways but had four important differences: (*1*) It emphasized "the sovereign and independent character" of each state. (*2*) It recognized and protected slavery. (*3*) It forbade protective tariffs. (*4*) It prohibited the use of government funds for internal improvements. The delegates chose Jefferson Davis of Mississippi as president of the Confederacy. Alexander Stephens of Georgia became vice president.

2. Buchanan's Position. During the last months of President James Buchanan's administration, secessionist forces seized most of the federal property in their states—forts, arsenals, customhouses, and post offices. They also took the New Orleans Mint, which contained $500,000 in gold and silver. Determined to keep the peace until his term was over, Buchanan did not interfere.

3. The Inauguration of Lincoln. On March 4, 1861, Abraham Lincoln took the oath of office as U.S. president. In his inaugural address he appealed to the South to preserve the Union. He said that he would not interfere with slavery in the states where it existed. He pointed out that no state could lawfully secede from the Union. Federal laws would be carried out in all the states, he claimed.

IDENTIFY OR DEFINE: Harriet Beecher Stowe, Kansas-Nebraska Act, "Bleeding Kansas," Dred Scott, John Brown, Jefferson Davis.

CRITICAL THINKING: Why did South Carolina and other Southern states secede from the Union after Lincoln's election?

Chapter Review

MATCHING TEST

Column A	Column B
1. "Fifty-four forty or fight!"	*a.* U.S. president during Mexican War
	b. founded a chain of Catholic missions
2. James K. Polk	*c.* Mormon leader after Smith
3. John C. Frémont	*d.* Democrats' slogan during
4. Junípero Serra	presidential campaign of 1844
5. Brigham Young	*e.* U.S. explorer of California

MULTIPLE-CHOICE TEST

1. U.S. claims to Oregon Country were settled by (*a*) an agreement with Spain (*b*) a war with Russia (*c*) a purchase from Mexico (*d*) a treaty with Britain.

2. The Mexican War was ended by the (*a*) Treaty of Guadalupe Hidalgo (*b*) Great Migration (*c*) Battle of Buena Vista (*d*) Gadsden Purchase.

3. The discovery of gold in California (*a*) was one of the causes of the Mexican War (*b*) helped bring about the Bear Flag Revolt (*c*) helped Zachary Taylor in his campaign for the presidency (*d*) drew 100,000 people to the region in the following year.

4. The main issue separating North and South in the 1850s was (*a*) tariffs (*b*) immigration policy (*c*) slavery (*d*) education.

5. The Compromise of 1850 dealt with all of the following *except* (*a*) New Mexico territory (*b*) Utah territory (*c*) the slave trade in Washington, D.C. (*d*) the status of Missouri.

6. The Kansas-Nebraska Act was passed in order to (*a*) help build a western railroad (*b*) guarantee more free states (*c*) aid Stephen A. Douglas in his debates with Lincoln (*d*) provide a home for Native Americans.

7. In the Dred Scott decision, the Supreme Court ruled that (*a*) Congress had the power to abolish slavery (*b*) Congress could not ban slavery in the territories (*c*) slavery was illegal north of 36°30′ (*d*) the slavery issue should be settled by popular sovereignty.

8. All of the following were presidential candidates in the election of 1860 *except* (*a*) Abraham Lincoln (*b*) John C. Breckinridge (*c*) Jefferson Davis (*d*) Stephen A. Douglas.

9. The secession of the first Southern states took place during the administration of President (*a*) Franklin Pierce (*b*) James Buchanan (*c*) Abraham Lincoln (*d*) Millard Fillmore.

10. The principle that allowed residents of a territory to decide whether to permit slavery when becoming a state was (*a*) the Wilmot Proviso (*b*) popular sovereignty (*c*) direct democracy (*d*) the Missouri Compromise.

 ESSAY QUESTIONS

1. How did the United States put the idea of manifest destiny into action in the 1840s?

2. What were the chief results of the conflict with Mexico?

3. (*a*) Why was a balance of free states and slave states important in the period before the 1860s? (*b*) How did this balance affect the admission of Missouri to the Union? (*c*) Of California?

4. How and why was sectional tension between North and South affected by *each* of the following? (*a*) the Kansas-Nebraska Act (*b*) the Dred Scott decision (*c*) John Brown's raid.

5. What was Buchanan's response to Southern secession? What attitude toward the South did Lincoln show in his inaugural address?

DOCUMENT-BASED QUESTION

This question is based on the accompanying documents (1–5). It will improve your ability to work with historical documents.

Historical Context:

The Missouri Compromise of 1820 and the Compromise of 1850 temporarily calmed the passions of most proslavery and antislavery Americans.

Task:

Using information from the documents and your knowledge of United States history, read each document and answer the question that follows it. Your answers to the questions will help you write the document-based essay.

Document 1. Excerpt from remarks by Elias Horry, a South Carolina plantation owner, 1826:

> [My slaves] enjoy a greater share of the blessings of life than falls to the lot of the laboring poor of most countries. Their dwellings on my plantation are built in such a manner as to afford them every protection and comfort, and are generally about forty feet in length and twenty feet wide, with a double brick chimney in the centre that forms two tenements; each tenement has two rooms and a hall. . . .
>
> Their labor is, comparatively, light and easy, so that an industrious negro can very easily accomplish his task early in the afternoon, and the rest of the time is at his own disposal.
>
> **Source**: Brown, Edward. *Notes on the Origin and Necessity of Slavery*. Charleston, South Carolina: A.E. Miller, 1826, pp. 56–57.

Name *one* of the benefits that Mr. Horry claimed his slaves enjoyed on his plantation.

Document 2. Excerpt from the description that Harry Grimes, an enslaved person from North Carolina, gave of his escape to the North, 1850s:

> In the woods I lived on nothing. . . . I stayed in the hollow of a big poplar tree for seven months. . . . I suffered mighty bad with the cold and for something to eat. One time a snake come to the tree

. . . and I took my axe and chopped him in two. It was a poplar leaf moccasin, the poisonest kind of snake we have. While in the woods all my thoughts was how to get away to a free country.

Source: Blockson, Charles L. *The Underground Railroad*. NY: Prentice-Hall Press, 1987.

What inspired Grimes to endure hardships as he traveled north?

Document 3. Excerpt from Henry David Thoreau's lecture "Resistance to Civil Government," 1848:

How does it become a man to behave toward this American government to-day? . . . I cannot for an instant recognize that political organization as *my* government which is the slave's government also . . . if the law is of such a nature that it requires you to be an agent of injustice to another, then, I say, break the law.

Source: www.vcu.edu/engweb/transcendentalism/authors/thoreau/civil

Why did the abolitionists welcome Henry David Thoreau's 1848 lecture?

Document 4. Excerpt from a speech of Senator John C. Calhoun protesting the plan to admit California as a free state, March 4, 1850:

I have, Senators, believed from the first the agitation of the subject of slavery would, if not prevented by some timely and effective measure, end in disunion. . . . It can no longer be disguised or denied that the Union is in danger. You have thus had forced upon you the greatest and the gravest question that can ever come under your consideration: How can the Union be preserved?

Source: www.nationalcenter.org/CalhounClayCompromise.html

What did Senator Calhoun say might happen to the United States if California were admitted to the Union as a free state?

Document 5. Study the map on page 172.

How many free states were there in 1854? How many slave states? Which territories were free and which were open to slavery?

DOCUMENT-BASED ESSAY

Using information from the above documents and your knowledge of United States history, write an essay in which you:

- Explain whether you agree with the idea that in 1854 it was only a matter of time before proslavery and antislavery Americans would reject compromise as a way to deal with their differences on the issue of slavery.

CHAPTER 10
The Civil War and Reconstruction

Even as Lincoln was giving his inaugural address in March 1861, the United States was moving toward civil war. Seven states had seceded from the Union, forming the Confederate States of America and seizing federal property.

The confederates had not yet seized Fort Sumter, located on an island off Charleston, South Carolina. In late March, the U.S. troops at the fort ran short of supplies. Lincoln ordered supply ships sent to the fort, When these ships approached on April 12, Confederate forces along the shore opened fire on the fort and forced it to surrender. The war had begun.

EARLY YEARS

In the North, Lincoln called for volunteers to join the Union army. Thousands did so. In the South, four more states—Virginia, Arkansas, North Carolina, and Tennessee—seceded and joined the Confederacy. Eleven states had now left the Union. Northerners waited anxiously to see if the remaining slave states—Maryland, Kentucky, Missouri, and Delaware—would follow. These states formed a border between North and South. If Maryland joined the Confederacy, Washington, D.C., the Union capital, would be cut off from the North.

All four border states rejected secession. Thousands of men from Kentucky and Missouri, however, enlisted in the Confederate army. The people of Virginia were also divided in their loyalties. The state joined the Confederacy, but its western part (which would soon become West Virginia) remained loyal to the Union.

1. War Leadership and Aims. The commanders in chief of the two sides had very different characters. Abraham Lincoln was a self-educated lawyer with practically no military experience. His wisdom, understanding, and humor, however, won him wide support. He played an active role in making military decisions and became an excellent strategist.

The Secession of States and Territories From the Union

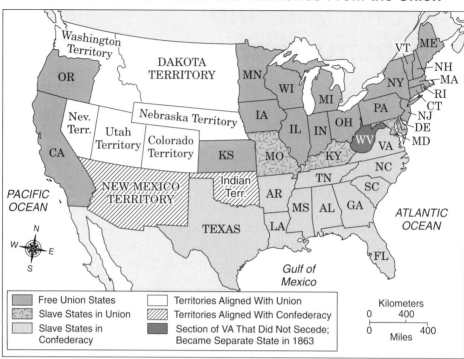

The Confederacy's president, Jefferson Davis, had graduated from West Point (the United States Military Academy) and served in the Mexican War. His intelligence and dignity were widely admired. But his aloof manner turned people away. Military leaders criticized him for being overly cautious and stubborn.

The two sides had different war aims. At the start of the war, the North's objective was not to free the slaves but to preserve the Union. This goal required the Union forces to take the offensive and strike at the South. The Southerners would be fighting on their own territory to defend their homes.

2. First Campaigns. Many Northerners believed that the war would be over in 90 days. To achieve a quick end, Army leaders hoped to capture the Confederate capital, Richmond. In July 1861, a Union force advanced into northern Virginia and attacked a Confederate army at a creek called Bull Run. The determination of the Confederate general Thomas J. Jackson won the day. His brave stand during that battle earned him the nickname "Stonewall." The Union defeat at Bull Run made Northerners realize that victory would not be won quickly.

a. The war at sea. At the outbreak of the war, Lincoln ordered Union ships to *blockade* the Southern coast from Virginia to Texas. The *blockade* was so effective that the exports of cotton from the South dwindled to 2 percent of their prewar volume. With its main source of income cut off, the South had difficulty buying the supplies it needed.

Southerners built a number of fast ships that could evade Northern patrols. These ships often succeeded in evading the blockade early in the war but were not so effective later. In another attempt to break the Northern blockade, the Confederates produced one of the first armored warships. They covered the sides of a standard wooden vessel, the *Merrimac*, with metal plates. On March 8, 1862, off the coast of Virginia, the *Merrimac* destroyed two Northern ships made of wood. The next day, however, it met its match in the North's *Monitor*. The *Monitor* had a flat iron hull topped by a revolving turret, from which powerful guns could be fired in any direction. The *Monitor* forced the *Merrimac* to withdraw. This battle saved the Northern blockade.

b. The war in the West. One of the main aims of Union forces in the West was to divide the Confederacy by gaining control of the Mississippi River. In February 1862, Union troops under Ulysses S. Grant moved against two Confederate forts in northern Tennessee. Grant was victorious in both cases and won control of western Tennessee and the upper Mississippi River.

In April, David G. Farragut led a fleet of Union warships from the Gulf of Mexico into the mouth of the Mississippi and took New Orleans. Except for a 200-mile stretch between Port Hudson and Vicksburg, all of the Mississippi was in Union hands by the end of 1862.

c. Further drives on Richmond. In the East, the Union was still trying to capture Richmond. George B. McClellan began a drive on the Southern capital through the peninsula formed by the York and James rivers. In his Peninsular Campaign, General McClellan got to within a few miles of Richmond. Stonewall Jackson, however, prevented nearby Union troops from helping McClellan. After a series of encounters (called the Seven Days' Battles) with the Confederate General Robert E. Lee, McClellan retreated northward.

d. A Confederate offensive. As McClellan moved north, Lee attacked another Union force in a second Battle of Bull Run (August 1862). This time the Confederates won. They then invaded

The Civil War in the East

Maryland and met McClellan's forces at Antietam in September 1862. Although neither side really won, some consider Antietam a Union victory because Confederate troops withdrew to Virginia. The final battle over Richmond that year ended in a crushing defeat for the Union.

IDENTIFY OR DEFINE: Fort Sumter, David Farragut, Robert E. Lee, Antietam.

CRITICAL THINKING: Compare the North and the South at the beginning of the Civil War in terms of population, industry, transportation, and leadership.

BEHIND THE LINES

The Civil War demanded more sacrifice from Americans than did any other war. Resources were strained to the limit, especially in the South.

1. Foreign Diplomacy. The British were undecided about which side in the U.S. Civil War to support. The upper classes generally sided with the South, while workers and people opposed to slavery tended to favor the North. The Confederates believed that Britain would help their side in order to keep receiving the raw cotton it needed for its textile industry. But British mill owners had a surplus of cotton at the start of the war and later obtained new supplies from India and Egypt. Britain remained neutral throughout the war but allowed Confederate ships to be built in British shipyards.

Although officially neutral, France tended to favor the South. French leaders believed that a divided United States would be less resistant to French expansion in the Western Hemisphere. France granted loans to the Confederacy and permitted French shipyards to build ships for the Southerners.

2. The Home Front. Most fighting took place on Southern soil, causing destruction to homes, businesses, and farms, and disrupting vital public services. The breakdown of the South's railroad network created serious supply problems after 1863. Many Southerners lacked food and clothes. Late in the war, prices soared. A barrel of flour cost $300; a pair of men's boots, $125. Another problem was Southern resistance to central authority. Many Southerners objected to wartime controls and, in some cases, refused to pay taxes to the Richmond government.

In contrast, the Northern economy boomed. Farmers and manufacturers stepped up production for both military and civilian needs. A number of measures passed by the Republican Congress stimulated this growth. These measures included a tariff to protect domestic manufacturers against foreign competition (Morrill Tariff), grants of land for homesteads in the West (Homestead Act), and inducements for building a railroad to connect the Pacific coast with the middle of the country. The arrival of more than 800,000 European immigrants during the wartime years provided labor for factories and farms, and swelled the ranks of people moving westward.

Like the South, the North was not completely united behind the war. One group of Northerners, the Peace Democrats, wanted peace

Peace Democrats in the guise of Copperheads threaten the Union cause.
(*Harper's Weekly*, 1863)

on almost any terms. The Democratic platform in the presidential election of 1864 called the war a failure. Lincoln won a huge electoral victory. But his popular majority was quite small.

3. The Draft. As a result of the huge casualties suffered in the war, both sides resorted to something new in U.S. history—the draft. (A *draft*, or *conscription*, requires people to register for compulsive military service.) The South adopted the draft in 1862; the North, in 1863.

Antidraft protests touched off violence. In July 1863, mobs of white laborers in New York City rioted in protest against being drafted into a war whose purpose (they believed) was to free the slaves. The riots resulted in the lynching of more than a dozen African Americans, the destruction of an orphan asylum for African-American children, and the death of some 120 rioters.

4. Role of African Americans. In the South, most able-bodied white men went off to fight, while enslaved people remained at home to work on the farms and in the factories. Thousands of African Americans joyfully abandoned their masters when Union forces approached. Some Southerners wanted African Americans to serve in the Confederate Army. But fear of what armed slaves might do delayed this move until early 1865. By then it was too late.

Northerners were also reluctant to arm African Americans. But in the summer of 1862, they allowed them to enlist. They restricted African Americans to all-black regiments, paid them less than whites, and gave them inferior supplies and weapons. Even so, African Americans served with distinction. About 180,000 enlisted in the Union Army, and some 29,000 joined the Union Navy.

During the early months of the war, Lincoln did not promise to emancipate the slaves, partly because he wanted to keep the support of the border states. But abolitionists, African-American leaders in the North, and the so-called "radical" wing of the Republican party pressured him to end slavery. On September 22, 1862, a few days after the Battle of Antietam, Lincoln announced that he would proclaim emancipation on January 1, 1863.

The Emancipation Proclamation freed those slaves living in states and districts then "in rebellion against the United States." The Proclamation did not apply to slaves in border states or in Confederate areas under Union control. Nor did it have any real affect on slaves in states still controlled by the Confederacy, since Southern slave owners ignored Lincoln's order. It did, however, give the Northern cause a moral force it had lacked earlier. It also paved the way for the total abolition of slavery after the war.

5. Role of Women. While Union and Confederate men were at the front, women ran farms and businesses and raised money for medical care. In both North and South, thousands served as professional and volunteer nurses in army hospitals. Dorothea Dix was appointed superintendent of female nurses in the Union Army. Mary Edwards Walker, a Northern physician, was commissioned an army surgeon. Clara Barton served as a Union field nurse and later founded the American Red Cross. Harriet Tubman, a former slave, acted as a Union spy behind Confederate lines.

Proud African-American soldiers of the Union Army posed for this photograph.

Women in both the North and the South supported the war effort of their side in many ways, such as sewing uniforms, caring for the wounded, and raising money.

LATER CAMPAIGNS

The Civil War has been called the first "modern" war because of its new weapons and military techniques. These included ironclad ships, mines, trenches, balloon observation, telegraphy, and rifles. It was the first American war to be photographed and the first in which railroads played a key role in transporting military personnel and supplies.

1. In the West. On July 4, 1863, Union General Ulysses S. Grant took Vicksburg—the last key Southern stronghold on the Mississippi—and Port Hudson, a few days later. These victories gave the North complete control of the Mississippi. States west of the river were now cut off from the rest of the Confederacy. In the fall of 1863, Union forces began another campaign in Tennessee. By the end of 1863, almost all of that state was in Union hands.

2. Sherman's March. The Northern successes in eastern Tennessee made possible a Union advance into the Deep South. The attack was

Western and Southern Theaters of War

led by William T. Sherman. His army invaded Georgia in May 1864 and advanced toward Atlanta, an important rail center. After capturing the city in September 1864, he began a march toward Savannah, Georgia. The advancing Union troops burned crops, killed cattle, wrecked railroads, and destroyed dams. They reached Savannah in December 1864.

3. In the East. Early in 1863, Lee resumed the offensive begun at Antietam the previous fall. In May, he defeated a Union army at Chancellorsville, in Virginia.

a. Gettysburg. In a second invasion of the North, Lee led his army into southern Pennsylvania. He was met by George G. Meade, in command of the Union army, at Gettysburg. The clash between the two forces began on July 1 and lasted three days. It was climaxed by a Confederate charge led by George E. Pickett. Union fire mowed down the Southerners by the thousands. The Confederate army was decisively beaten.

The Battle of Gettysburg proved to be the main turning point of the war. The Confederacy never again undertook a major offensive. Gettysburg is also linked with one of the most famous speeches in

U.S. history. When a national cemetery was dedicated at the site in November 1863, Lincoln delivered his famous Gettysburg Address.

b. End of the war. Early in 1864, Grant was given command of all Union armies. He set out to destroy Lee's army and capture Richmond. Union losses were staggering during this campaign. But Grant pressed on. By 1865, the South was beginning to crumble under furious attacks by the Union armies. Lee (now commander in chief of all Confederate forces) saw that he could no longer protect Richmond. After trying to join forces with other troops, Lee surrendered to Grant at Appomattox Court House on April 9, 1865. The long war was over.

Costs of the Civil War

	Union	*Confederacy*
Troops Killed in Battle	110,000	95,000
Troops Dead From Illness	250,000	165,000
Troops Wounded	275,000	100,000
Estimated Wartime Expenditures	$3 billion	$2 billion (plus cost of freed slaves)

IDENTIFY OR DEFINE: draft, Clara Barton, Ulysses S. Grant, George E. Pickett.

CRITICAL THINKING: Which battle is considered the main turning point of the Civil War? Why?

FIRST ATTEMPTS AT RECONSTRUCTION

In U.S. history, the term *Reconstruction* refers to the restoration of the South to the Union after the Civil War. The Reconstruction era, from 1865 to 1877, was a time of bitter political quarrels. When planning Reconstruction, political leaders asked themselves three major questions: (*1*) What was the relationship between the 11 seceded states and the Union? (*2*) How should Southern whites be treated? (*3*) What would become of the freed slaves? An additional question emerged during this time: Should the president or Congress decide the details of Reconstruction?

1. Lincoln's Plan. Late in 1863, Lincoln announced his plan to reconstruct Confederate areas occupied by Union troops:

- Southerners who had taken part in the war would be pardoned if they took an oath of allegiance to the United States. This offer excluded Confederate military and political leaders.
- The president would recognize the political restoration of a secessionist state that met the following conditions: (*1*) At least 10 percent of the men who had voted in the 1860 presidential election must take the oath of allegiance. (*2*) These voters must set up a new state government that guaranteed the abolition of slavery.

Under Lincoln's so-called "10-Percent Plan," new governments were set up in Louisiana, Arkansas, and Tennessee in 1864. But Congress, opposing Lincoln's plan, refused to recognize them. By mid-April 1865, the situation had reached a deadlock.

2. A New President. Less than a week after Lee's surrender at Appomattox, John Wilkes Booth, a Southerner, shot and killed the president. Andrew Johnson became the new president. A Democrat and former governor of Tennessee, Johnson had remained loyal to the Union when his state seceded. He had been nominated as Lincoln's running mate in 1864 to attract Democratic support for the Republican president's re-election.

3. Johnson's Reconstruction Policy. Congress was not in session during Johnson's first months in office, so he had a free hand in governing. Adopting Lincoln's plan of Reconstruction, Johnson recognized the state governments already restored—those in Louisiana, Arkansas, and Tennessee. He also recognized a pro-Union faction in Virginia as the official government of the state. In the other seven Confederate states, he appointed temporary governors and gave them power to hold elections and form state governments. Johnson pardoned almost all Southerners who took the oath of allegiance. The only exceptions were a few important ex-Confederates. These had to request special pardons, which Johnson granted.

By the end of 1865, all the Confederate states except Texas had set up new state governments and elected representatives to Congress. As required, these ten states had ratified the Thirteenth Amendment to the Constitution, which abolished slavery.

4. The Black Codes. The newly elected state legislatures in the South quickly passed a series of *black codes*. These laws aimed to restore much of the old order by regulating the status of *freedmen*, as freed slaves were known. (The term also referred to women and children.) The codes granted freedmen the right to own property, make contracts, and bring suits in court. But they prohibited them from serving on juries, testifying in court against whites, and bearing arms. Many of the codes restricted the kinds of jobs that African Americans could take and threatened arrest of those who were unemployed. No state gave African Americans the right to vote.

5. Attitude of Congress. When Congress reconvened in December 1865, it refused to admit the newly elected congressmen from the former Confederate states. (One of them was Alexander H. Stephens, vice president of the Confederacy.) It also declared that the Southern states had not been restored and that their newly formed state governments were invalid. Congress rejected Johnson's Reconstruction program. Instead, members of Congress favored one that would keep Southerners from running their states in the old ways and that would bolster their own political power.

Radical Republicans, a group led by Representative Thaddeus Stevens of Pennsylvania and Senator Charles Sumner of Massachusetts, favored a harsh policy that would punish Southerners for their disloyalty. Congress members also wished to curb the powers of the president, which had expanded greatly during the war. They claimed that only the legislative branch had the authority to readmit the states that had seceded.

Moderate and conservative Republicans in Congress, as well as radicals, viewed the enactment of the black codes as proof that Southern whites intended to re-enslave African Americans. All three groups were determined to postpone the readmission of the South until steps could be taken to protect the freedmen.

Southern whites, being almost the only voters in their states, chose Democrats to be their congressmen. Republicans feared that the admission of Southern Democrats to Congress would endanger their control of Congress.

CONGRESSIONAL RECONSTRUCTION

Early in 1866, Congress began to put into action its own plan of Reconstruction. The Freedmen's Bureau had been set up in 1865 to provide former slaves with the necessities of life and to organize schools and find jobs for them. Congress now proposed to give the Freedmen's Bureau the power to hold trials to protect the rights of African Americans. President Johnson thought that the expanded Freedmen's Bureau violated states' rights and was, thus, unconstitutional. He vetoed the Freedmen's Bureau Bill, but Congress overruled him.

1. Civil Rights. Over Johnson's veto, Congress also passed the Civil Rights Act of 1866. It granted African Americans all the legal rights of citizens. Congress also enacted the Fourteenth Amendment, which granted citizenship to African Americans. The amendment provided that no state should "deprive any person of life, liberty, or property, without due process of law; nor deny to any person within its jurisdiction the equal protection of the laws." In addition, the amendment contained these provisions: (*1*) Confederate officials who had held government positions before the war were barred from holding public office again. (*2*) The Confederate war debt was canceled, thus

Johnson, by his veto, administers a kick to the Freedmen's Bureau (depicted as a piece of furniture) and dislodges the African Americans it had sheltered. (Republican cartoon by Thomas Nast, *Harper's Weekly*, 1866)

punishing those who had lent money to the Confederacy. (*3*) Southern states were forbidden to compensate former slave owners for the loss of their slaves.

Congress pledged to restore to the Union any Southern state that ratified the Fourteenth Amendment. President Johnson urged the states not to ratify it. Only Tennessee ratified the amendment. It was readmitted to the Union in 1866.

2. Elections and the Reconstruction Acts. In the fall of 1866, Johnson's attacks against Republicans running for re-election to Congress were so extreme that he lost much public support and increased Republican opposition to him. The Republicans swept the elections, winning enough seats in Congress to override any future vetoes by Johnson.

Congress submitted a series of bills known as the Reconstruction Acts, which were passed over Johnson's veto. They provided for the following: (*1*) The ten unreconstructed states were divided into five military districts, each to be policed by federal troops under the command of a military governor. (*2*) Southerners who had voluntarily fought in the Confederate forces were deprived of the right to vote or hold office. (*3*) To be readmitted, a state had to hold a convention and frame a new constitution guaranteeing African-American suffrage. Delegates to this convention were to be chosen by all citizens eligible to vote, including African Americans. (*4*) After a state had organized a new government and ratified the Fourteenth Amendment, it would be restored to the Union.

Six Southern states met these requirements and were readmitted to the Union in 1868. In 1869, Congress passed the Fifteenth Amendment, granting former slaves the right to vote. The remaining unreconstructed states now had to ratify *both* the Fourteenth and Fifteenth amendments as a condition for readmission. They did so, and in 1870, they were restored to the Union.

3. The Impeachment of Johnson. Johnson regarded Republican Reconstruction as too harsh. Republican congressmen distrusted Johnson as a Southerner and a Democrat. His vetoes of the Reconstruction Acts convinced them that he had no interest in real changes for the South. To weaken the president's power, Congress passed the Tenure of Office Act early in 1867. It banned the president from dismissing, without the Senate's consent, any high official whose original appointment had been confirmed by that body. Believing that this law was unconstitutional, Johnson dis-

Military Reconstruction of Former Confederate States

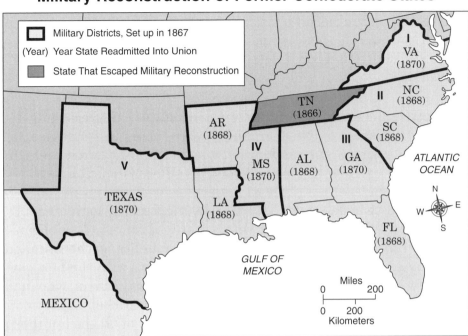

missed Secretary of War Edwin Stanton without consulting the Senate.

Early in 1868, Radical Republicans decided to remove Johnson from office. As a first step, the House of Representatives *impeached* the president—that is, charged him with wrongdoing. Charges against him included violation of the Tenure of Office Act and attempts to disgrace and belittle Congress. The Senate, sitting as a court, then tried Johnson on the impeachment charges. By a margin of one vote, the radicals failed to get the two-thirds vote necessary to remove Johnson. He remained in office until the end of his term.

IDENTIFY OR DEFINE: black codes, freedmen, Thaddeus Stevens, Freedmen's Bureau, Civil Rights Act of 1866, impeachment.

CRITICAL THINKING: How did the post-Reconstruction Southern state governments restrict the rights of the freedmen? Why did they do so?

THE RECONSTRUCTED SOUTH

After the war, Southern farms, cities, railroads, and factories lay in ruins. Thousands of soldiers had lost their lives, and thousands more suffered from wounds or illness. The economic system that had depended on slave labor had been destroyed.

1. Republican Rule. For some Southern states, congressional Reconstruction lasted only a short time—three years in Tennessee, for example. For others, such as Florida, it lasted more than ten years. In all these states, Republicans had control of Reconstruction, not only at the national level but at the state level as well. (Thousands of Democrats had been deprived of the vote by the Reconstruction Acts.)

The new African-American voters were, of course, Republicans. Two other groups in the South were also Republicans: the so-called *scalawags* (Southerners who wanted to cooperate with the new government) and the so-called *carpetbaggers* (Northerners who had moved south to aid freedman or to fill their own pockets).

African Americans served in the legislatures of all the Southern states but formed a majority in only one house, in South Carolina. Two African Americans from Mississippi—Hiram R. Revels and Blanche K. Bruce—were elected to the U.S. Senate. Fourteen African Americans served in the House of Representatives.

2. Charges of Corruption. At the time and for many years afterward, Southern Reconstruction governments were accused of waste

The 1873 South Carolina legislature, including African-American delegates, is shown passing an appropriation bill.

and corruption. They did spend more than prewar governments. But large sums were required to pay for war damage, to rebuild public facilities, and to provide badly needed services, such as public education for both African-American and white children.

Graft and swindles were widespread in the North as well—especially during Ulysses S. Grant's administration. Grant had been a great Civil War hero. But during his two terms as president (1869 to 1877), he chose advisers and appointed officials unwisely. As a result, his administration was marred by political and financial scandals.

3. The Democrats Regain Control. In a fairly short time, Southern Democrats again led the South. Adult white males who had not been in the war had the right to vote. Each year, more males who had been too young to fight reached voting age. A law passed by Congress in 1872 restored the right to vote and hold office to all but about 500 former Confederates.

To regain the political control that they had enjoyed before the war, Southern whites resorted to racist appeals. They urged whites to vote Democratic, the "white man's party." They also used economic pressure and terrorism to keep people—especially African Americans—from voting or to force them to vote Democratic. The best-known terrorist organization was the Ku Klux Klan. To prevent cooperation with the Republicans, Klan members destroyed the property of some African Americans and whites, beat them, and even resorted to lynchings. When Reconstruction ended in 1877, Southern states gradually deprived most African Americans of the vote.

The changing attitude of Northerners helped end Republican rule in the South. In Congress, moderate and conservative Republicans were tired of "the Negro question." Even Radical Republicans had lost some of their zeal. Many people in the North were racist and cared little about protecting the rights of people whom they considered inferior.

THE END OF RECONSTRUCTION

In the presidential election of 1876, Republican Rutherford B. Hayes of Ohio ran against Democrat Samuel J. Tilden of New York. Both candidates promised to end Reconstruction. Tilden won a larger popular vote than Hayes but was one electoral vote short of a majority. Twenty electoral votes from four states remained uncounted. Both parties claimed these votes. In January 1877, Congress appointed an electoral commission to settle the dispute. It consisted of eight

Republicans and seven Democrats. Voting strictly along party lines, the Republican-dominated commission gave every disputed vote to Hayes, thereby assuring his election.

Congress still had to ratify this decision, however. Fearing that Democrats in the Senate might start a *filibuster* (a tactic to delay legislative action), the Hayes forces appealed for Southern Democratic support by making several informal pledges: (*1*) to appoint a Southerner to the Cabinet, (*2*) to grant federal aid to Southern railroads, and (*3*) to withdraw the last federal troops from the South. The Southerners voted with the majority, and Hayes took office. Shortly after his inauguration in 1877, he ended military occupation of the South. Reconstruction was at an end.

The Republican-controlled governments remaining in the South were soon voted out of office. Southerners, however, continued to resent the Republican party. For the next 75 years, they voted overwhelmingly Democratic, thus earning their region the nickname of the "solid South."

IDENTIFY OR DEFINE: scalawag, carpetbagger, filibuster, solid South.

CRITICAL THINKING: What was the main criticism of Republican Reconstruction governments in the South? Do you think it was justified? Explain your answer.

Chapter Review

 MATCHING TEST

Column A	Column B
1. Stonewall Jackson	*a.* Lincoln's announcement on slavery
2. Emancipation Proclamation	*b.* Union commander at Gettysburg
	c. location of Lee's surrender
3. William T. Sherman	*d.* Confederate general at Bull Run
4. George G. Meade	*e.* victor at Atlanta in 1864
5. Appomattox Court House	

	MULTIPLE-CHOICE TEST

1. In 1861, Maryland decided to (*a*) join the Confederacy (*b*) stay in the Union (*c*) be annexed by France (*d*) break into two parts, with western Maryland joining the Confederacy.

2. The initial, main war aim of the North was to (*a*) free the slaves (*b*) build a railroad to the West (*c*) enact a higher tariff (*d*) preserve the Union.

3. A major objective of Union forces was the (*a*) annexation of Canada (*b*) capture of Richmond (*c*) invasion of Pennsylvania (*d*) control of the Hudson River.

4. After the battle at Vicksburg, the Confederacy (*a*) was split in two along the Mississippi River (*b*) defeated all Union forces in the West (*c*) sued for peace (*d*) was free to invade Washington, D.C.

5. Under Lincoln's plan for Reconstruction, the Confederate states were to be (*a*) readmitted to the Union after ratifying the Fourteenth Amendment (*b*) readmitted to the Union only by Congress (*c*) recognized when 10 percent of voters took an oath of allegiance (*d*) occupied by military troops for 20 years.

6. Radical Republicans in Congress (*a*) regarded the former Confederate states as conquered territory (*b*) passed the black codes (*c*) favored Lincoln's ideas on Reconstruction (*d*) introduced legislation to pardon Jefferson Davis.

7. The Fourteenth Amendment provided for all of the following *except* (*a*) citizenship for African Americans (*b*) equal protection of the laws for all Americans (*c*) cancellation of the Confederate war debt (*d*) military districts for the South.

8. Andrew Johnson was impeached by the (*a*) House of Representatives (*b*) Senate (*c*) electoral college (*d*) Supreme Court.

9. Southern state governments during Reconstruction were controlled by (*a*) African-American voters (*b*) groups of African-American and white Republicans (*c*) Northern Democrats (*d*) former Confederate army officers.

10. Andrew Johnson was succeeded in office by (*a*) Ulysses S Grant (*b*) Charles Sumner (*c*) Abraham Lincoln (*d*) Samuel J. Tilden.

ESSAY QUESTIONS

1. Why is the Civil War considered to be the first modern war?

2. Describe the background of the Emancipation Proclamation. What did it accomplish?

3. Describe the opposition to wartime government policies in the North and in the South.

4. What were the major questions facing government leaders in the Reconstruction period? What positions on these major questions were taken by (a) Lincoln (b) Johnson (c) Radical Republicans?

5. When and how did Reconstruction come to an end?

DOCUMENT-BASED QUESTION

This question is based on the accompanying documents (1–4). It will improve your ability to work with historical documents.

Historical Context:

The 12 years following Civil War make up the period known as Reconstruction. It was a time when the states of the former Confederacy came back into the Union. In addition, the South began to rebuild its economy. Americans disagreed on how Reconstruction should be carried out.

Task:

Using information from the documents and your knowledge of United States history, read each document and answer the question or questions that follow it. Your answers to the questions will help you write the document-based essay.

Document 1. Excerpt from a late 1930s interview with Toby Jones, a former slave, in which he described life in South Carolina immediately after the Civil War (1865):

> I don't know as I 'spected nothing from freedom, but they turned us out like a bunch of stray dogs, no homes, no clothing, no nothing, not 'nough food to last us one meal. . . . All we had to farm with was sharp sticks. We'd stick holes and plant corn, and when

it come up we'd punch up the dirt round it. We didn't plant cotton, 'cause we couldn't eat that. I made bows and arrows to kill wild game with, and we never went to a store for nothing. We made our clothes out of animal skins.

Source: www.stolaf.edu/courses/2000sem1/Africa_and_the_Americas/231/amfirst.htm

What problems did Jones face immediately after getting his freedom?

Document 2. Excerpt from a Mississippi law (one of the black codes), passed in November 1865, after the abolition of slavery in the United States:

[All] freedmen, free negroes, and mulattoes [people of mixed races] in this State, over the age of eighteen years, found on the second of Monday in January, 1866, or thereafter, with no lawful employment or business, or found unlawfully assembling themselves together, either in the day or night time . . . shall be deemed vagrants [drifters], and on conviction thereof shall be fined [a] sum . . . not exceeding . . . fifty dollars . . . and imprisoned at the discretion [judgment] of the court . . . not exceeding ten days.

Source: Hart, Albert Bushnell (ed.) *American History Told by Contemporaries*. NY: The Macmillan Company, 1901, IV, p. 479.

Based on what you read in Document 1, what social problem was the 1865 Mississippi law ignoring? Explain your answer.

Document 3. Excerpt from a speech by Thaddeus Stevens, in which he criticized the black codes, January 3, 1867:

We have broken the material shackles of four million slaves. We have . . . granted them the privilege of fighting our battles, of dying in defense of freedom, and of bearing their equal portion of taxes, but where have we given them the privilege of ever participating in the formation of the laws for the government of their native land?

Source: *Congressional Globe*, 39th Congress, 2nd Session (Jan. 3, 1867), I, p. 251.

According to Stevens, what right was being denied African Americans by the black codes?

Document 4. Excerpt from a 1907 speech by Senator Benjamin R. Tillman of South Carolina, in which he said that he supported the violent tactics of the Ku Klux Klan during Reconstruction:

There was a condition bordering upon anarchy. Misrule, robbery, and murder were holding high carnival. The people's substance was being stolen. . . . Our legislature was composed of a majority of Negroes, most of whom could neither read nor write. . . .

It was then that "we shot them [African Americans]"; it was then that "we killed them." . . . Then it was that "we stuffed ballot boxes," because desperate diseases require desperate remedies, and having resolved to take the state away, we hesitated at nothing.

> **Source**: *Congressional Record*, 59th Congress, 2nd Session (Jan. 21, 1907), p. 1440.

a. What did African Americans eventually attain in South Carolina that Stevens in Document 3 had said had been denied them?

b. What methods had Senator Benjamin R. Tillman supported as a way to rid the South Carolina legislature of African Americans?

DOCUMENT-BASED ESSAY

Using information from the above documents and your knowledge of United States history, write an essay in which you:

- Explain whether each Southern group (white and black) during Reconstruction could rightly claim to be the victim of the other. Give reasons for your choice.

UNIT V

THE NATION TRANSFORMED

11
The Age of Industrialization

The years between the Civil War and 1900 is often called the Age of Industrialization. Established businesses expanded their operations, and new industrial plants sprang up across the country. By 1900, the United States was the world's leading industrial nation.

INDUSTRIAL GROWTH

The Civil War created a huge demand for weapons, war supplies, and machinery of all kinds. Growth continued after the war for five main reasons: (*1*) The national government maintained high tariffs to protect American industry from foreign competition. (*2*) An ever-increasing population offered an expanding market for manufactured goods. (*3*) A continuous flow of immigrants provided an ample labor force. (*4*) Abundant natural resources supplied industry with raw materials. (*5*) A network of railroads opened up national markets to manufacturers.

1. Railroad Improvements. Beginning in the 1860s, rail lines were extended across the entire United States. Track mileage increased from about 30,000 miles in 1860 to almost 260,000 miles in 1900. For 50 years after the Civil War, railroad construction and operation was the nation's biggest nonagricultural business.

Railroads brought about standard time zones in the United States. Until the 1880s, each locality across the country set its own time, fixing as noon the moment when the sun was directly overhead. The resulting time differences made it difficult for railroads to work out schedules. In 1883, the railway companies agreed to divide the country into four standard time zones. This division remains in effect.

2. Better Communications. The telegraph, in wide use by the 1850s, was followed by other inventions that speeded up communication. Cyrus Field laid the first permanently successful underwater telegraph cable across the Atlantic in 1866. The line, from Newfoundland to Ireland, made possible telegraphic communication between North America and Europe. Cables were later laid across the other oceans, linking all the continents by the telegraph.

Another communications breakthrough, the telephone, was patented in 1876 by Alexander Graham Bell. By 1900, more than a million telephones were in use. Still another advance in communications was the wireless telegraph. Guglielmo Marconi, an Italian scientist, developed it in 1895. This invention made possible ship-to-ship, ship-to-shore, and *transoceanic* (across-an-ocean) communication without the use of cables. Typewriters, adding machines, and cash registers were also introduced in the 1870s.

3. New Industries. Although railroad construction offered the prime example of industrial growth in the late 1800s, other industries also expanded. They included meatpacking, flour milling, and the manufacture of clothing and shoes. Entirely new industries sprang up as well.

a. Steel. Although the early Industrial Revolution was an age of iron, steel dominated industry's later growth. This metal, stronger and more flexible than iron, can be shaped into a great variety of useful products. In the 1850s, William Kelly, a Kentucky blacksmith, discovered a new, cheaper method of making steel. In England, Henry Bessemer independently developed a similar technique. In the Bessemer process, cold air is forced through molten iron to remove its impurities. Then carbon is added to make the steel tough and elastic. The first Bessemer converter in the United States went into operation in 1864.

Once steel was inexpensive to produce, it replaced iron in trains, railroad tracks, bridges, ships, and many kinds of machinery. The steel industry was first centered in Pittsburgh but soon spread elsewhere.

b. Petroleum. In 1859, Edwin L. Drake drilled the world's first successful oil well near Titusville, Pennsylvania. Oil prospectors rushed to the area and drilled other wells. Special railroad cars and

California oil derricks, about 1898.

pipelines were built to transport the petroleum to refineries. There petroleum was processed into kerosene to fuel lamps or into oil and grease to lubricate machinery. Petroleum made possible the invention of the gasoline engine, which led to the growth of the automobile industry in the early 20th century.

c. Electrical power. In the 1870s, three important developments in the generation and use of electricity took place: (*1*) Charles F. Brush designed a practical *dynamo*, a machine that could produce a sustained flow of electric current. (*2*) Thomas A. Edison invented the electric lightbulb. (*3*) The electric motor came into use. Before long, power plants were built to generate electricity in commercial amounts. The first electric power plant in the United States opened in New York City in 1882.

Factories switched from steam power to electric power. Electric lights replaced kerosene and gas lamps, and electrically operated home appliances were invented. By 1900, patents had been granted for an electric iron, electric stove, and electric sewing machine.

IDENTIFY OR DEFINE: Cyrus Field, Alexander Graham Bell, Guglielmo Marconi, Edwin L. Drake.

CRITICAL THINKING: Why was the United States divided into four time zones in the 19th century?

CHANGES IN BUSINESS METHODS

After the Civil War, a group of strong business leaders gained control of the nation's leading industries and changed the structure of American business.

1. Vertical Integration. One of the most famous of these industrialists was Andrew Carnegie. In 1873, Carnegie founded his own steel company, using the Bessemer process to produce the metal in large quantities.

Carnegie gained control of every phase of steelmaking by buying mining companies, ore ships, and railroad lines. Owning the various stages of production from raw materials to finished products is called *vertical integration*. Petroleum refiners followed Carnegie's lead by acquiring oil fields, pipelines, and distribution facilities.

2. The Corporation. The Carnegie Steel Company was a *partnership*, meaning that it had only a few co-owners. But many of the new industrial companies were *corporations*, a type of business owned by all the people who buy shares in it. There can be thousands of *shareholders* (also called *stockholders*). They elect a board of directors to manage the business. Each shareholder receives a part of the profits in the form of *dividends*. The amount of the dividend is based on the number of shares a person owns.

An important advantage of the corporation is its ability to raise a large amount of capital by selling stock to investors. This enables the corporation to build huge factories, buy expensive machinery, and expand nationally and internationally. The corporation soon became the dominant form of business organization in the United States. By 1900, corporations controlled more than two-thirds of all manufacturing.

3. Combinations. Individual companies not only grew in size and wealth but also formed *combinations*—business alliances that increased their assets and power.

a. The merger. In one form of combination, the *merger*, two or more companies joined to form a larger one. In 1869, Cornelius Vanderbilt merged a number of short railroad lines between New York City and Buffalo. The result was the country's first great railroad system, the New York Central. Many business leaders arranged mergers to reduce or eliminate competition. Once they gained a monopoly on a product or service, they could then demand higher prices.

b. The pool. A *pool* was an informal agreement among competing companies to fix prices, share profits, or divide the market for their products. Rival railroads serving the Midwest set up the first pool in 1870. Pooling soon became a common practice among competing railroads and spread to other industries. But pools were not legally binding and were often broken. The pool was replaced by the trust.

c. The trust. A *trust* combined a number of corporations in the same field or in related fields. A small board of trustees managed the combination. Stockholders in each company signed over their stock to the trustees. In exchange, the stockholders received trust certificates that entitled them to a proportionate share of the trust's profits.

John D. Rockefeller organized the first successful trust. After starting an oil-refining business in the 1860s, he bought out competitors or ruined them by sharply lowering his own prices. In 1879, he formed the Standard Oil Trust, which controlled 90 percent of the oil refining business. During the next decade, trusts were formed in many other industries, including sugar, lead, whiskey, and

Nothing but Feed and Fight: Farmer Jonathan *(who has just been rooting out foreign thistles).* "I GUESS THIS NEW BREED OF CATTLE HAS GOT TO GO NEXT."

meatpacking. One of the biggest trusts was the American Tobacco Company, formed in 1890 by James B. Duke.

d. The holding company. The *holding company* did not produce or distribute goods or services. Instead, it held a controlling interest in the stock of several related companies, called *subsidiaries*, and concerned itself with directing their operations. A pioneer in this form of combination was the Bell Telephone Company. By the end of the century, 185 industrial holding companies controlled a third of all the capital invested in American manufacturing.

4. Investment Banking. *Investment bankers* raised capital for corporations by supervising the issue and sale of *securities* (stocks and bonds). They often sat on a corporation's board of directors. In the age of industrialization, the giant of U.S. investment bankers was J. Pierpont Morgan. He headed the country's largest private bank. When hundreds of railroads faced ruin after a business panic in 1893, Morgan reorganized and restored them. In 1901, he and his associates bought the Carnegie Steel Company, merged it with other companies, and formed the huge U.S. Steel Corporation, the nation's first billion-dollar company.

5. New Retailing Practices. Before the rise of big business, people had few choices about where to buy everyday supplies. The availability of mass-produced goods during the age of industrialization brought changes. Merchants developed new types of stores and new techniques of merchandising.

The *chain store*, a group of retail outlets owned by one company, could sell goods at lower prices because of centralized management and large-scale purchasing. The first grocery-store chain was founded in 1859. It later became known as the Great Atlantic and Pacific Tea Company (A&P). F.W. Woolworth opened the first unit in his chain of five-and-ten-cent stores in 1879.

Another retailing novelty was the *department store*, which sold goods of almost every description. Each kind of product—women's clothing, toys, kitchenware, and so on—was located in a separate department. The first department stores were founded in the 1860s and 1870s, including Macy's in New York City, Wanamaker's in Philadelphia, and Marshall Field in Chicago.

Mail-order companies published catalogs offering a wide variety of goods. Customers ordered and received merchandise by mail. Pioneers in this field were Montgomery Ward, founded in 1872, and Sears Roebuck, founded in 1895.

Selling techniques improved in the late 1800s. Foodstuffs, once sold in bulk, were now packaged and labeled. Brand names came into wide use. The number of trademarks registered at the U.S. Patent Office jumped from 121 in 1870 to 10,568 in 1906. Advertising appeared not only in magazines and newspapers but also on big electric signs. Another shopping innovation was *installment buying* (paying over a period of time).

The Free-Enterprise System

The United States' economic system is called the *free-enterprise system,* or *capitalism.* It is based on the following principles: (*1*) Private individuals should own and control a nation's resources. (*2*) Producers should be able to compete freely among themselves for a share of the market. Consumers should have the opportunity to make their own choices among the available products. Such competition would establish a firm foundation for a healthy economy and would benefit society as a whole. (*3*) Government should not interfere with the operation of the economic system. Such a policy is called *laissez-faire* (French for "let do"). This principle is not always strictly followed by governments, however.

The principles of capitalism dated back to the late 1700s. The U.S. system during the age of industrialization differed in many ways from the ideal. For instance, trusts and other business combinations severely limited free competition in many fields. But the economy was booming. Many Americans believed that a laissez-faire policy was the best way to sustain economic growth.

IDENTIFY OR DEFINE: vertical integration, corporation, merger, pool, trust, holding company.

CRITICAL THINKING: Why did industries form trusts in the late 19th century?

PROBLEMS OF LABOR

As the United States industrialized, the number of wage earners grew. Employees generally worked long hours for low pay. Working conditions were often poor and sometimes dangerous. Unemployment was an ever-present threat. Acting alone, a worker could do nothing about a bad situation except quit and look for another job.

1. Organizing Unions. Workers realized that they could make changes only by forming labor unions. A union's first objective was to win recognition by an employer as the official representative of the employees. Then it could engage in *collective bargaining*—negotiations between labor and management officials to settle such issues as wages, hours, and working conditions.

a. The Knights of Labor. The first important national union was the Knights of Labor, formed in 1869 by garment workers in Philadelphia. It aimed to unite all workers, skilled and unskilled, into one large union. Members included African Americans and women. The Knights hoped not only to better the worker's lot but also to reform society in general.

The Knights were active in the nation's first major strike. In 1877, workers on the Baltimore and Ohio and other railroads in the East walked off their jobs to protest a wage cut. The railroads replaced them with other workers. When angry strikers tried to halt the trains, riots broke out. A militia was called in and pitched battles resulted. President Hayes sent in U.S. troops to restore order. Unable to stop the trains and afraid of losing their jobs, the strikers accepted the wage cut.

Nevertheless, the Knights continued to grow, with membership reaching more than 700,000 by 1886. In that year, thousands of workers seeking an eight-hour workday went on strike in Chicago. Strikers and police clashed at the McCormick Harvester Company. A protest meeting was called at Haymarket Square to protest the killing of two strikers by the police. When police arrived to break up the crowd, someone threw a bomb, which killed or injured a number of people. Eight agitators among the strikers were convicted of conspiracy to commit murder. Although the evidence against them was flimsy, four were hanged and three were sentenced to long prison terms.

Although the Knights of Labor had not been involved in the Haymarket riot, the public blamed the union for the incident. As a result, its membership fell off sharply. Other factors that contributed to the decline of the Knights were unsuccessful strikes, internal disputes over political activity, and conflicting interests of skilled and unskilled workers within the organization.

b. The American Federation of Labor. Many of those who left the Knights of Labor joined the American Federation of Labor (AFL). Samuel Gompers, one of its founders, was the AFL's president from 1886 to 1924. He believed that unions should not reform society but win immediate benefits for their members. Under Gompers's leadership, the AFL's membership grew to about 550,000 in 1900. The AFL was made up of *craft unions*, ones in which skilled workers were grouped according to their trades. Unskilled workers, including most minority and women workers, were excluded. Each trade formed its own national union, with many locals throughout the country. The AFL was a union of unions rather than a union of individual workers.

2. A Time of Struggle. Although more successful than the Knights of Labor, the AFL represented less than 10 percent of American non-farmworkers in 1900. The times did not favor organized labor. Corporations often refused to recognize unions and fired employees who tried to organize other workers. They hired *strikebreakers* (sometimes called scabs) to work in place of strikers. When labor and management were at odds, government at all levels almost always sided with business. The courts, for example, often issued *injunctions* (court orders) against strikers. The public and the press also often supported business over unions.

In 1892, a particularly bitter dispute erupted at the Carnegie Steel Company's plant in Homestead, Pennsylvania. Refusing to accept a wage cut, union workers went on strike. To protect its property and break the strike, the company hired 300 armed guards from the Pinkerton detective agency. In a fight between strikers and guards, seven guards were killed and the rest driven off. A state militia then stepped in. Strikebreakers kept up production. The strike collapsed after five months, and the power of the union was broken.

Chicago stockyards. Strikers in the Great Railway Strike of 1894 jeered when a train passed escorted by the U.S. Cavalry.

Even more discouraging to organized labor was the Pullman strike. The Pullman Company, near Chicago, manufactured sleeping cars for trains. Its workers went on strike in 1894 to protest a wage cut. Members of the independent American Railway Union, headed by Eugene V. Debs, supported them by refusing to handle any trains hauling Pullman cars. Violence flared up when the railroads tried to keep the trains running. President Grover Cleveland sent in U.S. troops to restore order. Meanwhile, the railroads obtained an injunction forbidding strikers to interfere with the U.S. mail and interstate commerce. When Debs refused to call off the strike, he was arrested and jailed. Under the protection of federal troops, train service was restored, and the strike was broken.

IDENTIFY OR DEFINE: collective bargaining, Haymarket riot, craft union, injunction, Homestead strike, Pullman strike.

CRITICAL THINKING: Why was it difficult for unions in late 19th-century America?

THE GROWTH OF CITIES

In the years 1860–1900, there was a strong trend toward *urbanization*—the growth of cities. In 1860, less than 15 percent of all Americans lived in cities having a population of 10,000 or more. By 1900, more than 30 percent lived in such cities. Many Americans moved to urban areas to find jobs in factories and businesses. Cities also attracted most of the immigrants who arrived in the United States during this period.

1. The New Immigration. In 1886, the Statue of Liberty, a gift of the French people, was unveiled in New York Harbor. Located at the entrance to the biggest U.S. port, it became a symbol of the nation's promise to immigrants. During 1860–1900, the number of newcomers to the United States averaged more than 200,000 a year. In some peak years in the 1880s, there were three times as many.

Until the 1880s, most immigrants to the United States came from Northern and Western Europe. Most were Protestants. Then, this so-called "old" immigration gave way to a "new" immigration. More and more people came from Eastern and Southern Europe—

Poland, Russia, the Austro-Hungarian Empire, the Balkan states, and Italy. There were not only thousands of Catholics but also large numbers of Jews. Few of the newcomers spoke English, and many could not read or write. By 1900, immigrants from Eastern and Southern Europe outnumbered other immigrants.

READING A GRAPH

Immigration to the United States, 1840–1919

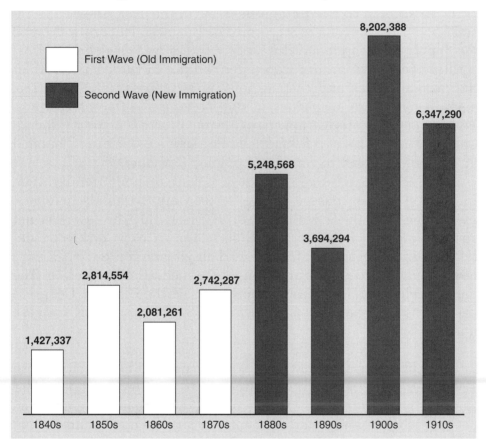

1. In which decade, was "old" immigration the highest?

2. In which decade, was immigration 5,248,568?

3. How many people immigrated to the United States in the 1890s?

---

a. Patterns of work and settlement. Many of the new immigrants, being poor and unskilled, tended to settle in large cities, where they could find factory or construction jobs. Italians worked on subways, bridges, and water systems in urban areas. Slavs mined coal, poured steel, and worked in the stockyards. Jews went into the garment industry or ran small stores. Chinese immigrants—who settled mainly on the West Coast—operated laundries and restaurants. The new immigrants felt more comfortable among their own people and often formed ethnic neighborhoods within cities. There they set up businesses and organizations to help their own group of people. Among these were welfare societies, newspapers, theaters, and sports clubs.

b. Response to the newcomers. As in the past, Americans' reactions to the newcomers were mixed. Business leaders welcomed the supply of cheap labor. But wage earners were less happy. Desperately poor immigrants were often willing to work for less than the normal wages and to take jobs as strikebreakers. Then, too, many people were suspicious of the foreigners' different customs. The strongest nativist opposition was directed against Roman Catholics. Members of the American Protective Association, founded in 1887, pledged not to vote for or employ Catholics.

Some Americans urged the government to limit immigration. In 1882, Congress passed a law to keep out criminals, paupers, the insane, and those with certain diseases. But the law was not strictly enforced. Inspectors at Ellis Island in New York—the nation's main immigration station—had only two minutes to ask each new arrival 32 questions and complete a medical examination. The main exception to free immigration involved the Chinese. Congress passed the Chinese Exclusion Act in 1882. It banned all Chinese immigration.

2. City Life. Between 1860 and 1900, the number of U.S. cities with 100,000 or more people jumped from 14 to 38. Cleveland, Ohio, for example, grew from 43,417 people to 381,768. Urban centers offered not only jobs but also entertainment, educational opportunities, and such conveniences as electric lights and running water.

Most American cities grew without plan. Since there was no zoning, builders might place houses next to a packing plant or a chemical factory. And since there were few building regulations, many structures were ugly, unhealthy, and dangerous.

a. Construction. Because city real estate was expensive, builders tried to cram as many people as possible into the space available. The result was the *tenement.* Originally, a tenement was any rental dwelling that housed many families. But it soon came to mean a crowded, run-down apartment building. Usually, several tenement apartments had to share toilet facilities, which might consist of one privy in a courtyard. Tenements had little light or air. Tenement neighborhoods quickly became slums.

Workspace, as well as living space, was limited. After the invention of the passenger elevator in the 1850s, buildings began to expand upward. At first, the outside walls had to be thick enough to support the floors. This limited a building's height to a few stories. A true skyscraper was possible only when builders started using iron frameworks to support both walls and floors. (Steel later replaced iron.) William LeBaron Jenney is generally credited with designing the nation's first skyscraper—the ten-story Home Insurance Building—in Chicago in 1884. Other skyscrapers soon rose in other cities. The greatest of the early skyscraper architects was Louis H. Sullivan. His motto "form follows function" pointed the way toward a more modern, less cluttered style.

b. Transportation. City transportation could not accommodate the number of city dwellers. Streets were too narrow to handle the traffic. Many of them were unpaved. In Chicago as late as 1890,

Recent immigrants lived in crowded areas of America's cities.

more than two-thirds of the street mileage consisted of rutted dirt roads.

Streetcars were the main form of public transportation. Horse-drawn at first, they were later powered by electricity. Because of traffic jams, several cities tried other ways of moving people. Chicago and New York raised trains above the ground to make "elevateds" (els). Other cities put railroad lines underground. In 1897, Boston opened the nation's first subway, a mile and a half long.

c. Services. Urban services were often inadequate. Wooden buildings were common and these often caught fire. In 1871, a great fire burned a huge area of Chicago, where even the sidewalks were made of wood. Volunteer fire companies were the rule until the mid-19th century. In the 1860s and 1870s, big cities like New York began to set up professional firefighting units.

Sanitation was a problem, too. Sewers often emptied into the same rivers that supplied drinking water. Many cities had no regular garbage pickup. Although several states and localities had established public health departments by 1900, conditions were still far from ideal.

3. Coping With City Problems. Most city governments had their hands full keeping order and providing minimum services. They could not offer welfare and the other benefits provided today. City dwellers in need of help turned to other resources.

a. Political machines. Strong political organizations called *political machines* first arose in the United States early in the 1800s. These groups were labeled "machines" because of their efficiency. By 1870, both Republicans and Democrats controlled city districts by means of political machines. Candidates of these parties could count on votes from such districts.

So-called *bosses* usually ran political machines. The party leaders supplied city jobs and city contracts in exchange for bribes. They rarely held major political office. Bosses offered business leaders a way of avoiding competitive bidding and other such procedures. They provided jobs, legal advice, and loans to ordinary citizens when times were hard. They gave much needed help to poor immigrants in exchange for their votes.

Almost every big city had its machine and its bosses. The most notorious big-city boss was William M. Tweed, who headed Tammany Hall, the Democratic machine of New York City. Tweed and his associates, known as the Tweed Ring, swindled the city

BRIBERY & CORRUPTION

NEW YORK

RIGHT UNDER HER NOSE, EVERY DAY IN THE WEEK

Thomas Nast: "The Spirit of Tweed Is Mighty Still"

out of $75 million or more. Convicted of fraud, Tweed was sent to prison.

b. Reformers and settlement houses. Reformers helped bring about changes in city living conditions. One was a Danish immigrant, Jacob Riis. As a police reporter in New York City, he became familiar with slums, vice, and crime. He publicized his findings in such books as *How the Other Half Lives* (1890). Pressured by the public reaction to Riis's books, the city cleaned up its water supply, built playgrounds, improved schools, and tore down some of its worst tenements.

Settlement houses were another response to city problems. These community centers in poor neighborhoods were usually supported by private contributors and run by volunteers. In 1889, Jane Addams founded Hull House in Chicago, and four years after that, Lillian Wald founded New York's Henry Street Settlement. A settlement house usually provided free classes in English, cooking, and child care. It also offered medical help and provided recreation in the form of clubs, sports teams, and theaters. The problems of city living gave rise to a new professional field, *social work*. Since dedicated amateurs and private charities were no longer able to handle all the pressing needs of ever-expanding city populations, local governments hired social workers.

EDUCATION

Many of the immigrants who came to America during the age of industrialization needed to learn to adapt to a new culture and the United States' political process. Reformers began to call for more and better public schools. City and state governments played key roles in the growth of education.

States passed laws requiring attendance at school. The first one to do so was Massachusetts, in 1852. Between 1870 and 1900, the number of pupils between ages 5 and 17 who attended public schools more than doubled, from 7 million to 15 million. In the same period, the number of high schools increased from 160 to 6,000.

Most of the new schools were in towns or cities. And many of the students were first-generation Americans. Public school was the main place where most of them learned what it meant to be an American. In fact, an important goal of public education was *Americanization*—teaching the immigrants English, U.S. history, and the values and traditions of their new homeland.

The first public kindergarten was opened in St. Louis in 1873. Soon, many other cities started classes for preschool children. The 1862 Morrill Act helped states found colleges and universities. The original purpose of this law had been to improve agricultural education. But its main result was the creation of the modern system of state universities.

John H. Vincent, a Methodist clergyman, organized the Chautauqua Institution for adult education. Each summer, thousands flocked to Chautauqua, New York, to attend concerts, operas, literary readings, and educational lectures presented by famous people. The idea spread, and "chautauquas" were organized in other parts of the country.

All these educational developments were aided by the growth of public libraries. The nation's first public libraries had been founded before the Civil War. But they became widespread later in the century. Andrew Carnegie donated more than $40 million for the building of libraries.

IDENTIFY OR DEFINE: urbanization, tenement, political machine, settlement house, Americanization.

CRITICAL THINKING: Some of the municipal services that are common today began developing in the late 19th century. Why do you think they developed then?

Chapter Review

 MATCHING TEST

Column A	Column B
1. Jane Addams	*a.* invented electric lightbulb
2. Thomas A. Edison	*b.* got rich as steel manufacturer
3. Andrew Carnegie	*c.* reporter who publicized big-city problems
4. Jacob Riis	*d.* founder of Hull House
5. Eugene V. Debs	*e.* head of American Railway Union

MULTIPLE-CHOICE TEST

1. Which was *not* a factor that contributed to industrialization after the Civil War? (*a*) abundant natural resources (*b*) high tariffs (*c*) a growing population (*d*) the formation of labor unions.

2. The biggest nonagricultural business in the United States between 1865 and 1915 was (*a*) railroad construction (*b*) shipbuilding (*c*) war armaments (*d*) telegraph.

3. The inventor who reduced costs for producing steel was (*a*) Cyrus Field (*b*) Samuel Gompers (*c*) Henry Bessemer (*d*) Thomas Edison.

4. A major factor in the development of the skyscraper was (*a*) strictly enforced zoning (*b*) the invention of the passenger elevator (*c*) regulations against tenements (*d*) the construction of elevated trains.

5. The first successful trust in the United States was organized by (*a*) James B. Duke (*b*) John D. Rockefeller (*c*) Andrew Carnegie (*d*) William Tweed.

6. A notorious 19th-century big-city political boss was (*a*) William Tweed (*b*) Thomas Edison (*c*) Lillian Wald (*d*) Jacob Riis.

7. The Knights of Labor lost support as a result of the (*a*) invention of the lightbulb (*b*) Haymarket riot (*c*) Homestead strike (*d*) rise of Tammany Hall.

8. Samuel Gompers founded the (*a*) American Federation of Labor (*b*) United Mine Workers (*c*) Knights of Labor (*d*) Transport Workers Union.

9. Andrew Carnegie gave more than $40 million to build (*a*) agricultural colleges (*b*) kindergartens (*c*) settlement houses (*d*) public libraries.

10. In 1882, Congress passed a bill that banned immigration from (*a*) Mexico (*b*) Germany (*c*) China (*d*) India.

    ESSAY QUESTIONS

1. Why did industrial growth accelerate during and after the Civil War?

2. What is a corporation, and how does it work? Why did corporations have an advantage in an age of industrial expansion?

3. What new industries developed during the age of industrialization? Name a person who was important in the development of *each* industry listed. Describe each person's contribution.

4. Compare the Knights of Labor and the AFL as to organization, membership, and aims.

5. How did the "new" immigrants differ from the "old"? For what reasons did nativists react negatively to the "new" immigrants?

DOCUMENT-BASED QUESTION

This question is based on the accompanying documents (1–4). It will improve your ability to work with historical documents.

Historical Context:

From 1860 to 1900, immigration to the United States was quite heavy—about 14 million people. The immigrants' arrivals made a great impact on the nation's political, social, and economic life. The immigrants' influence was especially strong in urban areas, as immigrants contributed to the rapid growth of American cities.

Task:

Using information from the documents and your knowledge of United States history, read each document and answer the question or questions that follow it. Your answers to the questions will help you write the document-based essay.

Document 1. Description of life for the poor in New York City in the 1880s, from Jacob Riis's book *How the Other Half Lives*:

> Be a little careful, please. The hall is dark and you might stumble over the children pitching pennies back there. Not that it would hurt them; kicks and cuffs are their daily diet. They have little else. . . . Close? Yes! What would you have? All the fresh air that enters these stairs is from the hall-door that is forever slamming. . . . Here is a door. Listen! That short hacking cough, that tiny helpless wail—what do they mean? . . . The child is dying with measles. With half a chance it might have lived; but it had none. That dark bedroom killed it.

> **Source**: Riis, Jacob. *How the Other Half Lives*. NY: Charles Scribner's Sons, 1890, pp. 43–44.

Judging from the title of Jacob Riis's book and the excerpt, why do you think he wrote the book?

Document 2. Study the graph on page 213.

During which decade shown was immigration to the United States the greatest?

Document 3. Study the cartoon of "Boss" William M. Tweed on page 217.

a. Why was "Boss" Tweed shown in jail?

b. Do you think that cartoonist Thomas Nast was trying to make fun of "Boss" Tweed? Explain your answer.

Document 4. Remarks by George Washington Plunkitt, a political "boss" in New York City, 1905:

> If there's a fire in Ninth, Tenth, or Eleventh Avenue, for example, any hour of the day or night, I'm usually there with some of my election district captains as soon as the fire-engines. If a family

is burned out I don't ask whether they are Republicans or Democrats, and I don't refer them to the Charity Organization Society, which would investigate their case in a month or two and decide they were worthy of help about the time they are dead from starvation. I just get quarters for them, buy clothes for them if their clothes were burned up, and fix them up till they get things runnin' again. It's philanthropy, but it's politics, too—mighty good politics. Who can tell how many votes one of these fires bring me?

Source: Riordon, William L. *Plunkitt of Tammany Hall*. Boston: Bedford/St. Martin's, 1994, p. 64.

What reason did Plunkitt give for not referring the burned-out family to the Charity Organization Society?

DOCUMENT-BASED ESSAY

Using information from the above documents and your knowledge of United States history, write an essay in which you:

- Explain whether conditions of the poor in cities in the late 1800s and early 1900s contributed to the rise of powerful political bosses and to the willingness of some poor people to overlook the illegal actions of bosses.

CHAPTER 12

The Last Frontier, Farmers, and Politics

At the end of the Civil War, one large part of the United States was still largely unsettled. This was the area between the Missouri River and the settlements in California, the Northwest, and the Southwest. Stretching more than 1,500 miles from east to west, the territory comprised two main regions. One, the Great Plains, lay between the Missouri and the Rockies. It was a dry, almost treeless expanse of land, covered with fields of high grass. The other region, west of the plains, included the Rocky Mountains and the arid plateaus beyond them.

In the 1860s, this huge territory was inhabited chiefly by Native Americans. But by 1900, many thousands of newcomers had settled there. Settlement of the "last frontier" was one of several developments that transformed the United States in the late 1800s.

MINES, TRAILS, AND RAILS

Lewis and Clark and other explorers had visited this area in the early 1800s. Fur traders and pioneers on their way to the Pacific Coast soon followed. Most of these visitors considered the area incapable of supporting civilized settlement. Beginning in the 1850s, however, attitudes changed.

1. The Lure of Wealth. The California gold rush of 1849 was the first of many mineral strikes. In the 1850s, gold was discovered near Pikes Peak, Colorado, and gold and silver in Nevada. In the 1860s, gold was found also in Idaho and Montana. Later, rich strikes were made in the Black Hills of South Dakota, in Arizona, and in Alaska. Miners and prospectors rushed to the mining sites and set up makeshift towns. Many of the ore deposits found were very valuable. At Virginia City, Nevada, the Comstock Lode alone yielded $300 million in gold and silver in 20 years.

Life in the mining camps was rough and lawless at first. Citizens formed local governments and organized groups of vigilantes to track down and punish lawbreakers. Some prospectors who failed to strike it rich settled down to ranching and farming. Others drifted

A Pony Express rider passed workers raising telegraph poles in the 1860s.

away or took jobs with mining companies. These mining companies replaced individual prospectors because mining below the surface required large amounts of money to sink shafts, dig tunnels, and buy machinery. Besides gold and silver, the companies found copper, lead, zinc, and other minerals.

2. Early Transportation and Communication. One of the first means of reaching the West was a *stagecoach* line called the Butterfield Overland Mail. Beginning in 1858, it carried mail and passengers from St. Louis, Missouri, to Los Angeles and San Francisco. The trip took at least three weeks.

To speed up mail delivery, a group of investors founded the Pony Express in 1860. Relays of riders traveled a central route from St. Joseph, Missouri, to Sacramento, California. Mounted on swift horses, Pony Express riders could carry mail from Missouri to California in ten days. But a new form of communication, the telegraph, was rapidly taking over. Lines to carry telegraph messages already linked most cities in the East. With the completion in October 1861 of the first telegraph line to the Far West, the Pony Express ceased operations.

3. Railroad Links. During the Civil War, the government licensed two railroad companies to build the first *transcontinental railroad*. (It did not actually cross the entire continent, but linked the Pacific coast with eastern lines already in place.) The government offered good terms to the companies: a free right-of-way across public land,

Many immigrants were hired to work laying the tracks of the Union Pacific Railroad.

financial assistance in the form of loans, and large grants of land for every mile of completed track.

One of the companies, the Union Pacific, began construction at Omaha and built westward across the Nebraska prairie into Wyoming and Utah. The other company, the Central Pacific, started at Sacramento and advanced eastward across the mountains into Utah. In May 1869, the two railroads met at Promontory Point, near Ogden, Utah. Finished goods could now be shipped by rail to Western markets. Moreover, Western raw materials and farm products could be sent eastward. The mineral and forest resources of the West were opened to development, and Western settlement was made easier.

Other railroads also built lines west. By the 1890s, they included the Great Northern; the Northern Pacific; the Atchison, Topeka and Santa Fe; and the Southern Pacific. The government encouraged the building of these transcontinental links by granting the companies some $60 million in loans and more than 150 million acres of public land. The railroads could sell much of this land to settlers.

THE CATTLE FRONTIER

Western railroads not only aided mining and forestry but also made large-scale cattle ranching practical. The first American settlers in Texas found huge herds of half-wild long-horned cattle. Originally brought to America by the Spaniards, these longhorns grazed freely over the *open range*—unfenced, unsettled grassland owned by the federal government. Texans established ranches and raised the longhorns for beef, hides, and *tallow* (rendered fat used in soap, candles, and lubricants). But the industry was a local one because of the difficulty of transporting cattle to Eastern markets.

In the 1860s, when railroads were extended into Kansas, Nebraska, and Colorado, Texas cattle raisers drove their animals north to rail centers and loaded them onto railroad cars for shipment to Eastern cities. In the 1870s, the introduction of the refrigerator car made it unnecessary to send live cattle halfway across the country. They could now be slaughtered in meatpacking centers, such as Kansas City and Chicago. From there, butchered beef could be sent to distant markets without spoiling.

During the 1870s and early 1880s, ranchers owned enormous herds of cattle. Each spring, cowboys chose the animals to be sold. They then herded these on the "long drive" north to "cow towns" along the rail lines. One favorite route was the Chisholm Trail, from San Antonio, Texas, to Abilene, Kansas. Another, the Western Trail, ended at Ogallala, Nebraska.

Ranching soon spread from Texas to other parts of the Great Plains. With the introduction of sheep into the plains, many areas of grassland became overgrazed. Conflicts between cattle ranchers and sheep owners led to a number of "range wars." The open range itself grew smaller as thousands of acres were sold to farmers. Worst of all, two terrible winters in the mid-1880s brought blizzards that killed thousands of cattle. By 1890, the era of the open range was over. Although cattle raising continued to be a big industry in the West, it was generally confined to fenced ranches in dry areas unsuited to farming.

FARMERS ON THE PLAINS

The largest group of newcomers to the last frontier were farmers. They settled mainly on the Great Plains. Many of them were Easterners and Midwesterners looking for a new start. Freedmen headed west, too, as did numerous Civil War veterans. And a large number of the new settlers were immigrants, especially Scandinavians.

The Homestead Act of 1862 gave settlers 160 acres of public land. In return, the settlers paid a small fee and promised to live on the land and work it for five years. Only about 20 percent of the farm families, however, were actually homesteaders. Most of the new

READING A MAP

The West and the Railroads

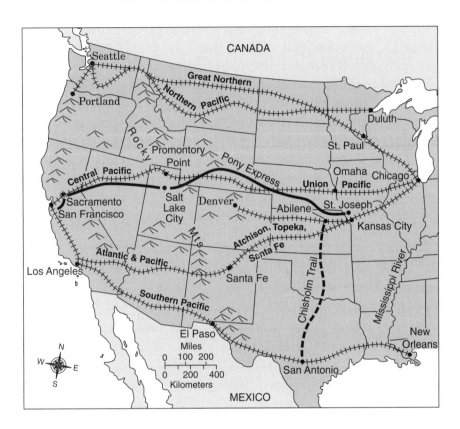

1. Name the eastern and western terminals of the Pony Express.

2. Name the location where the Central Pacific and Union Pacific railroads were linked in 1869.

3. Name the railroad that originated in New Orleans and serviced the southernmost section of Western United States.

4. What railroads were built to serve the band of states extending from Minnesota west to Seattle?

5. Name the route followed by Texas cowboys on their long drives north to Abilene, Kansas.

6. What railroad connected Santa Fe and Kansas City?

settlers bought land from railroads or from speculators who had obtained large tracts of homestead land illegally.

Winters on the Great Plains were bitter cold, and summers were extremely hot and dry. Few trees grew there, and underground water ran far below the surface. The pioneers built houses out of *sod* (chunks of earth), or they dug caves into hillsides. They burned dried cornstalks, corncobs, and animal dung for fuel. And they dug wells to a depth of 200 feet or more to obtain water.

Several techniques aided plains farmers. One was *dry farming*—plowing and planting in ways that conserved moisture. Another was using windmills to pump water from deep within the earth. A third was using barbed-wire fencing to keep out stray cattle and sheep. Barbed wire was first marketed in 1874. But no one could do much about dust storms, blizzards, and swarms of grasshoppers. Nor could anyone predict droughts. A series of dry years in the late 1880s forced many farm families off the land.

IDENTIFY OR DEFINE: stagecoach, refrigerator car, long drive, range war, Homestead Act.

CRITICAL THINKING: Explain how developments in transportation and communication helped open the "last frontier" to settlement.

TRAGEDY FOR NATIVE AMERICANS

Ever since the arrival of Europeans along the Atlantic coast of North America, Native Americans had been pushed westward. The Indian Removal Act of 1830 forced many Eastern groups to move west of the Mississippi. Most of present-day Oklahoma then became Indian Territory, reserved for the Five Civilized Tribes. Because these tribes sided with the Confederacy during the Civil War, the western half of the region was taken away from them and reserved for other Eastern tribes. In addition, huge tracts in the Dakotas, Wyoming, Montana, and elsewhere were set aside for Plains and other Western tribes. As miners, ranchers, and farmers moved West in the 1860s and 1870s, more conflicts with Native-American groups developed.

The federal government tried to ease tensions by setting aside *reservations* for Native Americans to live on. Some Native-American groups, no longer able to support themselves by hunting buffalo,

In the lava beds in northern California, Modoc people fought U.S. troops in 1873, inflicting heavy casualties on their attackers. The Modoc held off the U.S. troops for three months before finally surrendering. Earlier, the Modoc had been sent to a reservation in Oregon, but they did not like it there and had returned.

agreed to move to reservations. Others were forced to. With the extension of railroads westward, Americans from the East headed for the Great Plains to shoot buffalo. They killed thousands of these animals for their hides, leaving the carcasses to rot. In 1850, there had been some 20 million buffalo on the plains. By 1889, there were fewer than a thousand left.

1. Resistance to the Newcomers. Many Native-American groups, however, rebelled against being removed from their homes. The following episodes are just a few examples of the many conflicts between U.S. troops and Native Americans. In the summer of 1877, a group of Nez Percé under Chief Joseph refused to leave Oregon for a reservation in Idaho. Pursued by U.S. troops, they fled hundreds of miles toward safety in Canada. By late September, the Nez Percé had almost reached their goal. But many were hungry and sick, and the winter had begun. After a pitched battle early in October, Chief Joseph and his people surrendered. He and his band were then confined to a reservation far from their homeland.

The Sioux also resisted relocation. One group had been promised the Black Hills of South Dakota as a permanent hunting ground.

But when gold was discovered there in the 1870s, the promise was broken. Two Sioux leaders, "medicine man" Sitting Bull and war chief Crazy Horse, led armed resistance against the newcomers. U.S. troops then set out after the Sioux. In 1876, at the Little Bighorn River in Montana, the Sioux and Cheyenne completely destroyed a force under General George A. Custer. In the long run, however, the Native Americans were no match for the U.S. Army. Band by band, they gave up and moved to reservations.

In the 1880s, many Sioux turned to a new religion called the "Ghost Dance." It promised to end the rule of their enemies and to restore their freedom and way of life. Believers gathered to perform a dance that they thought put them in touch with their ancestors. Federal authorities feared that the new faith would lead to a Sioux uprising. They blamed Sitting Bull for the rapid spread of the Ghost Dance and sent an army unit to his reservation to arrest him in December 1890. In the confusion that followed, Sitting Bull was killed.

Fearing more violence, hundreds of Sioux fled the reservation, going to the Badlands area of South Dakota. The U.S. Cavalry went after them. The opposing forces met at Wounded Knee Creek on December 28. The next day, while the Sioux were being disarmed, fighting broke out. At least 250 Sioux—many of them women and children—were killed, as were some 25 of the cavalry. Wounded Knee was the last major incident in Native-American–U.S. Army conflicts.

2. Reservation Life. Life for Native Americans on reservations was demoralizing. With their traditional way of life no longer available to them, they lived mainly on government handouts. Non-native officials of the federal government ran the reservations. Many of them pocketed funds meant for the Native Americans.

In her book *A Century of Dishonor* (1881), Helen Hunt Jackson recounted how Native Americans had suffered for years from broken promises, cheating, and ill treatment. Public criticism of the government's policy led to the passage of the Dawes Act in 1887. It granted 160 acres of land to the head of each Native-American family. This land came out of former tribal holdings. What was left over was to be sold to non-Native Americans. The government hoped to encourage Native Americans to give up tribal culture and to support themselves by farming or ranching.

Unfortunately, much of the land granted to the Native Americans was not suitable for such purposes. In any case, many Native Americans regarded farming and ranching as unworthy of warriors. Thousands of them rented or sold their land to settlers for cash. When the money was gone, the Native Americans were worse off than before. Many succumbed to poverty, disease, alcoholism, and suicide.

New States and Native-American Reservations, 1864–1890

IDENTIFY OR DEFINE: reservation, Chief Joseph, George A. Custer, Sitting Bull, Wounded Knee.

CRITICAL THINKING: Why did the government pass the Dawes Act? What happened to Native Americans after its passage?

POLITICS AND PROTESTS

In 1890, the Census Bureau announced that unsettled areas of the United States had been "so broken into by isolated bodies of settlement that there can hardly be said to be a frontier line." In other words, the frontier no longer existed, at least officially. An era had come to an end.

Western settlement, industrialization, and the growth of cities created a number of new problems, but politicians did little to solve them. Congress, for example, largely ignored the growing power of corporations and political corruption. Segments of the population began to demand reform, however, and their influence led to some improvements in the 1880s and early 1890s.

The presidents during the late 19th century were not dynamic leaders. But even if they had wanted to effect sweeping changes, they would have met resistance. During Reconstruction, Congress had limited the power of the president and continued to overshadow the executive branch.

Although Congress was powerful, it was not respected. The Senate was called a "rich man's club." Many members of the House of Representatives ignored the proceedings and spent their time reading newspapers and answering letters. Some legislators accepted bribes from business groups in return for supporting bills favored by these groups.

1. The Role of Government. Most Americans in the late 19th century believed in laissez-faire. They felt that the government should not regulate the economy or provide financial help to people in need. Grover Cleveland, the only Democratic president of this period, once vetoed a bill intended to help farmers hurt by drought. His comment summed up a common attitude: "Though the people support the government, the government should not support the people."

2. Party Politics. During the late 1800s, both the Republican and Democratic parties were conservative. Both adhered to the theory of laissez-faire economics and employed the spoils system. Despite these similarities, Americans generally gave their loyalty and support to one of the parties. The percentage of eligible voters who voted in national elections was always more than 70 percent (sometimes higher than 80 percent). In the 20th century, the average fell below 60 percent.

Though the two parties had about equal strength nationally, each was stronger in certain regions than in others. In the "solid South," where Republicans were associated with Reconstruction, almost all white voters were Democrats. African Americans in the South were largely pro-Republican, but they were discouraged from voting. In New England and some Plains states, most voters were Republicans. Party strength was more evenly divided in the Middle Atlantic and Midwestern states. Campaigners for national office, therefore, made their major appeals in these regions. In the period from 1868 to 1896, almost all presidential candidates came from these key areas.

The two parties also appealed to different groups of voters. Most native-born white Protestants (except in the South) tended to identify themselves as Republicans. Most immigrants, especially Jews and Roman Catholics, joined the Democratic party.

A SPECIAL CASE: THE SOUTH

The South's economy and racial makeup made it different politically from the rest of the country.

1. Economic Development. After the Civil War, many Southerners felt that their economy relied too heavily on cotton and did not have enough industries. Farmers began to plant a variety of crops. Such industries as lumbering, mining, tobacco processing, and steel production began to expand. Since the South had raw cotton, a good supply of cheap labor, low taxes, and abundant waterpower, it was a good region in which to open cotton textile factories. Many New England textile mills moved to the South.

Southern leaders felt that these agricultural and industrial developments had created a "New South." But the South still lagged behind other U.S. regions economically and industrially. In fact, it actually had a smaller percentage of the nation's factories in 1900 than it had had in 1860.

After the Civil War, most big plantations were divided into small farms that were rented to landless farmers, many of whom were freedmen. The majority of tenants who worked these farms lacked the cash to rent the land, housing, and barns, or to buy seeds and tools. They therefore paid for these things with a share of the crop. This practice was called *sharecropping.*

Since landowners wanted crops that would bring them the highest profit, dependence on cotton persisted in the South despite efforts to diversify. If it is not rotated with other crops, cotton wears out the soil. In the rush for profits, landowners did not practice crop rotation. As a result, the land yielded less and less. Sharecroppers could rarely pay off their debts and have enough money to live on. Since they always owed money to their landlords, they were not free to leave the land and try something else.

2. Racial Discrimination. During Reconstruction, the federal government had taken steps to protect the rights of Southern African Americans, especially their right to vote. With the end of Reconstruction in 1877, there had been an informal agreement that the federal government would interfere less in Southern affairs. Southern African Americans were greatly harmed by this policy.

a. Jim Crow laws. Measures such as the 1866 Civil Rights Act and the Fourteenth Amendment did little to alter racism in either the South or the North. After Reconstruction, Southern states were determined to keep African Americans subordinate to whites. They passed laws to maintain *segregation* (separation of the races). These were called "Jim Crow laws" after a character in a popular minstrel song. The first Jim Crow laws were passed in the 1870s. They eventually imposed segregation in almost every social situation. Marriage between African Americans and whites was forbidden. Laws required separate schools, hospital facilities, and railroad accommodations for each race. Segregation was also the rule in hotels, restaurants, parks, theaters, and cemeteries.

When African Americans protested this discrimination, the courts ruled against them. In 1883, in the five so-called "Civil Rights cases," the Supreme Court ruled that the Fourteenth Amendment protected people against discrimination by states but not by individuals. This meant that the federal government could not intervene if, for example, a theater owner made African-American patrons sit in the balcony. A landmark decision of 1896, *Plessy* v. *Ferguson*, legitimized segregation. At issue was a state law that required separate accommodations for African Americans on railroads. The Supreme Court ruled that segregated facilities were legal if they were equal in quality. This ruling became known as the "separate but equal" doctrine. In reality, facilities for African Americans were almost always inferior to those for whites.

b. Disfranchisement. Southern whites also took steps to limit the political rights of African Americans. This limitation had not seemed necessary when Reconstruction first came to an end. Most white Southerners were willing to allow African Americans to vote, as long as they voted in support of white interests. White landlords used their economic power over their black sharecroppers to influence their voting. Force was also used at times.

By the 1890s, many African-American men threatened to vote in their own interests. Southern whites set out to *disfranchise* African Americans altogether—that is, to strip them of the vote. States used a number of methods to bypass the Fifteenth Amendment, which guaranteed all citizens the right to vote. As a requirement to vote, some localities imposed heavy *poll taxes* or set high property qualifications. Others required difficult *literacy tests*—memorizing or explaining the state constitution, for instance.

Ku Klux Klan aiming to shoot a black family in their cabin, 1870s. Violence or the threat of violence was another measure used by some Southern whites to control the behavior of African Americans.

Such measures, however, kept many whites from voting, too. A number of states, therefore, resorted to the so-called *grandfather clause*. This provision canceled other voting restrictions if the voter, his father, or his grandfather had been eligible to vote in 1867. Since Southern African Americans had not had the franchise then, only whites could make use of this clause. Statistics from Louisiana show how effective these policies were. Before the state adopted a grandfather clause, 130,344 African Americans had been registered to vote. Two years later, the number had been reduced to 5,320.

IDENTIFY OR DEFINE: segregation, *Plessy* v. *Ferguson*, poll tax, literacy test, grandfather clause.

CRITICAL THINKING: How did the sharecropping system affect the South?

REFORMS AND CONTROVERSIAL ISSUES

Political leaders in the late 1800s were not very interested in reform. But public pressure brought about some changes.

1. Civil Service Reform. The spoils system of rewarding faithful party members had been in effect since the early 19th century. After the Civil War, more government jobs began to require special skills. Reformers argued that government jobs should be awarded on the basis of merit rather than political connections. They wanted a *civil service*—a system of hiring government employees by means of competitive examinations.

a. Hayes. President Rutherford B. Hayes, a Republican, had pledged his support for a civil service when he was inaugurated in 1877. He appointed a leading reformer, Carl Schurz, as his secretary of the interior. Schurz filled jobs in his department on a merit basis, and so did some other Cabinet officers. In addition, Hayes issued an executive order—widely ignored—forbidding federal officeholders from taking part in political activities. The Hayes administration also began a reform of the U.S. Customs (the agency that collects import duties) office in New York City. At that time, corrupt political machines controlled Customs.

b. Garfield and Arthur. In the 1880 presidential election, the winners were both Republicans—James A. Garfield as president and Chester A. Arthur as vice president. Garfield favored a civil service. After only four months in office, however, he was fatally shot by a mentally deranged politician who had failed to obtain a government job in the new administration.

None of the reformers expected much from Arthur. As a New York-based custom official, he had been fired during the Hayes administration's cleanup. But Arthur, outraged by the attack on Garfield, pushed for change. In 1883, Congress passed the Pendleton Act. It had three main provisions: (*1*) Competitive examinations were to be used to hire workers for government jobs placed on a classified civil service list. (*2*) A Civil Service Commission was to draw up and give the exams. (*3*) Dismissal of federal employees for political reasons was forbidden. Only about 10 percent of the existing federal jobs were covered by the Pendleton Act, but more were added in the years that followed. By 1900, about 40 percent of federal jobs were filled on the basis of competitive tests.

c. Tariffs. Northern manufacturers favored high tariffs to protect U.S. industry from foreign competition. Since most Southerners bought imported goods from abroad, they wanted lower tariffs. During the Civil War, when the Southern states were not represented in Congress, the legislature adopted the highest tariff ever imposed.

For the next 40 years, the government followed a policy of *protectionism*—maintaining high protective tariffs. The policy suited

U.S. business interests, which were very powerful at the time. Both political parties favored protectionism, although Republicans supported it more vigorously than Democrats. Although protective tariffs meant that ordinary citizens had to pay higher prices for both domestic and imported goods, they believed that barriers to foreign imports kept their wages up.

President Grover Cleveland, the Democratic winner of the election of 1884, wanted a more moderate tariff. His main reason was that revenues from high tariffs had caused a surplus in the federal treasury. This not only kept money out of circulation but also tempted members of Congress to appropriate funds for pet projects. But Cleveland could not get a tariff reform bill through Congress. The tariff issue became the deciding factor in the next presidential election.

In 1888, Cleveland ran against Republican Benjamin Harrison. Harrison, a high-tariff supporter, won the election. Two years later, Congress passed the McKinley Tariff, which raised import duties to a new high. Since these rates drove up the cost of manufactured goods, consumers protested. In the 1892 election, Cleveland defeated Harrison, largely because of the unpopular tariff. Again, he tried to lower tariffs. But the bill that Congress passed—the Wilson-Gorman Tariff of 1894—reduced rates only slightly. Protectionism continued to prevail.

2. Business Regulation. Meanwhile, the government turned its attention to the massive power of big business.

a. Farmers' concerns. Because farm output expanded greatly after 1865, prices of farm produce fell. At the same time, the cost of manufactured goods and machinery remained high. Farmers also had to pay high fees to the owners of grain-storage elevators, to the dealers who marketed their crops, and to the railroads that shipped them. Farmers often borrowed heavily by mortgaging their farms. The many who failed to meet high interest payments on these loans lost their land through a legal procedure known as *foreclosure*.

To make their voices heard, farmers joined a national farmers' organization called the Grange. Founded in 1867 by Oliver H. Kelley, the Grange spread rapidly, particularly in the upper Mississippi Valley. By 1875, total membership exceeded 800,000.

The original aim of the Grange was to bring farm families together for social and cultural activities. In response to farmers' need for economic help, the Grange founded cooperatives. (A *cooperative*, or *co-op*, is a business owned and operated by those who benefit from its services. These groups market, produce, store grain, buy supplies and equipment, and manufacture machinery.) The cooperatives

The Grange attempts to alert an indifferent public to the threat of railroad monopolies.

failed because big business opposed them and many farmers lacked management skills or adequate capital.

The Grangers also involved themselves in politics as a way to fight abuses by railroads. In the late 19th century, railroads charged high rates to farmers and other small-scale shippers. In most cases, the rates were higher for short hauls in areas not served by other lines than for long hauls in competitive territory. The railroads also commonly granted *rebates* (refunds) to large shippers. In Illinois and several other Midwestern states, the Grangers influenced legislatures to pass laws regulating railroad freight rates. The constitutionality of these Granger Laws was then questioned. The Supreme Court upheld the laws in 1877 (*Munn* v. *Illinois*) and then reversed itself in 1886 (the *Wabash Railroad* case). In the later decision, the Court held that only the federal government, not the states, could regulate interstate commerce.

Farm groups then turned to the federal government for help. Congress responded in 1887 by passing the Interstate Commerce Act. It provided that railroad rates should be "reasonable and just."

It banned such practices as rebates and differing rates for short and long hauls. It also created the Interstate Commerce Commission (ICC), the nation's first regulatory agency, to carry out the law's provisions. At first, the railroads found several ways to get around the Interstate Commerce Act. Later, the law became more effective.

b. An antitrust law. Some Americans began to point out that the trusts' controlling many industries stifled competition, the lifeblood of free enterprise. Both political parties officially favored some regulation of trusts. As in the case of railroad reform, individual states tried to act, but without much success. Since monopolies operated interstate, it became apparent that only the federal government had the power to restrain them.

In 1890, Congress passed the Sherman Antitrust Act. It made illegal every "combination in the form of trust . . . in restraint of trade or commerce." But the Sherman Act, like the Interstate Commerce Act, had little effect at first. Presidents at that time did not enforce it. And businesses easily found loopholes in it. In the last decade of the 19th century, the act was used mainly as a weapon against labor unions.

IDENTIFY OR DEFINE: civil service, protectionism, the Grange, cooperative, rebate, antitrust law.

CRITICAL THINKING: Why was the Sherman Antitrust Act passed? How was it abused?

THE POPULIST MOVEMENT

In the late 1870s, the Grange lost members and influence. One reason was the failure of its co-ops. Another was a rise in farm prices, which made many farmers feel there was less need for joint action. But their troubles were not over.

1. Early Success. When farm prices fell once again in the 1880s, farmers began to form large regional organizations. The National Farmers' Alliance consisted of farmers in the Midwest and the Great Plains. The Southern Farmers' Alliance served the South's white farmers, and the Colored Farmers' Alliance, its African-American farmers. By 1890, the three groups claimed a combined membership of about 2 million.

READING A GRAPH

Urban and Rural Populations, 1870–1920

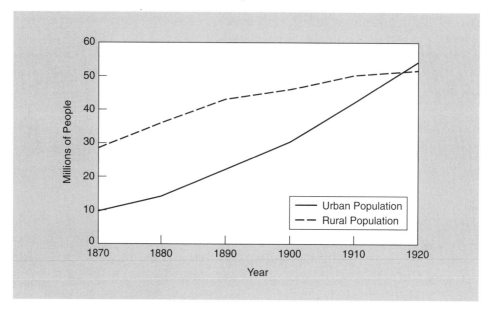

1. In 1870, which was larger—the nation's urban population or its rural population?

2. In 1920, which was larger—the nation's urban population or its rural population?

3. In what year were urban and rural populations equal?

Like the Grange, the alliances started out by providing social and educational programs for their members but soon began to call for political and economic reforms. In 1890, the alliances succeeded in electing a number of their supporters to state legislatures and to Congress. Thus encouraged, they decided to combine with labor groups to form a new political party.

In 1892, the newly organized Populist party held a national convention in Omaha, Nebraska. The Populist platform called for (*1*) *free silver* (increased coinage of silver); (*2*) an increase in the amount of money in circulation; (*3*) a *graduated income tax*—an income tax that would tax large incomes at progressively higher rates; (*4*) savings banks at post offices; (*5*) public ownership and operation of transportation and communication services; (*6*) election of U.S. senators by popular vote; (*7*) a one-term limit for presidents; (*8*) the secret ballot; (*9*) restrictions on immigration; and (*10*) a shorter work-day. In the election of 1892, the Populist candidate for president was James B. Weaver. Although he came in third, he received the impressive total of more than 1 million popular votes.

2. The Money Question. The first two Populist demands—increased coinage of silver and more money in circulation—concerned issues that were of great concern in the late 1800s. The United States was in a period of *deflation* (constantly falling prices). This was particularly hard on farmers and other people with debts. They had to pay back their loans with money that was worth more than the money they had borrowed. Debtors urged a policy that would bring about *inflation* (constantly rising prices). If the value of money fell, they would find it easier to repay what they owed.

One cause of inflation is an increase in the money supply. So farmers wanted the government to issue more money, and they wanted it backed by silver. For a long time, the government had bought both silver and gold to back its paper currency. But in 1873, new finds in Western mines led to a surplus of silver, and the government had stopped buying it. In response to pressure from farmers and mine owners, Congress passed the Bland-Allison Act (1878) and the Sherman Silver Purchase Act (1890). These laws required the government to buy and coin a certain amount of silver each month. Proponents of silver called for a further expansion of silver coinage. In the phrase of the time, they demanded "free silver." This plank in the Populist platform attracted members of other political parties.

THE ELECTION OF 1896

Soon after Cleveland began his second term, the financial panic of 1893 shook the country. It was followed by a depression. Hundreds of businesses and banks failed, and thousands of people lost their jobs. In 1894, Jacob S. Coxey, an Ohio businessman, led an "army" of some 500 unemployed people to Washington. They demanded that the government sponsor *public works* projects—building roads, bridges, and other public facilities—to create jobs. Coxey was arrested. Also in 1894, the Pullman strike took place.

The money issue was pressing, too. Like other conservatives of the day, Cleveland was a firm believer in the *gold standard* (gold as the only backing for paper money). Believing that the Sherman Silver Purchase Act had caused the panic of 1893, he persuaded Congress to repeal it. But the depression continued, and the treasury's

William Jennings Bryan delivering a speech at the Democratic national convention, July 1896: "We will answer their demand for a gold standard by saying to them: 'You shall not press down upon the brow of labor this crown of thorns, you shall not crucify mankind upon a cross of gold.' "

supply of gold decreased. In 1895, the government had to turn to J.P. Morgan and other private bankers for help. When they bought gold from abroad to add to the government's supply, Populists and others accused Cleveland of selling out to Wall Street. Americans now were sharply divided. For the "cheap money" supporters, free silver was the only answer. The "sound money" people were equally certain that the gold standard had to prevail.

1. The Conventions. In 1896, the Republicans nominated Governor William McKinley of Ohio for president. Their platform supported business interests and the gold standard.

The Democrats, who met in July, were divided into free-silver and "goldbug" factions. On the second day of their national convention, a former congressman from Nebraska named William Jennings Bryan made a rousing speech in support of free silver. The next day, the convention nominated him for president.

The Populists faced a difficult choice. Should they support the Democratic candidates or nominate their own? The Democratic platform advocated free silver, but it ignored many other reforms that the Populists wanted. Finally, they decided to support Bryan. But they put him on their own ticket with a Populist vice presidential candidate.

2. The Campaign. In the election campaign of 1896, McKinley stood for respectability and laissez-faire capitalism. Bryan championed the "toiling masses" against big business. He promised that a free-silver policy would bring back good times. Bryan's opponents denounced him as a revolutionist and predicted economic chaos if he were elected.

McKinley won by a sizable margin, the biggest in 20 years. Although Bryan carried the South and most of the West, he failed to gain the support of the industrialized Midwest and Northeast. In these regions, many Democrats crossed party lines to vote for McKinley. Bryan's defeat marked the virtual end of the free-silver issue and Populism.

IDENTIFY OR DEFINE: free silver, gold standard, graduated income tax, secret ballot, public works.

CRITICAL THINKING: Who wanted inflation in the period after the Civil War? Why did these people want it? How did they try to achieve it?

Chapter Review

MATCHING TEST

Column A	Column B
1. Promontory Point	*a.* unfenced, public grassland
2. Oliver H. Kelley	*b.* site of Custer's Last Stand
3. Little Bighorn	*c.* Apache leader
4. Geronimo	*d.* place where Union Pacific and Central Pacific railroads linked
5. open range	*e.* founder of the Grange

MULTIPLE-CHOICE TEST

1. The Pony Express became unnecessary after (*a*) the establishment of the Butterfield Overland Mail (*b*) the construction of the

Union Pacific Railroad (*c*) the opening of the Chisholm Trail (*d*) the completion of a transcontinental telegraph.

2. The first railroad line to cross the last frontier connected (*a*) Omaha and Sacramento (*b*) Santa Fe and Los Angeles (*c*) Kansas City and Santa Fe (*d*) New Orleans and Los Angeles.

3. Large-scale cattle ranching began in (*a*) Kansas (*b*) Texas (*c*) Arkansas (*d*) Nebraska.

4. After the Civil War, the main goal of the federal government policy toward Native Americans was to (*a*) move all Native Americans to Indian Territory (*b*) force Native Americans to migrate to Canada (*c*) move them to reservations (*d*) prevent settlers from taking Native-American lands.

5. All of the following were aims of most white Southerners after the Civil War *except* (*a*) protecting the civil rights of African Americans (*b*) industrializing (*c*) growing more kinds of crops (*d*) becoming less dependent on cotton.

6. The main issue in the presidential campaign of 1892 was (*a*) civil service (*b*) the tariff (*c*) regulating the railroads (*d*) restricting immigration.

7. Most farmers in the late 19th century were disturbed by all of the following *except* (*a*) inflation (*b*) railroad freight charges (*c*) high interest rates (*d*) loss of their farms.

8. The Grange was strongest in the (*a*) South (*b*) Northeast (*c*) Rocky Mountain states (*d*) Midwest.

9. All of the following were planks in the 1892 Populist platform *except* (*a*) more money in circulation (*b*) a gold standard (*c*) public ownership of railroads (*d*) graduated income tax.

10. The main campaign issue in the presidential election of 1896 was (*a*) free silver (*b*) the Interstate Commerce Act (*c*) labor unions (*d*) voting rights.

 ESSAY QUESTIONS

1. What attracted settlers to the "last frontier"?

2. Why was farming difficult on the Great Plains? Describe some techniques that helped farmers there.

3. What is a laissez-faire policy? What attempts were made to modify it in the United States late in the 19th century?

4. How and why did the Southern states restrict the rights of African Americans after Reconstruction?

5. Who wanted high tariffs in the period after the Civil War? Why?

DOCUMENT-BASED QUESTION

This question is based on the accompanying documents (1–5). It will improve your ability to work with historical documents.

Historical Context:

From 1880 to 1900, big industries could force weaker companies out of business by forming pools, trusts, and monopolies. Most small business owners lacked the legal weapons or economic power to combat cutthroat competition. Farmers, however, organized the Grange and persuaded state legislatures to regulate the unfair practices of railroad monopolies and grain elevator operators.

Task:

Using information from the documents and your knowledge of United States history, read each document and answer the question that follows it. Your answers to the questions will help you write the document-based essay.

Document 1. Excerpts from the *Declaration of Purposes of the National Grange*, 1874:

> We propose meeting together, talking together, working together, buying together, selling together, and, in general, acting together for our mutual protection and advancement, as occasion may require. . . .
>
> We desire proper equality, equity, and fairness; protection for the weak; restraint upon the strong; in short, justly distributed burdens and justly distributed power. These are American ideas, the very essence of American independence, and to advocate the contrary is unworthy of the sons and daughters of an American Republic.

Source: www.geocities.com/cannongrange/declaration_purposes.html

Would you say that the farmers who wrote the *Declaration of the Purposes* believed in "strength in numbers"? Explain your answer.

Document 2. Study the political cartoon on page 238.

Why do you think the member of the Grange (the young man) is shown as more aware of the trouble the oncoming train can cause than are the rest of the people in the cartoon?

Document 3. Quote attributed to Kansas populist Mary Elizabeth Lease, about 1890:

> What you farmers need to do is to raise less corn and more Hell! We want the accursed foreclosure system wiped out. . . . We will stand by our homes and stay by our firesides by force if necessary, and we will not pay our debts to the loan-shark companies until the Government pays its debts to us.

> Source: Barr, Elizabeth N. "The Populist Uprising," in W.E. Donnelley (ed.) *A Standard History of Kansas and Kansans*, II (1928), p. 1148, as reprinted in Bailey, Thomas A. and Kennedy, David M. *The American Spirit*. Boston: Houghton Mifflin, 1997.

What problem or problems was Lease describing?

Document 4. Excerpt from a letter of W.M. Taylor, a farmer, to the editor of *Farmer's Alliance* (published in Lincoln, Nebraska), January 10, 1891:

> We are cursed . . . not by the hot winds so much as by the swindling games of the bankers and money loaners. . . . I have borrowed for example $1,000. I pay $25 besides to the commission man. I give my note and second mortgage of 3 per cent of the $1,000, which is $30 more. Then I pay 7 per cent on the $1,000 to the actual loaner. . . . The time comes to pay. . . . If I can't get the money, I have the extreme pleasure of seeing my property taken and sold by this iron handed money loaner while my family and I suffer.

> Source: faculty.washington.edu/qtaylor/Coures/101_USH/101_manual_6.htm. Also Marcus, Robert D., Marcus, Anthony and Buner, David (eds.) *America Firsthand*. NY: Bedford/St. Martin's, 1989, II, p. 99.

What did Taylor think of bankers and money loaners he had to deal with? Explain your answer.

Document 5. Excerpt from the Populist party platform, which attacked the Democratic and Republican parties, 1892:

> We have witnessed, for more than a quarter of a century, the struggles of the two great political parties for power and plunder,

while grievous wrongs have been inflicted upon the suffering of the people. We charge that the controlling influences dominating both these parties have permitted the existing dreadful conditions to develop without serious effort to prevent or restrain them.

Source: *ibid*. Also Current, Richard N. and Garraty, John A. (eds.) *Words That Made American History Since the Civil War*. Boston: Little, Brown and Co., 1965, pp. 223, 226–227.

What did the Populist party platform accuse the Democratic and Republican parties of ignoring?

DOCUMENT-BASED ESSAY

Using information from the above documents and your knowledge of United States history, write an essay in which you:

- Explain why between 1874 and 1896 farmers became more frustrated with their lives.
- Explain to what extent they tried to improve their lives and tell how successful they were.

CHAPTER 13

The Progressive Era

From the beginning of Theodore Roosevelt's administration (1901–1909) until the entry of the United States into World War I in 1917, a spirit of active reform dominated national, state, and local politics. Those who sought change came to be known as *Progressives*.

VOICES OF PROTEST

Like the reformers of the Jacksonian era, Progressives were interested in a wide range of issues. In wanting to make politics more democratic, Progressives were like Populists. But there were important differences. Most of the Populists had been rural Americans from Southern and Western states. They were chiefly concerned with the problems of farmers. The majority of Progressives were middle-class city dwellers from the Midwest and Northeast. Their interests were broader than those of the Populists.

1. Muckrakers. Skillful reporters, popularly called *muckrakers*, exposed many of the conditions that the Progressives wanted to correct. One of the best-known muckrakers was Lincoln Steffens, an editor of *McClure's Magazine*. Steffens's descriptions of corruption in several cities were collected in *The Shame of the Cities* (1904). *McClure's* also printed the results of a full investigation of the Rockefeller oil trust and its business practices. Written by Ida Tarbell, these articles later appeared in book form as *The History of the Standard Oil Company* (1904). In *The Treason of the Senate* (1906), David Graham Phillips charged that most U.S. senators represented railroads and trusts rather than the American people. John Spargo, in *The Bitter Cry of the Children* (1906), described the dreadful working conditions of child laborers. Muckrakers also attacked living conditions in the slums, discrimination against African Americans, and unsanitary practices in the meatpacking industry.

2. Feminists. By 1900, a number of states had enacted laws to protect the property and earnings of married women. About 20 percent of American women were in the labor force. There were almost 130 women's colleges in the United States, and a fourth of the nation's college students were women.

Suffragists march in the nation's capital, April 7, 1913, the day before Woodrow Wilson took office as U.S. president.

Women, however, still did not the right to vote. From the 1860s on, the main aim of feminists was to get the vote for women. In 1890, such *suffragists* as Susan B. Anthony, Carrie Chapman Catt, and Anna Howard Shaw formed the National American Woman Suffrage Association. In the same year, Wyoming became the first state to provide for women's suffrage in its constitution. During the next three decades, several other states, most of them in the West, took similar steps. Progressives continued to urge the adoption of a constitutional amendment that would guarantee voting rights to *all* American women.

3. African-American Reformers. Several African-American leaders rose to prominence during the Progressive era. Booker T. Washington, a former slave, founded and headed Tuskegee Institute in Alabama. He advised African Americans to be patient and responsible laborers, even though their position in American society was humble.

Washington's approach was too conservative for another African-American leader, W.E.B. DuBois. Educated at Harvard University, he was a professor of economics and history at Atlanta University. DuBois urged African Americans to be neither content with menial jobs nor silent about unjust treatment. In 1905, he founded the Niagara Movement, the first organization of African Americans to protest racial discrimination.

Three years later, a race riot broke out in Springfield, Illinois. Two African Americans were lynched and four whites killed, but the ringleaders of the mob were never punished. The riot led to the formation, in 1909, of the National Association for the Advancement of Colored People (NAACP). This group aimed to put an end to discrimination by means of legislation and court decisions. Another organization, the National Urban League, was founded in 1910 to help African Americans get better jobs and housing, particularly in cities.

REFORMS AT CITY AND STATE LEVELS

One goal of the Progressives was to eliminate corruption in local and state governments. Their reforms aimed at reducing the power of political machines and making elected leaders more responsible to the people. A reform adopted by one city or state often spread to others.

1. Cities. Samuel Jones, a Progressive mayor of Toledo, Ohio, introduced civil service into the police department, set a minimum wage for city employees, built public parks in the city's poorer sections, and established kindergartens. Tom Johnson, mayor of Cleveland, Ohio, brought about greater *home rule*—that is, independence from outside (in this case, state) control. As a result of his efforts, the state passed a law guaranteeing home rule to all Ohio towns.

Progressives backed two new types of city government. (*1*) Under the *commission plan*, voters elect a small group of commissioners whose political affiliations are not stated. Each commissioner heads a government department. Together, they carry out both the executive and legislative duties of the city. In 1901, Galveston, Texas, became the first city to adopt this plan of government. (*2*) The other new form of city government was the *city-manager plan*. Here voters elect commissioners, who, in turn, hire a professional manager to run the city. The first city to introduce this plan was Staunton, Virginia, in 1908. By the end of the Progressive Era, some 400 cities had adopted the commission plan, and about 50, the city-manager plan.

2. States. Members of state legislatures, being poorly paid, were frequently bribed by big businesses and public utilities. To counter that, several Progressive reforms were enacted to increase citizen participation. One was the *direct primary*, which allowed voters to select a party's candidates for office. (Formerly, politicians at party conventions had chosen candidates.) Minnesota became the first state to require a statewide direct primary, in 1901. In the next few years, most other states also adopted it. Another reform was the secret ballot. Voting in private protected citizens against pressure from observers who might influence them or buy their votes.

Three other political reforms also came into use at this time. One, the *initiative*, provides that the legislature must consider passing a law if a certain percentage of voters sign a petition in its favor. Another, the *referendum*, requires that a law or constitutional amendment passed by a legislature be submitted to voters for their approval. The first state to adopt the initiative and referendum was South Dakota, in 1898. A third reform, *recall*, permits voters to petition for, and vote upon, the removal of elected officials before their terms expire. In 1908, Oregon became the first state to adopt the recall.

In the early 20th century, Progressives helped elect many reformers as state governors. One of them was Wisconsin's Robert La Follette. He brought in experts from the University of Wisconsin to draft laws that lowered railroad rates, regulated public utilities, established workers' compensation, and reformed the tax system. Another reforming governor, Charles Evans Hughes of New York, succeeded in regulating public utilities in his state. Hiram Johnson of California was elected governor on the slogan "Kick the Southern Pacific out of politics," and he did so. This powerful railroad had dominated the state's political life for four decades.

IDENTIFY OR DEFINE: Progressive, suffragist, Niagara Movement, Urban League, commission plan, city-manager plan.

CRITICAL THINKING: In what ways were Populists and Progressives similar? In what ways were they different?

THEODORE ROOSEVELT: PROGRESSIVE PRESIDENT

Roosevelt brought Progressivism to the White House. After replacing the assassinated McKinley in 1901, he was elected president in his own right in 1904. Roosevelt was fond of saying that every American deserved a square deal. His term in office is often labeled the "Square Deal."

Roosevelt's presidency emphasized foreign affairs. As will be discussed in Chapter 14, he acquired the Canal Zone, began

construction of the Panama Canal, issued the Roosevelt Corollary, and arranged the Treaty of Portsmouth. One of his favorite slogans was "Speak softly and carry a big stick." (By "big stick," he meant a powerful military force.) Eager to impress the world with U.S. naval might, he sent a force of 16 battleships and 4 destroyers on a round-the-world cruise in 1907.

1. Regulating Business. Progressives worried that business combinations seemed to be running the country. Although Roosevelt shared this concern, he made a distinction between good and bad trusts. (At this time, the word "trust" was generally used to refer to any business monopoly.) And he vowed to bring the bad trusts under control.

Under Roosevelt's direction, the Department of Justice succeeded in breaking up the Northern Securities Company, a powerful railroad holding company. Successful lawsuits were also brought against beef, oil, chemical, and tobacco trusts. Roosevelt became known as a trustbuster, although his approach was actually quite moderate. In fact, several big business owners made large contributions to his 1904 election campaign.

The Roosevelt administration also took action against railroad abuses. The Interstate Commerce Commission (ICC) had been unable to prevent such practices as rebates and unfair freight charges (discussed on page 239). The Elkins Act of 1903 made rebates illegal. And the Hepburn Act of 1906 gave the ICC the power to set railroad rates.

2. Public Health. Upton Sinclair's *The Jungle* (1906) brought the issue of unsafe food to the attention of the Roosevelt administration. This muckraking novel, set in and around the Chicago stockyards, described the ingredients used in sausage, including moldy meat, dirt, and dead rats. Horrified public reaction spurred passage of the Meat Inspection Act of 1906. This act gave the federal government power to enforce sanitary regulations in meatpacking plants and vehicles that shipped meat from state to state. The Pure Food and Drug Act (also 1906) banned the sale of harmful and impure foods and medicines and required truthful labels on foods and drugs.

3. Conservation. Roosevelt was the first president to take a role in preserving the environment. He worked for passage of the Newlands Act (1902), which provided that money from the sale of Western lands be used for irrigation projects. He stopped the public sale of about 80 million acres of mineral land and 1.5 million acres of land suitable for waterpower sites. During his administration, nearly 150 million acres of public land were set aside as national forest reserves.

In 1908, Roosevelt called the state governors to a national conference on how to preserve and develop the nation's natural resources. As a result of this meeting, Roosevelt appointed a National Conservation Commission, headed by Gifford Pinchot. It conducted the first scientific study of the country's water, forest, soil, and mineral resources.

4. Other Actions. Roosevelt was somewhat of a Progressive in his social policy. He invited Booker T. Washington to the White House for dinner. When coal mine owners refused to negotiate with the strikers in a 1902 Pennsylvania strike, Roosevelt appointed an impartial committee to try to settle the dispute. The miners won some of their demands and went back to work. But the mine owners did not have to recognize the union. For the first time, a president had intervened in a labor dispute without taking sides against labor.

Roosevelt tried to steer a middle course in immigration policy. The number of Japanese immigrants had begun to increase in the 1890s. Most of them settled in the Western states, where many people became concerned about increased competition for jobs. Nativists launched an emotional campaign against the "yellow peril," demanding that the government stop all Japanese immigration. In 1906, San Francisco announced plans to set up a segregated school for Japanese and other Asian students. When Japan protested, Roosevelt persuaded the city to cancel its plan. He then negotiated an informal agreement with Japan, by which that country agreed to restrict the migration of Japanese laborers to the United States.

TAFT IN THE WHITE HOUSE

After the election of 1904, Roosevelt announced that he would not seek another term. Four years later, he persuaded the Republicans to nominate his friend, Secretary of War William Howard Taft. Taft won a sweeping victory over William Jennings Bryan in the 1908 election.

1. Progressive Accomplishments. Taft achieved a number of Progressive reforms. He initiated many lawsuits against trusts. Ninety antitrust suits were started during Taft's term in office, compared with 44 in Roosevelt's time.

Government-operated savings bank facilities were set up in post offices, and a parcel post service was begun. The Publicity Act required that contributions to campaigns for federal election be made public. The Mann-Elkins Act of 1910 placed telephone, cable, and wireless companies under the supervision of the ICC. Taft also supported the Sixteenth Amendment, ratified in 1913. It authorized Congress to impose an income tax.

2. Foreign Policy. In foreign affairs, Taft favored what he called *Dollar Diplomacy*. This meant encouraging American businesspeople to invest in countries of strategic importance to the United States. Dollar Diplomacy would have a great deal of impact in Latin America, where Americans invested heavily. But many Latin Americans would come to resent U.S. military intervention in their countries to protect the investments of U.S. citizens.

3. Political Blunders. Taft's policy on the tariff won him political enemies at home. Progressives wanted to lower tariff rates in order to stimulate competition and reduce prices for consumers. Taft had promised to work toward this goal. The Payne-Aldrich Tariff, passed by Congress in 1909, lowered rates somewhat, but less than what Progressives had wanted. Taft not only signed the measure but praised it as a progressive piece of legislation.

Taft further angered the Progressives by his stand on conservation. Gifford Pinchot, a Roosevelt appointee in the Department of Agriculture, criticized Richard Ballinger, Taft's secretary of the inte-

The arithmetic of Democratic victory. (*Puck*, 1912)

rior, for reopening federal waterpower sites to private developers. Pinchot also accused Ballinger of mishandling Alaskan coal reserves. Taft ended up supporting Ballinger and firing Pinchot.

4. The Election of 1912. Roosevelt turned against Taft early in 1910. Later that year, he went on a speaking tour to proclaim what he called the New Nationalism. This program called for stricter regulation of corporations and such social reforms as *workers' compensation*. With the latter, employers had to buy insurance to cover workers in case they were injured on the job.

Roosevelt hoped to be the Republican nominee for president in 1912. But the national convention chose Taft instead. Roosevelt's supporters then broke away, formed the Progressive party (also called the Bull Moose party), and nominated him as their candidate. Roosevelt's platform included a host of Progressive objectives: women's suffrage; initiative, referendum, and recall; workers' compensation; and strict business regulation.

The Democratic party nominated Woodrow Wilson, the Progressive governor of New Jersey and a former president of Princeton University. Both Roosevelt and Wilson advocated reform. But Wilson's program—which he called the New Freedom—differed from Roosevelt's. Roosevelt wanted to regulate trusts, not destroy them. Wilson believed that monopolies were a threat to free enterprise and should be abolished. The Progressive party attracted many Republicans, thus splitting the party vote between Taft and Roosevelt. As a result, Wilson carried 40 states and won the election.

IDENTIFY OR DEFINE: Elkins Act, Pure Food and Drug Act, conservation, Dollar Diplomacy, workers' compensation.

CRITICAL THINKING: Why did big business favor high tariffs? Why were Progressives opposed to them?

WILSON'S ADMINISTRATION

A man of high moral purpose, Woodrow Wilson was able to in-spire the public. But he was rigid in his beliefs and reserved in his demeanor.

1. The New Freedom. During Wilson's two terms as president (1913–1921), he proposed, and Congress enacted, many Progressive laws. Wilson persuaded Congress to pass the Underwood Tariff in 1913. It reduced import duties to the lowest level since 1860. To make up for the expected loss of revenue, Congress levied an income tax, as permitted by the Sixteenth Amendment.

Another important financial measure, the Federal Reserve Act (1913), was designed to regulate credit and improve banking serv-ices. The law divided the country into 12 districts, each of which was assigned its own Federal Reserve Bank. A Federal Reserve Board controlled credit by increasing or decreasing the amount of money in circulation and by setting key interest rates.

The Structure of the Federal Reserve System

Open Market Committee

Federal Reserve Board

Advisory Council

Federal Reserve District Banks 12 Banks, 25 Branches

Local Banks 39,000

☐ National Level

☐ District Level

☐ Local Level

Although Wilson had campaigned on a platform of breaking up trusts, he took few steps to do so once elected. But he did favor two regulatory laws that Congress passed in 1914. One set up the Fed-eral Trade Commission to investigate and stop unfair business prac-tices. The other was the Clayton Antitrust Act. It broadened the Sherman Act by clearly defining unfair business practices and gave the federal government more power to deal with business combinations. The act also exempted labor organizations from its antitrust provisions, a step that encouraged unionization.

Other measures also helped labor. The La Follette Seamen's Act (1915) regulated working conditions of sailors on American ships. The Adamson Act (1916) set a shorter workday for railroad workers. Two laws were passed to end child labor, but the Supreme Court later declared both unconstitutional.

2. Three New Amendments. During Wilson's administration, three amendments were added to the Constitution.

a. 17th. The Constitution had specified that state legislatures elect senators, but this method had encouraged bribery. The Seventeenth Amendment (1913) made the Senate more democratic by providing that senators be elected directly by the people.

b. 18th. The Eighteenth Amendment (1919) established a nationwide prohibition on the manufacture, transportation, and sale of alcoholic beverages.

c. 19th. In 1920, the Nineteenth Amendment granted women throughout the nation the right to vote. By this time, 29 states had already allowed women to vote in some elections.

3. Foreign Affairs. Wilson did not approve of Dollar Diplomacy. But his policies led to much U.S. intervention overseas anyway. When trouble broke out in Haiti and the Dominican Republic, Wilson sent troops into both countries and took over management of their finances. U.S. marines remained in the Dominican Republic until 1924, and in Haiti until 1934.

Wilson's major foreign involvement (before U.S. entry into World War I) was with Mexico. Early in 1913, Victoriano Huerta led a successful revolution against Mexico's reform government. Mexican President Francisco Madero was murdered. When Wilson became president, he refused to recognize the new regime. In addition, he placed an embargo on American arms shipments to Mexico. To keep European military equipment from reaching Huerta, he stationed U.S. ships off the port of Veracruz.

In 1914, Huerta's troops arrested a group of U.S. sailors in Tampico. Then, when a German ship carrying a cargo of arms approached Veracruz, U.S. ships bombarded and captured the city. Only the combined diplomatic efforts of Argentina, Brazil, and Chile prevented war between Mexico and the United States. Huerta resigned, and a president more acceptable to the United States—Venustiano Carranza—took office. The United States then withdrew its troops.

But troubles continued. In 1916, one of Carranza's former generals, Pancho Villa, tried unsuccessfully to overthrow him. Villa then tried to start a war between the United States and Mexico by invading the American Southwest. Wilson sent an Army force under John J. Pershing into Mexico to punish Villa. Pershing's pursuit was unsuccessful. In 1917, the U.S. troops were recalled.

IDENTIFY OR DEFINE: Federal Trade Commission, Clayton Antitrust Act, Eighteenth Amendment, Mexican Revolution.

CRITICAL THINKING: Explain why the Seventeenth and Nineteenth Amendments can be considered extensions of democracy.

Chapter Review

MATCHING TEST

Column A	Column B
1. Lincoln Steffens	a. Mexican who led raids into Southwestern United States
2. Ida Tarbell	
3. Susan B. Anthony	b. leader in the struggle to gain women's suffrage
4. Pancho Villa	
5. Robert La Follette	c. Progressive governor of Wisconsin
	d. author of *The Shame of the Cities*
	e. author of *The History of the Standard Oil Company*

MULTIPLE-CHOICE TEST

1. The Progressive era lasted from (*a*) 1865 to 1900 (*b*) 1880 to 1917 (*c*) 1900 to 1950 (*d*) 1901 to 1917.

2. From the 1860s to 1920, the main feminist effort was to (*a*) increase the number of jobs open to women (*b*) broaden women's educational opportunities (*c*) gain the vote for women (*d*) elect more women to Congress.

3. The main aim of the Federal Reserve Act of 1913 was to (*a*) guarantee the safety of depositors' money (*b*) regulate credit by

increasing or decreasing the amount of money in circulation (*c*) make state banks illegal (*d*) make private banks unprofitable.

4. All of the following were political reforms adopted during the Progressive era *except* (*a*) election of U.S. senators by state legislatures (*b*) initiative and referendum (*c*) recall (*d*) the direct primary.

5. Theodore Roosevelt's administration is known as the (*a*) Square Deal (*b*) New Deal (*c*) New Freedom (*d*) New Nationalism.

6. Upton Sinclair's *The Jungle* led to passage of the (*a*) Interstate Commerce Act (*b*) Newlands Act (*c*) Meat Inspection Act (*d*) Hepburn Act.

7. Theodore Roosevelt was the first president to intervene in a labor dispute (*a*) on the side of labor (*b*) on the side of management (*c*) as an enemy of labor and management (*d*) in a neutral capacity.

8. The Sixteenth Amendment to the Constitution (*a*) provided for prohibition (*b*) allowed Congress to impose an income tax (*c*) created the Federal Reserve System (*d*) set aside millions of acres of land for national parks.

9. Taft lost the support of many Progressives when he (*a*) spoke out in favor of the Payne-Aldrich Tariff (*b*) persuaded Congress to pass the Underwood Tariff (*c*) fired Secretary of the Interior Richard Ballinger (*d*) advocated Dollar Diplomacy.

10. The election of Woodrow Wilson to the presidency in 1912 came about mainly because of (*a*) Taft's refusal to run (*b*) the death of Theodore Roosevelt (*c*) a split in the Republican party (*d*) the U.S. entry into World War I.

 ESSAY QUESTIONS

1. Who were the muckrakers? Where did their name come from? What goal did they have in common?

2. How did Booker T. Washington and W.E.B. DuBois differ in their approach to opposing discrimination against African Americans?

3. Briefly explain initiative, referendum, and recall. How did these three reforms help promote democracy?

4. Did the Clayton Antitrust Act broaden or narrow the Sherman Antitrust Act? Explain your answer.

5. Compare and contrast Theodore Roosevelt and Woodrow Wilson as Progressives.

DOCUMENT-BASED QUESTION

This question is based on the accompanying documents (1–5). It will improve your ability to work with historical documents.

Historical Context:

During the years 1901–1921, social reformers called Progressives asked for key changes in American society. The three U.S. presidents during these years were also reformers. Theodore Roosevelt attacked business trusts, promoted federal regulation of the food industry, and took steps to conserve natural resources. William Howard Taft continued the attack on trusts and the emphasis on conservation. Woodrow Wilson backed new laws to regulate businesses, aid factory workers and farmers, and create a new central banking system.

Task:

Using information from the documents and your knowledge of United States history, read each document and answer the question that follows it. Your answers to the questions will help you write the document-based essay.

Document 1. Study at the cartoon on page 252.

How did the cartoonist show that President Theodore Roosevelt was not going to give "good trusts" total freedom of action?

Document 2. Excerpt from *The Shame of the Cities* by Lincoln Steffens, 1904:

> Philadelphia is, indeed, corrupt. . . . The [political] machine controls the whole process of voting, and practices fraud at every stage. The [tax] assessor's list is the voting list, and the assessor is the machine's man. . . . The assessor pads the list with the names of dead dogs, children, and non-existent persons.

Source: Steffens, Lincoln. *The Shame of the Cities*. NY: Macmillan, 1904, pp. 193–194. Available at: http://faculty.washington.edu/qtaylor/Courses/101_USH/101_manual_6.htm

What did Steffens see as the shame of Philadelphia? Explain your answer.

Document 3. Excerpt from the "Principles of the Niagara Movement," written by W.E.B. DuBois, 1905:

> We repudiate the monstrous doctrine that the oppressor should be the sole authority as to the rights of the oppressed. The Negro race in America, stolen, ravished and degraded, struggling up through the difficulties and oppression, needs sympathy and receives criticism; needs help and is given hindrance; needs protection and is given mob violence; needs justice and is given charity; needs leadership and is given cowardice and apology; needs bread and is given a stone. This nation will never stand justified before God until these things are changed.

> **Source**: www.niagrafallsreporter.com/menagerie9.html

What do you think DuBois meant by the first sentence in the excerpt?

Document 4. Excerpt from Upton Sinclair's novel *The Jungle*, in which he described meatpacking plants in Chicago, 1910:

> There would be meat that had tumbled out on the floor, in the dirt and sawdust, where the workers had tramped and spit uncounted billions of consumption germs.... [R]ats were nuisances, and the packers would put poisoned bread out for them; they would die, and then rats, bread, and meat would go into the hoppers together [to make the sausages].

> **Source**: Upton Sinclair, *The Jungle*. NY: Amsco School Publications, n.d., p. 146.

Even though *The Jungle* was a novel, a work of fiction, Sinclair was trying to arouse the public to demand reforms. What problems did he portray?

Document 5. Look at the photograph on page 249.

What were the suffragists hoping to achieve by marching in Washington, D.C.?

DOCUMENT-BASED ESSAY

Using information from the above documents and your knowledge of United States history, write an essay in which you:

- Explain to what extent the debate on the issues raised in the above documents and the rest of the chapter led to real reforms by 1921.

CHAPTER 14

Overseas Expansion and World War I

Since colonial times, Americans had been pushing westward into new territories. Crossing the Allegheny Mountains and the Mississippi Valley, they reached the Pacific in the 1840s. Then they settled the last frontier—the Great Plains and the Rocky Mountain region. By the late 19th century, Americans began to show interest in lands beyond their borders.

ACQUIRING NEW TERRITORIES

The first land acquired after the Civil War was Alaska. Since 1741, it had belonged to Russia, which was more interested in it for its fur trade than as a territory to settle. Finding Alaska of little value and fearing that Great Britain might seize it in case of war, Russia offered to sell it to the United States. Secretary of State William H. Seward arranged the purchase in 1867 for $7.2 million. Alaska was one-fifth the size of the rest of the United States and had relatively few inhabitants. Many Americans of the 1860s were not interested in gaining far-away territories. They considered Alaska worthless, calling it "Seward's Folly."

1. Increased Interest in Expansion. Toward the close of the 19th century, American views on overseas expansion changed. As the output of U.S. factories increased, industrialists wanted to export their products to new markets abroad. They also needed to import such raw materials as rubber and tin. Businesspeople wished to take advantage of investment opportunities overseas. American farmers sought foreign markets for their surplus crops. And Christian missionaries sought new converts.

The practice of acquiring foreign territories, or of gaining political or economic control over such areas, is called *imperialism*. In the 1870s, Britain, France, and other European nations had begun to scramble for territory and influence in Africa. Some Americans wondered why the United States did not seek foreign colonies as well.

One of the most influential advocates of American imperialism was Alfred Thayer Mahan, a naval officer and historian. In his book

The Influence of Sea Power Upon History, 1660–1783, Mahan said that sea power was the key to the rise of all great nations. In his view, the mark of a great nation was not only a powerful navy but also colonial possessions, overseas bases, and *coaling stations* (harbors where steamships could refuel).

U.S. Possessions in the Pacific, 1899

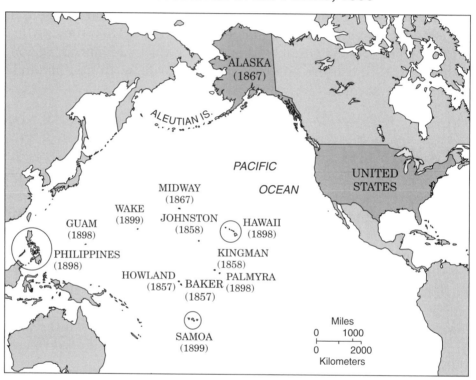

2. Hawaii. Starting in 1820, American missionaries began to go to Hawaii to teach Christianity, set up schools, and train native teachers. American merchant ships en route to China stopped at the islands for supplies. Fishing vessels used Hawaii as headquarters for whaling operations. Later, other Americans developed sugar and pineapple plantations there. And in 1887, the United States obtained the right to build a naval base at Pearl Harbor.

By the late 1800s, two-thirds of Hawaii was under the control of Americans or the U.S. Navy. In 1891, Queen Liliuokalani came to power. She took steps to reduce U.S. influence in the islands. In response, American planters led by Sanford Dole staged a revolt. They overthrew the queen and set up a new government in 1893. This group's request to Congress for annexation of the islands was denied at first. In 1898, though, Congress approved annexation.

3. Other Pacific Outposts. Americans also gained control over other Pacific islands, some 50 in all. Midway Island, for example, was occupied by U.S. troops in 1867. In 1898, the United States and Germany divided the Samoan Islands between them.

THE SPANISH-AMERICAN WAR

A turning point in U.S. expansionism was a war with Spain in 1898.

1. Trouble in Cuba. The Cubans had rebelled against Spanish rule early in the 19th century. At that time, the United States had shown little interest. But when they rebelled again in 1895, the United States was eager to prove itself a world power. Then, too, newspaper publishers Joseph Pulitzer and William Randolph Hearst had aroused the public's sympathy for the Cuban rebels. To boost circulation, they filled their papers with tales of Spanish atrocities in Cuba. Some of these accounts were accurate, but many others were exaggerated or untrue.

Although sympathetic to the Cubans, Americans did not want war. President Cleveland strongly supported neutrality. But in February 1898, Hearst's *New York Journal* published a secret letter in which a Spanish diplomat in Washington described President McKinley as weak. A week later, the U.S. battleship *Maine* mysteriously exploded in the harbor of Havana, Cuba. The ship had sailed to Cuba to protect American lives and property there. Americans blamed Spain for the disaster. To this day, no one knows who sank the *Maine*.

"Remember the *Maine*!" became the slogan of the day, as Congress and the public clamored for war. Although McKinley personally opposed such a move, he responded to the outcry by asking Congress to approve U.S. intervention in Cuba. On April 20, Congress adopted a resolution recognizing Cuban independence and authorizing the president to use force to drive the Spanish from the island. A few days later, both Spain and the United States issued formal declarations of war against each other.

2. Conflict in Two Hemispheres. The Spanish-American War (1898) was brief and decisive. Since the key battles of the war were

naval engagements and the Spanish were unable to match the Americans in sea power, Spain was easily defeated.

a. The Pacific. The first fighting took place halfway around the world from Cuba, in the Philippines. George Dewey, commander of the U.S. Navy in the Pacific, had been ordered to attack Spain's naval forces there in case of war. Immediately after war was declared, he headed for Manila Bay, where a Spanish fleet was stationed. On May 1, Dewey's squadron destroyed or captured all the Spanish ships and blockaded the city of Manila. After the arrival of U.S. troops in the summer of 1898, Manila fell and the Spanish land forces in the Philippines surrendered.

b. The Caribbean. Meanwhile, in mid-May, a U.S. naval squadron blockaded a Spanish fleet in Santiago harbor, Cuba. U.S. troops landed in Cuba in June and marched on the city of Santiago. By early July, they had captured two strategic heights overlooking the city. The Battle of San Juan Hill was noted for the exploits of a young New Yorker named Theodore Roosevelt. The Rough Riders— a volunteer cavalry regiment that he had organized and led—distinguished themselves in the engagement and won national acclaim.

During the U.S. siege of Santiago, the Spanish fleet tried to escape from the harbor. In the sea battle that followed, the entire Spanish fleet was destroyed. Santiago surrendered, and Spanish resistance in Cuba collapsed. At about the same time, another U.S. force invaded Spanish-held Puerto Rico. The troops soon occupied the island. The conflict ended in August 1898, when Spain asked for peace.

3. Results of the War. The Spanish-American War cost the United States some $250 million and about 5,000 lives. But in return, the United States gained a strong position of influence in the Caribbean. The peace treaty, signed in December 1898, provided for the independence of Cuba. But Cuba remained under U.S. protection for more than 30 years. The United States gained Puerto Rico and the small Pacific island of Guam. Spain was reluctant to cede the Philippines but did so when the United States offered $20 million for it.

When the war ended, some Americans opposed the idea of taking possession of the Philippines. Opponents of imperialism in the U.S. Senate argued that U.S. rule over others was not in the nation's democratic tradition. They also pointed out that it would be foolish to assume responsibility for a foreign people living 7,000 miles west of California. By contrast, expansionists stressed the economic and strategic importance of the Philippines to the United States. McKinley supported the expansionist position, declaring that Americans had a duty to "educate the Filipinos, and uplift and civilize and Christianize them." The expansionists won when the U.S. Senate ratified the treaty with Spain.

IDENTIFY OR DEFINE: Seward's Folly, imperialism, Alfred Thayer Mahan, Sanford Dole, George Dewey, Rough Riders.

CRITICAL THINKING: Summarize the arguments pro and con U.S. acquisition of the Philippines in 1898. Which side do you think was right? Why?

EXTENDING U.S. POWER

The United States' growing colonial empire led to problems. The nation had to increase military spending and become more involved in foreign affairs. It also had to find ways of dealing justly with colonial peoples, many of them with different cultures.

1. The Philippines. Many Filipinos wanted to be independent after Spain was defeated. Early in 1899, Filipinos led by Emilio Aguinaldo began a campaign of guerrilla warfare against the United States. U.S. forces fought the guerrillas for three years before suppressing the rebellion. The United States ruled the Philippines until the 1940s. William Howard Taft served as its first governor, from 1901 to 1904.

2. China. After acquiring the Philippines, the United States became more involved in Asian affairs.

a. Spheres of influence. China had long resisted foreign influences. By the late 19th century, however, the country had little military power to back up its policy of isolationism. China was helpless to resist the great powers—among them Britain, France, Germany, Russia, and Japan. All these countries were carving out their own *spheres of influence*—areas where they could dominate trade and the exploitation of economic resources.

b. Open Door Policy. Since colonial times, American merchants had carried on a brisk trade with the Chinese. American business leaders now hoped to expand their activities in the East Asia. But they were at a disadvantage in those areas where other foreign countries had special commercial privileges.

To protect U.S. interests, Secretary of State John Hay made a proposal in 1899 to six of the great powers. He asked them to agree to an *Open Door Policy* in China. What he meant was that all nations should have equal trading rights in the various spheres of influence. The six countries' replies were evasive, but he decided to treat their lack of opposition as consent. In 1900, Hay announced that all the leading powers had accepted the Open Door Policy.

c. Boxer Rebellion. In 1900, a group of Chinese patriots called "Boxers" organized a revolt. Their purpose was to drive the "foreign devils" from China. The Boxers killed more than 200 foreigners, destroyed foreign property, and laid siege to foreign settlements in the capital city of Peking (Beijing). In response, the great powers raised an international army to put down the Boxer Rebellion. The army included some 2,500 Americans.

The United States feared that the other powers would use the rebellion as an excuse to seize more Chinese territory. Hay stated that the United States opposed the creation of further spheres of influence in China. He proposed that, instead, the Open Door Policy should be extended to cover the whole country. The other powers agreed. But first, they forced China to pay a large *indemnity* (fine) for foreign losses during the rebellion.

3. Japan. Like the Chinese, the Japanese had kept foreigners out of their country for centuries. The United States opened Japan to trade by sending a naval expedition to Tokyo led by Matthew C. Perry. Commodore Perry arranged a treaty of friendship with the Japanese emperor in 1854.

Unlike the Chinese, the Japanese decided to modernize their country. They industrialized and built a strong army and navy. Japan defeated China in the Sino-Japanese War of 1894–1895. With this victory, Japan gained the island of Formosa (Taiwan) and a sphere of influence in Korea. Japan annexed Korea in 1910.

Japan also defeated Russia in the Russo-Japanese War of 1904–1905. Japan then asked U.S. President Theodore Roosevelt to help negotiate a peace treaty. Roosevelt won a Nobel Peace Prize for his work in arranging the Treaty of Portsmouth. But both the Japanese and the Russians accused the United States of favoring the other.

4. Intervention in Latin America. After the Spanish-American War, the United States had greater responsibilities in Latin America, especially in the Caribbean area.

a. Cuba. At the beginning of the war, the United States had stated that it would withdraw from Cuba when independence was won. U.S. military forces, however, occupied the island until 1902, when it became a republic. Even then, the Platt Amendment to the new Cuban constitution limited Cuba's independence. It authorized the United States to establish naval bases in Cuba. It also gave the United States the right to take action if Cuban law and order or independence were threatened. In the next 20 years, the United States intervened in Cuban affairs twice.

b. Puerto Rico. When Puerto Rico was ceded to the United States, the island was at first placed under military rule. Then in 1900 it became an unorganized U.S. territory. Congress authorized the U.S. president to appoint a civilian governor and an upper legislative house. A lower house would be elected by the people of Puerto Rico. In 1917, Congress (1) granted Puerto Ricans U.S. citizenship, (2) made the upper house of the legislature an elective body, and (3) changed the island's status to that of an organized territory of the United States.

c. Venezuela. Events in Venezuela led to further United States involvement in the Caribbean area. Venezuela was unable to pay its debts to European investors. Seeking repayment, Britain, Germany, and Italy blockaded Venezuela in 1902, bombarded several of its ports, and sank some of its naval vessels. President Theodore Roosevelt strongly criticized these European actions. The matter was then settled by peaceful arbitration.

U.S. Involvement in the Caribbean Region, 1902–1941

Map Code	Date	Location	U.S. Action
①	1902	Venezuela	Warning to European powers to stop interference
②	1903	Panama	Support of revolution to gain independence from Colombia
③	1904	Canal Zone	Beginning of U.S. control
④	1905–1941	Dominican Republic	Supervision of finances
⑤	1905–1941	Haiti	Supervision of finances
⑥	1906–1909	Cuba	Military occupation to supervise voting reforms and election
⑦	1911–1914	Nicaragua	Supervision of finances
⑧	1912–1933	Nicaragua	Military occupation to maintain order
⑨	1912	Honduras	Landing of marines to protect U.S. property
⑩	1914	Mexico	Occupation of Veracruz to prevent unloading of foreign arms
⑪	1915–1934	Haiti	Military occupation to support U.S. protectorate
⑫	1916–1917	Mexico	Dispatch of troops to pursue Pancho Villa
⑬	1916–1924	Dominican Republic	Military occupation to maintain peace
⑭	1917–1922	Cuba	Military occupation to end revolt and maintain peace

    d. Roosevelt Corollary. The possibility of further European interference still worried Roosevelt. In 1904, it seemed likely that the Dominican Republic too would be unable to pay its foreign debts. In his annual message to Congress, Roosevelt stated that the United States might have to intervene in the Western Hemisphere "in flagrant cases of . . . wrongdoing or impotence" and exercise "an international police power." This announcement became known as the *Roosevelt Corollary* to the Monroe Doctrine. The United States did take over the management of Dominican finances in 1905. During the next three decades, the United States was closely involved in the internal affairs of several other Caribbean countries as well.

U.S. Involvement in the Caribbean Region

THE PANAMA CANAL

For a long time, there had been great interest in digging a canal across Central America to connect the Atlantic and Pacific oceans. In 1881, a private French company started to construct such a canal across Panama, a province of Colombia. After seven years, however, the French company failed due to lack of funds and the deaths of workers from tropical diseases.

The United States realized that a canal connecting the Atlantic and Pacific oceans would shorten the water route from New York to San Francisco by some 8,000 miles. The waterway's usefulness was even more apparent after the United States became involved in the Spanish-American War. One U.S. battleship stationed in California had to sail all the way around South America to reach the fighting in Cuba.

In 1902, another French company offered to sell the property and canal rights in Panama to the United States for $40 million. Congress authorized President Roosevelt to accept the offer, with one condition. Colombia had to agree to U.S. control of the region through which the canal passed. Such a treaty was negotiated in 1903. The United States agreed to pay Colombia $10 million in cash and $250,000 in yearly rent. But then the Colombian Senate, hoping for better terms, refused to ratify the treaty. Both Roosevelt and the Panamanians were angry. The Panamanians wanted the canal to be built in Panama, and feared that the United States might switch to another route across Nicaragua.

A group of Panamanians decided to revolt. After secretly obtaining Roosevelt's pledge of support, they proclaimed their independence from Colombia. The revolution was successful largely because U.S. warships and marines prevented the entry of Colombian military forces into Panama.

The United States quickly recognized the new republic and drew up the Hay-Bunau-Varilla Treaty. It granted the United States full and permanent control over a strip of land 10 miles wide—the Canal

HELD UP THE WRONG MAN

Zone—through which a canal would be built. The United States guaranteed the independence of Panama and agreed to pay $10 million for the Canal Zone and an annual rent of $250,000. In 1921, the United States paid Colombia $25 million for the loss of its Panamanian province.

It took more than 40,000 workers to complete the 50-mile canal, at a cost of some $335 million. The Panama Canal opened to traffic in 1914. Before long, it became one of the great crossroads of the world.

IDENTIFY OR DEFINE: Emilio Aguinaldo, sphere of influence, Open Door Policy, Boxers, Roosevelt Corollary.

CRITICAL THINKING: Why did the United States want to construct a canal across Central America?

THE EUROPEAN CONFLICT

In the presidential election of 1916, Wilson campaigned and won on the theme "He kept us out of war." A terrible conflict had broken out in Europe two years earlier, in 1914. Americans still wanted no part of it. Wilson won supporters by maintaining the country's neutrality.

1. The Outbreak of War. World War I had started in 1914 soon after the assassination of Archduke Franz Ferdinand, heir to the throne of the Austro-Hungarian Empire. It took place on June 28 in the town of Sarajevo. The assassin belonged to a terrorist organization that wanted to bring southern Slavs in Austria-Hungary under Serbian rule. Blaming Serbia for the assassination, Austria-Hungary sent the Serbian government a list of harsh demands. Dissatisfied with Serbia's response, Austria-Hungary declared war.

Two alliance systems came into play. Russia, feeling close to fellow Slavic country Serbia, came to Serbia's defense. Soon, Russia's allies, Britain and France, joined Russia's side, while Austria-Hungary's ally, Germany, went to war against Russia, France, and Britain. By mid-August 1914, war was widespread. One side, the *Central Powers*, consisted of Germany and Austria-Hungary. They were eventually joined by the Ottoman Empire (Turkey) and Bulgaria. The other side, the *Allies*, included Britain, France, Russia, and a number of smaller countries.

READING A MAP

Allies and Central Powers, 1915

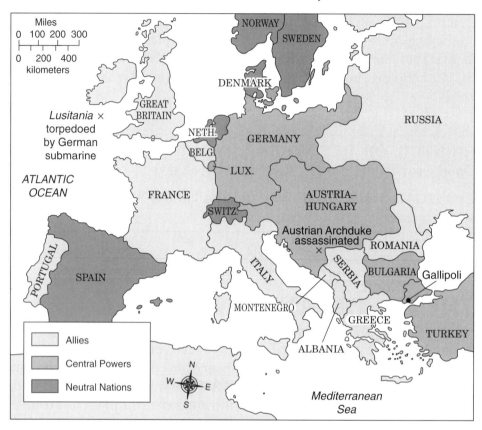

1. Which powers in 1915 were called the Central Powers?
2. Which other countries belonged to the Central Powers?
3. Which powers in 1915 were called the Allies?
4. Which countries were neutral?

The conflict, which involved millions of people, was called the Great War. (It became known as World War I only after a second worldwide conflict broke out in 1939.) The Central Powers fought the Allies on three main fronts. One was in the east, along the Russian border. Another was in the south, along the Italian border. The third front was in the west, in Belgium and northern France.

The new techniques of warfare—machine guns, poison gas, submarines, and tanks—caused vast destruction on both sides. The result was a stalemate, particularly on the Western Front. Here, the opposing armies, occupying huge networks of rat-infested trenches, faced each other across "no-man's-land." Time after time, one side or the other would try to take an enemy position. Thousands of lives were lost as soldiers fought to gain a few hundred feet of ground.

2. American Neutrality. Although Wilson had issued a proclamation urging Americans to be neutral, he and the majority of Americans sympathized with the Allies. There were several reasons:

a. Submarine warfare. The United States supplied the Allies with needed goods and equipment and loaned them millions of dollars. In retaliation, the Germans launched *U-boat* (submarine) attacks on U.S. and Allied supply ships as they crossed the Atlantic. The U-boats sank passenger vessels as well as merchant ships. A German attack on the British liner *Lusitania* in 1915 killed almost 1,200 people, including more than 100 Americans. After Wilson protested, Germany promised that it would not attack neutral countries' passenger liners and that it would give warnings before attacking other ships. But in early 1917, Germany returned to unrestricted submarine warfare even though it knew that the United States would retaliate by entering the war. Germans believed that they could defeat Britain and France before the Americans were ready to fight with them.

This drawing, by William A. Rogers, appeared in the *New York Herald* on August 4, 1915, a few weeks after the Germans sank the *Lusitania*. The German action (and this drawing) helped galvanize U.S. public opinion against the Germans.

b. Other factors. In February 1917, the British intercepted a secret message from German Foreign Secretary Arthur Zimmermann to the German representative in Mexico. They then turned it over to the Americans. The Zimmermann Note proposed that Mexico attack the United States if the Americans entered the war. In return, Mexico would get back its "lost territories" in the American Southwest. Hearing of this proposal brought Americans closer to war.

Another event concerned Russia, which was headed by a czar (emperor). Few U.S. leaders wanted to be allied with Russia's repressive government. But in March 1917, Russian moderates overthrew the czar and began to set up a democratic regime. The democratic nations began to see Russia as a compatible ally.

THE UNITED STATES AT WAR

In mid-March 1917, German U-boats sank four U.S. ships on the high seas. Early in April, Wilson sent a message to Congress condemning the German submarine policy and asking for a declaration of war. Congress passed a war resolution on April 6.

1. Efforts at Home. The United States immediately geared up to produce arms, munitions, and food to send to the hard-pressed Allies. By mid-June, almost 10 million men had registered for service in the armed forces. But it took months to train these new draftees. In the meantime, massive shipments of food and other supplies were sent overseas. To prevent attacks by German submarines, the Americans and British created convoys of merchant vessels protected by warships.

The U.S. government set up a number of agencies to coordinate war production. Farmers grew more crops. Workers kept strikes to a minimum. The government helped in this effort by encouraging unionization, fair working hours, and fair wages. Many African Americans and women found jobs in industry. Some 500,000 African Americans moved from the rural South to the industrial North, in part to search for jobs. The United States raised $33 billion to fight the war, about a third of it from taxes. The other two-thirds was raised through the sale of government war bonds. Americans also conserved fuel and food to allow the troops to have more.

Americans were exposed to an outpouring of anti-German propaganda. In posters, news stories, and speeches, the Germans were pictured as savage "Huns" who committed atrocities. The teaching of German in schools was forbidden. German music was banned from concert halls. People with German names were fired from their jobs.

Even common German foods were renamed. Sauerkraut, for example, became "liberty cabbage."

2. On the Western Front. After the United States declared war, John J. Pershing became commander of the American Expeditionary Force (AEF). By the summer of 1918, he had landed a million U.S. troops in France. The first troops went into action in the fall of 1917 on the Western Front, which passed through Belgium and France. This region had been the scene of a major German attack in 1914 that had come within 15 miles of Paris before being pushed back. Two years later, in 1916, assaults along the Somme River took more than a million lives.

In the spring of 1918, Germany launched another all-out offensive on the Western Front. Again, its army approached Paris. This time, though, U.S. troops were present. Their courageous fighting at Château-Thierry, Belleau Wood, and Cantigny stopped the German advance. The Allies then united under French Commander Ferdinand Foch. In July, they began a counteroffensive in which the Americans played a major role. By the end of October, the German army

Western Front and Allied Drives to Victory, 1918

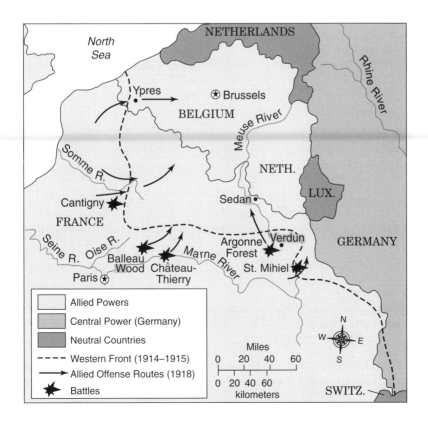

THE GRANGER COLLECTION, NEW YORK

Many soldiers on the Western Front found themselves fighting the war from trenches.

was retreating all along the Western Front. And the Central Powers were in even greater trouble in Southern and Eastern Europe. There, the Ottoman army had been destroyed, Bulgaria had surrendered, and Austria-Hungary was suing for peace. In addition, threats of revolution had begun to surface within Germany itself. Realizing that the war was lost, the Germans asked for an *armistice* (an end to the fighting). The German emperor, Kaiser Wilhelm II, abdicated and fled the country. On November 11, 1918, the armistice was signed, ending World War I.

IDENTIFY OR DEFINE: U-boat, Zimmermann Note, American Expeditionary Force, armistice.

CRITICAL THINKING: How did the United States contribute to the Allied war effort after April 1917?

AFTERMATH OF THE WAR

Both sides suffered enormous casualties in World War I—a total of 10 million killed and twice as many wounded. Some Americans boasted that the United States had won the war. Although this was an exaggeration, U.S. participation did tip the scale in favor of the Allies.

1. The Peace Conference. In December 1918, Wilson went to the Paris Peace Conference. He was the first U.S. president to travel to Europe while in office. All 23 of the Allies were represented. But the major players were President Wilson, Prime Minister David Lloyd George of Great Britain, and Premier Georges Clemenceau of France.

a. Wilson's Fourteen Points. Wilson felt that the aim of the Allies should be a just and lasting peace, a "peace between equals." In January 1918, he presented Congress with his Fourteen Points. Among other things, it called for (*1*) abolition of secret treaties, (*2*) freedom of the seas in peace and in war, (*3*) removal of all trade barriers between nations, (*4*) reduction in arms, (*5*) fair settlement of colonial claims, (*6*) recognition of the right of national groups to *self-determination* (self-government), and (*7*) formation of an international association of nations to protect the territory and guarantee the independence of all countries.

b. Aims of the Allies. On the surface, the Allies seemed to agree on Wilson's Fourteen Points as the basis for their negotiations. But they had different aims. Unlike the others, the United States had no territorial claims and no desire for revenge. France had suffered enormous casualties and considerable destruction of property. Britain, too, had been severely hurt. Both of them wanted Germany to make substantial *reparations* (payments for war damages).

Territories were also at stake. Italy had agreed to fight on the Allied side in exchange for land in southern Austria inhabited largely by Italians. Japan had joined the Allies in hopes of gaining Germany's Pacific possessions. Everywhere in Europe, national groups—Finns, Poles, Czechs, Hungarians—wanted their own countries.

c. The treaties. The treaties that were finally drawn up at Paris granted some wishes and denied others. What resulted was not a peace between equals. Instead, it was a settlement imposed by the winners on the losers.

There were five treaties in all. The most important one was the Treaty of Versailles between the Allies and Germany. German representatives signed it under protest in June 1919. The Versailles Treaty forced the Germans to accept responsibility for causing the war. They were to pay billions in reparations to the Allies. Germany returned Alsace and Lorraine to France and lost eastern territories to an enlarged, newly independent Poland. Germany gave up all its colonial possessions in Africa, Asia, and the Pacific. And the Germans were disarmed and forbidden to rebuild a strong military force. The Versailles Treaty also called for a new international organization, the League of Nations.

READING A MAP

Europe After World War I

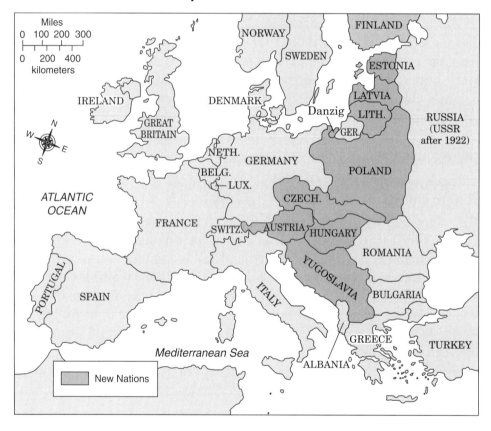

1. Name *five* of the new nations created after World War I that at least part of which had previously been in the Austro-Hungarian Empire.

2. Name at least *two other* new nations.

The Paris treaties drastically changed national boundaries in Europe. Poland, which had disappeared from the map in the 18th century, was re-created. Austria and Hungary were split apart. And a number of new nations came into being.

Wilson was able to soften some of the Allies' more extreme demands. For instance, he blocked French efforts to set aside part of western Germany as neutral territory. He was also successful in resisting Italian demands for the city of Fiume, a key seaport on the Adriatic. But he gave way on German reparations and on the "war guilt" clause that placed all blame on Germany.

2. Rejection of the League. Wilson believed strongly in the League of Nations. He hoped that it would prevent future alliances of the kind that had helped cause World War I. But the Treaty of Versailles, containing provisions for the League, had to be approved by the U.S. Senate. Some senators were opposed to the League. They feared that joining an international organization would weaken American democracy. Leaders of this group included Robert La Follette of Wisconsin, Hiram Johnson of California, and William Borah of Idaho. Henry Cabot Lodge of Massachusetts, among other senators, favored the League but wanted it to guarantee U.S. freedom to act.

Wilson's failure to take any prominent Republicans to Paris cost him the support of the Republican party. Wilson had also incurred Senate opposition by refusing to make any compromises with it. Wilson set out on a nationwide tour to appeal to the people. Partway through the trip, in September 1919, he collapsed. Early in October, he suffered a stroke from which he never fully recovered.

In the months that followed, the Senate held votes on the Versailles Treaty, both with and without changes. On each occasion, the treaty was defeated. By this time, Americans had lost interest in international issues. Thus, the United States did not become a member of the League of Nations. (In 1921, a joint congressional resolution ended the state of war between the United States and Germany, Austria, and Hungary.) Wilson left office in March 1921.

THE LEAGUE OF NATIONS

Although the United States never joined the League, more than 50 other countries did. They pledged to submit disputes to the League for settlement and to abide by its decisions. They also agreed that any member resorting to war would become the target of *economic sanctions* (such as a halt in trade) and, if necessary, military force.

1. Work of the League. For 25 years, the League performed many useful services. It carried on relief work in war-torn countries and aided war refugees. Its Mandates Commission supervised the former colonies of the Central Powers. The World Court settled a number of international disputes. The League also gathered statistics, published reports, and held international conferences to improve labor conditions, public health, education, communication, and transportation throughout the world. The United States took part in many of the League's nonpolitical activities.

2. Weaknesses of the League. In spite of its accomplishments, the League was unable to succeed at its major task—preventing aggression and war. There were four main reasons for this failure: (*1*) The League lost prestige when the United States, a leading world power, refused to join. (*2*) The League lacked the means to punish an aggressor nation. It could suggest that its members take action but could not force them to do so. (*3*) Member nations accused of aggression chose to withdraw from the League, rather than give in to its demands. (*4*) Leading members did not unite against aggression, unless their own interests were directly involved.

IDENTIFY OR DEFINE: Paris Peace Conference, national self-determination, freedom of the seas, reparations, war guilt.

CRITICAL THINKING: Why did the United States fail to join the League of Nations?

Chapter Review

 MATCHING TEST

Column A	Column B
1. Matthew C. Perry	*a.* proposed Open Door Policy
2. Arthur Zimmermann	*b.* commander of AEF
	c. arranged treaty of friendship with Japan
3. John J. Pershing	
4. John Hay	*d.* native Hawaiian leader
5. Queen Liliuokalani	*e.* German foreign secretary during World War I

> ## MULTIPLE-CHOICE TEST

1. The first new territory acquired by the United States after the Civil War was (*a*) Alaska (*b*) Puerto Rico (*c*) the Philippines (*d*) Hawaii.

2. A major cause of the Spanish-American War was (*a*) an uprising on the island of Puerto Rico (*b*) someone blowing up the battleship *Maine* (*c*) the Open Door Policy (*d*) the overthrow of Queen Liliuokalani.

3. After the Spanish-American War, Filipinos waged a guerrilla war against (*a*) Cuba (*b*) the United States (*c*) Spain (*d*) Puerto Rico.

4. Theodore Roosevelt won a Nobel Peace Prize for arranging the treaty that ended the (*a*) Sino-Japanese War (*b*) Spanish-American War (*c*) Korean War (*d*) Russo-Japanese War.

5. The Platt Amendment gave the United States the right to intervene in (*a*) Cuba (*b*) Nicaragua (*c*) Haiti (*d*) China.

6. At the time, the 1914–1918 war was called (*a*) World War I (*b*) the Franco-Prussian War (*c*) the War Between the States (*d*) the Great War.

7. All of the following were new weapons of warfare in World War I *except* (*a*) machine guns (*b*) tanks (*c*) battleships (*d*) poison gas.

8. U.S. participation in the fighting of World War I lasted (*a*) about a year (*b*) about 20 months (*c*) two years (*d*) three years.

9. The Treaty of Versailles included provisions for all of the following *except* (*a*) Italy taking Fiume from Austria (*b*) the return of Lorraine to France (*c*) the surrender of all German colonial possessions (*d*) the League of Nations.

10. When Wilson encountered Senate opposition to the League of Nations, he (*a*) compromised on all points (*b*) gave up the struggle for ratification (*c*) went on a nationwide speaking tour (*d*) made it an issue in his third presidential campaign.

 ## ESSAY QUESTIONS

1. Why did the United States become interested in expanding beyond its borders in the second half of the 19th century?

2. What was the Roosevelt Corollary? How did it come about?

3. What was the Open Door Policy? Why did the United States favor such a policy?

4. What developments led to the U.S. declaration of war on Germany in 1917?

5. How did the aims of the United States at the Paris Peace Conference differ from those of its allies?

DOCUMENT-BASED QUESTION

This question is based on the accompanying documents (1–5). It will improve your ability to work with historical documents.

Historical Context:

From 1867 to 1900, the United States was involved in foreign expansion. It purchased Alaska, took over Pacific islands, and expanded its trade network and naval power around the world. The most striking foreign expansion was a result of the U.S. war against Spain in 1898. According to the historian Frank Friedel, U.S. involvement in the Spanish-American War was a result of "a popular crusade to stop a seemingly endless revolution which was shattering Cuba."

Task:

Using information from the documents and your knowledge of United States history, read each document and answer the question that follows it. Your answers to the questions will help you write the document-based essay.

Document 1. Excerpts from a letter to the editor, *New York Evening Post*, by José Martí, a leader in the struggle to gain Cuban independence from Spain, March 25, 1889:

> [W]e have fought like men, sometimes like giants, to be freemen; we are passing that period of stormy repose, full of germs of revolt, that naturally follows a period of excessive and unsuccessful action. . . . [W]e deserve in our misfortune the respect of those who did not help us in our need. . . . [We will continue] the war that has been by foreign observers compared to an epic, the upheaval of a whole country, the voluntary abandonment of wealth, the abolition of slavery in our first moment of freedom, the burn-

ing of our cities by our own hands, the erection of villages and factories in the wild forests. . . . The struggle has not ceased.

Source: www.fiu.edu/~fcf/martilettertoeditor.html

In your opinion, what purpose did Martí have in writing this letter to the editor?

Document 2. Excerpts from comments by President Grover Cleveland about the revolution in Cuba against Spanish rule, 1895:

This government is constantly called upon to protect American citizens, to claim damages for injuries to persons and property, now estimated at many millions of dollars, and to ask explanation and apologies for the acts of Spanish officials whose zeal for the repression of rebellion sometimes blinds them to the immunities [protections] belonging to the unoffending citizens of a friendly power. It follows from the same causes that the United States is compelled to actively police a long line of seacoast against unlawful expeditions, the escape of which the utmost vigilance will not always suffice [be able] to prevent.

Source: Richardson, James D. (ed.) *Messages and Papers of the Presidents*. Washington, D.C., 1917, XIV, pp. 6150–6151.

According to President Cleveland, how was the revolution in Cuba affecting the United States?

Document 3. Excerpts from an article by James Creelman, a correspondent for the New York *World*, describing what he saw while traveling in Cuba in 1896:

Cuba will soon be a wilderness of blackened ruins. . . . The horrors of a barbarous struggle for the extermination of the native population are witnessed in all parts of the country. Blood on the roadsides, blood in the fields, blood on the doorsteps, blood, blood, blood! The old, the young, the weak, the crippled—all are butchered without mercy. . . . Is there no nation wise enough, brave enough to aid this blood-smitten land?

Source: New York *World*, May 17, 1896.

In your opinion, what did Creelman hope to achieve by writing his article? Explain your answer.

Document 4. Excerpt from President William McKinley's message to Congress, April 11, 1898:

The forcible intervention of the United States as a neutral to stop the war . . . is justifiable. . . . First, in the cause of humanity and to put an end to the barbarities, bloodshed, starvation, and horrible miseries now existing there. . . . Second, we owe it to our citizens in Cuba to afford them . . . protection. . . . Third, the right to intervene may be justified by the very serious injury to the commerce, trade, and business of our people. . . . Fourth, the present condition of affairs in Cuba is a constant menace to our peace, and entails upon this government an enormous expense.

Source: *Papers Relating to Foreign Affairs of the United States, 1898*, pp. 750–760. Found at: http://search.eb.com/elections/pri/Q00099.htm

On April 20, 1898, the U.S. Congress declared war on Spain and demanded Cuban independence. How did this April 20th declaration of war differ from what President William McKinley had asked Congress on April 11, 1898?

Document 5. Study the cartoon on page 266.

What is the view of the cartoonist regarding the U.S.-Spanish conflict? Explain your answer.

DOCUMENT-BASED ESSAY

Using information from the above documents and your knowledge of United States history, write an essay in which you:

- Explain whether you agree or disagree with the idea the United States went to war with Spain in 1898 mainly in order to help the Cuban people.

UNIT VI

TRIALS AND HOPE

CHAPTER 15
The Twenties and Thirties

With the end of World War I in 1918, a new era in U.S. history began. Although it lasted for more than a decade, it is commonly known as the Twenties. It was characterized by political conservatism, economic prosperity (for most), and great social change. The Twenties was followed by the Thirties, a time of economic upheaval and government intervention.

THREE REPUBLICAN PRESIDENTS

During the transition from war to peace, the United States experienced economic and social unrest. With the lifting of wartime controls in 1918–1919, prices rose sharply. Unionized workers, seeking to keep pace with the rising cost of living, struck for higher wages. Unemployment spread as many factories closed down to retool for peacetime production. The return of thousands of war veterans seeking jobs swelled the ranks of the unemployed. This was the situation as the presidential election of 1920 neared.

1. Harding in the White House. Since the Democrats were in power in 1920, they were blamed for the nation's problems. Then, too, the bickering over Senate ratification of the Versailles Treaty seemed to be a sign of Democratic party disunity. The Republicans chose as their presidential candidate in 1920 the amiable but otherwise undistinguished Senator Warren G. Harding of Ohio. The Democrats nominated Governor James M. Cox, also of Ohio.

Cox centered his campaign on favoring U.S. membership in the League of Nations. Americans, however, were more impressed with

Harding's pledge to return the country to "normalcy" (a time in the past without problems). Harding won by a landslide.

a. Turning back the clock. The Republican administration quickly reversed the Democratic policy of low tariffs. Congress passed an emergency tariff to raise rates on imported agricultural products. Then, in September 1922, it passed the Fordney-McCumber Tariff, which set high duties on manufactured imports. Without effective foreign competition, most American-made products rose in price.

The United States also acted to keep out foreigners. In 1921, Congress passed the Emergency Quota Act, the first law to set immigration quotas. It limited the total number of immigrants to 357,000 a year. It also limited the number of people from any one country who could enter the United States annually. The total was set at 3 percent of that country's nationals who were living in the United States in 1910. The Immigration Act of 1924 then lowered each country's quota from 3 to 2 percent, based on the census of 1890 instead of 1910. Far fewer people from Eastern and Southern Europe had lived in the United States at the earlier date. Thus, this law reduced immigration from those areas of Europe by nearly 85 percent, which was its intent. The 1924 law also put an end to all immigration by Asians.

b. Shady deals. Harding's chief qualification for high office was that—in the words of his campaign manager—"he looked like a president." He did choose some able advisers. Charles Evans Hughes became secretary of state; Herbert Hoover, secretary of commerce; and Andrew Mellon, secretary of the treasury.

While Harding was an honest man, some of his close associates were not. The head of the Veterans' Bureau and the Custodian of Alien Property were jailed for stealing huge sums of money from the government. Attorney General Harry Daugherty was charged with the illegal sale of pardons and liquor permits, and forced to resign. In the Teapot Dome scandal, Secretary of the Interior Albert B. Fall accepted bribes from oilmen in exchange for leasing them government oil reserves on good terms. Harding never knew the full extent of his friends' betrayals. He died of a heart attack in August 1923 before the story of their corruption became public knowledge. Vice President Calvin Coolidge was sworn in as his successor.

2. Coolidge as President. Coolidge was a native of Vermont and a resident of Massachusetts. Unlike the genial Harding, "Silent Cal" was severe, reserved, and frugal. But he was like Harding in his conservatism. People enjoyed Coolidge's homespun ways. When he ran for president in his own right in 1924, voters elected him by a wide margin.

Coolidge was a firm believer in a "hands-off" policy toward business and agriculture. He took steps to lower the cost of government and reduce the national debt. His tax policy was based on the advice of Secretary of the Treasury Andrew Mellon, who believed that the rich should pay low taxes. They would, he claimed, then invest more in industry and help the nation's economy to expand. This point of view led to a series of tax laws that reduced the taxes of the wealthiest Americans by two-thirds.

3. The Election of Hoover. When Coolidge decided not to be a candidate for re-election in 1928, the Republicans nominated Herbert Hoover for the presidency. Hoover had served as secretary of commerce in the Harding and Coolidge administrations. His supporters promised "a chicken in every pot, a car in every garage" if Hoover won the election. The Democratic candidate was the governor of New York, Alfred E. Smith. From the point of view of rural and small-town Americans, Smith had several disadvantages: (*1*) He was a Roman Catholic. (*2*) He opposed prohibition of alcohol (discussed on page 295). If elected, he said, he would do everything he could to have the Eighteenth Amendment repealed. (*3*) Smith was a "city slicker" with ties to Tammany Hall, New York City's political machine. All these factors worked to the advantage of Hoover, who won by a landslide.

4. The Economy in the "New Era." The 1920s was a time of business expansion. Industrial activity rose to a new high level. So did the *gross domestic product (GDP)*—the total value of goods and services produced by the nation. Jobs were plentiful, and the average city family had a larger income than ever before. Most Americans believed that the nation had entered a "New Era"—a time of ever-increasing prosperity.

5. Expanding Industries. The best symbol of industrial growth in the 1920s was the automobile. Europeans had pioneered its development. The first Americans to build and successfully market an automobile were Charles and Frank Duryea, in the 1890s. Henry Ford introduced his first car in the same decade.

Early automobiles were so expensive that, in 1900, there were only 8,000 motor vehicles registered in the United States. Henry Ford changed all that. In 1908, he developed the Model T and set up a factory to mass-produce it. He combined the use of interchangeable parts with the *assembly line*—a system made up of workers, tools, and a conveyor belt. As a car moved along the belt, each worker performed one or more operations on it. By 1916, a Ford could be made in 90 minutes and cost only $345.

During the 1920s, the yearly output of passenger cars rose from 1.9 million to nearly 4.8 million. The automotive industry also turned out hundreds of thousands of trucks, buses, and tractors. The automobile provided employment for millions of people. Some workers made cars. Others had jobs in related industries, including tires, glass, steel, and oil refining. Still others worked in gas stations and garages. Thousands more built and maintained new and improved roads.

The Wright brothers had developed the airplane early in the 20th century. Planes had played a limited role in World War I. After the war, they began to be used commercially. By the end of the 1920s, about 50 private airlines were in operation. They carried the U.S. mail and some passengers.

Other industries that thrived during the Twenties were construction and home appliances. New houses were built throughout the country. Big cities were transformed by skyscrapers. Among the

Amelia Earhart, the first woman to fly solo across the Atlantic, stands next to her airplane. She disappeared in 1937 in the Pacific while trying to fly around the world.

The Twenties were "boom times" for some—but not for the farmers. (Fitzpatrick in the *St. Louis Post-Dispatch*)

many tall structures that altered skylines in the 1920s were New York City's Chrysler Building and Chicago's Tribune Tower. The average middle-class family owned a car, a refrigerator, a vacuum cleaner, and an electric iron. Most people bought these items "on time," using the installment plan.

6. Business Growth. An increasing number of Americans were making quick profits by buying and selling corporate shares. A rise in speculation propelled the number of shares traded from 236 million in 1923 to more than a billion in 1928.

The trend toward business consolidation, which had begun after the Civil War, continued in the 20th century. During the 1920s, larger concerns absorbed about 8,000 manufacturing and mining companies. Holding companies swallowed up some 5,000 public utilities. By 1929, roughly half the corporate wealth of the country was controlled by 200 business enterprises.

7. Agriculture and Labor. American farmers did not share in the prosperity of the 1920s. They had made good money during the war and had expanded their acreage. But when European farm production increased after the war, the U.S. supply exceeded demand, and prices fell sharply. While other sections of the economy were booming, farmers had to cope with declining incomes due to surplus crops and heavy debts. Thousands went bankrupt. Many moved to cities and increased their already expanding populations. The census of 1920 showed for the first time that more people were living in urban areas than in rural ones.

Unions did poorly in the 1920s. Most individual workers earned a decent living. They made little progress, however, in the struggle for shorter hours and other benefits. Some companies, Ford among them, voluntarily raised wages. In general, however, business, government, and much of the public strongly opposed unions. Union membership declined from more than 5 million in 1920 to fewer than 3.5 million in 1929.

IDENTIFY OR DEFINE: Emergency Quota Act, Teapot Dome Scandal, GDP, assembly line.

CRITICAL THINKING: What was the U.S. government's attitude toward business in the 1920s? What specific actions and policies resulted from this attitude?

CHANGE AND TENSION

Society was being changed by the automobile. By making people more mobile, it fostered a sense of personal freedom, encouraged an exodus from central cities to suburban areas, and stimulated travel. The automobile reduced the isolation of rural dwellers. It also provided young people with freedom and privacy unknown to earlier generations. For some, the new ways were exciting. For others, they produced uncertainty and fear.

1. Attacks on Radicals. American society had long had its critics, such as the Populists and Progressives of the late 19th and early 20th centuries. But many critics of the Twenties had more extreme points of view.

One group, the *socialists*, opposed the capitalist economic system of free enterprise. They called for public rather than private ownership of factories, mines, utilities, and transportation systems. These changes, they believed, could be achieved through the democratic process. Eugene V. Debs, for example, helped form the Socialist party of America in 1901. Several crusading figures of the Progressive era, including Upton Sinclair, were socialists.

The *anarchists* believed in doing away with government altogether. Some resorted to terrorism. An anarchist had assassinated President McKinley in 1901. Some members of the political left, which included the socialists and anarchists, belonged to the Industrial Workers of the World (IWW), a labor union founded in 1905. These so-called "Wobblies" believed that the AFL was too timid to achieve real reform. All the various radical groups included sizable numbers of immigrants from Europe.

a. Wartime developments. Americans had always been suspicious of radicals, and World War I increased this distrust. During the war, *pacifists*—people opposed to all wars—were branded as "slackers" and even traitors for refusing to fight. Most radicals in Europe and the United States opposed the war, arguing that it would make capitalists rich at workers' expense. Congress passed laws that provided severe penalties for spying, obstructing the war effort, refusing to serve in the armed forces, and making disrespectful remarks about the U.S. government, Constitution, or flag. These laws authorized the government to arrest more than 1,500 persons. William Haywood, leader of the IWW, was sentenced to 20 years in prison; Debs, to 10 years.

In 1917, Russia was taken over by Bolsheviks. They were *Communists*—dedicated to achieving socialist aims by violence and by setting up a workers' dictatorship. They aimed to do this not only in Soviet Russia but all over the world. The American Communist party was organized in 1919.

b. The Red Scare. The so-called "Red Scare" in the United States began in the spring of 1919 and lasted about a year and a half. During this time, Americans of differing views clashed violently. Authorities took extreme steps to end the unrest. Most of the violence was blamed on "reds." Although people generally used this term to describe avowed Communists, they also applied it to union organizers, activist clergy, and other dissidents. Bitter strikes convinced many Americans that radical agitators wanted to destroy the country. In February 1919, one strike nearly shut down the city of Seattle, Washington. The following fall, Boston police went on strike. Coolidge, then governor of Massachusetts, gained nationwide fame when he spoke out firmly against the strike. An unexplained bombing in the nation's capital destroyed the home of Attorney General A. Mitchell Palmer. Another, on Wall Street in New York City, killed 38 people. Postal inspectors also discovered bombs in packages addressed to government officials.

Palmer set up a new division of the Justice Department to combat radicalism. (This division later became the FBI.) In November

1919 and in January 1920, Palmer ordered raids on the headquarters of radical organizations. Several thousand aliens were arrested. Some 800 of them were eventually deported. The "Palmer raids" ended when moderate leaders curbed the attorney general.

Nonetheless, suspicion and fear of radicals continued. Two Italian immigrants, Nicola Sacco and Bartolomeo Vanzetti, were anarchists accused of murdering the paymaster of a Massachusetts shoe factory and his guard. Tried and found guilty, Sacco and Vanzetti were sentenced to death in July 1921. Many people both in America and abroad felt that the two men had been convicted only because of their radicalism. In spite of repeated appeals and worldwide protests, Sacco and Vanzetti were executed in 1927.

2. African Americans: Problems and Achievements. Almost 400,000 African Americans served in the armed forces during World War I. Thousands of others moved north to take factory jobs. African Americans hoped that they would benefit from greater freedom and opportunity. Unfortunately, they still faced discrimination in jobs, housing, and civil rights. They also encountered racial antagonism and even violence. For the slightest of reasons, mobs lynched African Americans—many of them soldiers in uniform. Race riots broke out in more than 25 cities. The worst of them, in Chicago in 1919, left 38 dead.

Much of this brutality was the work of the newly revived Ku Klux Klan. The KKK had died out in the late 1800s. During the war, however, a new KKK began targeting Catholics, Jews, "reds," foreigners, and especially African Americans. The KKK worked secretly. White-robed and hooded members beat, tortured, and sometimes killed their victims. The organization was at its peak in the mid-1920s, with 5 million dues-paying members. In some states, Klansmen won election to high office and gained such political power that people were afraid to oppose them. Investigative reporters, however, began to publicize the Klan's terrorist activities. Charges of corruption within the movement finally led to its collapse in the late 1920s.

Although racial discrimination continued to make life hard for African Americans, they found ways to develop their vibrant culture. Many African Americans moved to the section of New York City called Harlem. There a group of writers started the movement known as the *Harlem Renaissance*. One of the best writers of this movement was Claude McKay. His poem "If We Must Die" is a passionate outcry against the racism that led to the postwar riots. Countee Cullen, another poet, wrote lyrical verses in the style of John Keats. The poems, novels, and plays of Langston Hughes display jazzlike verbal rhythms and a dry wit.

Langston Hughes (*left*) wrote in all forms of literature but is best known for his poetry. Bessie Smith (*right*) sang blues with a strong and beautiful voice.

African-American musicians, too, gained increasing fame during this period. They created the era's most distinctive style of music—jazz. It had moved from the South to the North with such early greats as Louis Armstrong, Joe "King" Oliver, and "Jelly Roll" Morton.

3. Prohibition. Early in 1919, the Eighteenth Amendment was ratified. It called for national prohibition, a ban on the manufacture, importation, and sale of all alcoholic beverages. Some Americans, determined to continue drinking these beverages, made liquor, wine, and beer at home. Many others bought from *bootleggers* (illegal sellers of alcohol). Bootleggers obtained their stock from American or foreign suppliers. Illegal bars, called "speakeasies," opened in almost every town. Because the federal bureau set up to enforce prohibition had fewer than 3,500 agents, it could not track down all the sources of illegal liquor.

Criminal gangs controlled most of the illegal alcohol business. As they grew in wealth and power, these gangs extended their operations into a number of legitimate businesses. Hoover refused to admit that prohibition was a failure. It took until 1933 for a Democratic-controlled Congress to pass the Twenty-First Amendment, ending prohibition.

4. Women's New Freedom. The Twenties brought less rigid standards of behavior for women—especially young women. Full, ankle-length dresses gave way to close-fitting, knee-length shifts. Long hair that had been worn in elaborate buns was cut short. Women began to use make-up and to smoke cigarettes. They went to speakeasies with their husbands and friends. The stylish young women of the period were known as "flappers."

Women's lives were changing in more important ways as well. More women than ever were going to college and working at salaried jobs. Although it was frowned on, some aimed at careers. Women's housekeeping chores became easier as electrical appliances, packaged foods, and other labor-saving improvements became available. And women had fewer children. The birthrate declined about 25 percent between 1915 and 1929.

5. The Roaring Twenties. Because earlier standards of sedate conduct gave way to daring and even scandalous behavior, the 1920s came to be called the "Roaring Twenties." Attracted by novelty and excitement, Americans idolized sports heroes, movie stars, and explorers. The most famous figure of the day was Charles Lindbergh, who made the first solo flight nonstop across the Atlantic in 1927.

Many people found the changes that took place during this decade to be troubling. The novelist F. Scott Fitzgerald describes the giddiness and anxiety that characterized the general mood of the period. His book *The Great Gatsby* (1925) describes the fate of a young bootlegger who fell in love with a rich, upper-class girl. Ernest Hemingway wrote of Americans living in Europe in *The Sun Also Rises*.

IDENTIFY OR DEFINE: socialist, anarchist, Communist, pacifist, Red Scare, Harlem Renaissance.

CRITICAL THINKING: How did American farmers fare in the 1920s? Explain your answer.

THE CRASH AND ITS AFTERMATH

Only about 1.5 million Americans were invested in stocks and bonds in the late 1920s. But market trading was important as a gauge of the nation's economy. By 1929, danger signals had appeared. One was unrealistically high stock prices that did not reflect what corporations were actually earning. Another was the practice of buying stocks *on margin* (paying only a small amount of cash to cover a stock purchase). Brokers lent the buyer the rest, with the stock as a security. Buying on margin drove stock prices up and led to a risky credit situation.

1. Panic on Wall Street. On October 24, 1929—a day that became known as "Black Thursday"—wave after wave of selling hit the stock market, and stock prices began to fall sharply. This was known as the *stock market crash*. In less than three weeks, the average price of stocks dropped by 40 percent. Speculators who had bought on margin were asked to put up more cash to secure their loans. Those who could not do so lost everything. Billions of dollars in paper profits were wiped out.

2. Beginning of the Depression. The stock market crash of 1929 marked the beginning of the Great Depression.

a. Causes. Although the crash did not cause the Depression, it revealed several problems. Not everyone had been prosperous during the 1920s. Farmers had been in trouble since the end of World War I. Members of the following minorities tended to be poor: African Americans, Mexican Americans, and Native Americans. According to one estimate, a third of the U.S. population was living in or near poverty in the 1920s.

Financial practices were unsound. Selling stocks on margin encouraged speculation. Banks granted risky personal and business loans and sought quick profits in stock market trading. Such practices threatened the financial stability of the banks and the safety of their depositors' funds. (Over 300 banks had failed in 1929 *before* the crash.) Many consumers went deeply into debt by buying expensive goods on the installment plan. When they could not meet their payments, their purchases were repossessed.

The most serious problem was a lack of balance in the economy itself. Industrial production kept rising, but wage earners' incomes did not. People could not buy all the goods being manufactured. Foreign demand for American products was limited, too. Europe was still recovering from the effects of World War I and had serious economic problems of its own. High protective tariffs added to the slowdown in international trade.

b. Effects. The Great Depression showed dramatically how all parts of an industrial society depend on one another. After the crash, funds for investments dried up. Many businesses then cut production or closed down. Thousands of workers lost their jobs. Unable to meet mortgage payments, many people were forced to give up their homes. Those with savings tried to withdraw them from banks. But many banks did not have ready cash because they had invested it. Hundreds of them simply closed their doors.

The worst year of the Depression was 1933. By that time, 100,000 businesses had gone bankrupt, and some 5,000 banks had failed. Farmers could no longer support their families. About 13 million people—25 percent of the workforce—were jobless. Thousands of those who still had jobs were forced to take pay cuts.

Homeless people jammed the country's roads, drifting from place to place looking for work. Makeshift villages of tar-paper shacks arose on the outskirts of cities. Local governments and private charities set up soup kitchens and tried to give some money to the destitute.

3. Hoover's Administration. In the beginning, President Herbert Hoover was optimistic. He knew that the country had recovered from earlier depressions in a year or two without government interference. The economy now, he said, was "fundamentally sound."

a. Government measures. Hoover's administration made several attempts to deal with the economy. Before the crash, it tried to solve the problem of falling farm prices by urging Congress to pass the Agricultural Marketing Act. This law aimed to stabilize farm prices by creating a federal farm board to buy and store crop surpluses. After three years, however, warehouses were full and farm prices were lower than ever.

After the crash, Congress passed the Hawley-Smoot Tariff (1930). It set rates at the highest level in U.S. history. The tariff was supposed to help manufacturers, but in fact it harmed them. Europeans reacted by raising their tariffs, and foreign trade almost stopped. At the same time, Americans cut back on investing overseas. In 1931, one of the biggest European banks failed. This led to a panic and *bank runs*. (A run occurs when depositors lose confidence in a bank and rush to withdraw their money.) A European depression followed.

As the Depression dragged on, the Hoover administration took a bold step. On its recommendation, Congress in 1932 created the Reconstruction Finance Corporation (RFC). It lent money to banks, insurance companies, farm groups, and railroads. It also helped states in their relief efforts. But Hoover vetoed a proposal for large-scale federal public works. He thought that the states should have control over such matters.

b. The Bonus Army. In the summer of 1932, thousands of unemployed veterans of World War I arrived in Washington, D.C., asking Congress for early payment of their bonuses (which were not due

Gross Domestic Product, 1929–1945

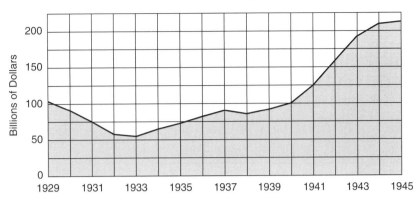

Unemployment, 1929–1945

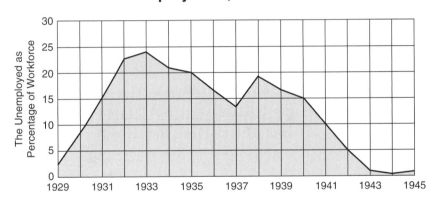

to be paid until 1945). When Congress failed to act, several thousand members of the Bonus Army stayed on in Washington, living in shanties. The administration used a U.S. Army unit under Douglas MacArthur to evict the veterans. The sight of soldiers attacking veterans shocked many Americans.

c. The Election of 1932. The Republicans, who renominated Hoover for the presidency in the summer of 1932, had little hope of winning. The public blamed the president for the Depression. The Democrats, on the other hand, had high hopes of regaining control of the White House. Their nominee was Franklin Delano Roosevelt (FDR), a distant relative of Theodore Roosevelt. He had served as assistant secretary of the navy under Wilson and had served as governor of New York since 1928.

The Democratic platform called for aid to the unemployed and farmers, banking and financial reforms, and repeal of prohibition. Roosevelt carried 42 states to Hoover's 6, and the Democrats gained control of both houses of Congress.

IDENTIFY OR DEFINE: on margin, stock market crash, bank run, Reconstruction Finance Corporation, Bonus Army.

CRITICAL THINKING: In what ways was the economy unsound during the 1920s before the stock market crash?

THE EARLY NEW DEAL

Hoover was the last president to remain in office for four months after his defeat. The Twentieth Amendment, ratified in February 1933, provided that future presidents would take over on January 20, instead of March 4.

1. Advisers and Aims. Roosevelt gathered around him a number of committed public servants. His Cabinet included Secretary of State Cordell Hull, a Southern supporter; Secretary of Labor Frances Perkins, the first woman to serve in a presidential Cabinet; and two Republicans: Secretary of Agriculture Henry A. Wallace and Secretary of the Interior Harold L. Ickes. Roosevelt also sought advice from many respected scholars and other professionals—a group that came to be known as the "brain trust." Another influence on Roosevelt was his wife, Eleanor. She worked hard on behalf of the poor, minorities, and women.

Roosevelt and his advisers put forward a series of programs and set up a number of agencies that, together, made up the New Deal. Its aims are often summarized as relief, recovery, and reform—relief for the needy, recovery from the Depression, and economic reform to prevent future depressions.

Many New Deal measures had their roots in Progressivism. Roosevelt had no intention of overturning the free-enterprise system. But his willingness to experiment with new ideas led to the government's taking a more active role in American life. Roosevelt's personal charm won him the support of conservatives as well as liberals. He changed the presidential press conference from a formal question-and-answer session to a relaxed exchange of views with reporters. He gave informal talks over the radio—"fireside chats," which won the trust of ordinary Americans.

2. The Hundred Days. During Roosevelt's first 100 days, he rushed a number of bills through Congress. First of all, he ordered all banks in the country to close. This four-day "bank holiday" stopped the rising tide of bank runs. Sound banks were then permitted to reopen. In his first fireside chat, the president told his listeners that the reopened banks were backed by the resources of the federal government. His statement helped ease the banking crisis. A few months later, the Glass-Steagall Act was passed. It created the Federal Deposit Insurance Corporation (FDIC) to insure depositors' accounts against loss in case of bank failure.

a. Relief. The Federal Emergency Relief Administration (FERA) distributed federal funds to state and local agencies for direct relief of the unemployed. Millions of families received cash to buy food, clothing, and shelter. The Civilian Conservation Corps (CCC) hired young men for such conservation projects as replanting forests, controlling floods, and improving national parks.

b. Recovery. More controversial were two recovery measures that aimed to raise prices by cutting production. The Agricultural Adjustment Act (AAA) of 1933 was designed to help farmers. It paid them to reduce their output of commodities such as wheat, corn, and cotton. Because the law was passed after the start of the growing season, thousands of acres had to be plowed under—a distressing practice when people were hungry.

The National Industrial Recovery Act suspended antitrust laws and encouraged manufacturers to cooperate in setting up codes of fair competition. These included industry-wide schedules of production and prices, as well as agreements on workers' wages and hours. The act also recognized the right of labor to form unions. The National Recovery Administration (NRA), created to administer the act, was criticized because its many regulations helped big businesses rather than small ones. And it did little to help the average consumer.

c. Reform. One of the most successful reforms of the hundred days was the Tennessee Valley Authority (TVA). This was a giant public power project in the valley of the Tennessee River. Designed to control floods, it also improved the region's standard of living by providing cheaper electricity, producing fertilizers, halting soil erosion, and improving river navigation. Opponents criticized the TVA as socialistic, but it did help people in its area.

3. After the Hundred Days. The early months of the New Deal did not bring the quick recovery everyone had hoped for.

a. New Deal critics. Some people argued that the New Deal had gone too far. Among these critics were wealthy Republicans and conservative Democrats, including 1928 presidential candidate Al Smith. A group of these anti-New Dealers formed the Liberty League to defend the free enterprise system from what they regarded as Roosevelt's attacks on it.

Other Americans believed that the New Deal had not gone far enough. Father Charles Coughlin (the "radio priest") advocated the Populist cure-all of silver inflation. Dr. Francis E. Townsend proposed government-funded pensions for the elderly. The critic with the biggest following was Senator Huey P. Long of Louisiana. His "Share Our Wealth" program promised to tax the rich and use the money to provide an annual income to the poor.

b. The Second New Deal. Roosevelt launched the so-called "Second New Deal" in 1935. It included a huge public works program, to be supervised by the Works Progress Administration (WPA). The WPA built and repaired highways, bridges, hospitals, schools, and parks. It also employed people in the arts. Writers produced state histories, painters created murals in public buildings, and entertainers toured the country in plays and musicals.

The Wagner Act (or National Labor Relations Act) was designed to protect workers' rights. It banned "unfair practices" by management, such as firing workers who joined unions. The act also set up the National Labor Relations Board (NLRB) to supervise collective bargaining and union elections.

The other major reform of the Second New Deal was the creation of the Social Security system. The Social Security Act provided for (*1*) pensions to retired workers or their survivors, (*2*) aid to states so that they could offer unemployment compensation, and (*3*) aid to states so that they could help support dependent and differently abled children.

IDENTIFY OR DEFINE: FDIC, CCC, AAA, NRA, TVA, WPA, Wagner Act.

CRITICAL THINKING: What were the three broad aims of the New Deal during the hundred days? Give an example of a measure in each of the three categories.

LATER YEARS

In the presidential election of 1936, Roosevelt ran against Alf Landon, the governor of Kansas and a former Progressive. FDR won 62 percent of the popular vote and the electoral votes of all but two states. Even so, Roosevelt's domestic policies met with greater resistance during his second term.

1. Trouble Over the Supreme Court. The Supreme Court had ruled against the NRA and the AAA in 1935 and 1936. Roosevelt was afraid it would do the same with the Wagner Act and Social Security. Early in 1937, Roosevelt sent a proposal to Congress that came to be called his "court-packing plan." He suggested that six new justices be added to the Supreme Court. Roosevelt presented his plan as a way to ease the Court's workload.

There was nothing unconstitutional about changing the number of Supreme Court justices. But both the public and the Democratic-controlled Congress considered the plan an attempt to destroy the independence of the judiciary. After five months of debate, the proposal was rejected.

"The Spirit of '37": Who is the man in the middle? What does he mean by saying, "Fall in"?

CARTOON BY FRED O. SEIBEL

Shortly afterward, the Supreme Court upheld the Social Security and Wagner Acts. Then a conservative justice resigned, and Roosevelt nominated a liberal. By 1941, he was to fill seven vacancies. Thus, on the Supreme Court issue, Roosevelt lost the battle but won the war.

2. Labor Problems. The Wagner Act encouraged labor unions to recruit new members. Union membership grew from fewer than 3 million in 1933 to almost 9 million in 1939. But some union leaders disliked the AFL because its member unions were made up of skilled workers only. Several leaders wanted to organize workers into *industrial unions*, ones that would admit all the workers (skilled and unskilled) in a given industry. In 1935, John L. Lewis, head of the United Mine Workers (UMW), and his supporters formed a committee within the AFL. Three years later, they broke away and formed the independent Congress of Industrial Organizations (CIO). It contained a number of industrial unions.

The Dust Bowl

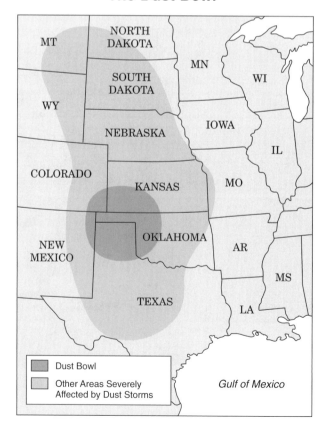

Industrial organizers faced opposition from both corporations and from the AFL. Workers in the auto industry could not gain recognition for their industrial union, the United Auto Workers (UAW). So in the winter of 1936–1937 they staged a series of *sit-down strikes*, staying in the auto plants but refusing to work. Afraid of property damage, management did not use force against the auto workers. Eventually, the strikers won recognition. So did steelworkers, after a number of pitched battles with the police.

3. Farm Problems. Despite New Deal efforts to help farmers, many of them were still very poor in the late 1930s. Beginning in 1933, several years of serious drought had led to severe dust storms in the southern plains. Winds swept away tons of topsoil. One region became known as the *Dust Bowl*. (See the map.) Thousands of families, unable to survive there, piled into their old cars and moved to California. There they looked for work, often as migrant farm laborers.

To fight the effects of the drought, Roosevelt introduced a series of conservation measures. Millions of trees were planted on the plains. They protected open fields from the force of the wind and held the topsoil down. To improve their land, farmers were urged to use contour plowing and crop rotation.

The federal government sent photographers around the country to document the results of the Great Depression.

To cope with the continuing problem of farm surpluses, Congress passed a second Agricultural Adjustment Act, in 1938. Like the first one, it paid farmers to limit production. The government stored surpluses for future use. Meanwhile, it made loans to farmers at rates that were below *parity* (a figure based on earlier prices—in this case, prices between 1909 and 1914). If the market price rose to parity or higher, farmers were allowed to sell their crops and repay the loans. If not, farmers kept the money and the government kept the crops. This method of keeping agricultural income fairly stable through farm subsidies was used for decades.

4. Final New Deal Legislation. In June 1938, Congress passed the Fair Labor Standards Act to help nonunion workers. It set maximum hours and minimum wages in industries that engaged in interstate commerce. It also banned the employment of children under 16, except on farms. In order to get the bill passed, Congress had to exempt several categories of workers, including farm laborers, domestic servants, and professionals. By this time, enthusiasm for the New Deal had waned. And events abroad were so threatening that Americans were more and more concerned with national defense.

THE NEW DEAL LEGACY

Roosevelt was feared, and even hated, by some people. They felt that he had endangered the American way of life by undercutting "rugged individualism." Business leaders and the wealthy denounced him as a "traitor to his class." But millions of other Americans admired, even idolized, FDR. They felt that he had saved the country from disaster.

The New Deal did not end the Great Depression. In 1939, there were still 9.5 million people out of work. Only the increased spending of the World War II era finally ended the depression. But the New Deal had a number of important consequences. Perhaps the most fundamental was the restoration of national confidence. Other lasting results may be summed up in four main areas.

1. Minority Participation. Segregation of African Americans continued, even in such New Deal programs as the CCC. But there were improvements. The Roosevelts had closer contacts with the African-American community than did earlier presidents or their wives. The government hired more African Americans. And African Americans benefited from relief and recovery programs.

Native Americans also benefited from relief measures. To correct the abuses caused by the Dawes Act, the Wheeler-Howard Act was enacted in 1934. It put an end to individual land sales and restored surplus reservation land to tribal ownership. It also encouraged Native Americans to form tribal cooperatives and maintain their ethnic traditions.

More than previous administrations, the New Deal brought Americans other than white, Anglo-Saxon Protestants into government. While only 3 percent of all the judges appointed by Harding, Coolidge, and Hoover were Catholics, under Roosevelt, the proportion rose to 26 percent. For the first time, an African American served as a federal judge (in the Virgin Islands). Opportunities in education and the professions also began to improve for minorities.

2. The New Deal Coalition. Roosevelt served longer than any other president in history. During his years in office (1933–1945), the Democrats became a majority party for the first time since the Civil War. FDR built a coalition that was to last nearly 50 years. (A *coalition* is an alliance of people or groups with different views.) The "old guard" of the New Deal coalition was made up of politicians from the Solid South and from big-city machines, such as that of Chicago. New Democrats included most African Americans, Catholics, Jews, and labor union members.

3. A Welfare State. The New Deal had created a *welfare state*—one in which the government assumes prime responsibility for the well-being of its citizens. Before the 1930s, only private or local charities helped victims of economic hardship. The New Deal convinced most Americans that the government had a duty to provide economic security for all citizens.

4. Big Government. A welfare state requires more personnel and more money than does a simpler type of government. Just as the late 1800s saw the rise of big business, the 1930s saw the rise of big government. The number of civilian federal employees grew from under 600,000 in 1929 to almost a million ten years later. Government expenses mounted, too. In 1932—Hoover's last year as president—the U.S. government spent about $4.6 billion for all purposes. In 1939, it spent about $9 billion. The government was spending more than it took in (a practice known as *deficit spending*). The government covers deficits by borrowing money through the sale of bonds. The national debt rose higher than ever during the Roosevelt administration. Most of this increase, however, was the result of wartime spending, rather than the cost of peacetime programs.

IDENTIFY OR DEFINE: industrial union, CIO, sit-down strike, Dust Bowl, maximum hours, minimum wage, welfare state.

CRITICAL THINKING: Why did some Americans dislike FDR and oppose the New Deal?

Chapter Review

 MATCHING TEST

Column A

1. Nicola Sacco and Bartolomeo Vanzetti
2. Louis Armstrong
3. Orville and Wilbur Wright
4. Charles and Frank Duryea
5. Charles Lindbergh

Column B

a. developers of first airplane
b. early jazz musician
c. radicals whose trial drew worldwide attention
d. first aviator to make solo nonstop flight across Atlantic
e. first Americans to produce commercially successful autos

MULTIPLE-CHOICE TEST

1. The chief targets of the revived Ku Klux Klan in the 1920s were (*a*) carpetbaggers (*b*) Catholics (*c*) Jews (*d*) African Americans.

2. The Great Depression began with the stock market crash of (*a*) 1928 (*b*) 1929 (*c*) 1932 (*d*) 1933.

3. A major agency created during the Hoover administration to combat the Depression was the (*a*) Reconstruction Finance Corporation (*b*) Civilian Conservation Corps (*c*) Civil Works Administration (*d*) Securities and Exchange Commission.

4. The Glass-Steagall Act set up the (*a*) FTC (*b*) FHA (*c*) FDIC (*d*) WPA.

5. The Second New Deal brought about all the following *except* the (*a*) Works Progress Administration (*b*) Wagner Act (*c*) Social Security Act (*d*) Tennessee Valley Authority.

6. Roosevelt's court-packing plan for the Supreme Court was aimed at (*a*) increasing the justices' workload (*b*) decreasing the total number of justices (*c*) ensuring a more favorable attitude toward New Deal legislation (*d*) creating a more conservative Court.

7. The NLRB (*a*) repairs highways and bridges (*b*) supervises union elections (*c*) provides unemployment compensation (*d*) halts soil erosion.

8. The purpose of the second AAA was to (*a*) increase agricultural production (*b*) keep farm income up (*c*) aid migrant farm workers (*d*) fight soil erosion.

9. The Great Depression ended (*a*) in 1935 (*b*) in 1938 (*c*) during World War II (*d*) in 1946.

10. The New Deal coalition included all of the following *except* (*a*) the Solid South (*b*) African Americans (*c*) organized labor (*d*) wealthy business leaders.

 ESSAY QUESTIONS

1. Why was Ford's Model T an important breakthrough? What effects did automobiles have on the American economy? On society?

2. What was the Red Scare? What events helped bring it about?

3. How did women's lives change in the 1920s?

4. In what ways did the New Deal help labor?

5. What were the most important consequences of the New Deal?

DOCUMENT-BASED QUESTION

This question is based on the accompanying documents (1–5). It will improve your ability to work with historical documents.

Historical Context:

The decade of the 1920s in the United States was a time of conservative politics. The policies of Presidents Warren G. Harding, Calvin Coolidge, and Herbert Hoover generally pleased business leaders. They all favored lower taxes, reduced government spending, and higher tariffs. Because of rising prosperity, the 1920s are sometimes called the "Golden Twenties."

Task:

Using information from the documents and your knowledge of United States history, read each document and answer the question that follows it. Your answers to the questions will help you write the document-based essay.

Document 1. Study the political cartoon and its caption on page 291.

According to the cartoon, who was enjoying the "boom" of the Twenties? Who was not?

Document 2. Excerpt from the book *Barrio Boy*, in which Ernesto Galarza described growing up in California in the 1920s:

> Ours was a neighborhood of leftover houses. The cheapest rents were in the back quarters of the rooming houses, the basements, and the run-down clapboard rentals in the alley. . . . Bed and meals were provided [to newcomers from Mexico] . . . on trust, until the new *Chicano* found a job.

> **Source**: Galarza, Ernesto. *Barrio Boy*. South Bend, IN: University of Notre Dame Press, 1971, pp. 201, 203.

Why do you think the people in the neighborhood were willing to provide bed and meals "on trust"?

Document 3. Excerpt from "The Klan's Fight for Americanism," by Hiram W. Evans, who became the leader of the Ku Klux Klan in 1926:

> The Ku Klux Klan, in short, is an organization which gives expression, direction and purpose to the most vital instincts, hopes, and resentments of the old-stock Americans, provides them with leadership, and is enlisting and preparing them for militant, constructive action toward fulfilling their racial and national destiny. . . . The Klan . . . attempts to build an America which shall fulfill the aspirations and justify the heroism of the men who made the nation. These are the instincts of loyalty to the white race, to the traditions of America, and to the spirit of Protestantism, which has been an essential part of Americanism ever since the days of Roanoke and Plymouth Rock.

> **Source**: Evans, Hiram W. "The Klan's Fight for Americanism," *North American Review*, No. 223 (March 1926), pp. 38–39.

Does this excerpt show that the Klan in the 1920s was opposed to more groups than just African Americans? Explain your answer.

Document 4. Excerpt from an article "Me and My Flapper Daughters," by W.O. Saunders in 1927:

I am the father of two flappers: trim-legged, scantily dressed, bobbed-haired, hipless, corsetless, amazing young female things, full of pep, full of joy, full of jazz. . . . Moving pictures bring to them every aspect of human society, at its worst as well as its best. The newsstands are loaded with cheap and trashy magazines in which these young people find frank discussions of phases of life in which they are by nature intensely interested, and about which we older folks maintain a prudish silence in the presence. . . . And so these amazing young folks . . . look down upon us older folks as a lot of old fogies. And having discovered much insincerity, much inconsistency and much hypocrisy in us as well, they flaunt our authority.

Source: W.O. Saunders, "Me and My Flapper Daughters," *The American Magazine*, CIV (Aug. 1927), pp. 27, 121–125.

Was W.O. Saunders praising his daughters? Explain your answer.

Document 5. Excerpt from a campaign speech by Herbert Hoover, the Republican party candidate in the 1928 presidential election:

By adherence to the principles of decentralized self-government, ordered liberty, equal opportunity, and freedom to the individual, our American experiment in human welfare has yielded a degree of well-being unparalleled [unequaled] in all the world. It has come nearer to the abolition of poverty, to the abolition of fear of want, than humanity has ever reached before. Progress of the past seven years is proof of it.

Source: *The New York Times*, October 23, 1928.

To what did Herbert Hoover give the credit for the "progress of the past seven years"?

DOCUMENT-BASED ESSAY

Using information from the above documents and your knowledge of United States history, write an essay in which you:

- Explain why the 1920s was or was not a good time to be living in the United States.

CHAPTER 16
World War II

A Second World War began in 1939, less than 21 years after the end of the Great War. The United States played a much larger role in World War II than it had in World War I. But it again escaped the devastation that left much of Europe and Asia in ruins.

U.S. FOREIGN POLICY BETWEEN WARS

After World War I, many ordinary Americans favored a policy of *isolationism*—remaining aloof from involvement overseas. Most of the nation's political leaders, however, realized that the United States was now a leading power and could not remain uninvolved in world affairs.

1. Republican Diplomacy. Although the United States was not a member of the League of Nations, it took part in international conferences and agreements.

   a. Washington Naval Conference. The Warren G. Harding administration organized the Washington Naval Conference of 1921–1922. Delegates from nine nations discussed Asian affairs and reductions in naval strength. The five leading naval powers—the United States, Britain, Japan, France, and Italy—agreed to limit the number of their battleships, aircraft carriers, and heavy cruisers for ten years. Conference delegates also pledged to guarantee China's independence and to continue an Open Door Policy there.

   b. Dawes Plan. The United States also played a role in European affairs. In the early 1920s, Germany had trouble making reparation payments to France. President Calvin Coolidge appointed a commission headed by Charles Dawes to work out a solution. The Dawes Plan provided for foreign loans to Germany so that it could make its payments.

   c. Kellogg-Briand Pact. A high point of international cooperation in the 1920s was the Kellogg-Briand Pact of 1928. It was sponsored by U.S. Secretary of State Frank Kellogg and the French

Foreign Minister Aristide Briand. Most nations signed this agreement to outlaw war as a way of settling international disputes. The Kellogg-Briand Pact, however, included no provision for enforcement of its provisions.

> ### d. Policy toward Latin America.
Under Harding and Coolidge, the United States continued to intervene in Latin America as it had during the Progressive era. (See the map and table on pages 270–271.) U.S. troops, in Nicaragua since 1912, were withdrawn in 1925 but were sent back a year later. Haiti remained a U.S. protectorate throughout the 1920s. U.S. Marines stationed in the Dominican Republic since 1916 were finally withdrawn in 1924.

President Herbert Hoover, however, opposed *interventionism*. As president-elect, he urged the nations of the Western Hemisphere to treat one another "as good neighbors." He later refrained from interfering when troubles broke out in Cuba, Panama, and El Salvador. He also ordered the withdrawal of U.S. troops from Nicaragua before he left office in 1933. Hoover's treatment of Latin American countries is called the *Good Neighbor Policy*.

2. Changes Under Roosevelt.
FDR became president in 1933, during the Great Depression. Many people felt that high U.S. tariffs (such as the Hawley-Smoot Tarriff of 1930) had contributed to the Depression. The Roosevelt administration set up the Export-Import Bank, which made loans to stimulate foreign trade. The Trade Agreements Act allowed the president to lower tariffs on specific items by as much as 50 percent, without congressional approval. By 1939, tariffs had been reduced by about 30 percent.

Ever since the Bolshevik revolution of 1917, Americans had been suspicious of the Soviets. Between 1918 and 1920, U.S. troops had even aided anti-Soviet Russians in their attempt to overthrow the Bolsheviks. Over the years, however, fear of a Communist revolution in the United States had lessened. In 1933, at the urging of farmers and business leaders who wanted to trade with the Soviet Union, Roosevelt established diplomatic relations with that country.

Roosevelt expanded the Good Neighbor Policy. In 1934, he pulled U.S. troops out of Haiti. That same year, the United States also revoked the Platt Amendment, thereby surrendering its right to intervene in Cuba.

THE COMING OF WAR

In spite of its domestic problems, the United States maintained a stable government. Japan, Italy, Germany, and other countries, however, experienced upheavals.

1. Militarism in Japan. After World War I, a prosperous Japan began to move toward democracy. Its *Diet* (Japanese parliament) gained greater power, and all men over 25 were granted the vote. Unfortunately, the Great Depression all but wiped out Japan's silk trade. People lost faith in the ability of the Diet to restore their prosperity. Many Japanese viewed as a national insult their country's 1922 agreement at the naval conference in Washington to limit its warships.

In 1931, Japanese military units seized the Chinese province of Manchuria. When the League of Nations condemned this aggression, Japan withdrew from membership. From then on, Japan's military leaders gained greater control over the country. Weakened by a revolution in 1911, China became a target for Japan's militarism. In 1937, Japanese troops moved south from Manchuria into China. When the United States protested against this violation of the Open Door Policy, Japan declared that it no longer accepted that policy. For the next eight years, Japan waged an undeclared war against China.

The Japanese invasion of Manchuria in 1931 signaled a new policy of militarism that would bring Japan and the United States into direct conflict within ten years.

2. Fascism in Europe. Dictatorships that rose to power in Europe during the 1920s and 1930s also adopted an aggressive foreign policy.

    a. Italy's Mussolini. After World War I, Italy was disrupted by labor unrest and fear of a Communist revolution. A political leader named Benito Mussolini gained wide support by promising order and a return to the glories of the ancient Roman Empire. In 1922, he led his private soldiers in a march on Rome and was soon made prime minister.

    Mussolini preached a doctrine called *fascism*, which glorified the nation at the expense of the individual. Citizens were expected to fight and die for the state. Fascist Italy was one of the first *totalitarian states*. Regimes of this type keep a close watch over people's activities, often through spies and hidden microphones and cameras. Government-controlled mass media subject citizens to constant propaganda.

    b. Germany's Hitler. Like Italy, Germany had troubles after the war. It was greatly weakened by the worldwide depression. Many Germans deeply resented the Versailles Treaty. It had branded Germany as the sole power responsible for World War I and had burdened the Germans with heavy reparations.

    Adolf Hitler, an Austrian-born veteran of World War I, argued that political leaders, foreigners, and Jews had sold out the German people. Hitler's new party, called the National Socialists, or Nazis, aimed to revive the German Empire. During the early 1930s, the Nazis became a powerful force in the *Reichstag* (German parliament). Because of that, Hitler became the German chancellor in 1933. Within a year, he ruled Germany as dictator.

    Nazism, a form of fascism, was particularly vicious because of its racial policies. According to Hitler, the Germans were a master race, destined to control such "inferior peoples" as Slavs, Jews, and Gypsies. Hitler exploited German *anti-Semitism*—hatred of Jews and discrimination against them—and made laws that deprived Jews of their rights and property.

3. A String of Aggressions. From 1935 through 1939, Mussolini and Hitler made a series of aggressive moves that brought on World War II.

    a. Initial moves. In 1935, Mussolini attacked the African state of Ethiopia. Italy's advanced weapons enabled it to defeat the Ethiopians in a few months. The League took little action. That same year, Hitler defied the Versailles Treaty by announcing that he would rearm Germany. He had already taken his country out of the League of Nations. The following spring (1936), Hitler marched troops into the Rhineland. This German area along the French border was supposed to be free of military installations. But Hitler built fortifications there.

b. The Spanish Civil War. During the summer of 1936, Francisco Franco led the Nationalists in an uprising against the forces of the Spanish government, known as Loyalists or Republicans. Both Italy and Germany sent troops and planes to help Franco. Although many people in the United States, Britain, and France sympathized with the Loyalists, the three democracies declared themselves neutral. None sent aid. Only the Soviet Union sent arms to the Loyalist cause. It also helped organize an International Brigade of volunteer soldiers from several countries, including the United States. Franco's forces defeated the Loyalists in 1939 and set up a Fascist dictatorship.

c. Final march to war. In 1936, Mussolini and Hitler signed an alliance called the Rome-Berlin Axis. In 1940, Japan joined the alliance, which then became known as the Rome-Berlin-Tokyo Axis. Early in 1938, Hitler annexed Austria with the support of Nazis in Austria. The *annexation* (takeover), in violation of the Versailles Treaty, gave Germany a better position from which to control the rest of Central Europe.

Hitler then demanded that Germany be allowed to annex the Sudetenland, border areas of Czechoslovakia where many Germans lived. Representatives of France, Britain, and Italy met with Hitler in the fall of 1938. Britain and France were so afraid of provoking war that, without consulting Czechoslovakia, they let Hitler have his way. This policy of making concessions to aggressors to keep the peace became known as *appeasement*. The German dictator promised that this would be his last territorial demand. Six months later, Germany took over the rest of Czechoslovakia.

By early 1939, France and Britain realized that Hitler and Mussolini would have to be stopped by force. In the spring of 1939, Italy invaded Albania and soon annexed it. Hitler's next target was Poland. In August, he signed a *nonaggression pact* with Joseph Stalin, dictator of the Soviet Union. The two countries agreed not to attack each other. This pact left Hitler free to act against Poland, the Soviet Union's western neighbor. On September 1, 1939, Germany launched an all-out attack on Poland. Two days later, Britain and France declared war on Germany. World War II had begun.

Axis Aggression in Europe, 1935–1939

IRELAND

DENMARK

LITH.

GREAT BRITAIN

NETH.

GERMANY
Hitler seizes power (1933) 1939

World War II begins

USSR

BELG.

1936

1938

Sudetenland

POLAND

LUX.

Rhineland

1939

CZECH.

FRANCE

1938

SWITZ. AUSTRIA HUNGARY

ROMANIA

ITALY

YUGOSLAVIA

BULGARIA

SPAIN
Civil War (1936–1939)

Rome
1939

Mussolini seizes power (1922)

GREECE

TURKEY

ALBANIA

Axis Powers in Europe in 1937

To ETHIOPIA (1935)

Axis Drives

0 100 200 300 Miles

0 200 400 kilometers

IDENTIFY OR DEFINE: isolationism, Good Neighbor Policy, fascism, Nazism, anti-Semitism, Sudetenland, appeasement.

CRITICAL THINKING: What is the relationship between economic problems and the rise of Nazism in Germany and fascism in Italy?

EARLY YEARS OF THE CONFLICT

Germany battered Poland with dive bombers, artillery, and tanks. The Germans called such a combined assault *blitzkrieg* (lightning war). While the Germans attacked Poland from the west, Soviet troops attacked it from the east. Poland surrendered late in September. The two invaders then divided the nation between them.

1. Western Europe. In the spring of 1940, Germany suddenly launched other blitzkriegs, toward the north and west. By the end of May, the Germans had overrun Denmark, Norway, Luxembourg, the Netherlands, and Belgium. German forces then pushed into France, which fell in 17 days.

Britain now stood alone. The bravery of their new prime minister, Winston Churchill, inspired the British to withstand punishing attacks. In the fall of 1940, the German *Luftwaffe* (air force) began a series of massive air raids on London and other British industrial centers and ports. This Battle of Britain was designed to knock out the country's defenses and soften British resistance to an invasion. Foiled by the Royal Air Force's valiant defense, the Germans abandoned their plan.

2. Fighting Elsewhere. German forces now occupied Romania, and Italy invaded Greece. By the spring of 1941, both Greece and Yugoslavia had fallen. At the same time, the Axis began to attack British possessions in North Africa. The Axis goal was to gain control of the Suez Canal and the oil fields of the Middle East. For months, the advantage swung from one side to the other.

Meanwhile, Hitler, ignoring his treaty with Stalin, invaded the Soviet Union in June 1941. German armored divisions quickly overran Ukraine and reached the outskirts of Moscow and Leningrad. The Soviet Union, now an ally of Britain, fought the Germans to a standstill during the winter of 1941–1942. But the Axis could look back on two years of warfare and see little but success.

3. U.S. Neutrality. Between 1935 and 1937, Congress passed several Neutrality Acts. Among other things, they (*1*) banned the export of arms to countries at war, (*2*) authorized the president to require warring powers to pay cash for U.S. goods and to transport the cargoes in their own ships, and (*3*) banned loans to nations at war.

In 1939, when World War II broke out, Congress revised the neutrality laws. The Allies could now buy weapons as well as other U.S. goods on a cash-and-carry basis. In 1941, Congress passed the Lend-Lease Act. It authorized the president to sell, exchange, lease, or lend articles of defense to any nation he considered vital to U.S. security. It extended to the Allies lend-lease aid valued at more than $50 billion.

The United States also prepared for its own defense. Congress set aside money to strengthen the armed forces. In 1940, it passed the Selective Service Act, the first peacetime program of compulsory military service in U.S. history. The United States traded 50 old destroyers to Britain in return for the lease of naval and air bases on British possessions in the Western Hemisphere.

4. Pearl Harbor. In 1940, after the fall of France, the Japanese had started moving into French Indochina in Southeast Asia. Soon afterward, Japan joined the Axis alliance. In response, the United States banned the export of steel and scrap iron to Japan. Later, the U.S. embargo was extended to include oil and airplane fuel as well. The United States also stepped up its aid to China.

U.S. neutrality came to an abrupt end in December 1941. On December 7, Japanese planes launched a surprise attack on Pearl Harbor, the U.S. naval base in Hawaii. They killed more than 2,000 Americans and destroyed 15 ships and 150 planes. The next day, President Roosevelt asked Congress to declare war on Japan. He called December 7 "a date which will live in infamy." On December 11, Germany and Italy declared war on the United States.

5. The American Home Front. Americans mobilized for World War II more completely than they had for World War I. All men between 18 and 45 were now subject to military service. During the war, more

Many African-American workers, such as these at a shipyard, made valuable contributions to the war effort.

than 16 million served in the armed forces, most of them overseas. A total of about 285,000 women joined the military, performing non-combat duties. Some 75,000 women served as Army and Navy nurses.

a. War production. American industry tooled up to produce airplanes, guns, tanks, and ships. War plants operated 24 hours a day, 7 days a week. More than 20 million people worked in key war industries. This total included millions of women. They took over many jobs that had previously been open only to men. The GDP rose to more than $200 billion, and the national debt to some $260 billion.

To finance the war, Americans invested billions of dollars in war bonds. Taxes were increased. A part of each worker's earnings was deducted in the form of withholding taxes. This system replaced the older method of paying income taxes in one lump sum. The government rationed such items as food, shoes, gasoline, and fuel oil. Millions of Americans collected paper and scrap metal for the war effort.

b. Relocation of Japanese Americans. Early in 1942, U.S. government authorities decided that people of Japanese ancestry living near the Pacific Coast might aid Japan if it invaded the U.S. mainland. Orders were issued to move them to *internment camps* inland. More than 110,000 Japanese Americans were uprooted. Given short notice of the transfer, many of them had to sell their homes and businesses at rock-bottom prices. Two-thirds of them were Ameri-

After the attack on Pearl Harbor, the U.S. government moved many Japanese Americans away from the West Coast. Most had to spend the rest of the war in internment camps.

can-born citizens. No Japanese American anywhere in the United States was ever found guilty of working for an enemy. In fact, thousands of Japanese Americans enlisted in the U.S. armed forces and fought with distinction.

After the war, Japanese Americans who had been interned received compensation for their sufferings that amounted to roughly 10 percent of the value of their claims. In 1983, a congressional commission blamed "racial prejudice, war hysteria, and failure of political leadership" for the internment. Five years later, the government granted $20,000 tax-free to each living former internee.

IDENTIFY OR DEFINE: blitzkrieg, Neutrality Acts, Lend-Lease, Selective Service, Pearl Harbor, internment camp.

CRITICAL THINKING: To what extent was the United States at war with the Axis powers before its official declaration of war in December 1941?

ALLIED VICTORY IN EUROPE AND AFRICA

When the United States entered the war in 1941, Britain and the Soviet Union had their backs to the wall. Soon, however, thousands of U.S. merchant ships carrying weapons and supplies were steaming across the Atlantic in Navy-protected convoys. And millions of GIs (U.S. soldiers) were arriving in the British Isles.

In the spring and summer of 1942, the Allies began massive bombing raids of their own. Their targets were enemy industrial centers and military installations. This was the first step in the Allied counteroffensive.

1. The Soviet Union. By the fall of 1942, a huge Axis army had driven 1,000 miles into the Soviet Union to the outskirts of Stalingrad. There, the Soviet Army made its stand, defeating their German attackers in February 1943 at the Battle of Stalingrad. The Germans alone lost 200,000 to 300,000 troops. After this decisive victory, the Soviet forces began to drive the enemy back toward Germany.

2. North Africa. Early in 1942, Axis forces in North Africa commanded by Erwin Rommel were threatening Britain's hold on Egypt. In the fall, the British, led by Bernard L. Montgomery, defeated Rommel at El Alamein, in northern Egypt. They then pursued the retreating Germans westward across Libya. Meanwhile, in November 1942, British and U.S. troops under Dwight D. Eisenhower landed at Casablanca, Oran, and Algiers. Axis forces in North Africa were caught between Eisenhower's troops in the west and Montgomery's in the east. Rommel surrendered in May 1943. All of North Africa was now in Allied hands.

Allied Campaigns in Europe and North Africa, 1942–1945

3. Italy. In July 1943, a combined force of U.S., British, and Canadian troops captured the Italian island of Sicily. The attack brought on a political crisis in Italy, and Mussolini resigned. In September, the Allies invaded the Italian mainland. The Italian government surrendered, but German troops continued to defend the Italian peninsula. The Allies struggled northward, taking Naples in 1943 and Rome and Florence in 1944. At the very end of the war, in April 1945, Italian resistance fighters captured and executed Mussolini.

4. The Invasion of France. In 1944, the Allies crossed the English Channel for a full-scale attack on the Germans in France. The Allied forces stormed ashore onto the beaches of Normandy, France, on *D-Day* (June 6). Eisenhower directed this invasion, the largest land-air-sea operation in history.

After a beachhead had been set up along the coast, reinforcements poured in. The Allies freed Paris in August. Next came Brussels and Antwerp, in Belgium. In September, the Allies invaded the Netherlands. More than 2 million Allied troops took part in the final push toward Germany.

5. German Surrender. In December 1944, the Germans launched a counterattack on the Allies at Bastogne in the Battle of the Bulge. The Allies won and pressed forward into Germany. At the Elbe River in April 1945, they joined forces with the Soviet Army, which had fought its way across Poland. The Soviets now occupied most of eastern Germany.

On May 1, German radio announced that Hitler had committed suicide in an underground bunker in Berlin. The following day, the Russians entered Berlin. Germany's armies were now destroyed, its territory overrun, and its major cities in ruins. It surrendered unconditionally on May 8. The war in Europe was at an end.

6. The Holocaust. After the defeat of Germany, the world became aware of the true horror of Nazism. As the Germans overran Europe, they forced hundreds of thousands of Europeans into slave labor. This was a common fate for Slavs and other peoples whom the Germans regarded as "inferior."

For Jews, the Germans reserved their most barbaric treatment. The Nazis first deprived Jews of their property and citizenship, and isolated them in ghettos. Later, they sent many to *concentration camps*, such as Dachau and Buchenwald in Germany. In January 1942, Hitler adopted what he called the "final solution of the Jewish question"—a program that aimed to kill every European Jew.

In some areas, all the Jewish residents were gathered together and shot. More commonly, Jews were sent by train to extermination camps. The most notorious of these were Auschwitz, Majdanek, and Treblinka, all in Poland. Here, the Germans killed their victims with poison gas and then burned their bodies. This organized murder of some 6 million European Jews came to be called the *Holocaust*. An equal number of other victims (homosexuals, Poles, Gypsies, resistance workers, political prisoners, and the handicapped) also died in the camps.

A long tradition of anti-Semitism helped make the Holocaust possible. In France, for instance, local authorities cooperated with the Germans by seizing Jews and sending them off to die. Britain and the United States were slow to react when they heard about the extermination policy. For instance, Allied planes, in their raids on German-held territory, did not bomb the concentration camps, an act that might have put them out of operation. Many historians believe, however, that little could have been accomplished in the face of Hitler's insane determination.

ALLIED VICTORY IN THE PACIFIC

By the time the Allies defeated the Axis in Europe, they were nearing a hard-won victory in the Pacific.

1. Japanese Successes. The Japanese attack on Pearl Harbor in December 1941 temporarily crippled U.S. naval and air power in the Pacific. The other Allies were also unable to withstand Japanese military attacks.

A few weeks after Pearl Harbor, the Japanese seized Guam, Wake Island, and Hong Kong. They also invaded the Philippines. The city of Manila fell in January 1942. Led by Douglas MacArthur, the outnumbered U.S. and Filipino troops withdrew to Bataan Peninsula across Manila Bay. There, they resisted the enemy for more than three months. On Roosevelt's order, MacArthur retreated to Australia, where he was given command of Allied forces in the southwest Pacific. The Japanese soon overran all the Philippine Islands. (See the map on page 326.)

The Japanese went on to take French Indochina, Thailand, Burma, the Dutch East Indies (Indonesia), and Singapore. From New Guinea and the Solomon Islands, the Japanese were menacing Australia. They also seized Attu and Kiska, the westernmost of the Aleutian Islands and hence had a base of operations against Alaska. By the middle of 1942, Japan had won control of a vast empire, rich in oil, rubber, tin, and other vital natural resources.

2. Stopping the Advance. Two U.S. victories began to turn the tide for the Allies in the Pacific. One was the Battle of the Coral Sea, off the eastern coast of Australia, in May 1942. The U.S. force defeated the Japanese, removing a threat to Australia.

The other turning point was the Battle of Midway, a month later. A large enemy fleet steamed out to seize Midway Island—the first step in a planned Japanese invasion of Hawaii. The United States, however, had recently broken the Japanese naval code. Therefore, U.S. leaders knew of the attack plan in advance. U.S. ships defeated the Japanese naval force decisively.

3. Taking the Offensive. By late summer 1942, the Allies were taking the offensive in the Pacific. They had three major objectives: (*1*) to cut Japan's lines of communication with its possessions, (*2*) to retake the Philippines, and (*3*) to attack Japan. The first Allied offensive was a U.S. attack on the enemy-occupied island of Guadalcanal, in the Solomon Islands. U.S. Marines landed in August 1942. After six months of sea, air, and land battles, they drove off the Japanese.

a. Island-hopping. Allied planners decided that a campaign to win back every enemy-held island would be too costly. Instead, they used the tactic of *island-hopping* (taking only certain strategic islands and leaving the others to the enemy). The bypassed islands would eventually surrender for lack of supplies. Heavily fortified Tarawa in the Gilbert Islands fell to the Allies in November 1943. Their next leap was to Kwajalein and Eniwetok, in the Marshall Islands, and then to Saipan and Guam, in the Marianas. From Saipan, U.S. long-range planes began to bomb industrial centers in Japan.

b. The Philippines. MacArthur opened a drive to retake the Philippines by landing troops on the island of Leyte in October 1944. The Japanese hurled their main fleet at the invasion forces in the Battle of Leyte Gulf, the largest naval-air engagement in history. The U.S. force won a decisive victory and gained control of Philippine waters. MacArthur then captured Manila in February 1945, and by July had regained the entire Philippines.

4. The Final Assault. In February 1945, U.S. Marines stormed the island of Iwo Jima, 750 miles from Japan. In April, U.S. troops landed on Okinawa, just 360 miles from Japan. The United States lost more than 10,000 men before defeating the Japanese. During the three-month campaign, the U.S. fleet suffered severe damage from *kamikaze* attacks. These were suicide missions in which Japanese pilots crashed their bomb-laden planes into enemy warships.

a. Truman in charge. In April 1945, shortly before the end of the war in Europe, President Roosevelt died of a brain hemorrhage. Vice President Harry S Truman became the new president. Truman had taken no part in high-level planning or decision-making regarding the war.

After he was sworn in as president, Truman learned that U.S. and foreign scientists had been working together to develop the world's first atomic bomb. Their research, called the Manhattan

World War II in the Pacific, 1942–1945

Project, had been carried on in total secrecy. In July 1945, the first successful atomic bomb test took place at a remote desert site in New Mexico.

b. To bomb, or not to bomb? Should Truman use the atomic bomb now that it was available? The alternative, as he saw it, was a full-scale invasion of Japan. Believing that such a campaign would cost the United States many thousands of lives, Truman chose atomic attack.

On July 26, Allied leaders issued an ultimatum to Japan: surrender unconditionally or suffer total destruction. The Japanese did not reply. On August 6, a single U.S. plane dropped an atomic bomb on the city of Hiroshima. The explosion killed at least 66,000 people immediately and injured even more. It destroyed every structure within a four-square-mile area of the city. Still, Japan would not surrender. When a second A-bomb was dropped on Nagasaki three days later, Japan gave up. The formal surrender took place on September 2, 1945, aboard the U.S. battleship *Missouri* in Tokyo Bay. World War II was over.

IDENTIFY OR DEFINE: D-Day, concentration camp, Holocaust, atomic bomb, island-hopping.

CRITICAL THINKING: What was the Nazis' "final solution" in regard to European Jews and how was it implemented?

Chapter Review

MATCHING TEST

Column A
1. Kellogg-Briand Pact
2. Lend-Lease Act
3. El Alamein
4. Auschwitz
5. Midway

Column B
a. a Nazi death camp
b. site of a decisive Allied victory in the Pacific
c. an international treaty that outlawed war
d. an agreement that allowed the U.S. president to provide military aid to nations important to U.S. security
e. the site of a decisive Allied victory in North Africa

MULTIPLE-CHOICE TEST

1. At the Washington Naval Conference, all of the following nations agreed to limit the size of their navies *except* (*a*) the United States (*b*) Great Britain (*c*) China (*d*) France.

2. The Kellogg-Briand Pact was not very effective because (*a*) few nations signed it (*b*) it could not be enforced (*c*) the United States refused to take part in the agreement (*d*) it went into effect after Hitler had begun to rearm Germany.

3. A Good Neighbor Policy was first advocated by (*a*) Warren Harding (*b*) Calvin Coolidge (*c*) Herbert Hoover (*d*) Franklin D. Roosevelt.

4. Hitler's rise to power in Germany was aided by all of the following *except* (*a*) widespread prosperity (*b*) the Great Depression (*c*) bitterness toward the Versailles Treaty (*d*) anti-Semitism.

5. In their relations toward Hitler and Mussolini through most of the 1930s, the European democracies followed a policy of (*a*) isolationism (*b*) intervention (*c*) appeasement (*d*) aggression.

6. The United States was brought into World War II when Japan attacked (*a*) Guam (*b*) Hawaii (*c*) Midway (*d*) the Philippines.

7. Allied troops invading Italy met heavy resistance from (*a*) the Italian army (*b*) Italian resistance fighters (*c*) Mussolini's private troops (*d*) German forces.

8. By mid-1942, Japan controlled all of the following *except* (*a*) Indochina (*b*) Australia (*c*) Burma (*d*) Singapore.

9. Beginning in 1942, the key to the Allied war effort against Japan was (*a*) kamikaze attacks (*b*) island-hopping (*c*) fire bombing of Tokyo (*d*) dropping atomic bombs on Japanese cities.

10. A new kind of warfare used by the Japanese in the final months of the war was (*a*) poison gas (*b*) guided missiles (*c*) atomic warheads (*d*) suicide attacks by pilots.

 ESSAY QUESTIONS

1. What is fascism? Who originated the term? Name *three* countries that had fascist governments during the 1930s.

2. In the early 1930s, what were Roosevelt's policies toward each of the following? (*a*) the Soviet Union (*b*) Latin America

3. Describe how the United States mobilized to fight in World War II.

4. What was the Holocaust? When did Hitler begin carrying it out? How many victims did it claim?

5. Explain why President Truman decided to use atomic bombs against Japan.

DOCUMENT-BASED QUESTION

This question is based on the accompanying documents (1–6). It will improve your ability to work with historical documents.

Historical Context:

The Japanese attack on Pearl Harbor in late 1941 put an abrupt end to U.S. isolationism. During World War II, the United States fought in both the Western European/North African theater and the Pacific theater. After driving German forces out of North Africa and Southern Europe, the Allies invaded German-occupied France in 1944. In the Pacific, through island-hopping, Allied naval forces steadily advanced toward Japan beginning in 1942. In 1945, Japan surrendered after U.S. planes dropped two atomic bombs on two Japanese cities.

Task:

Using information from the documents and your knowledge of United States history, read each document and answer the question that follows it. Your answers to the questions will help you write the document-based essay.

Document 1. Excerpt from U.S. Marine E.B. Sledge's description of what it was like to be sent into battle in the Pacific during World War II at age 19:

> There was nothing macho about the war at all. We were a bunch of scared kids who had to do a job. . . . We were in it to get it over with, so we could go back home and do what we wanted to do with our lives. . . . But I was afraid so much, day after day, that I got tired of being scared.

> **Source**: Terkel, Studs, *"The Good War": An Oral History of World War II.* NY: Ballantine Books, a Division of Random House, 1984, pp. 56–59.

What was Sledge's attitude toward serving as a Marine in the Pacific during World War II?

Document 2. Excerpt from an article written in 1942 by an African American, J. Saunders Redding, in which he explained why he supported the war effort:

> I do not like these "race incidents" in the [military] camps. . . . I do not like the constant references to the Japs as . . . "yellow bellies" and "yellow monkeys," as if color had something to do with treachery, as if color were the issue and the thing we are fighting rather than oppression, slavery, and a way of life hateful and nauseating. These and other things I do not like, yet I believe in the war. This is a war to keep men free. The struggle to broaden

and lengthen the road of freedom—our own private and important war to enlarge freedom here in America—will come later.

Source: Redding, J. Saunders, "A Negro Looks at This War," *American Mercury*, LV (Nov. 1942), pp. 585–592.

What did Redding hope that victory in World War II would do for African Americans?

Document 3. Study the photograph on page 319.

Is it likely that if a photograph of shipyard workers had been taken before World War II, it would *not* have shown so many women? Explain your answer.

Document 4. Study the photograph on page 320.

What happened to many Japanese Americans during World War II?

Document 5. Poem written by an anonymous U.S. sailor, fall of 1945:

Remember

The guns of the third fleet in silence lay,
Across the Pacific in Tokyo Bay.
The horrors of war have come to cease,
The world at last can rest in peace.

We've stopped the invader, we've won the fray
Without much time for fun or play
But the flag of freedom once more can fly
Remember those who fought to die.

Remember him Buddie, remember him,
Remember Jack, remember Jim?
They fought beside you on bloody sands,
You couldn't help them much, just hold their hands.

They're gone now Buddie, no more to roam
They'll not come back to a dreamed of home,
But what they fought for shall not die,
The flag of freedom will always fly.

What message or messages was the author of the poem trying to convey?

Document 6. A sample of American motion pictures made 1942–1945:

Across the Pacific (1942)
Mrs. Miniver (1942)
Action in the North Atlantic (1943)
Bataan (1943)
Destination Tokyo (1943)

Guadalcanal Diary (1943)
We've Never Been Licked (1943)
The Fighting Seabees (1944)
Ladies Courageous (1944)
God Is My Co-Pilot (1945)

Take an educated guess: How do you think these motion pictures contributed to the war effort?

DOCUMENT-BASED ESSAY

Using information from the above documents and your knowledge of United States history, write an essay in which you:

- Explain how true Franklin D. Roosevelt's December 9, 1941, statement "We are now in this war. We are all in it—all the way" turned out to be.

POSTWAR CONCERNS

CHAPTER 17
The Cold War

World War II was the most destructive war in history. It took the lives of 14 million soldiers and more than 20 million civilians. Millions more were wounded. There was widespread suffering from disease and starvation, and many people were left homeless. At the war's end, thousands of cities, villages, factories, and farms lay in ruins.

The war also changed the balance of power. It had left Britain and France too weak to play a decisive role in the postwar world. Two superpowers, the United States and the Soviet Union, now dominated international affairs. It also caused a surge of nationalism, especially in colonial regions. Between 1945 and 1960, more than 30 former colonies became independent countries.

After World War II, many people found it difficult to believe that humanitarian ideals played a part in international relationships. What would the future hold now that the United States had used the atomic bomb against civilians?

PLANNING THE POSTWAR WORLD

After World War I, most Americans had wanted to concentrate on their own affairs. The World War II generation was willing to commit the nation to foreign alliances, foreign aid, and other forms of international involvement.

1. Wartime Conferences. In 1941, four months before Pearl Harbor, Roosevelt and Churchill issued the Atlantic Charter. Though not binding, it set forth a number of aims that other anti-Axis countries later endorsed. These included the right of people to choose their own form of government, free trade, and the disarmament of aggressor nations.

a. Tehran Conference. After the United States entered World War II, there were several important meetings of the leaders of the "Big Three"—the United States, Great Britain, and the Soviet Union. At Tehran, Iran, in November 1943, Roosevelt, Churchill, and Stalin not only discussed the Normandy invasion but also talked about reducing the power of Germany after the war.

b. Yalta Conference. In February 1945, the three leaders met again at Yalta, a Soviet resort on the Black Sea. With the war in Europe nearly over, postwar planning could now be more specific. The Big Three agreed on a joint military occupation of Germany after the war. They promised to support free elections to create "broadly representative" governments in liberated countries. Roosevelt and Churchill also secretly promised Stalin territory in Asia if the Soviet Union would enter the war against Japan. In addition, Roosevelt and Churchill approved the Soviet annexation of eastern Poland and the transfer of a part of eastern Germany to Poland.

c. Potsdam Conference. A final Big Three meeting took place at Potsdam, Germany, in July 1945. Since Roosevelt had died in April, the United States was now represented by Harry S Truman. Near the end of the conference, Clement Attlee, Britain's new prime minister, replaced Churchill. At this meeting, the Allied leaders made plans for the occupation of Germany. They set up a council of foreign ministers to draw up peace treaties and issued the "unconditional surrender" ultimatum to Japan that would precede the planned atomic bombing of Hiroshima.

2. The Question of Germany. By the end of the war in Europe, eastern Germany had become a Soviet zone of occupation. Western Germany was divided into British, U.S., and French zones. Berlin, in the Soviet zone, was divided into four sectors. (Austria and its capital, Vienna, were divided and occupied in a similar fashion.)

a. Resettlement and reparations. During the war, the Allies had agreed to give the German territory east of the Oder and Neisse rivers to Poland. This agreement forced millions of Germans to resettle within the new German borders.

The Allies had more trouble agreeing on German reparations. The original plan was to take payment in valuable goods, such as factories, rather than money. Realizing, however, that a permanently weakened Germany would create future problems for Western Europe, they discontinued the plan. The United States adopted a new policy of supporting Germany's economic recovery.

b. Punishing the Nazis. In their wartime meetings, the Allies had made plans to root out Nazism in Germany. One goal was *denazification*—the removal of all Nazis from positions of authority in Germany. Courts were set up to judge individual cases. But the program was abandoned because it was too expensive and difficult to implement.

Public trials of major Nazi leaders were held in Nuremberg, Germany, in 1945–1946. The main trial involved 22 officials charged with waging aggressive war and committing "crimes against humanity." A panel of judges representing the Soviet Union, Britain, France, and the United States sentenced 12 of the accused to death and 7 to prison. (Three others were acquitted.)

3. The United Nations. In 1944, representatives of the United States, Great Britain, the Soviet Union, and China met in Washington, D.C. There they drew up plans for a postwar international organization to replace the League of Nations. It was to be called the United Nations (UN). A UN charter was created in the spring of 1945. By October, the organization had been established in New York City with 51 members.

Senator Tom Connaly, a member of the U.S. Delegation to the San Francisco Conference on creating the Charter to the UN, signed the Charter on June 26, 1945. On the left, President Truman observed.

The United States became a charter member of the UN. Many Americans felt that their isolationism after World War I had helped bring on World War II. Then, too, Roosevelt's methods of seeking *bipartisan* support (that is, the support of both major political parties) swayed many Americans in favor of the UN. He sent Republicans *and* Democrats to help create the UN charter. After Roosevelt's death, Truman continued the same bipartisan approach.

a. Structure of the UN. The *General Assembly* is the democratic forum of the United Nations. Each Assembly member has an equal vote. The *Security Council* has a more active role. Unlike any group within the League of Nations, the UN Security Council can take military action against aggressors. Decisions on important matters, however, require the support of the United States, Russia, the United Kingdom, France, and China. Each can veto any action being considered.

Other UN departments and their duties are as follows: (*1*) The *Secretariat* does the UN's administrative and clerical work; (*2*) The *Economic and Social Council* makes recommendations and coordinates activities in a wide variety of fields, from trade and development to population and human rights; (*3*) The *International Court of Justice* settles legal disputes between nations; (*4*) The *Trusteeship Council* was set up to supervise colonial possessions. Over the years, as former colonies became independent, its field of responsibility steadily diminished.

b. The UN in action. The UN has been more successful at listening to members' problems than at solving them. Nonetheless, it has many accomplishments to its credit. In 1948, it issued a Declaration of Human Rights, which supported the rights of all people to life, liberty, and safety. The UN also outlawed *genocide*—the mass killing of a national, racial, or religious group. It helped formulate an international agreement banning nuclear weapons in outer space and the setting up of military bases on the moon or the planets. And it sent peacekeeping forces to maintain order in a number of trouble spots, including the Congo, Lebanon, East Timor, and the Balkans.

Specialized agencies have worked to aid refugees, to care for child victims of war or poverty, and to fight epidemics. Technical advice and aid have been extended to developing countries. The UN has also made loans for public works; improved worldwide weather forecasting; and set international standards and regulations for civil aviation, shipping, and postal services.

IDENTIFY OR DEFINE: Big Three, resettlement, Security Council, General Assembly, genocide.

CRITICAL THINKING: Why did the Allies want to set up the United Nations after World War II?

BEGINNING OF THE COLD WAR

During World War II, the Soviet Union had taken over Estonia, Latvia, and Lithuania. When the war ended, the Soviets occupied not only eastern Germany but also Poland, Hungary, Romania, Bulgaria, and eastern Czechoslovakia.

1. The Iron Curtain. Shortly after the war, Communists controlled the governments of all the countries of Eastern Europe. In some cases, Communists came to power through elections. But in these elections, only Communists had been allowed to run or vote. In other cases, the Communists seized power by force and imprisoned or murdered members of opposition parties. As early as March 1946, Britain's former prime minister, Winston Churchill, spoke of an "iron curtain" separating Communist from non-Communist countries. The last Eastern European country to fall under Communist domination was Czechoslovakia, in 1948.

Poland, East Germany, Czechoslovakia, Hungary, Bulgaria, and Romania had close political and economic links to the Soviet Union. These nations became known as *satellites*, since they depended on the Soviet Union as the planets in our solar system depend on the sun. Albania and Yugoslavia also set up Communist governments but broke away from Soviet domination.

Serious tension developed between the two *superpowers*, the United States and the Soviet Union. The result was the *Cold War*— a conflict fought mainly with economic, political, and diplomatic weapons. It pitted the non-Communist (Western) bloc against the Communist (Eastern or Soviet) bloc.

The West distrusted the Soviet Union because, since the Bolshevik Revolution, Soviet leaders had been calling for world revolution to overthrow capitalism. The Soviet Union was generally distrustful of the West. Since the USSR had suffered such severe damage in the two world wars, its leaders wanted to protect it from future attack by surrounding its borders with satellite states.

2. Containment. During this time of mutual suspicion, U.S. leaders were influenced by a State Department expert, George Kennan, who predicted that the Soviet Union would expand wherever it could. He urged the United States to adopt a policy of *containment* (policy of restricting Soviet aggression and influence).

a. The Truman Doctrine. Containment was first put into action in Greece and Turkey. Neighboring Communist countries were aiding Greek revolutionaries in a war against their government. Britain had been helping the Greek government, but by 1947, it could no longer do so. At the same time, the Soviets were demanding that Turkey allow them to share control of the straits between the Black Sea and the Mediterranean.

Afraid that both Greece and Turkey would fall under Communist control, President Truman declared that the United States must "support free peoples who are resisting attempted subjugation by armed minorities or by outside pressures." This principle became known as the *Truman Doctrine*. To reinforce it, the United States sent military equipment, supplies, and advisers to Greece and Turkey. The Greek government put down the rebellion, and Turkey successfully resisted Soviet demands.

b. The Marshall Plan. Secretary of State George E. Marshall proposed a financial aid plan in 1947 that was also intended to contain Soviet expansion. Concerned that Communists might exploit war-devastated countries, he asked European leaders to draw up a blueprint of their needs. In response, 16 nations adopted a four-year, multibillion-dollar plan to provide participating nations with food, fuel, raw materials, and machinery. In 1948, Congress approved this European Recovery Program, now called the *Marshall Plan*. The Soviet Union and its satellites refused to take part in the plan. They organized strikes in participating nations and sabotaged U.S. foreign aid shipments.

The United States spent more than $12 billion on the Marshall Plan. The plan helped participating nations raise their industrial and agricultural production above prewar levels and stimulated their international trade. It also helped the United States by reviving the European market for American goods. And it held communism in check by reducing the economic and political instability on which communism thrives.

The continuation of the Cold War kept the United States from ending foreign aid in 1952. Gradually, U.S. shifted aid from Europe to developing countries in Asia, Africa, and Latin America. To these, the United States provided food, raw materials, machinery, and scientific and industrial know-how.

3. Crisis in Germany. The Western powers and the Soviet Union could not agree on a peace treaty for Germany or to the setting up of a unified German government. In 1948, the United States, Britain, and France acted without the Soviet Union and combined their zones of occupation in western Germany to create a single republic. In retaliation, the Soviet Union refused to allow trucks and trains from the West travel through its zone in East Germany to Berlin. Cut off from their main source of supplies, 2 million West Berliners faced starvation.

The Western Allies broke the Berlin Blockade with a gigantic airlift. For 11 months starting in June 1948, cargo planes flew food, coal, and other supplies into Berlin. The Soviets finally lifted the Berlin Blockade in May 1949. In that same month, the new Federal Republic of Germany (West Germany) came into being. Its capital was Bonn. West Germany received Marshall Plan aid and was slowly brought into the ranks of the Western powers. In 1955, the Western Allies granted the country full independence. They also allowed West Germany to rearm by creating an army of up to 500,000 troops. In addition, it was permitted to manufacture its own military equipment (except atomic weapons, guided missiles, and large warships).

European Military Alliances, 1982

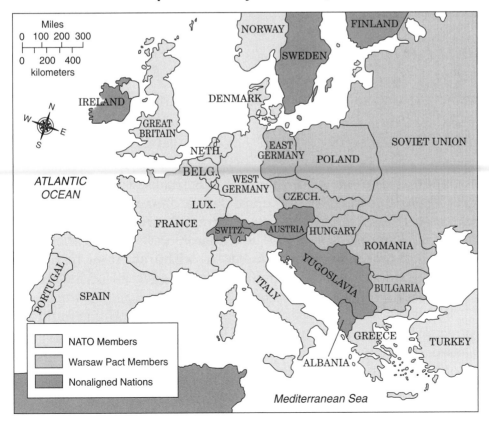

4. Military Alliances. In 1949, Western powers organized the North Atlantic Treaty Organization (NATO). Its original members were the United States, Canada, Belgium, Denmark, France, Iceland, Italy, Luxembourg, the Netherlands, Norway, Portugal, and Britain. The NATO nations agreed to treat an armed attack on one member as an attack on all. They set up a unified military force, to which each member contributed funds and personnel. Greece and Turkey became members in 1952, West Germany in 1955, and Spain in 1982.

After West Germany joined NATO, the Communist bloc announced its own military alliance, the Warsaw Pact. When organized in 1955, it had eight members—the Soviet Union, Poland, Czechoslovakia, Bulgaria, Hungary, Romania, Albania, and East Germany. The armed forces of these nations were placed under a unified command, with headquarters in Moscow. Albania withdrew from the pact in 1968, and Yugoslavia (another Communist country of Eastern Europe) never joined.

IDENTIFY OR DEFINE: iron curtain, superpower, Cold War, containment, Berlin Blockade, NATO, Warsaw Pact.

CRITICAL THINKING: How and why did the United States policy toward the Soviet Union change soon after World War II?

FOCUS ON ASIA

The Cold War extended to the Far East, where events threatened to plunge both superpowers into a "hot" war again.

1. Japan. At the end of World War II, U.S. troops, with General Douglas MacArthur in charge, occupied Japan. Japan was disarmed, its war industries dismantled, its war criminals tried, and its government made more democratic. (The emperor, however, was allowed to keep his throne.) Japan was forced to withdraw from territories it had seized during the war and to surrender all of its prewar acquisitions.

For five years, the Western Allies and the Soviet Union could not agree on a peace treaty for Japan. In 1951, the United States bypassed the Soviet Union and (with 48 other countries) signed a treaty with Japan. The treaty gave Japan back its independence. Japan promised to abide by the principles of the UN charter, and became a UN member in 1956.

2. China. Since the 1920s, Chinese Communists, led by Mao Zedong, had fought a civil war against the Nationalist government of Chiang Kai-shek. When the Japanese invaded China in 1937, the two Chinese blocs suspended their civil war so that they could both fight the invaders. But after Japan's defeat in 1945, they resumed their struggle.

At the end of the war, the Soviets gave huge quantities of captured Japanese weapons to the Chinese Communists. Although aided by the United States, the Nationalists were unable to withstand the stepped-up Communist attacks. In 1949, the victorious Mao's forces set up the People's Republic of China. Chiang and his Nationalist followers withdrew to Taiwan. The United States and the United Nations refused to recognize the new Communist government on the mainland. It regarded the Taiwan regime as the legitimate government of China.

3. The Korean War. Annexed by Japan in 1910, Korea came under Soviet and U.S. control in 1945 after Japan's defeat. The Soviet Union occupied Korea north of the 38th parallel; the United States, south of it. A single government was supposed to be set up after national elections. Instead, two rival nations emerged: North Korea, backed by the Soviet Union, and South Korea, with ties to the United States.

More than 500,000 U.S. troops served in the Korean conflict, 1950–1953.

a. Beginning of the conflict. In June 1950, North Korea invaded South Korea. The UN Security Council ordered North Korea to withdraw, but it refused. The Council called on all UN members to help enforce its demands. (The Soviet Union could not veto the resolution because it was boycotting UN meetings at the time.) Although other UN members besides the United States pledged aid, the war was fought mainly by South Korean and U.S. troops. Douglas MacArthur commanded the UN forces in Korea.

After capturing the capital city of Seoul, the North Koreans pushed the UN forces southward. In September 1950, with only a small area around the southeastern city of Pusan remaining in UN hands, MacArthur launched a counterattack. He landed 50,000 U.S. troops 150 miles north of enemy lines. UN troops in the Pusan area began to drive northward. MacArthur forced the invaders back across the 38th parallel and captured the North Korean capital of Pyongyang. Then he moved toward the boundary between North Korea and China.

b. Chinese intervention. In November 1950, more than 200,000 Chinese soldiers from the People's Republic entered North Korea from Manchuria. They drove the UN armies south, crossing the 38th parallel, and advancing 70 miles into South Korea. In the spring of 1951, UN troops counterattacked and forced the enemy back into North Korea. The opposing lines continued to face each other about 25 miles north of the 38th parallel.

To drive Chinese troops from Korea, MacArthur wanted to bomb military targets in China and allow Nationalist Chinese troops from Taiwan to invade China. Truman opposed this plan because it might involve the United States in a large-scale war with China and the Soviet Union. MacArthur persisted and attempted to gain the support of Congress. Truman responded by removing MacArthur from his command.

c. Negotiating peace. In July 1951, the two sides in the Korean War began to discuss a cease-fire. They soon came to a deadlock over the issue of exchanging prisoners. The Communists demanded the forced *repatriation* (return) of all prisoners held by the UN side. The UN insisted on voluntary repatriation—prisoners themselves deciding whether to go back to their homeland. After two years of negotiations, the Communists accepted the principle of voluntary repatriation.

A *cease-fire* agreement was signed in July 1953. Each side withdrew 1 1/4 miles from the final battle line, thus forming a 2 1/2-mile

READING A MAP

The Korean War

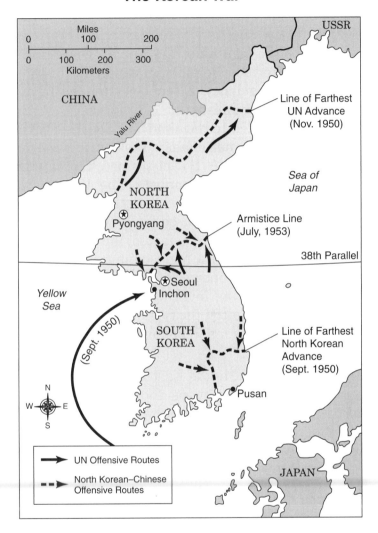

1. Name the Asian countries in this map that are separated by the Yalu River.

2. Name the capitals of North and South Korea.

3. What has been the significance of the 38th parallel?

wide *demilitarized zone* between them. U.S. troops have remained in South Korea to help maintain the uneasy truce.

FURTHER CHALLENGES TO PEACE

Six months before the signing of the Korean cease-fire, Dwight D. Eisenhower, the victorious Republican candidate in the 1952 election, assumed the presidency. Eisenhower tended to avoid armed confrontation with Communists.

When the French tried to reclaim their Southeast Asian possessions after World War II, nationalists there who wanted independence resisted the French. A Soviet-trained Communist, Ho Chi Minh, led the Vietnamese nationalists. The United States aided France with money and supplies, but by 1954, the French cause seemed doomed. Eisenhower refused to allow direct intervention by U.S. troops, and the French were defeated. Vietnam was then divided into a Communist north and a non-Communist south. The United States became the main supporter of South Vietnam.

When a popular uprising in Hungary in 1956 threatened Communist control of that country, the Soviets brutally put down the rebellion. The United States made no military response.

1. Southwest Asia. The Middle East was important to the United States because of its vast oil fields and its location, and because it contained the Suez Canal, one of the world's main shipping routes. It was also the home of the Jewish state of Israel, re-established in 1948. As the only democracy in the region, Israel developed a friendly relationship with the United States.

a. The Suez Canal. In 1956, President Gamal Abdel Nasser of Egypt sought international support to build a huge dam at Aswan on the upper Nile River. It would supply irrigation and hydroelectric power and help control flooding. The United States and Britain withdrew promised financial help after Nasser strengthened ties with the Soviet Union. Nasser then seized control of the Suez Canal, which had been owned and operated by a private company with mostly British and French shareholders. Nasser planned to operate it and use the toll money to pay for the Aswan Dam.

Israel, meanwhile, had been troubled by border raids from Egypt. (The Egyptians and other Arab nations in the region had sworn to destroy the Jewish state.) In October 1956, Israel invaded Egypt and advanced to within a few miles of the Suez Canal. A British-French force also invaded Egypt and seized the northern part of the canal. The Egyptians then scuttled a number of their own ships in the waterway, making it unusable. The United Nations, with U.S. and Soviet support, criticized the actions of Israel, Britain, and France. The three countries agreed to a cease-fire, and a UN emergency force went to Egypt to supervise the truce. UN engineering teams cleared the Suez Canal, which was reopened to shipping in 1957.

b. The Eisenhower Doctrine. After the Suez crisis, President Eisenhower authorized economic and military aid to any Southwest Asian nation requesting help against Communist aggression. This policy became known as the Eisenhower Doctrine. It was the basis for U.S. intervention in Lebanon in 1958 to help put down a civil war there.

2. Soviet-U.S. Relations. Relations between the United States and the Soviet Union shifted several times in the 1950s. The first "thaw" grew out of the death of Stalin in 1953. The new Soviet leader, Nikita Khrushchev, brought some increase in freedom within the Soviet Union and a spirit of greater cooperation abroad.

In 1949, the Soviet Union successfully tested an atomic bomb. Early in the 1950s, both the Soviets and the Americans developed

"Don't Mind Me—Just Go Right On Talking"

even more powerful hydrogen bombs. In 1955, the leaders of the United States, Britain, France, and the Soviet Union met to discuss nuclear arms control. This summit conference resulted in an increase in cultural exchanges between East and West. Improved relations led to a visit by Khrushchev to the United States in the summer of 1959.

Eisenhower planned to visit the Soviet Union in 1960, after another summit conference in Paris. Just before this meeting, though, Khrushchev announced that a U.S. spy plane had been shot down over the Soviet Union. The United States admitted that it had been flying such planes, called U-2s, over the Soviet Union for several years. Khrushchev broke up the Paris meeting and canceled his invitation to Eisenhower.

3. Latin America. During World War II, all the Latin American nations but Argentina actively supported the Allied cause. After the war, they all joined the United Nations. They also allied themselves with the United States in the Organization of American States (OAS), founded in 1948 to promote cooperation and prevent disputes.

Despite these alliances, relations between the United States and Latin America during the Cold War period were not always friendly. Many Latin Americans felt that the United States was too overbearing. Americans controlled much of the wealth in Latin America. They cooperated with wealthy landowners and with local rulers, who were often dictators. The majority of Latin Americans were poor. But most U.S. government aid was going to Europe and Asia, not to Latin America.

Revolts and military takeovers were common. In 1959, Fidel Castro overthrew the Cuban dictator Fulgencio Batista. At first, most Americans were sympathetic to Castro. But they changed their minds when he seized U.S. property, executed hundreds of opponents, and announced that he was a Communist. Soon, Khrushchev pledged Soviet military aid to Cuba. The United States then broke off diplomatic relations with Cuba (1961), and the OAS excluded Cuba from active membership (1962).

IDENTIFY OR DEFINE: Mao Zedong, Chiang Kai-shek, Ho Chi Minh, Gamal Abdel Nasser, Nikita Khrushchev, Fidel Castro.

CRITICAL THINKING: Do you think General Douglas MacArthur was correct in wanting to bomb China and allow Nationalist troops to invade the Chinese mainland? Why or why not?

Chapter Review

MATCHING TEST

Column A	Column B
1. denazification	*a.* Western military alliance
2. George Kennan	*b.* plan aimed at preventing spread of communism in the Middle East
3. NATO	
4. George C. Marshall	*c.* secretary of state under President Truman
5. Eisenhower Doctrine	*d.* author of containment policy
	e. program aimed at removing Hitler's followers from important posts in Germany

MULTIPLE-CHOICE TEST

1. In 1946, Winston Churchill used the term iron curtain to describe (*a*) the Ruhr River Basin (*b*) the imbalance between developed and developing countries (*c*) opposition by colonial powers to independence movements in their colonies (*d*) a division between Soviet-dominated countries of Eastern Europe and democratic countries of Western Europe.

2. The "Big Three" leaders met in (*a*) Tehran, Yalta, and Potsdam (*b*) Moscow, London, and Washington, D.C. (*c*) Berlin, Tokyo, and Rome (*d*) Reykjavik, Geneva, and Vienna.

3. The UN agency that has the power to approve military actions is the (*a*) Security Council (*b*) General Assembly (*c*) Trusteeship Council (*d*) Secretariat.

4. Two countries that were the object of U.S. military and economic aid under the Truman Doctrine were (*a*) Great Britain and France (*b*) the Soviet Union and Poland (*c*) Spain and Italy (*d*) Greece and Turkey.

5. Two permanent members of the Security Council are (*a*) the United States and Canada (*b*) Russia and China (*c*) Great Britain and India (*d*) France and Austria.

6. A Communist nation that never joined the Warsaw Pact was (*a*) Hungary (*b*) Poland (*c*) Yugoslavia (*d*) Romania.

7. The followers of Chiang Kai-shek in China were known as (*a*) Communists (*b*) Boxers (*c*) Nationalists (*d*) Fascists.

8. The Communist nation that sent over 200,000 troops to help North Korea during the Korean War was (*a*) Cuba (*b*) East Germany (*c*) the Soviet Union (*d*) China.

9. The general in charge of UN forces in Korea was (*a*) George Patton (*b*) Dwight Eisenhower (*c*) Bernard Montgomery (*d*) Douglas MacArthur.

10. In the Suez Crisis, the United States sided with (*a*) the Soviet Union (*b*) Great Britain (*c*) France (*d*) Israel.

 ESSAY QUESTIONS

1. What was the Cold War? When, how, and why did it come about?

2. What was containment? How effective was it as a policy?

3. One historian has written: "The Marshall Plan was a superb blend of ideals and self-interest in diplomacy." Explain.

4. What were some achievements of the United Nations?

5. Describe the main events of the Korean War.

DOCUMENT-BASED QUESTION

This question is based on the accompanying documents (1–5). It will improve your ability to work with historical documents.

Historical Context:

After World War II, the United States had close relations with Western European countries, Japan, and South Korea. It provided them with large amounts of economic and military aid. Through NATO, the United States became a military ally of many of these countries. In contrast, U.S. relations with the Soviet Union, its Warsaw Pact allies, China, and North Korea were poor, partly because of the Communist governments these countries had. Perhaps more important was the aggressive foreign policies of the Soviet Union, China, and North Korea.

Task:

Using information from the documents and your knowledge of United States history, read each document and answer the question that follows it. Your answers to the questions will help you write the document-based essay.

Document 1. Excerpt from President Harry Truman's announcement that the United States would help South Korea resist armed attack from North Korea, June 27, 1950:

> The attack upon Korea makes it plain beyond all doubt that communism has passed beyond the use of subversion to conquer independent nations and will now use armed invasion and war. It has defied the orders of the Security Council of the United Nations.
>
> Source: *Congressional Record*, 81st Congress, 2nd Session, p. 9228.

In what new way did President Truman see communism as a threat to world peace?

Document 2. President Truman wanted to fight a limited war in Korea. But U.S. Army General Douglas MacArthur, the commander of UN forces in Korea, openly challenged Truman's limited war strategy. Instead, he called for an invasion of China. As a result, the president relieved MacArthur of his command. Excerpt from President Truman's explanation to the American people on why he supported a limited war, April 11, 1951:

> So far, by fighting a limited war in Korea, we have prevented aggression from succeeding and bringing on a general war. . . . We are trying to prevent a world war—not start one. . . . If we were to [extend the war into China], we would become entangled in a vast conflict on the continent of Asia and our task would become immeasurably more difficult all over the world. What would suit the ambitions of the Kremlin [Soviet Union] than for our military forces to be committed to a full-scale war with Red China?
>
> Source: *The New York Times*, April 12, 1951, p. 4.

What reasons did President Truman give for not wanting to extend the war into China?

Document 3. Excerpt from a letter sent to President Truman in response to his "firing" of General MacArthur:

April 11, 1951

Dear Mr. President:

AMVETS [American Veterans] support your painful decision to relieve General Douglas MacArthur of his command. . . . AMVETS recognize . . . that the issue here is not whether General MacArthur is right or wrong or whether administration policies are right or wrong. The issue clearly and simply is whether the ultimate civil authority of the United States can tolerate, no matter what the motives, actions in contempt of constitutional lines of authority. Any lessening of civil power over military power must inevitably lead away from democracy.

Sincerely yours,

Harold Russell
National Commander

Source: www.pbs.org/wgbh/amex/macarthur/filmmore/reference/primary/letters01.html

What is the reference to "constitutional lines of authority" about?

Document 4. Excerpt from another letter sent to President Harry S Truman:

April 12, 1951

Dear Mr. President:

You have thrown into the trash-pile all that has been accomplished in Japan in the last five years. . . . You have sold us out, just as your noble predecessor sold us out at Yalta. . . . Your dismissal of Douglas MacArthur confirms your devotion to Communist Russia. . . . You have fired a man whose first and whole devotion has been to the best Interest of our country.

Yours sincerely, (and don't bother with the form letter reply)
Elizabeth Wood

Source: *ibid.*

What is the reference to Yalta about?

Document 5. Excerpt from General MacArthur's remarks to Congress, April 19, 1951:

The Communist threat is a global one. Its successful advance in one sector threatens the destruction of every other sector. . . . I made it clear that if not permitted to destroy the enemy built-up bases north of the Yalu, if not permitted to utilize the friendly Chinese force of some 600,000 men on Formosa, if not permitted to blockade the China coast to prevent the Chinese Reds from getting succor [aid] from without, and if there were to be no hope of major reinforcements, the position of the command from the military standpoint forbade victory. . . . War's very object is victory, not prolonged indecision. In war there can be no substitute for victory.

Source: *The New York Times*, April 20, 1951, p. 4.

What is the reference to the "friendly Chinese force" on Formosa about?

DOCUMENT-BASED ESSAY

Using information from the above documents and your knowledge of United States history, write an essay in which you:

- Explain whether you would have supported President Truman's actions regarding General Douglas MacArthur. Give reasons for your answer.

CHAPTER 18

Prosperity, Idealism, and Commitment

The United States experienced some readjustment problems after World War II. It soon overcame them, however, and entered the greatest era of prosperity it had ever known.

TRUMAN'S PRESIDENCY

When Truman became president in April 1945, he had definite ideas about what he hoped to achieve. But he met stiff opposition to many of his proposals.

1. Return to a Peacetime Economy. To ease the return of U.S. servicemen to civilian life, Congress passed the GI Bill of Rights. It provided them with cash payments, education at government expense, unemployment benefits, and loans to buy homes and businesses.

Instead of war materials, industries began to produce peacetime goods. The removal of price controls and the great demand for consumer goods caused a sharp rise in prices. Demanding pay increases to keep up with the rising cost of living, workers in several major industries went on strike. The higher prices and strikes, together with mounting production costs, led to inflation.

2. A Mixed Record. Unlike Roosevelt, Truman did not start out with solid Democratic support in Congress. He was further weakened after the Republicans won majorities in both houses of Congress in 1946.

a. Labor issues. Congress was able to pass the Taft-Hartley Act (1947) over Truman's veto. It aimed to curb the power of labor unions and to correct labor abuses, such as misuse of union funds. Among other things, it banned (*1*) the *closed shop* (a plant where only union members may be hired), (*2*) union contributions to political campaigns, and (*3*) *jurisdictional strikes* (strikes called when two unions dispute the right to represent workers). The law compelled unions to file annual financial reports. It required union leaders to take an oath that they were not members of the Communist party. In addition, the law provided for a "cooling-off" period of 60 days before a strike could be called. The Taft-Hartley Act did not end labor abuses, as its backers had hoped. Nor did it decrease union membership, as its opponents had feared.

b. Twenty-Second Amendment. Congress disapproved of Roosevelt's length of service, which broke the two-term tradition established by George Washington. It introduced the Twenty-Second Amendment, limiting future presidents to election to two terms in office. The amendment was ratified in 1951.

c. Civil rights and the election of 1948. Aiming to help African Americans, Truman asked Congress to enact laws against lynching and poll taxes, and to set up a commission to combat discriminatory hiring practices. Southern senators blocked these proposals by threatening to *filibuster*. Acting on his own, Truman appointed the first African-American federal judge, named African Americans to other federal offices, and began to desegregate the armed forces.

When Truman ran for election in his own right in 1948, Southern Democrats formed the States' Rights ("Dixiecrat") party. Its presidential candidate, Strom Thurmond, was extremely conservative. The Democratic party was further split by leftists who found Truman too conservative. They favored Henry Wallace, candidate of a new Progressive party. The Republicans nominated Thomas E. Dewey, governor of New York. Few people expected Truman to win the election. But he won a surprise victory, and the Democrats regained control of Congress.

d. The Fair Deal. After his 1948 election win, Truman launched a domestic reform program that he called the Fair Deal. He expected the Democratic majority in Congress to help pass his proposals. These included an increase in the minimum wage, an expansion of Social Security, increased public housing and slum clearance, federal aid to education, and national health insurance. But Congress enacted only the first three proposals. Concern over helping religious schools blocked federal aid to education. The American Medical Association criticized national health insurance as "socialistic."

THE HUNT FOR SUBVERSIVES

The Cold War made Americans extremely concerned about subversives. (*Subversives* are people who try to weaken or overthrow a government.) As early as 1947, Truman set up loyalty boards to investigate federal employees. Workers could be fired if there were "reasonable grounds" to believe that they were disloyal. By 1951, more than 3 million employees had been cleared, about 2,000 had resigned, and some 200 had been fired.

1. Important Trials. A series of trials in the late 1940s and early 1950s increased concern over Communist subversion.

a. Hiss. One case involved Alger Hiss, a former high-ranking State Department employee. Journalist Whittaker Chambers accused Hiss of having been a Communist spy in the 1930s. When Hiss denied the charge, he was tried for *perjury* (lying in court under oath). Too much time had passed since the alleged crime had occurred to try him for spying. Hiss was convicted, serving almost four years in prison. This Hiss-Chambers affair cast doubts on the Democratic administration.

b. Rosenbergs. More sensational was the trial of Ethel and Julius Rosenberg. They were accused of passing atomic secrets to the Soviet Union. The Rosenbergs had been involved with left-wing politics for years. In their trial, they refused to discuss whether they were Communists but denied that they had been spies. They were found guilty of treason in 1951 and were executed.

2. McCarthyism. Widespread fear of subversion prompted Congress to pass the McCarran Act (1950). It required Communist groups to

A 1954 HERBLOCK CARTOON, COPYRIGHT BY THE HERB BLOCK FOUNDATION

"I have here in my hand—"

register with the Justice Department and barred Communists from employment in defense plants. It also allowed the deportation of any alien who was a member of a Communist, Nazi, or Fascist organization and forbade the entry of such persons into the United States. Most of the act's provisions were later declared unconstitutional.

In 1950, Senator Joseph R. McCarthy of Wisconsin charged that there were 205 Communists (later reduced to 57) in the State Department. A special Senate subcommittee conducted an investigation and declared his charges false. But by then, he had moved on to other targets.

For some four years, McCarthy was constantly in the public eye. He made sweeping attacks on various branches of the government, the Protestant clergy, higher education, and the media. Fearful of being accused of employing subversives, many organizations carried out "witch hunts" of their own. They fired the innocent, along with the guilty. "McCarthyism" came to mean hysterical anticommunism.

McCarthy eventually went too far. He accused the U.S. Army of harboring Communists. Televised hearings before a Senate committee convinced many viewers that McCarthy was a bully and a liar. His influence waned in 1954 when the Senate finally *censured* (officially reprimanded) him for his conduct.

The hysteria finally died down. But it had damaged or destroyed the reputations and careers of many Americans. It also weakened the influence of moderate anti-Communists trying to alert the public to real threats from the Soviet Union.

IDENTIFY OR DEFINE: GI Bill of Rights, filibuster, States' Rights party, subversives, McCarthyism.

CRITICAL THINKING: How can President Truman be considered a reformer?

EISENHOWER IN THE WHITE HOUSE

When Truman decided not to run again in 1952, the Democrats nominated Governor Adlai Stevenson of Illinois as their candidate for president. The Republicans chose Dwight D. Eisenhower, a popular hero of World War II. Republicans campaigned on the theme that it was "time for a change" (and time to end the war in Korea). "Ike" Eisenhower scored an overwhelming victory, receiving 442 electoral votes to Stevenson's 89. In 1956, Eisenhower ran against Stevenson a second time. The president won re-election by an even greater margin than before: 457 to 73.

1. The Middle of the Road. Eisenhower tried to steer a course between extremes. He disliked McCarthy but did not take a public stand against him until late in the senator's career. In foreign affairs, he wanted to keep the Soviets in check without going to war.

Eisenhower's attitude toward the role of the federal government was contradictory. He attacked the Tennessee Valley Authority as an example of "creeping socialism." In his view, state and local ownership of natural resources was preferable to national ownership. And yet, his administration was responsible for two giant federal projects: (*1*) One was a program for interstate highways. A 41,000-mile network of new, limited-access roads would link most of the nation's cities at a cost of more than $100 billion. (*2*) The other was the St. Lawrence Seaway, a huge transportation and hydroelectric project undertaken jointly with Canada. Completed in 1959, it enabled oceangoing vessels to travel from the Atlantic to ports on the Great Lakes.

2. The Warren Court. Probably the most significant appointment of Eisenhower's presidency was that of Earl Warren, former governor of California, as chief justice of the United States. The Warren Court, which lasted from 1953 until 1969, handed down a number of controversial decisions.

a. School desegregation. An African-American girl, Linda Carol Brown, was not allowed to enroll in an all-white public school in Topeka, Kansas. Her father, backed by the NAACP, sued on the grounds that she was being denied equal protection of the laws. In *Plessy* v. *Ferguson* (1896), the Supreme Court had ruled that "separate but equal" accommodations for African Americans and whites

EISENHOWER ON THE MILITARY-INDUSTRIAL COMPLEX

In the councils of Government, we must guard against the acquisition of unwarranted influence, whether sought or unsought, by the *military-industrial complex*. The potential for the dangerous rise of misplaced power exists and will persist.

—Dwight D. Eisenhower, Farewell Address, January 1961

were constitutional. In *Brown* v. *Board of Education of Topeka* (1954), the Court reversed the earlier decision. The justices ruled unanimously that "Separate educational facilities are inherently unequal."

The Court recommended in 1955 that local school districts carry out *desegregation* "with all deliberate speed." But many Southerners, including 100 members of Congress, vowed to resist desegregation. Every September brought tension, and often violence, as African-American children tried to enroll in white schools. Eisenhower remained silent on the issue until the fall of 1957. When rioting broke out in Little Rock, Arkansas, he sent in federal troops to maintain order. Desegregation in schools and in other public institutions came about slowly.

b. Other decisions. The Warren Court also made far-reaching decisions regarding criminal justice. In *Gideon* v. *Wainwright* (1963), the Court ruled that persons accused of a felony have a right to free legal services if they are too poor to pay for a lawyer. In *Escobedo* v. *Illinois* (1964), the justices declared that a criminal suspect cannot be denied a lawyer during questioning. The *Miranda* v. *Arizona* decision (1966) held that suspects must be warned of their rights to be silent or to have a lawyer present when they are questioned. Many Americans opposed these rulings, arguing that they made law enforcement too difficult. Widespread opposition was also touched off by Supreme Court decisions that forbade organized prayer and Bible reading in public schools. Conservative groups even demanded Warren's impeachment.

3. Progress Against Discrimination. Eisenhower completed the desegregation of the armed forces, begun under Truman. In 1957, Congress passed the first civil rights law since Reconstruction. It removed some of the obstacles that prevented African Americans from voting and set up a special division in the Justice Department to protect the rights of African Americans.

But the efforts of African Americans working on their own made the greatest difference in desegregation. Pressure from the NAACP and similar groups spurred the integration of schools and other institutions. In Montgomery, Alabama, in 1955, Rosa Parks was arrested for not giving her bus seat to a white man. African Americans then organized a boycott of the local bus system that eventually led to its desegregation. The boycott's leader, the Reverend Martin Luther King, Jr., gained national prominence as a civil rights activist.

America's first lunch counter sit-in, February 2, 1960, in Greensboro, North Carolina.

A VARIETY OF ACHIEVEMENTS

By the mid-20th century, Americans were excelling in almost every field of human endeavor. The products of their ingenuity and creativity, ranging from soft drinks and movies to automobiles and computers, were in demand all over the world.

1. The "Affluent Society." Beginning in the late 1940s, the United States entered a 20-year period of unmatched prosperity. The GNP rose to levels undreamed of earlier. Americans attained one of the highest standards of living the world had ever known. Employment was up and so were wages. Consumer goods, in short supply during the war, now enjoyed record sales. By the mid-1950s, nine out of ten American families owned a refrigerator, three out of four owned at least one car, and three out of five owned a house.

Another postwar phenomenon was a *baby boom*. The soaring birthrate caused the nation's population to grow almost 20 percent between 1950 and 1960. Many families moved to suburbs, attracted by government housing aid, new highways, cheap gasoline, and open spaces.

Economist John Kenneth Galbraith called the United States in the 1950s an "affluent society." But he was very critical of this

READING A TABLE

Immigration to the United States, by World Areas, 1951–1980

Area	1951–1960	1961–1970	1971–1980
Europe	1,492,200	1,238,600	801,300
Asia	157,000	445,300	1,633,800
Latin America	841,300	1,579,400	1,929,400
Africa	16,600	39,300	91,500
Australia and New Zealand	5,000	13,600	19,600
Other areas	3,300	5,500	17,700
Total	2,515,400	3,321,700	4,493,300

1. In the period 1951–1960, immigration to the United States was greatest from which area?

2. In the periods 1961–1970 and 1971–1980, immigration to the United States was greatest from which area?

3. After 1960, an area that showed a decline in the number of immigrants coming to the United States was which one?

4. Of the total number of immigrants to the United States in the period 1951–1960, Europeans made up about what percent?

---

wealth. Many Americans lived well in private, he said, but skimped on public services. Schools, hospitals, parks, and transportation systems were consistently run-down and badly maintained. Furthermore, Galbraith wrote, the affluence was far from universal. In 1957, over 32 million people, nearly one-fifth of the total population, had incomes below the poverty level.

2. Science and Technology. During and after World War II, the government, large corporations, and universities worked together to achieve scientific and technological breakthroughs. The most notable advance was the development of atomic energy, in which refugees from fascist Europe played a key role. They included Albert Einstein from Germany, Enrico Fermi from Italy, and Leo Szilard

and Edward Teller from Hungary. One milestone was the 1954 launching of the first nuclear-powered submarine, the *Nautilus*. Another milestone that same year was the opening of the first U.S. nuclear power plant, at Shippingport, Pennsylvania.

a. Medicine. Advances in medicine helped bring hope to millions. None was more welcome than a polio vaccine developed by Jonas Salk in the early 1950s. Beginning in 1955, millions of Americans took the vaccine. Incidence of the disease dropped 80 percent. It was further reduced after the introduction in 1961 of an oral vaccine developed by Albert Sabin.

In 1963, John Enders got a license for a vaccine that reduced the incidence of measles. Antibiotic drugs developed by Selman Waksman proved useful in treating serious bacterial infections. Antihistamines eased the discomfort of allergy sufferers, while cortisone helped combat such crippling diseases as rheumatoid arthritis.

b. Space. Americans were shocked in 1957 when the Soviet Union sent the first artificial satellite, *Sputnik*, into orbit around the Earth. The United States then stepped up its own space program. In 1958, the National Aeronautics and Space Administration (NASA) was created, and the first U.S. satellite, *Explorer I*, was launched.

The Soviet Union continued to achieve a number of "firsts" in space. It sent a cosmonaut into orbit in 1961, and three cosmonauts in one vehicle in 1964. A Russian made the first "space walk" in 1965.

The United States quickly matched these feats. In 1962, John Glenn became the first American to orbit the Earth. Three years later, the first U.S. space walk was carried out, and two U.S. spaceships completed the world's first meeting in space. In the mid-1960s, NASA began Project Apollo, designed to land astronauts on the moon. In 1969, Neil Armstrong and Edwin Aldrin became the first humans to set foot on the moon's surface.

After Project Apollo, NASA focused on a *space shuttle* program. Unlike earlier projects, this one featured reusable launch vehicles, promising greater economy and, thus, more frequent voyages. American astronauts piloted the world's first reusable space shuttle in 1981.

In 1995, astronaut Norman Thagard joined the crew of an orbiting Soviet space station. From this cooperative venture, NASA learned firsthand how humans react to extended periods in space.

The many space probes—with and without astronauts—have yielded much new data about weather, the sun's rays, and the other planets in our solar system. Orbiting communications satellites now aid in relaying international radio, telephone, and television signals.

c. Electronics. Several innovations, such as X-ray tubes and radio, grew out of the branch of electrical engineering called electronics. But electronics came into its own only with the replacement of bulky vacuum tubes by tiny transistors.

One electronic device that took firm hold in the United States after World War II was television. The first sets for home use were sold in the 1930s, but output was held down by World War II. In 1947, some 14,000 U.S. families owned television sets. The first presidential inauguration to be televised was Truman's in 1949. The national nominating conventions of 1952 were the first to be televised nationally. The new medium demonstrated its power when televised hearings by a Senate committee helped end Senator McCarthy's career in 1954.

Even more revolutionary in its impact on U.S. society was the computer. This electronic device could store huge quantities of data and process it in seconds. The first mass-produced computer went on the market in 1951. Within 20 years, computers were being used to direct space flights; set type; book airline seats; keep inventories; and prepare payrolls, bills, and bank statements. In industry, computers took over many complex operations, from making aspirin to pouring steel. This industrial development, known as *automation*, had a serious drawback—a decrease in the demand for unskilled labor. Computer applications, however, opened up many new jobs for skilled technicians.

3. Entertainment. After World War II, television replaced radio as the nation's favorite home entertainment. Night after night, whole families sat watching comedy shows, variety programs, and movies. Television excelled in drama, sports, and news. An estimated 600 million people in 49 countries watched Neil Armstrong step out onto the moon. But TV's prime purpose was to sell products, and the general level of programming was low. The chairman of the FCC once called television a "vast wasteland."

Television made spectator sports a bigger business than ever. Millions of fans watched football, baseball, and basketball games. One of the most important sports milestones of the immediate postwar era had little to do with television, however. This was the end of segregation in professional sports. In 1947, Jackie Robinson, hired by the Brooklyn Dodgers, became the first African-American player in major league baseball. In succeeding years, African-American and Hispanic athletes won fame in nearly all sports—from track and basketball to golf and tennis.

Musical entertainment also flourished during and after the war. Outstanding Broadway shows of the period included *Oklahoma!* (1943), *South Pacific* (1949), *The King and I* (1951), and *West Side Story* (1957). These and many similar shows were later produced as movies. A new kind of music, rock and roll, became popular in the 1950s. It combined elements of country music and rhythm and blues, always with an insistent beat. In the 1960s, as rock, this music became more sophisticated, louder (with electronic help), and more elaborately performed.

IDENTIFY OR DEFINE: military-industrial complex, *Brown* v. *Board of Education*, baby boom, John Glenn, Rosa Parks.

CRITICAL THINKING: How did electronics change American life after World War II?

THE KENNEDY YEARS

In 1960, the Republicans nominated Eisenhower's vice president, Richard M. Nixon, for president. The Democratic candidate was a young senator from Massachusetts, John Fitzgerald Kennedy (JFK). Millions of Americans watched the two candidates in a series of televised debates. Kennedy projected an image of youth and vigor, while Nixon looked awkward and insecure. Some people wondered if

Kennedy's Roman Catholicism would lose him votes among Protestants. In the end, his religion seemed not to have made a big difference.

In the election, the popular vote was very close. Kennedy received 34,227,000 votes to Nixon's 34,109,000. But Kennedy carried most of the larger states, winning 303 electoral votes to Nixon's 219. Kennedy was the youngest man ever elected president.

1. Foreign Affairs. Soon after his inauguration, Kennedy proposed two new foreign aid programs. Both went into effect in 1961.

a. Peace Corps. The Peace Corps was designed to promote world friendship. Since its founding, the Peace Corps has sent more than 175,000 volunteers to developing countries. They live among the people, teach English, train workers to operate modern machinery, and demonstrate improved methods of farming and sanitation.

b. Alliance for Progress. Much of Latin America suffered from economic distress and political instability. Kennedy asked the countries of the Western Hemisphere "to join a new Alliance for Progress." The project was to use U.S. capital and technical skill to foster Latin American domestic reform and self-help. Unfortunately, funds from the United States were limited and Latin American countries were slow to enact reforms.

c. Bay of Pigs. After the 1959 revolution in Cuba, many Cubans fled to the United States to escape Castro's oppressive rule. The U.S. Central Intelligence Agency (CIA) trained a small army of these exiles to overthrow Castro. In April 1961, with President Kennedy's approval, some 1,500 of these troops were landed at the Bay of Pigs in Cuba. But Kennedy had second thoughts about the invasion and called off planned air support at the last minute. Also, an expected uprising of anti-Castro Cubans did not take place. Within three days, Castro's army had crushed the invaders.

d. Tensions in Germany. Since 1948, the Soviet Union had made periodic attempts to force the United States, Britain, and France to withdraw their troops from West Berlin. In 1961, the Soviets tried again. They also insisted that, before the end of the year, the Allies sign a peace treaty confirming the existing division of Germany. The Allies rejected these demands. Kennedy called for an increase in NATO forces and a buildup of U.S. military strength. Suddenly, the East Germans put up a fortified wall between East and West Berlin. The Berlin Wall closed off an escape route that some 3 million East Germans had used since 1949 to flee to the West.

In response, Kennedy ordered additional U.S. troops to Berlin. He also sent Vice President Lyndon Johnson to assure West Berliners that the United States would not abandon them. Faced with this display of U.S. force and determination, the Soviets backed down on their demands.

e. Cuban Missile Crisis. In the fall of 1962, photographs taken by U.S. planes showed that Soviet technicians were building missile-launching sites and airfields for long-range jet bombers in Cuba. Medium-range missiles were already in place, and installations for intermediate-range missiles were nearing completion. These would be capable of delivering nuclear warheads to most targets in North America.

Kennedy set up a blockade of Cuba by ordering U.S. armed forces to turn back any ship carrying offensive military equipment to the island. He also demanded that existing missiles be dismantled and removed immediately. The Soviet leaders called back ships that were carrying offensive weapons to Cuba and agreed to dismantle their

In August 1963, some 200,000 people assembled in Washington, D.C., to demonstrate for the passage of civil rights laws and legislation to provide more jobs. Rev. Martin Luther King, Jr., spoke at the rally: "I have a dream that my four little children will one day live in a nation where they will not be judged by the color of their skin but by the content of their character. . . ."

missile bases and remove the missiles. Kennedy, in turn, promised to lift the blockade and assured the Soviets that the United States would not invade Cuba. Secretly, the United States agreed to dismantle some missiles in Turkey that were aimed at the USSR.

After the Cuban Missile Crisis subsided, the two superpowers agreed to set up a telephone hotline between Moscow and Washington, D.C. Its purpose was to permit instant communication between the two capitals. The two nations, along with Great Britain, signed the Nuclear Test-Ban Treaty in 1963. It banned the testing of nuclear weapons in the atmosphere, in outer space, and underwater (but not underground).

2. The New Frontier. Kennedy called his ambitious domestic program the New Frontier. It included aid to education, medical care for the aged, and tax reforms to encourage economic growth. Although Democrats controlled Congress, its leading members had little interest in reform. As a result, most of Kennedy's proposals bogged down in Congress.

a. Civil rights. Kennedy tried to achieve progress in civil rights without confronting Congress. For instance, when the University of Mississippi refused to admit a black student, he sent in troops to protect the student's right to enroll. The government brought suit in several state courts to secure voting rights for blacks deprived of the franchise. Using his executive powers, Kennedy issued an order barring racial and religious discrimination in federally aided housing.

Civil rights groups continued to fight discrimination. Inspired by the leadership of Rev. Martin Luther King, Jr., they followed a policy of *nonviolent civil disobedience*—peaceful refusal to obey laws regarded as unjust. They held *sit-ins* at segregated public eating places and transportation facilities. In August 1963, peaceful protesters staged a vast March on Washington.

b. Assassination. On November 22, 1963, while riding in an open car to address a luncheon gathering in Dallas, Texas, Kennedy was shot by a sniper and killed. Lee Harvey Oswald was charged with the slaying. But Oswald was murdered before he could be brought to trial. Vice President Johnson was immediately sworn in as president. His confidence and firmness reassured the nation and helped ease the shock of the sudden change in leadership.

IDENTIFY OR DEFINE: Bay of Pigs, Berlin Wall, Cuban Missile Crisis, Rev. Martin Luther King, Jr., nonviolent civil disobedience, sit-in.

CRITICAL THINKING: What were the aims of the Peace Corps and the Alliance for Progress? How successful was *each* of these programs?

JOHNSON AND THE GREAT SOCIETY

Lyndon Baines Johnson declared his intention to build a "Great Society." His goals included peace and freedom throughout the world, improved living conditions for Americans, and encouragement and support of the arts and sciences. In the first few years of his administration, Johnson won congressional approval for several key Kennedy proposals and for a number of his own Great Society recommendations.

The Civil Rights Act of 1964 had been one of Kennedy's proposals. It contained some of the broadest guarantees of equal rights for African Americans ever passed by Congress. The federal government gained additional authority to speed school desegregation, curb violations of voting rights, and end racial discrimination by employers and unions. The act also outlawed segregation in such public places as hotels, restaurants, stores, and theaters.

1. Democratic Victory in 1964. Johnson was the natural Democratic choice for president in 1964. Senator Hubert H. Humphrey of Minnesota was picked as his running mate. The Republicans chose Senator Barry M. Goldwater of Arizona, a conservative, as their presidential candidate.

Goldwater called for a more aggressive policy toward communism abroad. On domestic matters, he felt that the expanding powers of the federal government were destroying Americans' self-reliance and freedoms. He was particularly critical of social welfare programs. Goldwater also believed that civil rights issues should be handled by the states and local communities.

Johnson emphasized the need for restraint in foreign policy in order to prevent the outbreak of nuclear war. He defended the welfare state and pledged to expand the federal programs already in effect. Johnson won by a landslide. He received a record-breaking popular vote of 43 million to Goldwater's 27 million, and 486 electoral votes to his opponent's 52. The Democrats also strengthened their hold on Congress.

2. New Programs. Before his victory in 1964, Johnson had declared a "War on Poverty" and set up an Office of Economic Opportunity to coordinate this many-sided effort. A Job Corps aimed to train un-employed youths. A domestic peace corps, called VISTA, sent volunteers into poor regions of the United States. After the election, Johnson persuaded Congress to pass Project Head Start, which offered preschool learning programs for poor children, and a Community Action Program, which was designed to help city neighborhoods. Johnson also focused his attention on securing laws to broaden civil rights, provide medical care for the aged, improve education, reduce environmental pollution, and revitalize inner cities.

The Immigration Act of 1965 would change the face of immigration to the United States. It provided that the former system of national quotas be eliminated by July 1968. Instead, it set up a new quota system, one that especially favored immigrants from the Western Hemisphere and from Asia. (See the table on page 359.)

Conservatives opposed the growth in federal programs. Even Americans who favored Johnson's aims felt that many of the projects were poorly planned and administered. When ambitious schemes did not succeed, people became disappointed and angry. Beginning in 1964, urban riots destroyed buildings and took lives summer after summer, particularly in poor African-American neighborhoods.

WAR IN VIETNAM

The main reason for Johnson's limited success with his Great Society programs was the country's increasing involvement with the war in Vietnam.

1. Background. In 1954, France gave up Vietnam, its former colony in Southeast Asia. The country was then divided into two states—a Communist one in the north and an anti-Communist one in the south. In North Vietnam, Ho Chi Minh led the Vietminh party, which ruled with Soviet and Chinese support. In South Vietnam, the United States supported a pro-Western government that was fighting local Vietminh sympathizers there (known as the Vietcong). U.S. leaders feared a *domino effect* in Southeast Asia. They believed that if one non-Communist country there became Communist, nearby countries would topple until the whole region was in the Communist camp.

In 1956, South Vietnam refused to permit an election aimed at uniting all of Vietnam. South Vietnamese officials became increasingly dictatorial in their efforts to suppress the Vietcong. In 1959, North Vietnam began to arm and train the Vietcong to overthrow the South Vietnamese government. In response, the United States increased its aid to South Vietnam. The Kennedy administration sent more military equipment and more advisers to the South Vietnamese army. But South Vietnam was unable to curb the Vietcong.

2. Increased U.S. Involvement. Lyndon Johnson was determined not to let South Vietnam fall to communism. In 1964, two U.S. destroyers reported that North Vietnamese gunboats had fired on them in the Gulf of Tonkin. Johnson asked Congress to pass a resolution authorizing the president to "take all necessary measures to repel any armed attack against forces of the United States and to prevent further aggression." Armed with this *Tonkin Gulf Resolution*, Johnson poured troops into South Vietnam. North Vietnam countered by sending its troops into the south. The United States then bombed strategic targets in North Vietnam. By mid-1968, more than 500,000 U.S. troops were fighting in South Vietnam. Thousands more were stationed on ships offshore and at nearby bases. U.S. war costs rose sharply—from $6 billion in 1966 to $29 billion in 1969.

3. Opposition to the War. By 1967, there was widespread opposition in the United States to the increasing *escalation* (stepping up) of the war. Nightly TV newscasts showed U.S. "search-and-destroy" missions causing Vietnamese civilians great suffering. A growing number of Americans felt that the United States should not inter-

CANFIELD IN THE NEWARK EVENING NEWS

"When I started, he was just about so big."

fere in what they considered a civil war. Some criticized the South Vietnamese government as corrupt and undemocratic, and thus not worth defending. Opponents of the war held peace demonstrations and protested against the draft.

Johnson's popularity declined. In the presidential campaign of 1968, antiwar Democrats challenged him for the party's nomination. In March of that year, Johnson ordered a halt to U.S. bombing of North Vietnam. He also stated that he would neither seek nor accept nomination for another term.

The presidential campaign of 1968 centered largely on the war in Vietnam. The Democrats nominated Johnson's vice president, Hubert Humphrey, who defended the administration's record. The Republicans chose former Vice President Richard Nixon, who pledged to end the war but offered few concrete suggestions for doing so. A Democratic split aided Nixon. Antiwar Democrats gave Humphrey only lukewarm support. Many conservative Democrats favored George Wallace's American Independent party. In the election, Nixon's popular margin was not large, but his electoral votes were substantial—302 to Humphrey's 191.

Four years later, Nixon ran for a second term. His Democratic opponent was Senator George McGovern of South Dakota. Nixon scored an overwhelming victory, carrying 49 states.

4. Continuing Conflict. Nixon continued cease-fire talks that had begun late in Johnson's term. And he urged "Vietnamization" of the war. By this he meant that the South Vietnamese should begin to assume a larger share of the fighting. From 1969 to 1972, almost 500,000 U.S. soldiers were pulled out of Vietnam, leaving about 60,000. Protests against the war died down in 1969.

Then in the spring of 1970, Nixon sent thousands of U.S. troops to destroy North Vietnamese supply sites in Cambodia. Massive antiwar demonstrations sprang up again in Washington, D.C., in other cities, and on college campuses. At Kent State University in Ohio, members of the National Guard killed four students taking part in an antiwar rally.

Later in the year, Congress repealed the Gulf of Tonkin Resolution. Nixon, however, ignored this move. In the spring of 1972, the North Vietnamese launched an all-out drive against key South Vietnamese positions. Nixon then resumed the bombing of strategic targets in North Vietnam. He also authorized the mining of North Vietnamese ports and the bombing of rail and highway links with China. The heaviest U.S. bombings of the war occurred in December 1972.

READING A MAP

War in Southeast Asia, 1964–1976

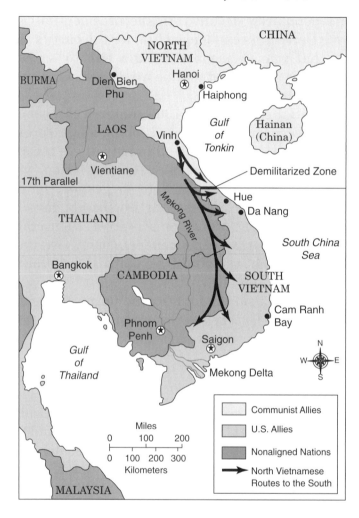

1. Name *three* Southeast Asian countries that were officially neutral or nonaligned.

2. What river flows past the capital cities of two of these countries?

3. Which location would more likely have been the site of a large U.S. military base in the 1960s—Haiphong or Cam Ranh Bay?

4. Through which non-Vietnamese countries did North Vietnam send soldiers and supplies to South Vietnam?

5. Cease-Fire and Final Withdrawal. Formal peace talks had been going on in Paris since 1968. Finally, in January 1973, the delegates hammered out an agreement that was acceptable to all. Despite this cease-fire, fighting soon erupted again throughout South Vietnam. Early in 1975, the North Vietnamese launched a major offensive. The South Vietnamese army retreated. At the end of April, South Vietnam surrendered. In 1976, North and South Vietnam were reunited as the Socialist Republic of Vietnam. Hanoi was made its capital. Native Communist groups, aided by North Vietnam, also gained control of two neighboring countries—Laos and Cambodia.

By war's end, U.S. casualties totaled more than 57,000 dead and 150,000 wounded. U.S. war costs were in excess of $100 billion. At least a million Vietnamese, both southerners and northerners, died as a result of the war. Countless others were wounded or made homeless. The Vietnam War was the longest war in U.S. history.

IDENTIFY OR DEFINE: War on Poverty, Job Corps, VISTA, Tonkin Gulf Resolution, Vietnamization.

CRITICAL THINKING: What problems at home and abroad limited the effectiveness of President Johnson's domestic reform programs?

Chapter Review

 MATCHING TEST

Column A	Column B
1. Jonas Salk	*a.* first African American in major league baseball
2. Jackie Robinson	*b.* person responsible for famous bus boycott in 1955
3. John Glenn	*c.* chief justice of United States from 1953 to 1969
4. Rosa Parks	*d.* first U.S. astronaut in space
5. Earl Warren	*e.* inventor of polio vaccine

> ### MULTIPLE-CHOICE TEST

1. The Taft-Hartley Act was an attempt to (*a*) legalize the closed shop (*b*) curb the power of big labor (*c*) prohibit collective bargaining (*d*) prevent the growth of craft unions.

2. The Twenty-Second Amendment (*a*) abolished prohibition (*b*) changed the date of presidential inaugurations (*c*) limited presidents to two terms (*d*) lowered the voting age.

3. Truman's Fair Deal proposals included all of the following *except* (*a*) school desegregation (*b*) increased public housing (*c*) national health insurance (*d*) federal aid to education.

4. The Bay of Pigs is in (*a*) Vietnam (*b*) Cuba (*c*) Germany (*d*) Russia.

5. The Alliance for Progress was aimed at ending economic hardship in (*a*) Southeast Asia (*b*) Africa (*c*) Latin America (*d*) Southwest Asia.

6. All of the following took place during Eisenhower's administration *except* (*a*) the beginning of an interstate highway program (*b*) construction of the St. Lawrence Seaway (*c*) the *Brown* v. *Board of Education* decision (*d*) the Rosenbergs' trial.

7. In the case of *Miranda* v. *Arizona*, the Supreme Court ruled that (*a*) legislative districts should be redrawn (*b*) organized school prayer is unconstitutional (*c*) criminal suspects have to be told of their rights before they are questioned (*d*) everyone being tried for a felony is entitled to a lawyer.

8. U.S. astronauts first set foot on the moon in (*a*) 1957 (*b*) 1958 (*c*) 1964 (*d*) 1969.

9. The use of computers to direct industrial operations is known as (*a*) miniaturization (*b*) electronics (*c*) automation (*d*) the factory system.

10. One outcome of the Cuban Missile Crisis was the establishment of a telephone hotline between Washington, D.C., and (*a*) London (*b*) Havana (*c*) Berlin (*d*) Moscow.

 ### ESSAY QUESTIONS

1. What was McCarthyism? When and why did it flourish? What were its main results?

2. Describe the background of the *Brown* v. *Board of Education* decision. What did the Supreme Court rule? Why was its decision important?

3. Describe *two* other major decisions of the Supreme Court under Chief Justice Warren. Why were they controversial?

4. What led to the Cuban Missile Crisis of 1962? How was the crisis resolved?

5. What was an argument in support of U.S. involvement in Vietnam? Against U.S. involvement? Formulate a position on the war as if you were a college student in 1970.

DOCUMENT-BASED QUESTION

This question is based on the accompanying documents (1–6). It will improve your ability to work with historical documents.

Historical Context:

During the 1950s and 1960s, the United States entered a period of prosperity it had never known before. But it was a prosperity that could not hide discontent.

Task:

Using information from the documents and your knowledge of United States history, read each document and answer the question that follows it. Your answers to the questions will help you write the document-based essay.

Document 1. Study the cartoon on page 354.

The person in the cartoon was so well known to the public in the early 1950s that the cartoonist did not have to identify him. Who is the person in the cartoon and what was the cartoonist accusing him of doing?

Document 2. Excerpt from Jack Kerouac's book *On the Road*, first published in 1957:

> [T]he only people for me are the mad ones, the ones who are mad to live, mad to talk, mad to be saved, . . . the ones who never yawn or say a commonplace thing, but burn, burn, burn like fabulous yellow roman candles exploding like spiders across the stars.

Source: Kerouac, Jack. *On the Road*. NY: Penguin Group (USA), 2002, p. 8.

What do you think Kerouac meant by the word "mad," which he used four times?

Document 3. Study the photograph on page 358.

What is the significance of what is happening in the photograph?

Document 4. Excerpt from Michael Harrington's book *The Other America*, first published in 1962:

> The poor live in a culture of poverty. . . . The poor get sick more than anyone else in the society. . . . When they become sick, they are sick longer than any other group in the society. Because they are sick more often and longer than anyone else, they lose wages and work, and find it difficult to hold a steady job. And because of this, they cannot pay for good housing, for a nutritious diet, for doctors . . . [and] their prospect is to move to an even lower level . . . toward even more suffering.
>
> **Source**: Reprinted with permission of Scribner, an imprint of Simon & Schuster Adult Publishing Group from *The Other America: Poverty in the United States*, by Michael Harrington, p. 15. Copyright © 1962, © 1969, © 1981 by Michael Harrington; copyright renewed © 1990 by Stephanie Harrington.

What do you think Harrington meant by the term "culture of poverty"?

Document 5. Excerpt from Betty Friedan's book *The Femine Mystique*, 1963:

> The problem lay buried, unspoken, for years in the minds of American women. It was a strange stirring, a sense of dissatisfaction, a yearning that women suffered in the middle of the twentieth century in the United States. Each suburban wife struggled with it alone. As she made the beds, shopped for groceries, matched slipcover material, ate peanut butter sandwiches with her children, chauffeured Cub Scouts and Brownies, lay beside her husband at night—she was afraid to ask even of herself the silent question—"Is this all?"
>
> **Source**: Friedan, Betty. *The Feminine Mystique*. NY: Dell Publishing Co. Copyright © 1983, 1974, 1973, 1963. Used by permission of W.W. Norton & Company, Inc.

What did Friedan think women in the 1950s were yearning for?

Document 6. Excerpt from a speech by Rev. Martin Luther King, Jr., in which for the first time he publicly opposed U.S. involvement in the war in Vietnam, April 4, 1967:

Somehow this madness must cease. We must stop now. I speak as a child of God and brother to the suffering poor of Vietnam. I speak for those whose land is being laid waste, whose homes are being destroyed, whose culture is being subverted. I speak for the poor of America who are paying the double price of smashed hopes at home, and dealt death and corruption in Vietnam. I speak as a citizen of the world, for the world as it stands aghast at the path we have taken. I speak as one who loves America, to the leaders of our own nation: The great initiative in this war is ours; the initiative to stop it must be ours.

> **Source**: www.mousemusings.com/musings/social/text_beyond_vietnam.html

Why did King feel that he had to speak out against the war?

DOCUMENT-BASED ESSAY

Using information from the above documents and your knowledge of United States history, write an essay in which you:

- Explain whether U.S. prosperity in the 1950s and early 1960s could hide discontent among Americans.

CHALLENGES OF THE MODERN ERA

19
Political Concerns in a Troubled Period

The 200th anniversary of U.S. independence in 1976 led to serious discussions about the national purpose. As one historian put it, "Americans seemed to be discovering limits for the first time—the limits of their own national virtue and the limits of their world power."

Observers noted that the balance of power in the United Nations was shifting. In earlier years, the majority of UN members had belonged to either the Western bloc or the Communist bloc. The *Western bloc* (sometimes called the Free World or the First World) consisted of the United States and most of the countries of the Western Hemisphere and Western Europe. The *Communist bloc* (sometimes called the Second World) was made up of the Soviet Union and its satellites. By the 1970s, a third group, made up mostly of newer members from Asia and Africa, tried to pursue a course independent of either of the superpowers. The *Third World*, as these nonaligned states were called, dominated the General Assembly, which began to have more power than the Security Council.

THE NIXON YEARS

As the United States entered the 1970s, Richard Nixon was president. He came to the presidency after serving as a representative and senator in Congress and then as vice president under Dwight D. Eisenhower.

Nixon was especially interested in foreign affairs. In this field, he worked closely with his national security adviser (later secretary of state), Henry Kissinger. Among other things, Kissinger negotiated the Vietnam cease-fire in 1973. Nixon and Kissinger wanted to downplay Cold War divisions and tensions. They concentrated their efforts on the two most powerful Communist nations, the Soviet Union and China.

1. Détente With the Soviet Union. During Nixon's administration, relations between the United States and the Soviet Union entered a phase referred to as *détente*. (This French word means "easing of tension.") One sign of détente was an attempt to reduce armaments. Since the 1950s, both the United States and the Soviet Union had been developing ever more powerful nuclear weapons. Some, known as *intercontinental ballistic missiles* (*ICBM*s) were offensive weapons, capable of reaching targets thousands of miles away. Others, intended for defense, were *antiballistic missiles* (*ABM*s). Each superpower was capable of completely destroying the other. When people were not worrying about a possible nuclear war, they worried about the enormous cost of the arms race.

In 1969, the United States and the Soviet Union agreed to begin Strategic Arms Limitation Talks (SALT). In 1972, President Nixon became the first U.S. president since World War II to visit the Soviet Union. He and Soviet Premier Leonid Brezhnev officially signed the SALT I agreement, which froze the number of long-range missiles each could have. The two leaders also planned joint space efforts, further arms reductions, and cultural and scientific exchanges. Nixon agreed to end a U.S. trade ban with the Soviet Union that had been in place since 1949. The Soviet Union, faced with serious food shortages, soon ordered $750 million worth of American grains.

2. Recognizing China. Ever since 1949, the United States had regarded the Nationalist regime on Taiwan, instead of the People's Republic, as the legitimate government of China. As time went by, this policy seemed to make less sense. The People's Republic ranked first in world population and third in size.

In 1971, the president announced to a startled world that he would visit China the following year. Nixon's trip began a long process of normalizing relations between the United States and the People's Republic. Trade and travel restrictions were eased, and a brisk exchange of people and goods developed. In 1971, the UN accepted the People's Republic as a member and expelled the Nation-

President Nixon (second from left) in China, 1972.

alists. In 1979, during President Jimmy Carter's administration, the United States cut its formal ties with Nationalist China and established full diplomatic relations with the People's Republic.

3. Domestic Strategies. Nixon's domestic policy was conservative. He believed that the pace of reform in the 1960s had been too fast. Government, he said, was interfering too much in people's lives. He appealed to what he called "Middle America" or the "silent majority."

a. The Supreme Court. Nixon felt that some Supreme Court justices had become "super-legislators with a free hand to impose their social and political viewpoints upon the American people." Before leaving office, he appointed four Supreme Court justices, including Chief Justice Warren Burger. But the Burger Court's decisions did not always please Nixon. One of its most controversial was *Roe* v. *Wade* (1973). It stated that a woman had a constitutional right to an abortion during her first three months of pregnancy.

b. Economic problems. By the time of Nixon's administration, the U.S. economy was not as stable as it had been in the 1950s and early 1960s. Inflation was at a record high, mainly because Johnson had spent a great deal on war and social reforms without increasing taxes. Economic growth was slow, and unemployment was rising. This combination of economic stagnation and inflation is known as *stagflation*.

Then, too, in 1973 the Organization of Petroleum Exporting Countries (OPEC)—a group of major oil-producing nations—suddenly decided to limit their exports of oil. They also raised the price of oil higher than it had ever been. Higher oil prices led to higher costs for many basic necessities, including gasoline, heating oil, electricity, plastics, and synthetic fibers.

c. Attempted solutions. Beginning in August 1971, Nixon tried a system of wage and price controls to halt inflation. As a result, the inflation rate did fall, only to rise when controls were lifted in April 1974. By the late 1970s, Americans experienced *double-digit inflation* (the cost of living rose 10 percent or more a year).

Nixon also tried to lower federal spending by cutting social welfare programs. He abolished the Office of Economic Opportunity and reduced funds for job training, urban renewal, and education assistance. Nixon introduced what he called the New Federalism. States and localities were to assume greater responsibility for social services. To help them do so, Nixon proposed a system of *revenue sharing*. Under this program, the federal government returned to the states, counties, and cities some of the taxes it had collected. This money could be used for ordinary operating expenses, as well as for needed improvements. Many localities found, however, that these federal funds did not cover all the services they were now expected to provide.

4. The Watergate Crisis. Nixon's presidency is remembered less for its accomplishments than for a domestic scandal that abruptly ended his administration.

a. The beginnings. During Nixon's 1972 reelection campaign, five men were arrested for breaking into the Watergate building in Washington, D.C., where the Democratic National Committee headquarters were located. James McCord, the security coordinator of the Republican Committee for the Re-election of the President (CREEP), led the intruders. They had cameras and electronic "bugging" devices.

In January 1973, the five Watergate intruders and two higher-ups accused of directing the break-in were convicted of conspiracy, burglary, and wiretapping. But two months later, the trial judge, John Sirica, disclosed a letter from McCord. It charged that McCord and the other defendants had been pressured to plead guilty and remain silent. It also stated that "others" were involved in the spying and that government witnesses had committed perjury during the trial.

b. Unfolding scandal. A special Senate committee chaired by Sam Erving of North Carolina and a Justice Department investigation led by Archibald Cox began to reexamine the case. It came to light that White House staff members and CREEP officials had planned the Watergate break-in. To sabotage activities of Democratic candidates, money raised by CREEP had been illegally used for the break-in. The money was also used to buy the silence of the Watergate defendants during their trial. The administration also seemed to have been involved in other illegal operations to collect damaging evidence about its opponents. The president fired a number of high-ranking administration officials. Many of them were later brought to trial, found guilty, and sent to jail.

c. The White House Tapes. During the Senate committee hearings in the summer of 1973, one witness revealed that Nixon had secretly tape-recorded many conversations at the White House and elsewhere. The Senate committee and Special Prosecutor Cox asked to hear certain tapes. Nixon refused on the grounds that surrendering them would injure national security, the doctrine of separation of powers, and the integrity of the presidency.

In October 1973, a court ordered Nixon to turn over to Cox some key tapes. The president offered him written summaries instead. When Cox rejected the offer, Nixon ordered that he be fired. The attorney general resigned rather than dismiss Cox. The deputy attorney general did likewise. This "Saturday Night Massacre" prompted calls for Nixon's impeachment. He then agreed to surrender the disputed tapes.

d. Agnew's resignation. As the Watergate Affair was unfolding, the Justice Department was also investigating Vice President Spiro Agnew for extortion and tax fraud and for accepting bribes while governor of Maryland and vice president. Agnew resigned in October 1973. He pleaded "no contest" to a charge of federal income tax evasion. Then he was given three years probation and fined $10,000. Nixon nominated Representative Gerald R. Ford of Michigan to succeed Agnew.

e. Nixon's resignation. Nixon responded to demands for additional tapes by supplying only *transcripts* (written versions), with many deletions. But in July 1974, the Supreme Court ordered him to surrender the requested tapes. These revealed that Nixon had been involved in the Watergate events almost from the beginning.

After six months of investigation, the Judiciary Committee of the House of Representatives recommended that the House vote to impeach the president. The grounds for this action were that Nixon had

(1) misused the powers of his office, *(2)* violated the constitutional rights of citizens, and *(3)* refused to cooperate with the committee. Impeachment by the House and conviction by the Senate seemed likely. Therefore, Nixon resigned on August 9, 1974. He was the first president in the nation's history to resign from office.

FORD'S PRESIDENCY

Gerald Ford became president immediately after Nixon resigned. Ford named Nelson A. Rockefeller, former governor of New York, as his vice president. He continued Nixon's basic foreign and domestic policies. Most important, Ford presided over the final U.S. withdrawal from Vietnam.

In September, Ford granted Nixon "a full, free, and absolute pardon" for all federal crimes that he "committed or may have committed or taken part in" while in office. Ford explained that he wished to avoid the "prolonged and divisive debate" that might have resulted from the indictment and trial of a former president. He also wanted to spare Nixon further punishment. Some Americans hailed the pardon as an act of mercy. Others felt that pardoning the chief offender in the Watergate Affair and punishing his underlings violated the constitutional principle of equal justice for all.

The Ford administration had a major accomplishment in foreign affairs. In 1975, after three years of talks, representatives of the United States, Canada, and 33 European nations (including the Soviet Union) met in Helsinki, Finland. In the Helsinki Agreement, they promised *(1)* greater East-West economic cooperation, *(2)* respect for human rights, *(3)* the freer movement of people and ideas from one country to another, and *(4)* acceptance of the changes that had taken place in European boundaries since World War II. Despite the Helsinki Agreement, the Soviet Union continued to suppress free speech by exiling or imprisoning Soviet dissidents who publicly criticized the government. It also denied exit visas to many Soviet Jews who wanted to emigrate to Israel. And it harassed foreign correspondents whose reports displeased Soviet authorities.

IDENTIFY OR DEFINE: détente, SALT, *Roe* v. *Wade*, OPEC, revenue sharing, White House Tapes.

CRITICAL THINKING: What was the Saturday Night Massacre and why was it significant in the Watergate Affair?

CARTER IN THE WHITE HOUSE

Gerald Ford ran for election as president in his own right in 1976. The Democrats nominated James Earl (Jimmy) Carter, a former governor of Georgia. Carter was little known outside his state. But his promise to make government "as good and decent as are the American people" struck a responsive chord. He won by a slim margin, receiving 297 electoral votes to his opponent's 240. His running mate, Senator Walter Mondale of Minnesota, became vice president.

1. An Outsider in Washington. During his campaign, Carter had stressed that he was an outsider in Washington—unspoiled by "politics as usual." Once elected, however, he realized that to accomplish anything he would have to deal with the existing institutions of government. His sincerity was genuine, but he could not win Congress's support for his proposals to reform the welfare system and the tax structure.

Early in his administration, Carter proposed a national energy bill designed to conserve domestic oil supplies and reduce dependence on imports. But opposition in Congress to various parts of the bill prevented its passage. Congress did, however, approve the creation of the Department of Energy in 1977.

The cost of foreign oil continued to rise, and a political upheaval in Iran cut off imports from that country. In 1979, Carter consulted about the problem with experts in many fields. He proposed an ambitious energy program that would take ten years and cost $142 billion. Included were proposals to develop synthetic fuels and solar energy. The public reacted unfavorably to Carter's gloomy outlook, and Congress passed only a scaled-down version of his proposals.

Carter's most serious domestic problem was the economy. By the end of his term, inflation had reached almost 12 percent a year. To bring it down, the Federal Reserve Bank raised interest rates to high levels. These were especially damaging to the construction and automobile industries because loans to home buyers and auto buyers were more expensive.

2. Foreign Affairs. Respect for individual *human rights* became a key element in the Carter administration's foreign policy. The United States warned South Africa that it could lose U.S. support if it continued to deny equal rights to its black majority. The administration reduced foreign aid to Argentina, Uruguay, and Ethiopia because of human rights violations there. It barred exports of advanced computers and specialized oil equipment to the Soviet Union because that country suppressed free speech and restricted its citizens' right to emigrate. When the Soviets suddenly invaded Afghanistan in 1979, Carter cut off sales of grain and high-tech equipment to the USSR.

a. The Panama Canal treaties (1977). For decades, the people of Panama had resented U.S. control over the Panama Canal. In 1964, violent anti-American riots led to negotiations on a new treaty that would satisfy Panama's demands and safeguard U.S. interests. An agreement was reached 13 years later. Two Panama Canal treaties provided for the transfer of control of the waterway by the end of 1999. The United States would retain the right to use about a third of the former Canal Zone for military bases, canal operations, and employee housing.

b. Two Israeli-Arab wars. Tense relations between Israel and its Arab neighbors were a continuing concern throughout the world. After the Suez crisis of 1956, there was an uneasy peace until 1967, when Israel was threatened by a joint Arab invasion. In the so-called "Six-Day War," Israel defeated Egypt, Jordan, and Syria. As a result, the Israelis gained complete control over Jerusalem, which had formerly been split between Israel and Jordan. They also took the Sinai Peninsula and the Gaza Strip from Egypt, the Golan Heights from Syria, and land along the West Bank of the Jordan River from Jor-

From the left, Egyptian President Anwar Sadat, President Jimmy Carter, and Israeli Prime Minister Menachem Begin shake hands during a White House announcement, September 18, 1978, of the accord reached at the Camp David summit.

dan. War broke out again in 1973, when Egypt and Syria launched a surprise attack on the Israelis in the Sinai and on the Golan Heights. The Soviet Union gave aid to the Arab side, while United States helped the Israelis. A UN emergency force supervised a cease-fire and thus prevented a major confrontation between the two superpowers.

c. The Camp David Accord (1978). In 1977, President Anwar Sadat of Egypt agreed to discuss a peace settlement with Israel—the first to be negotiated by an Arab state. But the talks between Sadat and Menachem Begin, Israel's prime minister, faltered in 1978. This failure prompted President Carter to meet privately with the two leaders at Camp David in Maryland. There they agreed on a tentative accord. The 30-year state of war between Egypt and Israel ended in March 1979, when Sadat and Begin signed a formal peace treaty in Washington, D.C.

d. The Hostage Crisis. After Iran in 1979 deposed its ruler, Shah Mohammed Reza Pahlevi, Islamic fundamentalists took over the country. The Shah had been a longtime ally of the United States. In October 1979, he entered the United States for medical treatment. In protest, Iranian militants stormed the U.S. Embassy in the capital city of Tehran. They took more than 60 hostages and vowed to keep them until the Shah was returned to Iran to stand trial.

When months of diplomacy failed to obtain the release of the hostages, Carter approved a helicopter rescue mission. It failed, too. Even after the Shah's death in July 1980, the captivity continued. Only after the election of a new U.S. president did Iran return the hostages to the United States, in January 1981.

IDENTIFY OR DEFINE: Helsinki Agreement, Panama Canal treaties, Camp David Accord, Iranian Hostage Crisis.

CRITICAL THINKING: How important was President Carter's role in normalizing relations between Egypt and Israel?

REAGAN: A SHIFT TO THE RIGHT

The Republican candidate for the presidential campaign of 1980 was Ronald Reagan, a former movie actor and governor of California. He appealed to conservative interests. Carter, on the other hand, had been damaged by the long hostage crisis, the lagging economy, and continuing high inflation. He fared poorly. Reagan won an overwhelming victory in the electoral vote—489 to 49. Four years later, running against Democratic candidate Walter Mondale, Reagan won reelection by an even greater landslide—525 to 13.

Reagan's victories marked the end of the New Deal coalition that had held together for nearly 50 years. Many who voted for Reagan had formerly thought of themselves as traditional Democrats—union members, the lower middle class, and members of certain ethnic groups. As a bloc, only African-American voters remained firmly in the Democratic camp. Since the New Deal, the federal government had assumed more and more responsibility for the well-being of citizens. Reagan's policies aimed to reverse these trends, which he and his supporters felt had harmed the nation. Above all, he wanted to cure the nation's economic ills and strengthen its position in world affairs.

1. Dealing With the Nation's Economy. Reagan proposed a policy known as *supply-side economics*. It was based on the idea that the government should provide financial incentives and benefits to producers and investors—the suppliers of goods and services. If this were done, corporations and wealthy individuals would have more funds to invest. The economy would then expand, new jobs would open up, and prosperity would "trickle down" to the population at large.

a. The plan in action. To advance Reagan's economic program, Congress passed tax cuts in the early 1980s and again in 1986. Since the tax cuts reduced federal income, it became necessary to reduce government expenses. This reduction was accomplished by keeping some social programs from expanding and cutting back on others, such as welfare. Another aspect of Reagan's economic policy was *deregulation*. Started first during the Carter administration, deregulation meant eliminating or not enforcing government regulations by bodies such as the Environmental Protection Agency and the Food and Drug Administration. Federal financial aid to states and cities was also cut back.

b. Mixed results. The rate of inflation fell during the Reagan administration from 16 percent in 1980 to 4 percent in 1988. Unemployment generally remained low, too. When Reagan took office, the rate was 7.1 percent; when he left, it was down to 5.5.

But Reagan's economic policies had unfortunate effects as well. Deregulation led to a relaxation of antitrust prosecutions, which brought a rash of business mergers. Many companies were swallowed up or wiped out. Savings and loan institutions (S&Ls), allowed to broaden their investments, made many unwise loans. Numerous S&Ls failed. Since S&Ls were insured by the government, paying off insured S&L depositors cost taxpayers billions of dollars.

Another problem was huge budget deficits. When Reagan took office, he promised a balanced budget by 1984. But slashes in government spending did not make up for the money lost by cutting taxes. In addition, defense spending grew tremendously. The result was a growing gap between government income and expenses. During his administration, the national debt rose from $908 billion to $2.6 trillion.

2. Foreign Problems. Reagan and his supporters believed that Carter's foreign policy had endangered the nation. One remedy they proposed was the Strategic Defense Initiative (nicknamed "Star Wars"), a shield of laser weapons and space stations to intercept enemy missiles. Because of its huge projected costs and uncertain reliability, SDI had many critics, but work on it continued.

a. Central America and the Caribbean. Reagan tried to reassert U.S. authority in three countries of Latin America: (*1*) Revolt against the military regime of El Salvador began in 1980. The United States supported the Salvadoran government with money, military advisers, and intelligence. (*2*) In Nicaragua, Marxist rebels (called *Sandinistas*) overthrew the country's dictator in 1979. The

United States aided counterrevolutionary forces (the *contras*) after they attacked the government. (*3*) In 1983, the United States claimed that the island of Grenada was falling under Cuban Communist control. U.S. forces invaded Grenada and installed a new government more favorable to U.S. interests.

b. The Middle East. The United States was also involved in the Middle East. In the 1970s, a civil war in Lebanon broke out between Muslims and Christians. In 1982, Israel invaded Lebanon because Palestinian guerrillas based on Lebanese soil had been attacking Israel. U.S. marines participated in a multinational effort to restore peace. But after 241 U.S. Marines were killed as a suicide terrorist drove an explosive-laden truck into their barracks, Reagan ordered U.S. forces withdrawn from Lebanon.

A complex series of events linking Lebanon, Iran, and Nicaragua came to light in 1986. Some American hostages were still being held in Lebanon. Moreover, it was widely believed that Iran supported the terrorists who held them. In an effort to obtain their release, U.S. representatives secretly sold weapons to Iran for its ongoing war with Iraq. Profits from the sales were then used to buy arms for the Nicaraguan contras. All of these activities were illegal because U.S. laws prohibited both arms sales to Iran and military aid to the contras.

U.S. government investigations of the Iran-Contra Affair implicated members of Reagan's National Security Council, some of whom were convicted of acting illegally. Reagan denied knowledge of the arms deal, and no evidence pointed to his involvement.

c. Relations with the Soviet Union. When he first became president, Reagan called the Soviet Union an "evil empire." Reagan changed his approach toward the USSR after Mikhail Gorbachev came to power in 1985. Although a committed Communist, Gorbachev wanted sweeping changes in the Soviet Union. He advocated *glasnost* (openness), which meant, among other things, relaxing censorship, allowing dissidents and others to emigrate, and candidly discussing the economic and social problems of the nation. Gorbachev also introduced *perestroika* (restructuring)—reforms to lessen central control of the economy. He hoped that elements of capitalism would improve the Soviet economy and the lives of ordinary Soviet people.

Gorbachev and Reagan met several times and established a friendly working relationship. They signed a treaty (INF) in 1987 that limited intermediate-range nuclear weapons in Europe.

IDENTIFY OR DEFINE: supply-side economics, deregulation, S&L Crisis, Sandinistas, contras, *glasnost, perestroika.*

CRITICAL THINKING: What effects were President Reagan's economic policies suppose to have on inflation, unemployment, and business?

A BUSH TAKES OVER

The Republican presidential candidate in 1988 was George H.W. Bush, Reagan's vice president. The Democrats nominated Michael Dukakis, the governor of Massachusetts. Bush benefited from Reagan's continued popularity and won a solid victory, with 54 percent of the popular vote and an electoral margin of 426 to 112.

1. Domestic Issues. A difficult issue facing Bush was an economy with a growth rate slower than at any time in the previous 45 years. Unemployment rose, and U.S. car and electronics manufacturers had trouble competing with Asian rivals, particularly those of Japan. A recession that began in 1990 limited funds needed to cope with urban decay, crime, drugs, and inadequate education and health-care systems. Bush had made a campaign pledge of "no new taxes." But he broke his pledge by raising income taxes on the wealthiest and taxing such items as gasoline, cigarettes, and liquor. Nevertheless, the gap between government income and expenses continued. In 1991, the U.S. budget deficit climbed to $268 billion, the highest to that time.

2. Foreign Concerns. Easing tensions in several regions of the world gave hope for a more peaceful future. While the United States did not play a prominent role in all instances, its careful diplomacy enabled it to steer a moderate course in difficult times. In Central America, the civil wars in both Nicaragua and El Salvador ended. In South Africa, white and black leaders negotiated to create a less racist, more democratic regime.

    a. The Middle East. The early 1990s saw an apparent end to the bloody civil war in Lebanon. Israeli-Palestinian negotiators seemed to settle long-standing differences between the two people.

    The West came to see Iraq as a serious menace to security in the region. Although Iraq's long war with Iran (1980–1988) had depleted its military forces, Iraqi dictator Saddam Hussein quickly rebuilt

During the Persian Gulf War of 1991, U.S. Marines patrolled near burning oil wells near Kuwait City. Iraqi forces had set fire to Kuwaiti oil fields before retreating north into Iraq.

them. In the summer of 1990, he suddenly invaded one of Iraq's oil-rich neighbors, Kuwait.

With UN approval, the United States organized an army of more than 500,000 Americans and some 265,000 others, including Egyptians, Saudi Arabians, British, and French. When the Iraqis ignored a UN deadline to withdraw from Kuwait by January 15, 1991, the U.S.-led forces launched a massive air and missile attack. This was followed by a 100-hour ground war, which led to Iraq's surrender and withdrawal from Kuwait. The six-week Persian Gulf War cost the allies about 300 combat deaths. Iraqi casualties totaled at least 100,000. Despite his defeat, Hussein remained in power. The United States and its allies refused to invade Iraq and drive him out.

b. End of the Cold War. Probably the most dramatic foreign development during the Bush administration was the end of the Cold War. The change began in 1980 with developments in Poland. There, an independent trade union called Solidarity won wide popular support. Its activities led to free elections in 1989 that forced out the Communist dictatorship and initiated a return to a free-market economy.

The Soviet Union allowed Poland, a former satellite, to determine its own future. The USSR also refused to intervene in a series of events that transformed Eastern Europe beginning in late 1989. In East Germany, widespread demands for reform and free access to the West led to the downfall of the hard-line Communist regime and the opening of the Berlin Wall. West and East Germany reunited as a single nation in 1990.

Meanwhile, revolutionary forces were at work in other Soviet satellites. In a few months, Hungary, Bulgaria, Czechoslovakia, and Romania overturned their dictatorships and set up more democratic regimes. The Warsaw Pact disbanded in July 1991. Yugoslavia came to an end as a unified country after ethnic violence split it apart into separate national units.

Turmoil swept the Soviet Union itself. In the Baltic region, Lithuania, Latvia, and Estonia declared their independence. Other Soviet republics began to break away as well. In late 1991, the Soviet Union officially disbanded. Gorbachev resigned. Most former Soviet republics formed a loose union, the Commonwealth of Independent States (CIS). Russia, the largest republic in the CIS, assumed the Soviet Union's seat on the UN Security Council. Russian President Boris Yeltsin became the dominant leader of the region after Gorbachev's resignation. Early in 1993, he and George Bush signed a far-reaching disarmament pact providing for big cuts in long-range nuclear missiles.

In 1989, demonstrators stood on top of the Berlin Wall as East German border guards looked on. The demonstration symbolized the opening of the Berlin Wall and movement of people between East and West Germany.

IDENTIFY OR DEFINE: Persian Gulf War, Kuwait, Iraq, Commonwealth of Independent States, Boris Yeltsin.

CRITICAL THINKING: How and when did the Persian Gulf War come about?

Chapter Review

 MATCHING TEST

Column A	**Column B**
1. Henry Kissinger	*a.* Soviet leader who came to power in 1985
2. Mikhail Gorbachev	
3. contras	*b.* association of oil-producing nations
4. OPEC	*c.* secretary of state under Nixon
5. Walter Mondale	*d.* vice president under Carter
	e. anti-Communist force in Nicaragua

▶ **MULTIPLE-CHOICE TEST**

1. A Communist country with which President Nixon made dramatic breakthroughs in improving relations was (*a*) Cuba (*b*) China (*c*) North Korea (*d*) Albania.

2. President Nixon attempted to curb inflation by (*a*) setting up wage and price controls (*b*) cutting taxes (*c*) increasing spending on domestic programs (*d*) encouraging greater investment.

3. Stagflation is a combination of (*a*) high oil prices and high unemployment (*b*) low unemployment and low inflation (*c*) economic stagnation and high inflation (*d*) economic stagnation and low inflation.

4. Nixon's vice president who resigned after criminal investigations were under way was (*a*) Archibald Cox (*b*) James McCord (*c*) Warren Burger (*d*) Spiro Agnew.

5. President Ford selected as his vice president (*a*) Nelson Rockefeller (*b*) Barry Goldwater (*c*) Ronald Reagan (*d*) Robert Dole.

6. A key element of President Carter's foreign policy was (*a*) rolling back communism (*b*) promoting human rights (*c*) reducing dependence on foreign aid (*d*) turning control of the Panama Canal over to Panama's government.

7. The arms control treaty that President Reagan signed with the Soviet Union was (*a*) SALT II (*b*) START I (*c*) ABM (*d*) INF.

8. Reagan's economic policies (*a*) balanced the budget by 1984 (*b*) reduced military spending (*c*) substantially increased the national debt (*d*) led to bankruptcy for the U.S. government.

9. Which was a campaign pledge President George H.W. Bush broke? (*a*) enact no new taxes (*b*) improve relations with Cuba (*c*) impose tariffs on Japanese imports (*d*) conclude no more arms control treaties with Russia.

10. The CIS is made up of most of the former lands of (*a*) Yugoslavia (*b*) Austria-Hungary (*c*) the Soviet Union (*d*) the United Arab Emirates.

 ESSAY QUESTIONS

---

1. Why did President Richard Nixon resign in 1974?

2. Do you think President Gerald Ford was correct to pardon Nixon? Explain your answer.

3. Why did Iranian militants seize and hold Americans as hostages in 1979? Why did they eventually release the hostages?

4. How and why did the Cold War come to an end?

5. What was President Clinton's main domestic achievement? Explain your choice.

DOCUMENT-BASED QUESTION

These questions are based on the accompanying documents (1–5). They will improve your ability to work with historical documents.

Historical Context:

From 1969 to 1992, the United States faced a number of domestic and international problems: Watergate, impeachment, a president never elected to a national office, inflation, assassination attempts, the Iranian Hostage Crisis, the end of the Cold War, and the Persian Gulf War. Some historians say that the Watergate Crisis was the country's major problem.

Task:

Using information from the documents and your knowledge of United States history, read each document and answer the question that follows it. Your answers to the questions will help you write the document-based essay.

Document 1. The following is an excerpt from John Dean's book *Blind Ambition: The White House Years* (1976). Dean, who served as President Richard Nixon's lawyer and later went to jail for obstruction of justice, recalled a meeting he had had with the president on March 21, 1973:

> "I think there's no doubt about the seriousness of the problem we've got," I said. "We have a cancer within—close to the Presidency—that's growing. It's growing daily. It's compounding. It grows geometrically now, because it compounds itself."

Source: Dean, John. *Blind Ambition: The White House Years*. NY: Simon and Schuster, 1976, p. 201.

What was the "cancer" that Dean was talking about?

Document 2. Excerpt from President Gerald R. Ford's speech of September 8, 1974, announcing a full and unconditional pardon for President Richard Nixon for any crimes he committed while in his office:

> After years of bitter controversy and divisive national debate, I have been advised, and I am compelled to conclude that many months and perhaps more years will have to pass before Richard Nixon could obtain a fair trial by jury in any jurisdiction of the United States under governing decisions of the Supreme Court. . . .
>
> During this long period of delay and potential litigation, ugly passions would again be aroused. And our people would again be polarized in their opinions. And the credibility of our free institutions of government would again be challenged at home and abroad. . . .
>
> Finally, I feel that Richard Nixon and his loved ones have suffered enough.

Source: http://www.ford.utexas.edu/library/speeches/740060.htm

How did Ford justify his decision to pardon Nixon?

Document 3. Excerpt from President Jimmy Carter's televised address to the nation, July 15, 1979:

In little more than two decades we've gone from a position of energy independence to one in which almost half the oil we use comes from foreign countries, at prices that are going through the roof. Our excessive dependence on OPEC has already taken a tremendous toll on our economy and our people. This is the direct cause of the long lines which have made millions of you spend aggravating hours waiting for gasoline. It's a cause of the increased inflation and unemployment that we now face. This intolerable dependence on foreign oil threatens our economic independence and the very security of our nation. The energy crisis is real. It is worldwide. It is a clear and present danger to our nation. These are the facts and we simply must face them. . . .

To give us energy security, I am asking for the most massive peacetime commitment of funds and resources in our nation's history to develop America's own alternative sources of fuel— from coal, from oil shale, from plant products for gasohol, from unconventional gas, from the sun.

Source: http://www.pbs.org/wgbh/amex/carter/filmmore/ps_crisis.html

Why did President Carter believe that dependence on foreign oil was "a clear and present danger" to the nation?

Document 4. Excerpt from President Ronald Reagan's speech at the Brandenburg Gate in West Berlin, June 12, 1987:

We hear much from Moscow about a new policy of reform and openness. Some political prisoners have been released. Certain foreign news broadcasts are no longer being jammed. Some economic enterprises have been permitted to operate with greater freedom from state control.

Are these the beginnings of profound changes in the Soviet state? Or are they token gestures, intended to raise false hopes in the West, or to strengthen the Soviet system without changing it? We welcome change and openness; for we believe that freedom and security go together, that the advance of human liberty can only strengthen the cause of world peace. There is one sign the Soviets can make that would be unmistakable, that would advance dramatically the cause of freedom and peace.

General Secretary Gorbachev, if you seek peace, if you seek prosperity for the Soviet Union and Eastern Europe, if you seek liberalization: Come here to this gate! Mr. Gorbachev, open this gate! Mr. Gorbachev, tear down this wall!

Source: http://www.reaganfoundation.org/reagan/speeches/wall.asp

What more did Reagan say the Soviets could do if they were serious about their new policies of reform and openness?

Document 5. Excerpt from President George H.W. Bush's televised address on January 16, 1991, announcing the beginning of military operations to expel Iraq from Kuwait:

> This conflict started August 2nd when the dictator of Iraq invaded a small and helpless neighbor. Kuwait—a member of the Arab League and a member of the United Nations—was crushed; its people, brutalized. . . .
>
> This military action, taken in accord with United Nations resolutions and with the consent of the United States Congress, follows months of constant and virtually endless diplomatic activity on the part of the United Nations, the United States, and many, many other countries. Arab leaders sought what became known as an Arab solution, only to conclude that Saddam Hussein was unwilling to leave Kuwait. . . .
>
> Now the 28 countries with forces in the Gulf area have exhausted all reasonable efforts to reach a peaceful resolution—have no choice but to drive Saddam [Hussein] from Kuwait by force.

> **Source:** http://www.historyplace.com/speeches/bush-war.htm

What efforts to resolve the crisis peacefully were taken but, in the opinion of the president, failed?

DOCUMENT-BASED ESSAY

Using information from the above documents and your knowledge of United States history, write an essay in which you:

- Explain how the presidents of the United States from Nixon to George H.W. Bush exercised leadership such as making decisions, pursuing certain policies and initiatives, and using their influence to win public and even international support for their policies.
- Explain what successes and failures they had and what, in your opinion, they should have done differently.

CHAPTER 20

Political Partisanship and the War on Terrorism

The Democratic President Bill Clinton and his Republican successor, George W. Bush, had different methods of handling a growing ideological split between liberal Democrats and conservative Republicans. Clinton tried to establish common ground between the two parties on issues such as the economy and foreign policy. He tried to avoid direct confrontation with his opponents by compromising with them. Nonetheless, partisanship increasingly damaged his administration. By embracing some of the more conservative values and policies, President George W. Bush widened the split between conservatives and liberals. After the September 11, 2001, terrorist attacks on New York City and Washington, D.C., the country united behind Bush. But this unity began to dissipate with disagreements over Bush's handling of foreign policy issues.

CLINTON, A "NEW DEMOCRAT"

The 1992 presidential election returned the Democrats to the White House. The winner, Bill Clinton, the longtime governor of Arkansas, distanced himself from the image many Americans had of Democrats as "tax-and-spend" liberal politicians who were weak on crime and national defense. As a so-called "New Democrat," Clinton said he favored a balanced budget, welfare reform, tough anticrime measures, and an active foreign policy, most of which had not been considered Democratic policies for decades.

1. A Three-Man Race. In 1992, the first President Bush ran for a second term as the Republican candidate. The Democrats nominated Clinton, who picked another Southerner, Senator Al Gore of Tennessee, as his running mate. A third major candidate was H. Ross Perot, a billionaire Texas businessman. Perot ran as an independent who tapped into substantial voter dissatisfaction with both parties and with the performance of the federal government.

The campaign's major issue was the economy. The national debt had increased to almost $4 trillion, and the budget deficit was continuing to rise as well. The economy was in a *recession* (extreme, short-term slowdown), and many Americans were unemployed. Clinton emphasized change, portraying the "New Democrats" as a moderate party dedicated to helping people "who work hard and play by the rules." Perot won support from many who distrusted professional politicians.

The biggest election turnout in 30 years resulted in a Clinton victory. He achieved a sizable margin in the Electoral College: 370 to 168 (with no votes for Perot). Clinton narrowly won the popular vote with 43 percent. Bush, meanwhile, got 38 percent; and Perot received 19 percent, which was surprisingly large for an independent.

2. Change at Home. In the 1992 election, the Democrats retained control of Congress, which was now more diverse than ever before. The number of women, African Americans, and Hispanics in Congress almost doubled. Among the six women elected to the Senate was its first African-American one, Carol Moseley-Braun of Illinois. Winners also included the first member of Congress of Korean descent and the first Native-American senator in 60 years.

a. Early initiatives. More liberal on social issues than his Republican predecessors, Clinton used executive orders to make some changes early in his administration. For instance, he lifted a "gag rule" that had prevented abortion counseling by clinics that received federal aid. The president also gained congressional approval for some measures, including a family-leave bill. It required companies with 50 or more employees to give unpaid leave to workers facing family or medical emergencies.

Clinton's 1993 budget, designed to reduce the deficit by almost $500 billion through 1998, curbed Medicare and Medicaid funding and raised taxes for the wealthy. Congress passed it without a single Republican vote. At the president's urging, Congress approved the Brady Bill, which set up a five-day waiting period for handgun purchases in order to allow for background checks.

By the early 1990s, medical costs were soaring. More than 35 million Americans lacked health insurance. A task force headed by the president's wife, Hillary Rodham Clinton, worked several months to draft a *national health insurance* plan that would both contain expenses and broaden coverage. Every American would be covered by some sort of health insurance. This plan, announced by the president in September 1993, aroused strong objections from many private health insurers, doctors, and employers. Unable to win congressional support for his health-care plan, Clinton abandoned it in 1994.

In 1994, Congress passed (and the president signed) a tough new crime-control law. It provided for the hiring of 100,000 additional po-

Because so many people lacked health insurance, President Clinton proposed in 1993 a national health insurance plan. It was not passed by Congress.

lice officers over the next six years. It expanded the number of federal crimes punishable by death and required life sentences for people convicted of three serious felonies ("three strikes and you're out").

b. The 1994 congressional elections. As the congressional elections approached late in 1994, Republicans sensed victory. The health-care defeat had hurt Clinton's popularity. Also plaguing the president were issues dating back to his Arkansas days, specifically allegations of sexual misconduct and financial illegalities.

Led by Congressman Newt Gingrich of Georgia, the House Minority Whip, Republicans in 1994 captured both houses of Congress for the first time since 1954. Most of the new Republican elected officials pledged to carry out their platform, the Contract With America. It called for tax cuts, congressional term limits, a stronger military, and a constitutional amendment requiring a balanced budget. Although some Contract provisions became law, a Balanced-Budget Amendment was defeated.

Budget issues divided the president and Congress throughout 1995. The president wanted a balanced budget but argued that cuts in *entitlements* (guaranteed government benefits, such as Social Security) proposed by Republicans were too drastic.

c. The 1996 elections. Clinton's legislative strategy in the election year of 1996 was to avoid head-on collisions with Republicans.

One compromise was a welfare-reform act that ended federal income guarantees to the poor. They were replaced by a work-orientated, time-limited system run by the states. After a certain amount of time had lapsed, recipients of state income programs were expected to look for a job and go to work.

The Democrats renominated Clinton for the presidency in the 1996 election. The Republicans chose a longtime senator from Kansas, Robert Dole, as their candidate. Dole ran on a conservative platform that called for a 15-percent tax cut. He also made thinly-veiled references to Clinton's ethical troubles. Perot ran once again as an independent.

Clinton benefited from a strong economy and low unemployment. His 379-to-159 margin in the electoral college (with Perot receiving no votes) made him the first Democrat to be re-elected for a second full term since Franklin Roosevelt. In a three-way race, Clinton won 49 percent of the vote. The Republicans retained their hold on Congress.

3. Impeachment and Acquittal. Many scandals dogged Clinton during his presidency. During Clinton's first term, he and his wife had been subjects of a federal investigation into questionable financial dealings while he had been governor of Arkansas. In addition, Paula Jones, a former Arkansas state employee, charged Bill Clinton with sexual harassment.

As the Jones lawsuit proceeded, a former White House intern, Monica Lewinsky, was called to testify about an alleged affair with Clinton. She denied having such an affair. But Linda Tripp, a former coworker of Lewinsky's, had secretly recorded telephone conversations with her in which Lewinsky discussed having an affair with the president. Clinton denied under oath that he had an affair with Lewinsky. Kenneth Starr, the special prosecutor appointed to look into the Clintons' financial dealings, also probed the Lewinsky matter and obtained the recordings.

Jones withdrew her lawsuit after Clinton agreed to settle her claim for $850,000, but with no admission of wrongdoing or any apology on his part. Starr believed that Clinton had abused his power as president, committed perjury, and obstructed justice in an attempt to keep his affair with Lewinsky secret. Starr turned over his evidence to the House of Representatives for possible impeachment proceedings.

In December 1998, the House voted to impeach the president for perjury and obstructing justice. The issue was not only whether there was substantive evidence that Clinton had broken the law, but also whether such conduct was serious enough to remove him from office. In early 1999, the Senate tried the president on the impeachment charges. He was acquitted by the Senate.

IDENTIFY OR DEFINE: national health insurance, family leave, entitlements, welfare reform, "three strikes and you're out."

CRITICAL THINKING: In what sense could Bill Clinton be considered a "New Democrat"?

---

4. Relations With Other Countries. During his two terms in office, Clinton conducted a very active foreign policy.

a. NAFTA. Early in his first term, Clinton voiced support for the North American Free Trade Agreement (NAFTA), which had originated in the Bush administration. This pact called for a huge *free-trade zone* comprising the United States, Mexico, and Canada. Many Democrats opposed NAFTA, fearing major losses of U.S. jobs to Mexico. When Congress passed the legislation in 1993, it did so only because of widespread Republican support.

b. Haiti. In the Caribbean region, the United States acted to restore order to Haiti. In 1990, Jean-Bertrand Aristide had been elected president of the country. But he was later expelled by a military coup and took refuge in the United States. Intervention by the UN and the United States restored Aristide to power in 1994.

c. Former Yugoslavia. U.S. leaders had long been concerned about violence in the former Yugoslavia. This Communist country had broken up as various nationalities agitated to form their own national governments. Beginning in the early 1990s, clashes among Serbs, Croats, and Bosnian Muslims led to widespread death and devastation. In 1995, the United States sponsored cease-fire negotiations among the warring factions in Bosnia. Americans then formed part of a NATO multinational force stationed in the Balkans to supervise a return to peaceful relations.

Meanwhile, Serbian president Slobodan Milosevic sent forces into the Serbian province of Kosovo, where ethnic Albanians were the majority and wanted independence. Because Milosevic refused to join peace talks on Kosovo, NATO in 1999 launched an air offensive against Serbia. Soon Serbia withdrew its forces from Kosovo. Milosevic and his political party lost the 2000 election. He was then turned over to stand trial before the International War Crimes Tribunal for his alleged role in the atrocities committed during the conflict in Bosnia. (He died in 2006 while still on trial.)

d. Russia. Under Vladimir Putin, Russia was making a difficult transition to democratic rule and a capitalist economy. The United States supported a multibillion-dollar loan proposed by the international financial community to keep the Russian government and the economy afloat. But the task was complicated by the war for independence waged in Chechnya, a small, mostly Muslim region of Russia to the west of the Caspian Sea.

e. Asia. The Clinton administration made some progress with Communist countries of Asia. It negotiated with North Korea to limit the latter's nuclear capability. And it resumed diplomatic relations with Vietnam.

Bill Clinton visited China in 1998, but relations between China and the United States remained uneasy. The United States continued to condemn human rights abuses in China. Then, too, Clinton threatened to use sanctions to force a crackdown on the black market sale in China of American computer programs, films, and music recordings.

f. Middle East. Clinton continued to play a personal role in finding a diplomatic solution to the conflict in the Middle East. At the White House in 1993, he welcomed Israeli Prime Minister Yitzhak Rabin and Yasir Arafat, the chairman of the Palestine Liberation Organization (PLO). The two Middle East leaders signed an unprecedented peace agreement. In 2000, Clinton sponsored a Mid-

President Clinton, Yitzhak Rabin, and Yasir Arafat at the White House in 1993.

dle East summit meeting between the Israeli Prime Minister Ehud Barak and Arafat. In the end, these talks collapsed. Then Palestinian militants resumed their suicide bombing attacks, which the Israelis answered with harsh reprisals.

In 1993, a month into Clinton's first term, followers of radical Sheik Omar Abdel Rahman exploded a truck bomb in the World Trade Center in New York City. This group's goal was to force the United States to end its support of Israel and Egypt. In 1998, Islamist fundamentalist groups launched terrorist attacks against U.S. embassies in Africa. It was believed that the Saudi Arabian religious extremist Osama bin Laden orchestrated the attacks. He operated out of Sudan first and then Afghanistan. Clinton ordered missile strikes on targets in Sudan suspected of being connected to bin Laden.

Following the Persian Gulf War, Iraq's leader Saddam Hussein had been forced to allow the UN to inspect and destroy Iraq's *weapons of mass destruction* (chemical, biological, and nuclear weapons). The process dragged on for years, with Hussein alternating between defiance and cooperation. After Iraq in 1998 refused to give the UN inspectors documents related to its weapons. Clinton launched four days of air strikes on Iraq in an effort to force compliance.

g. Africa. A civil war has long raged in Somalia. In 1994, efforts at peacekeeping in this East African nation resulted in the deaths of 26 U.S. soldiers. As a result, Clinton pulled all U.S. forces out of that country.

In this same year, a civil war in Rwanda between the two major ethnic groups of Hutus and Tutsis resulted in the genocide of over half a million people, mostly Tutsis. Haunted by the failure of the U.S. mission in Somalia, U.S. leaders hesitated and then abandoned any plans to intervene in Rwanda. In 1998, Clinton made a tour of Africa in an effort to mend the tattered U.S. relations with that continent.

IDENTIFY OR DEFINE: Jean-Bertrand Aristide, Kosovo, Vladimir Putin, Chechnya, Sudan, Somalia.

CRITICAL THINKING: Do you think that the United States should have helped restore Jean-Bertrand Aristide to power in Haiti in 1994? Why or why not?

THE 2000 AND 2004 ELECTIONS

Vice President Al Gore was the Democratic candidate for president in 2000, while Connecticut Senator Joseph Lieberman was the vice presidential candidate. George W. Bush, the two-term governor of Texas and the son of former President George H.W. Bush, won the Republican nomination. Dick Cheney, the former secretary of defense and Wyoming congressman, was picked as his running mate.

The major policy issues of the 2000 campaign were financing Social Security and prescription drug coverage. Issues of personality and personal integrity, however, played a large role in the campaign. Bush highlighted his "outsider" status and attempted to link Gore to scandals of the Clinton presidency. Gore stressed his political experience and vast knowledge of public policy issues. He also criticized Bush for his lack of experience.

The 2000 election, in which Bush and Gore ran neck and neck up to Election Day, was perhaps the most controversial in U.S. history. In Florida, the extremely close count, faulty voting machines, and voter registration problems made George W. Bush's victory seem questionable. Both candidates insisted on recounts and made legal challenges right up to the Supreme Court. It was not until mid-December that Bush was officially declared the winner in Florida. This gave him enough votes in the electoral college to win the election, even though he had fewer popular votes than Gore.

The 2004 election was not as close as the 2000 one. Massachusetts Senator and Vietnam War veteran John Kerry won the Democratic nomination for president. Kerry picked Senator John Edwards of North Carolina as his running mate. President George W. Bush and Vice President Dick Cheney were renominated by the Republican Party. With a high voter turnout, Bush received 51 percent of the popular vote and 286 out of a possible 538 electoral votes.

ANOTHER BUSH IN THE WHITE HOUSE

After George W. Bush took the oath of office for the first time as president in January 2001, he faced significant challenges at home and abroad. At home were the issues of maintaining a robust economy and dealing with the changes that an aging population brings. On the world scene, an increase in terrorist attacks and the threat of nuclear conflict in the Korean Peninsula and India/Pakistan also demanded attention.

1. The Tragedy of September 11, 2001. On September 11, 2001, terrorists belonging to the al Qaeda network established by Osama bin Laden hijacked four jetliners. They flew two into the Twin Towers of the World Trade Center and one into the Pentagon near Wash-

Smoke billowed from the towers of the World Trade Center in New York on September 11, 2001, in the most horrifying terrorist attack against the United States.

ington, D.C. The fourth crashed in a field in Pennsylvania. Some 3,000 people lost their lives.

In response to the September 11 attacks, Congress passed the Patriot Act of 2001. Its purpose was to make it easier to fight terrorism. Critics claimed that the act dangerously expanded law enforcement's surveillance and investigative powers. Moreover, they claimed, it denied hundreds of individuals jailed under the act access to lawyers or family. In response to lawsuits, U.S. courts declared only some provisions of the law unconstitutional. To coordinate all government agencies in the fight against terrorism, President Bush set up a Cabinet-level Department of Homeland Security, which officially began operations in January 2003.

In January 2006, it was learned that Bush had authorized the National Security Agency (NSA) to *wiretap* U.S. citizens and groups without a warrant. The president defended himself by saying that these people were believed to have terrorist connections. He argued that the Constitution and the emergency powers passed by Congress after the terrorist attack on the World Trade Center legalized this action.

2. Foreign Affairs. During his two terms of office, President Bush took measures to root out al Qaeda havens around the world and to work to resolve international conflicts, some of which (it was feared) could spark new acts of terrorism.

a. Afghanistan. Almost immediately after September 11, the Bush administration demanded that the Taliban, a fanatical group of Islamic clerics ruling Afghanistan, turn over Osama bin Laden.

The Taliban's refusal resulted in their downfall as anti-Taliban Afghan forces and U.S. troops launched attacks. Bin Laden, however, managed to escape capture.

In January 2004, delegates to the newly installed Afghan grand council approved a charter that set up a presidential system and a national assembly, and granted equal rights to women. Despite on-going turmoil in the country, Hamid Karzai in October won Afghanistan's first-ever presidential election. The Taliban still have rebel forces in the country's southern provinces. NATO forces are slowly taking over the U.S. military role in Afghanistan.

b. Iraq. Suspecting Iraq of aiding al Qaeda in attacking the World Trade Center, some U.S. leaders wanted to invade Iraq. Another reason they gave was their suspicion that Iraq had weapons of mass destruction (WMDs). Iraqi officials had been uncooperative with the UN inspectors who were looking for these weapons. Then diplomatic efforts obtained a resumption of UN inspections for WMDs in that country. Despite opposition from a number of countries (including France, Germany, and Russia), the United States and its allies attacked Iraq in March of 2003. They overthrew Saddam Hussein in a matter of weeks.

The war was not over, however. Insurgents hostile to the U.S. presence in Iraq turned to terror and violence to try to force the

United States and its allies to leave Iraq. Ambush attacks and continuing military operations have resulted in increasing numbers of U.S. soldiers dead and wounded. Insurgents have also kidnapped and killed Iraqis and foreigners sympathetic to the U.S. presence.

Meanwhile, a scandal increased the already considerable resentment of the U.S. presence in Iraq. In April 2004, disturbing accounts of abuse in Iraq's Abu Ghraib prison surfaced. Preliminary reports stated that U.S. soldiers had beaten, terrorized, and humiliated Iraqi prisoners of war. President Bush ordered an investigation of the abuses and promised to demolish the prison as soon as replacement facilities become available.

In December 2003, Saddam Hussein was captured. But neither his trial nor the January 2005 Iraqi legislative elections brought about immediate peace and stability. In April 2006, Iraqi government leaders chose Shiite Nuri Kamal al-Maliki as prime minister. Since some Kurdish and Sunni factions supported this choice, it generated hope that Iraq was moving toward an effective and cohesive government.

Many Americans began to express doubts that the protracted war in Iraq would have a successful outcome. By the beginning of 2006, Iraq seemed on the brink of a civil war between the Shiites and Sunnis (the two major sects of the Islamic religion). Ordinary Iraqis live in constant fear of violence.

c. Africa. Beginning in the mid-1950s, rebels in southern Sudan waged civil wars against their government. Although the country is rich in oil reserves, its civil wars caused Sudan to become poor and destabilized. Beginning in 2003, the government and rebel leaders held peace talks. In 2005, they signed a peace agreement.

In early 2003, a new rebellion broke out in Sudan, in its western part (Darfur). Rebels there hoped to secede from Sudan. Both government forces and the rebels committed atrocities against the civilian inhabitants of Darfur. Moreover, observers claimed that Arab militias hired by the government were engaging in ethnic cleansing against the indigenous population. Because of the fierce fighting in this area, it has been difficult to extend aid to the victims. Hundreds of thousands of people have fled from Darfur to neighboring Chad.

At first, President Bush relied on peace talks and long-term solutions to deal with the Darfur conflict. In early 2006, however, he called for increasing the number of UN and NATO troops in Darfur. He also proposed sending $500 million in aid to the ravaged country.

d. Latin America. Venezuela possesses rich reserves of oil and gas. The United States is one of the major buyers of these natural resources. In 2002, Venezuela's leftist president Hugo Chávez accused the United States of having sponsored an unsuccessful coup d'état against him. As a member of OPEC, he has joined other members of that group in raising oil prices. But he has agreed to provide 198,000 barrels a day of oil to 13 Caribbean countries at comparatively low prices. And he has joined with other left-leaning countries in Latin America in an anti-United States stance.

Jean-Bertrand Aristide's return to power in Haiti in 1994 did not bring about the economic and social reforms that the Haitian people—and the United States—had hoped for. His reelection as president in 2000 was met with charges of fraud and corruption. As opposition to his government steadily increased, so did the level of violence in the streets. Under U.S. pressure, Aristide left Haiti in February 2004. But once in exile, he maintained that he was still the legitimate president and that U.S. forces had kidnapped him. U.S. troops remain in Haiti as part of a UN peacekeeping force.

e. Fear of nuclear proliferation. In May 2002, the United States and Russia reached a historic arms agreement to cut their nuclear arsenals by up to two-thirds over a ten-year period. But at the same time, other countries were preparing to acquire nuclear weapons. In October 2002, for example, North Korea admitted to developing nuclear arms. The United States, Russia, and China have since been negotiating with North Korea to try to convince that country to give up its nuclear ambitions. A bright spot came in December 2003 when Libyan leader Muammar Qaddafi announced that he would dismantle Libya's nuclear weapons program. This task was accomplished with U.S. help, and U.S.-Libyan relations have improved.

In February 2004, the International Atomic Energy Agency (IAEA) discovered that Iran had been concealing nuclear activities and possibly building nuclear weapons. The EU and the United States pressed Iran to give up its nuclear ambitions. In spite of Western disapproval, Iran has defiantly refused. Some U.S. commentators warned that Bush might seize the occasion to attack Iran. But Bush declared that these warnings were wild speculation. He said that he planned to use all diplomatic means to deal with Iran—although military force would remain an option as a last resort.

f. Middle East. In 2002, the United States joined Russia, the European Union, and the United Nations in proposing a "road map" for peace to resolve the Israeli-Palestinian conflict. In signing on to the "road map" process, President Bush became the first U.S. president to call for the creation of an independent Palestinian state. But he refused to work with Palestinian leader Yasir Arafat. Bush claimed that Arafat had failed to stop Palestinian attacks against Israel.

Continued violence, however, has kept the peace process from becoming a reality. Yasser Arafat's death in November 2004 (and the subsequent election of Mahmoud Abbas as the new Palestinian president) inserted new factors in the equation of peace talks. The 2006 parliamentary election victory of Hamas, an anti-Israel party that grew out of a fighting organization, sparked outrage in Israel and among the nations that support both Israel and the idea of a Palestinian state. Hamas leaders continued to deny Israel's right to exist.

In July 2006, the situation in the Middle East worsened when hostilities between Israel and Hezbollah, a militant Arab guerilla organization that controls southern Lebanon, escalated into war. During a cross-border attack, Hezbollah captured two Israeli soldiers. Calling the attack an "act of war," Israel responded with air strikes on Hezbollah targets in southern Lebanon. Hezbollah then began launching rocket attacks in Israel, striking the port city of Haifa and other towns. It was widely believed that Syria and Iran, which are hostile to Israel, supplied Hezbollah with advanced weapons.

In order to weaken Hezbollah, Israel quickly expanded its military campaign throughout Lebanon, bombing targets in Beirut, Lebanon's capital, and near the Syrian border. On July 30, an Israeli air strike in the Lebanese town of Qana killed dozens of civilians, including many children. Many observers expressed concerns that the crisis could topple Lebanon's democratically elected government and could drag Syria into a war with Israel.

President Bush defended Israel's right to defend itself against Hezbollah attacks but called on Israel to exercise restraint. Israel withdrew from Lebanon after the UN agreed to send its forces there to keep the peace.

3. Domestic Issues. The 2001 inauguration of George W. Bush sparked a new round in the long-running debate over the role of government in people's lives. Liberals continued to urge more government programs to guarantee a "safety net" for the poor, sick, and elderly. President Bush's views were more in line with those of conservatives who continued to be suspicious of large government (and its social programs) but who thought that government had a role in enforcing traditional moral values.

a. The economy. One of the first domestic issues President Bush had to face in 2001 was the sluggish economy. His solution was to propose a $1.35 trillion, ten-year tax cut program that he believed would stimulate the economy. Critics argued that Bush's tax cuts

Gross Domestic Product Since 1940

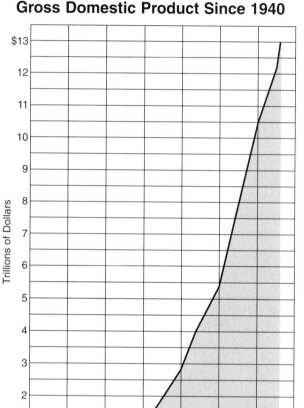

would favor the rich. But most Americans favored the plan. Congress passed major tax cut packages in 2001 and 2003.

Did the tax cuts accomplish their goal? More jobs were created, but most did not have the same high salary that the lost jobs had. In 2002, businesses began to have increased sales and profits. But lower tax revenues and the cost of wars in Afghanistan and Iraq increased the budget deficit.

By 2003, the economy was in good shape. The GDP rose from $12 trillion in October 2004 to almost $13 trillion in March 2006. In 2006, economists worried that rising oil prices (due to Hurricane Katrina and turmoil in the Middle East) would cause inflation. Many experts also pointed out the uneven distribution of wealth in U.S. society. And they expressed concern about the trade deficit between the United States and China and the high national debt.

INTERPRETING A CARTOON

BY PERMISSION OF MIKE LUCKOVICH AND CREATORS SYNDICATE, INC.

1. Who is the man on the left and what is he doing?

2. What is the significance that the vehicle is a Hummer?

3. Who do the men on the right represent?

4. What does the man on the left want of the other two men?

5. What is supposed to be funny or ironic about what the man on the left is saying?

---

b. Social Security. Because of increased life expectancy, more and more elderly people will become beneficiaries of Social Security. At the same time, because of a dropping birthrate, fewer and fewer young people will be making contributions to the system. Democrats say that the system will start running a deficit many decades from now and that the problem can be fixed by higher taxes. By contrast, Republicans claim that the system will collapse much sooner.

Early in his administration, President Bush sought a plan that would permanently strengthen Social Security without raising payroll taxes. One of his proposals was to permit younger workers to put some money into personal investment accounts instead of into the Social Security fund. This method would allow workers to take advantage of (sometimes) rising stock prices. But critics argued that any diversion of funds to personal accounts would weaken the Social Security System, not help it. A stock market slump in 2003 put talk of Social Security reform on hold. It seems that more people came to believe that putting their retirement savings in the stock market was too risky.

c. Prescription drugs. The new medicines that have enabled Americans to live longer are expensive, especially when a person needs to take several kinds every day. For senior citizens on a limited budget, the high cost of medicine threatens economic ruin.

In December 2003, President Bush signed into law legislation that makes Medicare prescription drug coverage available to 40 million seniors and people with disabilities. Even though the drug plan covers only part of beneficiaries' costs, many Americans welcomed it. Critics charge that the new law still forces beneficiaries to use a large a part of their limited income to buy medicine.

d. Improving education. From the earliest days of his presidency, George W. Bush proposed sweeping reforms in America's schools. His No Child Left Behind Act of 2002 requires states to make all students proficient in reading and math and to close achievement gaps between students of different socioeconomic backgrounds. All states are required to test students in these subjects at several grade levels. Critics of the law claim that it focuses too narrowly on math and reading at the expense of other school subjects. They also claim that teachers have to spend too much time preparing students for the tests instead of using more creative and effective teaching strategies.

e. Scandals in the financial world. On December 2, 2001 a Texas-based energy company named Enron shocked the financial community by filing for bankruptcy. The event rose to the level of a scandal when it was learned that the company had for several years concealed billions of dollars of debt from shareholders through fraudulent accounting and illegal loans. Thousands of Enron workers lost their jobs and their pensions, and thousands of investors in Enron lost billions of dollars.

Other companies soon came under federal investigation for fraud and misleading accounting. In response to these scandals, Congress in 2002 passed a corporate reform bill.

f. Scandals in the Bush administration. Several key Republican leaders were entangled in scandals. In the spring of 2006, for example, House Majority Leader Tom DeLay resigned from Congress when he was indicted for conspiracy to violate election laws. Also in 2006, Vice President Cheney's former chief of staff, Lewis Libby, was officially accused of having leaked the identity of a CIA agent, Valerie Plame. Critics charged that the leak was an attempt to discredit the agent's husband, Joseph Wilson. Wilson had published an opinion article in *The New York Times* alleging that the Bush administration had manipulated intelligence about the status of Iraq's weapons holdings in order to justify declaring war on Iraq.

g. Hurricane Katrina. Many people lost faith in the Bush administration when Hurricane Katrina struck the coasts of Louisiana, Alabama, and Mississippi on August 29, 2005. During the storm, the levies that protected the low-lying city of New Orleans were unable to hold back the water. The resulting flood devastated much of the city. More than 1,800 people in several states were confirmed dead, and many remain listed as missing. People were appalled at the slow, incompetent response of the Federal Emergency Management Agency (FEMA) and other federal agencies. (Louisiana and New Orleans government officials also received criticism.) To help the people in the region, Bush promised $200 billion in federal aid to rebuild the city and communities in Louisiana, Alabama, and Mississippi.

h. The 2006 elections. Many voters saw the 2006 congressional elections as a plebiscite on the George W. Bush administration, especially in its handling of the war in Iraq. Many candidates of the Democratic party for U.S. House and Senate seats criticized Bush's antiterrorism and war policies. Some called for an immediate withdrawl of U.S. troops from Iraq. President Bush countered, saying that some mistakes had been made by the United States in Iraq, but that it would be foolhardy and dangerous to set a timetable for withdrawl of troops.

The results of the elections were that for the first time since 1994 Democrats controlled both the House and the Senate. Democrats did well in many state elections also. Also noteworthy was the post-election selection of Representative Nancy Pelosi of California as the Speaker of the House. This was the first time that a woman has held the top position in the House of Representatives.

IDENTIFY OR DEFINE: Darfur, Enron, Hamas, Hugo Chávez, Katrina.

CRITICAL THINKING: Study the photograph on page 405? How did the event shown change the United States both domestically and internationally?

Chapter Review

MATCHING EXERCISE

Column A

1. Department of Homeland Security
2. IAEA
3. Brady Bill
4. Contract With America
5. NAFTA

Column B

a. Republican congressional election platform in 1994
b. a law that mandates five-day waiting period for all handgun purchases
c. new Cabinet-level agency created to combat domestic terrorism
d. trade agreement signed by the United States, Mexico, and Canada
e. international body that investigates nuclear activities of certain countries

MULTIPLE-CHOICE TEST

1. The major candidate in the 1992 presidential election who ran as an independent was (*a*) George Wallace (*b*) John Anderson (*c*) H. Ross Perot (*d*) John Edwards.

2. Bill Clinton's vice president was (*a*) Al Gore (*b*) Walter Mondale (*c*) Kenneth Starr (*c*) Monica Lewinsky.

3. The first African-American woman elected to the U.S. Senate was (*a*) Patty Murray (*b*) Barbara Jordan (*c*) Carol Moseley-Braun (*d*) Barbara Boxer.

4. The nation torn apart by civil war among its main ethnic groups during the 1990s was (*a*) Yugoslavia (*b*) Albania (*c*) Greece (*d*) Italy.

5. President Clinton withdrew U.S. peacekeeping forces from the African nation of (*a*) Rwanda (*b*) Somalia (*c*) South Africa (*d*) Angola.

6. The architect of the Republicans' successful campaign to recapture control of the House of Representatives in 1994 was (*a*) Lewis Libby (*b*) Newt Gingrich (*c*) Tom DeLay (*d*) Bob Dole.

7. The founder of the al Qaeda terrorist network was (*a*) Osama bin Laden (*b*) Saddam Hussein (*c*) Yasser Arafat (*d*) Sheik Omar Abdel Rahman.

8. In response to the September 11, 2001, terrorist attacks, Congress passed the (*a*) Taft-Hartley Act (*b*) National Security Act (*c*) Smith Act (*d*) Patriot Act.

9. President George W. Bush's vice president is (*a*) Hillary Clinton (*b*) Dick Cheney (*c*) John Edwards (*d*) Tom DeLay.

10. President Bush's education initiative is called the (*a*) Head Start Program (*b*) Patriot Act (*c*) Tuition Assistance Program (*d*) No Child Left Behind Act.

 ESSAY QUESTIONS

1. Why did President Clinton's national health insurance proposal fail? Do you think it was a good idea? Why or why not?

2. How well did President Clinton deal with Somalia, Haiti, and Yugoslavia?

3. Why was President Clinton impeached by the House of Representatives?

4. How well did President Bush respond to the September 11, 2001, terrorist attacks?

5. Why were President George W. Bush's approval ratings lower in his second term than during his first?

DOCUMENT-BASED QUESTION

This question is based on the accompanying documents (1–5). It will improve your ability to work with historical documents.

Historical Context:

Since 1993, the United States has faced a number of domestic and international problems. The solutions to these problems will affect our society and those of other nations of the world for years to come.

Task:

Using information from the documents and your knowledge of United States history, read each document and answer the question that follows it. Your answers to the questions will help you write the document-based essay.

Document 1. Study the photograph on page 402.

What role did President Clinton play in the 1993 peace agreement between Israel and the PLO?

Document 2. Excerpt from President Clinton's *State of the Union Address*, February 17, 1993:

A part of our national economic strategy must be to expand trade on fair terms, including successful completion of the latest round of world trade talks. A North American Free Trade Agreement with appropriate safeguards for workers and the environment. At the same time, we need an aggressive attempt to create the hi-tech jobs of the future; special attention to troubled industries like aerospace and airlines, and special assistance to displaced workers like those in our defense industry.

Later this spring, I will deliver to Congress a comprehensive plan for health care reform that will finally get costs under control. We will provide security to all our families, so that no one will be denied the coverage they need. We will root out fraud and outrageous charges, and make sure that paperwork no longer chokes you or your doctor. And we will maintain American standards—the highest quality medical care in the world and the choices we demand and deserve. The American people expect us to deal with health care. And we must deal with it now.

Later this year, we will offer a plan to end welfare as we know it. No one wants to change the welfare system as much as those who are trapped by the welfare system.

We will offer people on welfare the education, training, child care and health care they need to get back on their feet. Then, after two years, they must get back to work—in private business if possible; in public service, if necessary. It's time to end welfare as a way of life.

Our budget will, by 1997, cut 140 billion dollars from the deficit—one of the greatest real spending cuts by an American president. We are making more than 150 difficult, painful reductions which will cut federal spending by 246 billion dollars. We are eliminating programs that are no longer needed, such as nuclear power research and development. We are slashing subsidies and canceling wasteful projects. Many of these programs were justified in their time. But if we're going to start new plans, we must eliminate old ones. Government has been good at building programs, now we must show that we can limit them.

Source: http://www.washingtonpost.com/wp-srv/politics/special/states/docs/sou93.htm

What did President Clinton plan to do in his first term as president?

Document 3. Excerpt from President George W. Bush's *Address to the Nation* on September 11, 2001:

These acts of mass murder were intended to frighten our nation into chaos and retreat. But they have failed; our country is strong. . . .

The functions of our government continue without interruption. Federal agencies in Washington which had to be evacuated today are reopening for essential personnel tonight, and will be open for business tomorrow. Our financial institutions remain strong, and the American economy will be open for business, as well. The search is underway for those who are behind these evil acts. I've directed the full resources of our intelligence and law enforcement communities to find those responsible and to bring them to justice. We will make no distinction between the terrorists who committed these acts and those who harbor them.

Source: http://www.c-span.org/executive/bush_terror.asp?Cat=Current_Event&Code=Bush_Admin

How did President Bush attempt to reassure the American people following the terrorist attacks?

Document 4. Study the cartoon on page 406, published after the United States had led a coalition into Iraq to depose the Saddam Hussein regime.

What was the cartoon's message regarding the aims of the war in Iraq?

Document 5. Excerpt from a speech by President George W. Bush to soldiers and their families at Fort Hood, Texas, April 12, 2005:

From the beginning, our goal in Iraq has been to promote Iraqi independence—by helping the Iraqi people establish a free country that can sustain itself, rule itself, and defend itself. And in the last two years, Iraqis have made enormous progress toward that goal. Iraqis have laid the foundations of a free society, with hundreds of independent newspapers and dozens of political parties and associations, and schools that teach Iraqi children how to read and write, instead of the propaganda of Saddam Hussein. Iraqis have laid the foundation of a free economy, with a new currency and independent central bank, new laws to encourage foreign investment, and thousands of small businesses established since liberation.

Source: www.whitehouse.gov/news/releases/2005/04/20050412.html

What did President Bush say has been the goals of U.S. policy in Iraq?

DOCUMENT-BASED ESSAY

Using information from the above documents and your knowledge of United States history, write an essay in which you:

- Explain the goals that Presidents Clinton and George W. Bush had during their terms in office.
- Evaluate how well each president achieved his goals.

GLOSSARY

abolition before the Civil War, reformers' goal of ending slavery

abstinence refraining from drinking alcohol

adobe sun-dried brick

alien person who is not a citizen of the country in which he or she resides

Americanization teaching of American culture to immigrants

anarchist person who believes in the abolition of all government

annexation taking over territory of another country

antiballistic missile (ABM) defensive missile used to shoot down other missiles

anti-Semitism hostility to Jews and discrimination against them

antitrust law legislation designed to limit the power of trusts or ban them

appeal taking of a case to a higher court for rehearing

appeasement policy of making concessions to aggressors in order to maintain peace

appellate jurisdiction authority of court to review decisions of lower courts

apprentice person who works with a master to learn a trade

armistice temporary halt to fighting by an agreement between opposing sides

assembly line arrangement of workers, machines, and equipment in which the product being manufactured passes along a moving belt from one operation to the next until it is completed

assumption accepting responsibility for someone else's debts or other obligations

automation automatic control of manufacturing processes by mechanical or electronic devices such as computers

bank run rush of depositors to withdraw money from banks

bipartisan supported by two political parties

black codes laws that restricted the lives of freedmen

blitzkrieg fast-moving battle combining bombers, artillery, and tanks

blockade to cut off access to or from a port, coastline, or other vital area by means of naval patrols or other armed forces

"blue laws" laws forbidding certain practices regarded as sinful, especially violations of the Sabbath

bond certificate issued by a government in exchange for a long-term loan

bootlegger illegal seller of alcohol

boss in politics, party head who controls a political machine

boycott to refrain from buying or selling something in order to force a change in a policy

Cabinet in the United States, a presidential advisory group composed mostly of heads of executive departments

capitalism economic system based on private ownership of resources and means of production, and free competition among producers; also known as **free enterprise**

carpetbagger Northerner who worked for the Freedmen's Bureau or ran for office in the South during Reconstruction

cash crop one grown for sale rather than for a farmer's private use

caucus political meeting to select candidates for nomination and/or to decide on policy

cease-fire temporary suspension of hostilities in a war

censure in U.S. Congress, official reprimand of a member

chain store one of many similar stores owned by the same company

charter royal patent to govern an area and control its trade

checks and balances system of limiting power of each branch of government through controls exercised by the other branches

circuit rider traveling preacher who spread a faith in rural areas

circumnavigate to go completely around something

city-manager plan form of city government in which voter-elected commissioners hire a professional manager

civil disobedience *see* **nonviolent civil disobedience**

civil rights (civil liberties) guarantees against abuse of government power; also, protection against discrimination

civil service system of hiring government employees by means of competitive exams

clipper ship fast-sailing, 19th-century ship with tall masts and large sails

closed shop workplace that hires only union members

coaling station port where steamships could refuel

coalition alliance, often temporary, of people or groups with differing views

Cold War ongoing conflict between two powers that falls short of actual fighting

collective bargaining negotiations between labor and management

combination alliance of businesses to increase their assets and power

commission plan form of city government in which voters elect heads of various city departments; acting together, department heads also serve as city's legislature.

Communist one who wants a system in which government controls all economic activity

concentration camp a brutal and degrading prison camp; some (**death camps**) were designed to kill all the prisoners.

concurrent powers under U.S. Constitution, powers shared by national and state governments

conservation protection of natural resources, especially against commercial exploitation

containment policy of restricting Soviet influence and territorial expansion

cooperative (co-op) business owned and operated by those who benefit from its services

corporation business organization owned by investors who purchase shares of stock in it

count coup act of bravery by a Plains brave

craft union labor union with membership limited to skilled workers practicing the same craft

culture way of life of a group of people

culture area geographic region inhabited by peoples with a similar way of life

decimal system one based on the unit of ten, such as U.S. money

deficit spending government spending more than it receives as income

deflation constantly falling prices

delegated powers those given to the federal government by the U.S. Constitution

demilitarized zone area kept free from all military forces

denazification process of removing Nazi personnel and dismantling Nazi institutions

department store large store in which each category of goods is sold in its own department

depression long period of slow business activity and high unemployment

deregulation removing government restrictions and regulations

desegregation removal of barriers that cause separation of races, as in education or housing

détente relaxation of tensions, especially between the United States and the Soviet Union

dictatorship government in which all power is concentrated in a single individual or a small group

direct democracy form of government in which people rule themselves directly rather than being governed by elected representatives or others

direct primary election in which voters select party candidates to run in a general election

discrimination practice of treating minority groups less favorably than the majority

disfranchise to deprive people of the right to vote

dividend part of corporation profits paid to shareholders

domesticate to tame animals for human use

double-digit inflation cost-of-living increase of 10 percent or more

draft (conscription) compulsory enrollment for military service

draft animal one used to draw loads

dry farming type of agriculture using special methods of plowing and planting to conserve moisture in the soil

duty tax on imports

dynamo small generator that makes electricity

earth lodge structure built partly underground with a roof of logs and hides

economic sanction government economic policy (such as an embargo) used against another government

"elastic clause" Article I, Section 8, Clause 18 of the U.S. Constitution; gives Congress authority to pass laws in addition to those specified in preceding clauses

electoral college group of individuals elected by voters to vote on their behalf for president and vice president

emancipate to free from bondage, slavery, or oppression

embargo official ban on trade with a country

entitlement guaranteed government benefit

enumerated article one of many colonial goods that could be sold only to Britain and its colonies

escalation speeding up of something

established religion official church (or religion) of a state or nation, recognized by law and often supported by public taxes

expansionism increasing the size of a country

family leave arrangement whereby an employee may take an unpaid leave of absence to take care of a member of his or her family

fascism political system that glorifies an all-powerful state at the expense of individuals

federalism system whereby power is shared by a central (national) government and regional (state) governments

feminism movement aimed at achieving equality for women

filibuster in U.S. Senate, a member's attempt to prevent passage of a bill by talking indefinitely

flax crop grown to make linen

foreclose to seize property when its owner fails to make mortgage payments

forty-niners migrants to California during the gold rush of 1849

Founders the 55 delegates to the Constitutional Convention

freedmen former slaves who had been freed

free enterprise *see* **capitalism**

free silver demand that unlimited amounts of silver be purchased by the government for coinage

free-trade zone a city or region of a country where there are no tariffs

fugitive slave one who has run away from his or her master

genocide mass killing of a national, racial, or religious group

glasnost Soviet policy of allowing more criticism of the government and society

gold rush rapid movement of people into California after the discovery of gold there in 1848

gold standard use of gold as the only backing for paper money

graduated income tax a tax that takes proportionately more from higher incomes

grandfather clause law of several Southern states that restricted voting to those whose male ancestors (grandfathers or fathers) had been qualified to vote in 1867

gross domestic product (GDP) total annual value of goods and services produced by a country

hogan Navajo eight-sided house

holding company business combination in which a central organization controls several member companies through stock ownership

home rule situation whereby a local government is free from control by a higher level of government

hornbook one-page book mounted on a board

humanitarian person dedicated to improving human welfare and promoting social reforms

human rights those regarded as belonging to all people

hunter-gatherer person who survives by gathering seeds and fruits and/or by hunting

immigration population movement into a country for purpose of settlement

impeach to bring charges of wrongdoing against a government official by the House of Representatives

imperialism policy of acquiring foreign territories and/or assuming political or economic control over them

implied power one that is not spelled out in the Constitution but is implied by the document's words

impressment practice of forcing people into service, especially seamen of one country into the navy of another

indentured servant person who agreed to work for a certain number of years in exchange for passage to America

indigo plant that is a raw material for making blue dye

industrialization (Industrial Revolution) change from manufacture by hand to large-scale machine production in factories

industrial union one made up of all workers, skilled and unskilled, in a given industry

infant industry a new business in competition with established foreign ones

inflation constantly rising prices

initiative procedure by which voters ask a legislature to consider a proposed law

injunction court order directing that an action be carried out or stopped

installment buying purchases of goods and services through periodic, partial payments

interchangeable parts separate elements of a manufactured product that are made exactly alike to facilitate assembly and repair

intercontinental ballistic missile (ICBM) long-range offensive missile

internment camp one of several camps in which many Japanese Americans were confined during World War II

investment banker one who raises capital for corporations by supervising the selling of stocks and bonds

iron curtain a political, military, and ideological barrier that isolated the area under Soviet control

irrigation watering land by artificial means

island-hopping Allied strategy of seizing some Japanese-held islands and temporarily bypassing others, with the ultimate goal of invading Japan

isolationism policy that favors keeping a nation aloof from foreign entanglements

"Jim Crow" laws and customs that segregated African Americans from whites; term derived from a character in popular minstrel shows.

joint-stock company business organization set up and owned by a group of stockholders who pool their money to finance a new venture

judicial review power of the Supreme Court to declare laws and presidential actions unconstitutional

jurisdictional strike one called when two unions dispute each other's right to represent workers

kachina ancestral spirit

kamikaze an airplane containing explosives flown in a suicide crash into a target

laissez faire policy advocating little or no government interference in an economy

language family group of related languages

literacy test reading test for qualifying to vote

lobby special-interest group that tries to influence public officials to make favorable policy decisions, or exerts pressure on lawmakers to pass laws that the group supports

long drive movement of cattle to a railway junction by cowboys on horses

long house rectangular, one-story building housing many families

longitude distance east or west of prime meridian (at Greenwich, England)

loose construction belief that government may exercise powers beyond those specifically listed in the Constitution in order to carry out authorized functions

McCarthyism tactics used by Senator Joseph McCarthy and others of making charges against people without proof and assuming people to be guilty unless it is proven otherwise

mail-order company business that sells products by mail

manifest destiny mid-19th-century belief that U.S. expansion to the Pacific was right and inevitable

maximum hours the total number of hours that employees could work in a day or week without having to be paid overtime

mercantilism economic theory advocating national self-sufficiency and accumulation of gold and silver

merger business combination in which two or more companies are combined

militia armed force made up of civilians who serve only in emergencies

minimum wage the lowest hourly rate that certain workers could be paid legally

Minutemen Massachusetts colonial militia

Morse code system of dots and dashes that represent letters and numbers used to transmit messages via telegraph

mountain man 19th-century American frontiersman who was at home in the wilderness

muckraker writer, especially in the Progressive era, who exposed conditions needing reform

national health insurance government program to provide health insurance for all Americans

national self-determination self-rule for national minorities

nativism movement whose main goal is to limit immigration

naval stores items used in building wooden ships, such as masts, pitch, and tar

Nazism German fascism

nomad member of a group that moves from place to place, usually in search of food

nominating convention meeting of political party delegates to choose candidates to run for office

nonaggression pact treaty whereby participating nations agree not to attack one another

nonviolent civil disobedience peaceful refusal to obey laws regarded as unjust

northwest passage desired route from the Atlantic through or around North America to the Pacific

nullification doctrine that claims that a state can declare invalid (**nullify**) any federal action it considers unconstitutional

on margin paying only a small percentage of the purchase price in buying stocks

open range unfenced, unsettled land in the West owned by the federal government

pacifist one who opposes all wars

packet boat passenger vessel that also carries mail and cargo

panic widespread fear of business collapse that leads to hasty financial transactions and a sharp drop in the value of stocks, bonds, and other property

parity price for farm products based on the price in an earlier period

partnership business organization owned by two or more individuals

pay certificate government document that promises to pay soldiers their back pay

penitentiary place to keep convicted criminals (in 19th century usually in solitary confinement)

perestroika Soviet policy of reforming the economic system by allowing elements of free enterprise

perjury lying in a court of law while under oath to tell the truth

political machine party organization devoted to getting members to vote and rewarding loyal supporters with jobs

poll tax fee required to vote

pool informal agreement among competing companies to fix prices, share profits, or divide markets

popular sovereignty idea that voters in a territory that was becoming a state could decide for or against allowing slavery there

post road one built to transport mail (post)

potlatch Northwest native ceremony to display and give away one's wealth

privateer privately owned merchant or fishing vessel authorized to attack or capture enemy ships in wartime

Progressive person who sought social and political reforms, 1900–1917

prohibition ban against manufacturing and selling alcoholic beverages

proprietary colony one sponsored by one or more individuals who had obtained a grant of overseas land from the British monarch to set up and govern settlements

protectionism policy of maintaining protective tariffs

protective tariff high tax placed on imports in order to protect domestic producers from foreign competition

public works roads, bridges, schools, and other structures built for public use and paid for by a government

pueblo Spanish word for village

quarter to provide funds, living quarters, and supplies to British troops

racism belief that certain races are superior to others; prejudice and discrimination based on this belief

range war conflicts between cattle ranchers and farmers over land use

ratify to approve constitutional amendments proposed by Congress or treaties proposed by the president

realism in literature, attempts to describe life as it is; in art, attempts to portray things accurately and realistically

reaper machine used for cutting grain

rebate refund

recall procedure by which voters can remove elected officials before their term expires

recession period of moderate business decline

Reconstruction restoration of the Confederate states to the Union after the Civil War

referendum practice of allowing voters to approve or disapprove proposed laws

reformatory penal institution for young offenders

refrigerator car railroad car that is cooled to preserve food

reparations payments imposed on defeated nations for war damages

repatriation return of people to their homeland

repeal to revoke or cancel a law or tax

representative assembly lawmaking body whose members are chosen by the voters

reprieve postponement of a sentence or punishment

reservation land set aside for groups of Native Americans

reserved powers under the U.S. Constitution, powers retained by the states

resettlement return of war refugees to their homes

revenue sharing policy of the federal government to give states, counties, and cities part of its tax revenue

right of deposit right to deposit in New Orleans goods shipped down the Mississippi and to transfer them there to oceangoing vessels without paying duties

rotation in office periodic replacement of employees in government jobs

royal colony in U.S. colonial period, a colony supervised by the British monarch through an appointed governor and council

sachem 50-man governing council of the Iroquois Confederacy

salutary neglect British government policy of not enforcing its trade laws in the colonies

satellite in the post-World War II era, a country dominated by the Soviet Union

scalawag Southerner who cooperated with efforts of the Radical Republicans

sea dog pirate

secession formal withdrawal from membership in an organization, as a state from the Union

secret ballot one that does not allow others to see how a voter votes

securities stocks and bonds

sedition treasonable behavior, especially incitement to disorder or rebellion

segregation separation of groups of people, especially along racial lines

seigneur lord in New France

separation of church and state principle whereby a government cannot interfere with subjects' religious beliefs or practices, and religious groups cannot impose their views on the country or state

separation of powers division of governmental authority and duties among legislative, executive, and judicial branches

settlement house community center that aids city dwellers, especially poor immigrants

sharecropping Southern system whereby farmers rent land, paying landowners back with a share of crops

shareholder (stockholder) person who owns shares of stock

sit-down strike a situation in which workers refuse both to leave the workplace and to work

sit-in demonstration, such as at a segregated lunch counter

slash-and-burn agriculture type of farming that involves clearing land by cutting and then burning shrubs, bushes, vines, and trees

socialist person who believes in an economic system based on public (rather than private) ownership of the means of production

sod chunk of earth

solid South situation beginning in late 19th century whereby Democrats could count on winning most elections in the South

space shuttle reusable rocket carrying people and equipment that can circle the Earth for months

specie gold or silver (rather than paper) money

speculator person who makes risky investments in hope of gaining big profits

sphere of influence area dominated by a foreign power

spoils system practice of rewarding party workers with government jobs

stagecoach horse-drawn, covered passenger vehicle with large wheels

stagflation combination of weak economic growth and inflation

states' rights doctrine favoring state over national authority

steamboat vessel powered by steam

stock market exchange where stocks and bonds are traded

strict construction belief that government is limited by the Constitution to exercise only the powers specifically granted to it

strikebreaker person hired to replace a striking worker; **scab**

subscription library book-lending association supported and used only by its members

subversive person who tries to weaken or overthrow a government

suffrage right to vote

suffragist one who worked to gain the vote for women

superpower one of the two strongest countries in the world

supply-side economics policy of favoring producers and investors, rather than consumers, in formulating programs to stimulate economic growth

tariff tax on imported goods

temperance moderation in drinking alcoholic beverages

tenement crowded, run-down apartment building

tepee cone-shaped hut covered with hides

terrorism use of violence to intimidate or instill fear

Third World developing nations of Asia, Africa, and Latin America

"three strikes and you're out" law requiring life term after three felony convictions

thresher machine used to separate grain from stalks

totalitarian state dictatorial political regime that attempts to control every aspect of citizens' lives

town meeting general gathering of a town's inhabitants for purpose of self-government

township unit of land six miles square

transcript written record of an audio recording

treason betrayal of one's country, especially in wartime

triangular trade any three-sided pattern of commerce

trust large business combination consisting of several corporations in the same field; especially a combination formed for purpose of reducing competition or creating a monopoly

turnpike private road with tolls

U-boat German submarine

ultimatum final demand, not subject to negotiation

unconstitutional contrary to the Constitution

urbanization formation of cities in previously rural areas

vertical integration business practice of acquiring control over all stages of production of something, from raw materials to finished product

veto to reject something or declare it invalid

war guilt being blamed for starting a war

weapons of mass destruction (WMDs) nuclear, biological, and chemical weapons

welfare state nation in which the government assumes prime responsibility for citizens' well-being

wickiup brush hut

wigwam dome-shaped hut covered with bark

wiretap to tap a telephone line to get information

workers' compensation government program whereby employers buy insurance to cover workers being injured on the job

writs of assistance in colonial America, legal documents that served as general search warrants

INTERNET SOURCES IN U.S. HISTORY

The Internet offers extensive information and resources on the topics covered in this book. The following pages provide a list of search engines, online encyclopedias, and Web sites that link you to sources of information, primary sources, visuals, and suggested sites that enable you to conduct research on selected topics from each unit of *Essential U.S. History*.

Search Engines

http://www.google.com
http://www.ask.com
http://www.msn.com
http://www.dogpile.com
http://www.refdesk.com/

U.S. History Sites

Digital History
http://www.digitalhistory.uh.edu/

Chronology of U.S. Historical Documents
http://www.law.ou.edu/hist/

History Matters
http://historymatters.gmu.edu/

Spartacus
http://www.spartacus.schoolnet.co.uk/USA.htm

U.S. History (on the Colonial and Revolutionary Periods)
http://www.ushistory.org

Several Online Encyclopedias

Wikipedia
http://www.wikipedia.org

MSN Encarta
http://encarta.msn.com/

Columbia Encyclopedia
http://www.bartleby.com/65/

Suggested Web Sites for Researching Selected Topics Found in *Essential U.S. History*

Unit I

Native Americans: Site provides information on early Native-American groups. Includes primary-source documents.
http://www.nativeamericans.com

European Explorers: Site profiles the explorers who traveled to North America. Includes links to other sites.
http://www.chenowith.k12.or.us/TECH/subject/social/explore.html

Unit II

Early America: Site gives information on America before the foundation of the United States. Includes many primary-source documents.
http://www.earlyamerica.com

American Revolution: Site provides information on the American Revolution.
http://www.americanrevolution.com

The Constitution: Site has information on the development of the U.S. Constitution, including debates among the Framers.
http://www.usconstitution.net

Bill of Rights: Among other features, site provides daily headlines on Bill-of-Rights issues.
http://www.billofrightsinstitute.org

Unit III

Lewis and Clark: Site offers the text of the journals of the Lewis and Clark Expedition. Includes maps and links to other sites.
http://lewisandclarkjournals.unl.edu/

War of 1812: Site provides information on this war with Britain.
http://members.tripod.com/~war1812/index.html

Andrew Jackson: Site gives information on President Jackson and the expansion of democracy during his two terms.
http://www.digitalhistory.uh.edu/modules/jacksonian/index.cfm

Unit IV

Slavery: Site offers information on slavery in the United States from its precolonial origins until after the Civil War.
http://www.cwc.lsu.edu/links/slave.htm

Civil War: Site offers information on the Civil War.
http://www.civil-war.net

Reconstruction: Site provides information on the Reconstruction period.
http://www.americaslibrary.gov/cgi-bin/page.cgi/jb/recon

American West: Student-created site provides information about the settling of the American West during the 19th century. Includes primary-source documents and links to other sites.
http://www.americanwest.com

Unit V
Immigration: Site chronicles the history of immigration to the United States up to the present. Includes numerous statistics.
http://www.bergen.org/AAST/projects/Immigration/

The Progressive Era: Site provides information on the Progressives.
http://www.americaslibrary.gov/cgi-bin/page.cgi/jb/progress

Women's Suffrage: Site offers information on the suffragists.
http://teacher.scholastic.com/activities/suffrage/

World War I: Site provides information on World War I.
http://www.firstworldwar.com/

Unit VI
Prohibition: Site provides information on Prohibition, 1919–1933.
http://prohibition.osu.edu

The New Deal: Site offers information, documents, and photos on the New Deal.
http://newdeal.feri.org/

World War II: Site provides information on World War II.
http://www.spartacus.schoolnet.co.uk/2WW/htm

Unit VII
Cold War: Site provides information on the Cold War. Includes primary sources.
http://www.coldwar.org/index.html

Civil Rights: Site provides information on the history of the Civil Rights Movement.
http://www.voicesofcivilrights.org/

Cuban Missile Crisis: Site offers information on the Cuban Missile Crisis. Includes documents such as transcripts of tape-recorded meetings of President Kennedy's advisors.
http://www.hpol.org/jfk/cuban/

Unit VIII

Watergate Affair: Site discusses the Watergate Affair during the Richard Nixon administration.
http://www.watergate.info

Ronald Reagan: Site offers information on the presidency of Ronald Reagan. Includes speeches and other documents.
http://www.reagan.utexas.edu

The Impeachment of President Bill Clinton: Site provides information and documents on the events that led to President Clinton's impeachment.
http://www.washingtonpost.com/wp-srv/politics/special/clinton/clinton.htm

September 11, 2001: Site provides many documents on the terrorist attacks of that day.
http://www.yale.edu/lawweb/avalon/sept_11/sept_11.htm

INDEX

Abbas, Mahmoud, 409
Abolition movement, 153, 154, 172, 174, 187
Adams, John, 59, 99, 102–103
  administration of, 105–106
  in election of 1800, 107
Adams, John Quincy, 143
Adams, Samuel, 67, 68, 71
Adamson Act (1916), 257
Addams, Jane, 217
Afghanistan, 405–406
African Americans
  abolition movement and, 153, 154, 172, 174, 187
  civil rights movement and, 353, 356–357, 365, 366
  in Civil War, 186–187
  enslaved, 43, 167–168
  as freedmen, 192, 193
  Harlem Renaissance and, 294–295
  Ku Klux Klan and, 197, 235, 294
  in labor unions, 210
  political parties and, 232
  populist movement and, 239
  as reformers, 249–250
  religion and, 150
  segregation of, 234, 306–307
  in sports, 362
  voting rights for, 194, 196–197, 233, 234, 235
  in World War I, 276
  in World War II, 319
Agnew, Spiro, 381
Agricultural Adjustment Acts (AAA) (1933), 301, 303, 306
Agricultural Marketing Act, 298
Agriculture, 3–4, 7, 8
  colonial, 44–45
  cotton, 130, 169
  Grange and, 237–238
  in Great Depression, 305–306
  in Hawaii, 264
  improvements in, 130
  indigo, 35
  rice, 43
  Shays's Rebellion and, 87
  tobacco, 28, 43
  in Western settlements after World War I, 291–292
Aguinaldo, Emilio, 267
Airplanes, 290, 296
  in World War II, 318, 323
Alabama, 123, 124
  secession of, 174
Alamo, 135
Alaska, 117
  acquisition of, 263
  mining in, 223
Albania
  Communist government in, 337

in World War II, 316
Albany Plan of Union, 62
Alien and Sedition Acts (1798), 106, 108
Allen, Ethan, 72
Alliance for Progress, 363
Al Qaeda, 404–406
American Federation of Labor (AFL), 210–211, 293, 304–305
Americanization, 218
Anarchists, 293
Andros, Sir Edmund, 52
Anglican Church, 26, 48
Anthony, Susan B., 249
Antiballistic missiles (ABMs), 378
Antietam, Battle of, 184
Anti-Federalists, 92–93
Anti-Semitism, 315–316, 323–324
Antitrust laws, 239, 256–257
Appeasement, 316
Appomattox Court House, 190
Arafat, Yasir, 402–403, 408–409
Aristide, Jean-Bertrand, 401, 408
Arizona, 163, 223
Arkansas
  Reconstruction in, 191
  secession of, 181
Armstrong, Louis, 295
Armstrong, Neil, 361, 362
Arthur, Chester A., 236
Articles of Confederation, 85–87, 125
Assumption of debt, 100
Atlanta, Georgia, 189
Atlantic Charter, 333–334
Atomic bomb, 325
  decision to drop on Japan, 326
  Soviet testing of, 345–346
Attlee, Clement, 324
Attucks, Crispus, 67
Austin, Stephen, 135
Austria, 281
  Hilter's annexation of, 316
Austria-Hungary, 273, 278, 280
Automation, 361
Automobiles, first, 289–290
Aztec empire, 21

Bacon's Rebellion, 51–52
Ballinger, Richard, 254–255
Bank(s)
  Federal Reserve and, 256
  First National, 100–101
  in Great Depression, 297–298
  "pet," 146, 147
  Second National, 129, 145–146
Banneker, Benjamin, 108
Baptists, 48, 150
Barak, Ehud, 403
Barbed wire, 228
Begin, Menachem, 384, 385

Belgium
  in World War I, 274, 276
  in World War II, 318, 323
Bell, Alexander Graham, 204
Berkeley, William, 51–52
Berlin Blockade, 339
Berlin Wall, 363–364
  opening of, 391
Bill of Rights, 49, 93
Bin Laden, Osama, 403, 404, 405–406
Black codes, 192
Blackwell, Elizabeth, 152
Bland-Allison Act (1878), 241
Blue laws, 56
Bolsheviks, 293. 276, 313
Bonus Army, 298–299
Boone, Daniel, 123
Booth, John Wilkes, 191
Borah, William, 281
Boston, Massachusetts, 29
  growth of, 59, 150
  newspaper in, 54
  police strike in, 293
  revolutionary activities in, 67, 68, 69, 72–73
  transportation in, 216
  unions in, 151
Bowie, Jim, 135
Boxer Rebellion, 268
Bradford, William, 29, 54
Brandywine, Battle of, 75
Brazil, 19
Breckinridge, John C., 174
Brezhnev, Leonid, 378
Briand, Aristide, 313
Britain
  American Revolution against, 70–79
  Civil War and, 185
  Industrial Revolution in, 127–128
  interference with U.S. shipping, 112
  Jay Treaty and, 104
  Monroe Doctrine and, 117
  territorial disputes and, 85, 115, 136
  War of 1812 and, 113–115
  in World War I, 273, 275
  in World War II, 316, 318–319.
  See also England
British East India Company, 68
Brown, John, 172, 174
Brown v. Board of Education of Topeka, 357
Bruce, Blanche K., 196
Brush, Charles F., 205
Bryan, William Jennings, 242–243, 254
Buchanan, James, 172
  administration of, 175
Bulgaria, 337

Bull Moose party, 255
Bull Run, battles of, 182, 183
Bunker Hill, Battle of, 72
Burger, Warren, 379
Burgoyne, John, 75
Burke, Edmund, 70
Burma, 324
Burr, Aaron, 107
Bush, George H.W.
　administration of, 389–391
　in election of 1988, 389
　in election of 1992, 397–398
Bush, George W., 397
　administration of, 404–413
　in election of 2000, 403–404
　in election of 2004, 404

Cabeza de Vaca, Álvar Núñez, 20
Cabinet, 90. *See also specific* ad-
　ministrations
Cabot, John, 25, 31
Cabral, Pedro, 19
Cabrillo, Juan Rodriguez, 21
Calhoun, John C., 179
　nullification and, 144
　as War Hawk, 112
California, 281
　Bear Flag Revolt in, 163
　gold rush in, 164–165, 223
　native culture in, 12
　settlement of, 22, 162–163
Calvert, Cecilius (Lord Balti-
　more), 33, 35
Camp David Accord (1978), 384,
　385
Canada, 12
　English conquest of, 63
　Revolutionary War and, 75
　Rush-Bagot Agreement and,
　115
Canal(s), 131
　Panama, 251–252, 271–273,
　384
　Suez, 344–345
Carnegie Steel Company, 206,
　208, 211
Carolinas, settlement of, 35. *See
　also* North Carolina, South
　Carolina
Carpetbaggers, 196
Carranza, Venustiano, 257–258
Carson, Kit, 134, 162
Carter, Jimmy
　administration of, 379,
　383–385, 387, 394–395
　in election of 1976, 383
　in election of 1980, 385-386
Cartier, Jacques, 23
Castro, Fidel, 346, 363
Catholic Church, 150
　Anglican Church split from, 26
　in Maryland, 33, 35, 48
　missions of, 22, 24
Catt, Carrie Chapman, 249
Cattle ranching, 225–226
Caucus, 142
Central Intelligence Agency
　(CIA), 363
Chain stores, 208
Champlain, Samuel de, 23
Charles II, King of England, 30,
　32, 52

Charles Town (Charleston), South
　Carolina, 35
　in Civil War, 181
　in Revolutionary War, 73, 78
*Charter of Liberties and Privi-
　leges,* 32
Chautauqua Institution, 218
Chávez. Hugo, 407–408
Chechnya, 402
Checks and balances, 90–92
Cheney, Dick, 404
Cherokees, 9, 126–127
Chicago
　1874 fire in, 216
　Hull House in, 217
　labor relations in, 210, 212
　skyscrapers in, 215, 291
　transportation in, 215–216
Chickasaws, 9, 126
Child labor, 151, 306
China
　Boxer Rebellion in, 268
　Communism in, 341
　intervenes in Korean War,
　342
　Japanese aggression against,
　314
　Nationalist, 378
　Open Door Policy and, 268,
　312, 314
　U.S. recognition of, 378–379
Chinese Exclusion Act (1882),
　214
Chisholm Trail, 226
Choctaws, 9, 126
Churchill, Winston, 318
　iron curtain speech of, 337
　at wartime conferences, 333,
　334
Circuit riders, 150
Cities, 129, 212–218
　life in, 214–215
　political machines in, 216–217
　reforms in, 217–218, 250
　transportation in, 215–216
　types of government in, 250
Civilian Conservation Corps
　(CCC), 301, 306
Civil Rights Act (1866), 193,
　234
Civil Rights Act (1964), 366
Civil Rights cases, 234
Civil rights movement, 373
　under Eisenhower, 356–357
　under Kennedy, 365
　under Lyndon Johnson, 366
Civil service, 235, 236–237
Civil War, 181–190
　African Americans in, 186–187
　costs of, 190
　draft in, 186
　foreign diplomacy in, 185
　home front in, 185–186
　industrial growth and, 203
　Native Americans in, 228
　women in, 187–188
Clark, George Rogers, 77
Clay, Henry, 143
　compromise of 1850 and, 170
　nullification and, 145, 146
　as War Hawk, 112
　as Whig, 146, 161

Clayton Antitrust Act (1914), 256
Clemenceau, Georges, 279
Cleveland, Grover, 212, 232, 237,
　241, 242
Clinton, Bill, 397
　administration of, 398–403
　in election of 1996, 399–400
　impeachment and acquittal of,
　400–401
Clinton, De Witt, 131
Clinton, Hillary Rodham, 398
Clinton, Sir Henry, 77
Clipper ships, 132
Coercive Acts, 69, 70
Cold War, 337–340
　in Asia, 340–344
　containment in, 337–338
　détente in, 378
　domino effect in, 367
　end of, 390–391
　in Latin America, 346
Collective bargaining, 210
Colleges
　colonial, 53–54
　later, 152
Colombia, 251–252, 271–272
Colonial America
　African Americans in, 43
　commerce in, 47–48
　education in, 53–54
　farming in, 44–45
　food in, 56
　government in, 49–51
　growth of, 41
　homes in, 55–56
　industry in, 45–46
　libraries in, 55
　militia in, 51, 70
　newspapers in, 54–55
　recreation in, 56
　relations with England, 64–70
　relations with Native Ameri-
　cans, 27, 28, 29, 33, 43,
　51–52
　religion in, 48–49
　social classes in, 41–42
　travel and communication in,
　56
Columbus, Christopher, 3, 18–19,
　38–39
Commission plan, 250
Committee for the Re-election of
　the President (CREEP),
　380–381
Committees of correspondence, 68
Commonwealth of Independent
　States (CIS), 391
Communism
　in China, 341
　fear of, in U.S., 293–294, 313,
　354–355
　in Soviet Union, 293
Compromise of 1850, 170–171
Comstock Lode, 223
Concentration camps, 323–324
Concord, Battle of, 71, 72
Confederate States of America
　formation of, 174–175.
　See also Civil War
Confederation Period, 85–87
Congregationalism, 48
Congress, U.S., 90

powers of, 89
Reconstruction and, 192, 193–195
Congress of Industrial Organizations (CIO), 304–305
Connecticut, 30, 113
Conservation
   in New Deal, 305–306
   under Roosevelt, T., 253, 254–255
Constitution, U.S., 89–91
   amending, 91–92
   checks and balances in, 90–92
   commerce and 89
   elastic clause in, 91, 101
   executive branch in, 90–91
   implied powers in, 91
   judicial branch in, 90, 91
   legislative branch in, 90
   loose construction of, 101, 102
   necessary and proper clause in, 91
   Preamble to, 89
   ratification of, 92–93
   separation of powers in, 90
   strict construction of, 101, 102
Constitutional Convention, 87–89
Containment, 337–338
Continental Army, 71
   foreign volunteers in, 76–77, 83–84
   under Washington, 71, 72–73, 74–75, 79, 83
Contract With America, 399
Coolidge, Calvin, 293
   administration of, 288–289, 312, 313
Cooperatives, 237–238
Coral Sea, Battle of, 324
Cornwallis, Lord, 75
Coronado, Francisco Vásquez de, 20
Corporations, 206
Cortés, Hernando, 21, 39
Cotton gin, 130, 169
Coughlin, Charles, 302
Cox, Archibald, 381
Cox, James M., 287–288
Coxey, Jacob S., 241
Crawford, William H., 143
Crazy Horse, 230
Creeks, 9, 126
Crime, 295, 398–399
Criminals, treatment of, 148
Crockett, Davy, 135
Crown Point, Battle of, 72
Cuba, 19
   Bay of Pigs invasion of, 363
   Castro's takeover of, 346
   Missile Crisis in, 364–365
   Platt Amendment and, 269, 313
   Spanish-American War and, 265, 266, 267, 269, 284–286
Cullen, Countee, 294
Cumberland Road, 131
Custer, George A., 230
Czechoslovakia, 280
   as Soviet satellite, 337
   in World War II, 316

Da Gama, Vasco, 18
Darfur conflict, 407

Davis, Jefferson, 175, 182
Dawes, William, 71
Dawes Act (1887), 230, 307
Dawes Plan, 312
D-Day invasion, 322–323
Debs, Eugene V., 212, 292
Declaration of Human Rights, 336
Declaration of Independence, 73, 108, 153
Declaration of Rights, 70
Declaration of Sentiments, 153
Declaratory Act, 66
Deficit spending, 307, 416
Deflation, 241
De Grasse, Count, 79
Delaware, 33
   as border state, 181
DeLay, Tom, 412
Democratic party, 143
   in Civil War, 185–186
   in late 1800s, 232–233
   tariffs and, 237.
   See also specific Elections
Democratic-Republicans, 102–103
   Alien and Sedition Acts and, 106
   in election of 1800, 107
   in election of 1824, 143
   in power, 108–109
Denazification, 335
Denmark, 318
Department stores, 208
Depressions, 147
Deregulation, 387
De Soto, Hernando, 20
Détente, 378
Dewey, George, 266
Dewey, Thomas E., 353
Direct democracy, 51
Direct primary, 250–251
Disabled, training for, 148
Disciples of Christ, 149
Dix, Dorothea, 148, 152, 187
Dole, Robert, 400
Dole, Sanford, 264
Dollar Diplomacy, 254, 257
Dongan, Thomas, 32
Douglas, Stephen A., 171–172
   debate with Lincoln, 173–174
Douglass, Frederick, 154
Draft
   in Civil War, 186
   in World War I, 276
   in World War II, 319
Drake, Edwin L., 204–205
Drake, Sir Francis, 25
Dred Scott v. Sanford, 173
DuBois, W.E.B., 249, 261
Dukakis, Michael, 389
Duke, James B., 208
Duryea brothers, 289
Dutch East Indies, 324
Dutch Reformed Church, 48, 53

Earhart, Amelia, 290
East Germany, 337
Edison, Thomas A., 205
Education
   in Colonial America, 53–54
   desegregation of, 356–357

improvements in, 151–152, 218, 412
Edwards, John, 404
Egypt
   conflict with Israel, 344–345
   peace with Israel, 384, 385
Eighteenth Amendment, 257, 289, 295
Eighth Amendment, 93
Eisenhower, Dwight D.
   administration of, 344, 355–358
   in election of 1952, 344, 355
   in election of 1956, 355–356
   on military-industrial complex, 356
Eisenhower Doctrine, 345
Elastic clause, 91, 101
Elections
   of 1788, 99
   of 1796, 105
   of 1800, 107
   of 1804, 112
   of 1808, 113
   of 1816, 116
   of 1824 and 1828, 143
   of 1832, 146
   of 1840, 147
   of 1844, 161
   of 1856, 172
   of 1860, 174–175
   of 1864, 191
   of 1876, 197
   of 1888, 237
   of 1892, 237, 241
   of 1896, 241–243
   of 1904, 251, 254
   of 1908, 254
   of 1912, 255
   of 1916, 273
   of 1920, 287
   of 1924 and 1928, 289
   of 1932, 299–300
   of 1936, 303
   of 1948, 353
   of 1952, 355
   of 1956, 355–356
   of 1960, 362–363
   of 1964, 366
   of 1968, 369
   of 1972 380
   of 1976, 383
   of 1980 and 1984, 385–386
   of 1988, 389
   of 1992, 397–398
   of 1994, 399
   of 1996, 399–400
   of 2000, 403–404
   of 2004, 404
   of 2006, 413
Electoral college, 91, 107, 142
Electrical power, 205
Elkins Act (1903), 252
El Salvador, 387–388, 389
Emancipation Proclamation, 187
Embargo Act (1807), 112
Emergency Quota Act (1921), 288
Emerson, Ralph Waldo, 150
Enders, John, 360
England
   colonies of, 26–35
   conquest of Canada, 63

England *(continued)*
   Parliament in, 35, 50, 66, 70
   pirates of, 25
   relations with colonies, 64–70
   rivalry with France, 61–64
   search for northwest passage,
     25–26
   slave trade and, 22.
   See also Britain
Enumerated articles, 65
Environmental Protection
   Agency, 387
Episcopal Church, 48
Era of Good Feelings, 116
Ericson, Leif, 18
Erie Canal, 131
Erving, Sam, 381
Escobedo v. *Illinois,* 357
Export-Import Bank, 313

Factories, 127, 128
   assembly lines in, 290
   automation in, 361
   switch to electric power, 205
   textile, 128
Fair Deal, 353
Fair Labor Standards Act (1938),
   306
Fallen Timbers, Battle of, 113,
   126
Farragut, David G., 183
Fascism, 315
Federal Deposit Insurance Corpo-
   ration (FDIC), 301
Federal Emergency Relief Admin-
   istration (FERA), 301
Federalism, 91
Federalists, 92
   Alien and Sedition Acts and,
     106
   decline of, 107, 116
   in election of 1800, 107
   Hartford Convention and, 113
   origin of, 102–103
Federal Reserve Act (1913), 256
Feminists, 152, 248–249
Fermi, Enrico, 359
Field, Cyrus, 204
Fifteenth Amendment, 194, 234
Fifth Amendment, 93
Filibuster, 198
Fillmore, Millard, 172
First Amendment, 93
First Continental Congress,
   69–70
Fitch, John, 132
Fitzgerald, F. Scott, 296
Five Civilized Tribes, 126–127,
   228
Florida, 22, 116
   acquisition of, 116–117
   secession of, 174
Foch, Ferdinand, 277
Food and Drug Administration,
   387
Force Bill (1833), 145
Ford, Gerald, 381, 382, 394
Ford, Henry, 289
Ford Motor Company, 290, 292
Fordney-McCumber Tariff (1922),
   288
Fort Christina, 33

Fort Duquesne, 63
Fort McHenry, 114
Fort Sumter, 181
Fort Ticonderoga, 75
Fourteen Points, 279
Fourteenth Amendment,
   193–194, 234
Fourth Amendment, 93
France, 22–24
   Civil War and, 185
   foreign relations with, 103,
     105–106, 112
   Louisiana Purchase and,
     110
   in Revolutionary War, 76
   rivalry with England, 61–64
   in World War I, 273, 274, 275,
     276
   in World War II, 316, 322–323
Franco, Francisco, 316
Franklin, Benjamin, 54, 55, 59,
   62, 88
Franz Ferdinand, assassination
   of, 273
Freedmen's Bureau, 193
Freeport Doctrine, 174
Free silver, 241–242
Frémont, John C., 162, 172
French and Indian War, 61–64,
   65, 110
   treaty ending, 63–64
French Indochina, 324, 367
Friedan, Betty, 374
Fugitive Slave Law, 171–172
Fulton, Robert, 132
*Fundamental Orders of Connecti-
cut,* 30
Fur trade, 24, 31, 46, 61, 134

Gadsden Purchase, 166
Gage, Thomas, 69, 71
Galbraith, John Kenneth,
   358–359
Gallaudet, Thomas H., 148
Garfield, James A., 236
Garrison, William Lloyd, 154
Genêt, Edmond, 103
George III, King of England, 71,
   73, 74
Georgia, 35
   in Civil War, 189
   secession of, 174
Germans, immigration of, 133,
   134
Germany
   Hitler and, 315
   nonaggression pact with Rus-
     sia, 316
   postwar crises in, 337, 339,
     363–364
   question of, in wartime confer-
     ences, 334–335
   reunification of, 391
   Versailles Treaty and, 279–280
   in World War I, 273, 275,
     277–278
   in World War II, 316, 317–319,
     323
Gettysburg, Battle of, 189–190
Ghent, Treaty of (1814), 115
GI Bill of Rights, 352
Gideon v. *Wainwright,* 357

Gilbert, Sir Humphrey, 26–27
Gingrich, Newt, 399
Glass-Steagall Act (1933), 301
Glenn, John, 361
Gold rush, 164–165, 223
Gold standard, 241
Goldwater, Barry M., 366
Gompers, Samuel, 210–211
Good Neighbor Policy, 313
Gorbachev, Mikhail, 388, 391
Gore, Al, 397
   in election of 2000, 403–404
   in election of 2004, 404
Grandfather clause, 235
Grange, the, 237–238, 239, 240,
   245
Grant, Ulysses S.
   as Civil War general, 183, 190,
     197
   as president, 197
Great Awakening, 49
Great Compromise, 88–89
Great Depression, 297
   effects of, 297–298
   end of, 306
Great Law, 33
Great Society, 366–367
Greece
   Truman Doctrine and, 338
   in World War II, 318
Green Mountain Boys, 72
Greene, Nathanael, 78
Grimké sisters, 153, 154
Gross Domestic Product (GDP),
   299, 410
Guadalcanal, Battle of, 325
Guadalupe Hidalgo, Treaty of
   (1848), 163
Guam, 264, 324

Haiti, 270, 313, 401, 408
Hall, John, 129
Hamas, 409
Hamilton, Alexander
   as delegate to Constitutional
     Convention, 88
   election of 1800 and, 107
   as Federalist, 93
   as secretary of the treasury,
     99, 100–102
Hamilton, Andrew, 55
Hancock, John, 71
Harding, Warren G., 287–288,
   312, 313
Harlem Renaissance, 294
Harpers Ferry, Virginia, 174
Harrison, Benjamin, 237
Harrison, William Henry, 147
Hartford Convention, 113
Hawaii, 264–265
   in World War II, 319, 324
Hawley-Smoot Tariff (1930), 298,
   313
Hay, John, 268
Hay-Bunau-Varilla Treaty,
   272–273
Hayes, Rutherford B., 197–198
   administration of, 235
   labor relations and, 210
Haymarket Square, 210
Hayne, Robert, 145
Haywood, William, 293

Head Start, 367
Hearst, William Randolph, 265
Helsinki Agreement (1975), 382
Hemingway, Ernest, 296
Henry, Patrick, 66, 88
Henry Street Settlement, 217
Henry VII, King of England, 25
Hepburn Act (1906), 252
Hessians, 73, 75, 83–84
Hezbollah, 409
Hiroshima, Japan, 326
Hiss, Alger, 354
Hitler, Adolf, 315
    aggressive actions of, 316–318
    suicide of, 323
Ho Chi Minh, 344, 367
Holding company, 208
Holocaust, 323–324
Home rule, 250
Homestead strike, 211
Homestead Act (1862), 185, 226
Hoover, Herbert, 288
    administration of, 295,
        298–299, 307, 313
    in election of 1928, 289, 311
    in election of 1932, 299–300
Horseshoe Bend, Battle of, 123
House of Representatives, U.S.,
    89, 90, 232, 399, 413. *See also*
    specific Elections
Houston, Sam, 135–136
Howe, William, 74, 75
Hudson, Henry, 24–25
Huerta, Victoriano, 257
Hughes, Charles Evans, 251, 288
Hughes, Langston, 294, 295
Hull, Cordell, 300
Hull House, 217
Humphrey, Hubert H., 366, 369
Hungary, 281
    1956 conflict in, 344
    as Soviet satellite, 337
Hurricane Katrina, 410, 413
Hussein, Saddam, 389–390, 403,
    406–407
Hutchinson, Anne, 30, 31

Ice Age, 1–2
Ickes, Harold L., 300
Idaho, 223, 281
Immigrants
    education of, 218
    political parties and, 233,
        221–222
    work of, on the railroads, 225
Immigration
    Civil War and, 185
    Irish, 133, 134, 150
    Japanese, 253–254
    new, 212–214
    old, 132–134, 213
    quotas on, 288
    after 1965, 367
Impeachment, 90
    of Clinton, 400–401
    of Johnson, 194–195
    Nixon and, 381–382
Implied powers, 91
Impressment, 104
Independent Treasury System,
    147
Indian Territory, 127, 145, 228

Industrial Revolution, 127–128,
    204
Industrial Workers of the World
    (IWW), 293
Industry. *See also* Factories
    growth of, 203–205, 289–291
    Hamilton's encouragement of,
        101
    infant, 129
Inflation, 241, 380
Initiative, 251
Installment buying, 209
Interchangeable parts, 128–129
Intercontinental ballistic missiles
    (ICBMs), 378
International Brigade, 316
Interstate Commerce Act (1887),
    238–239
Interstate Commerce Commis-
    sion (ICC), 239, 252–253
Intolerable Acts, 69
Iran
    hostage crisis in, 384, 385
    Israeli-Palestinian conflict
        and, 409
    nuclear activities in, 408
    war with Iraq, 389–390
Iran-Contra Affair, 388
Iraq
    invasion of Kuwait, 390
    U.S. wars with, 390, 406–407,
        410
    war with Iran, 389–390
    weapons of mass destruction
        in, 403, 406
Irish, immigration of, 133, 134,
    150
Iron Curtain, 337
Iroquois Confederacy, 9
Isabella, Queen of Spain, 18
Israel
    Arab conflict and, 344–345,
        384–385
    conflict with Lebanon, 388,
        409
Israeli-Palestinian conflict,
    402–403, 408–409
Italy
    fascism in, 315
    in World War I, 279
    in World War II, 318, 322
Iwo Jima, Battle of, 325

Jackson, Andrew
    administration of, 142–146,
        158–159
    Cabinet of, 143
    in election of 1824, 143
    Native Americans and, 117,
        123, 145
    nullification and, 144–145
    political parties and, 142–143
    in War of 1812, 142
Jackson, Helen Hunt, 230
Jackson, Thomas J. "Stonewall,"
    182, 183
James II, King of England, 32, 52
Jamestown, 27–28
    Bacon's Rebellion in, 51–52
Japan
    attack on Pearl Harbor, 319,
        324

decision to drop atomic bomb
    on, 326
    militarism in, 314
    post-World War II, 340
    U.S. expedition to, 268–269
    in World War I, 279
    in World War II, 319, 324–326
Japanese Americans, relocation
    of, 320–321
Japanese immigrants, 253–254
Jay, John, 93, 99, 104
Jay Treaty, 104, 105
Jefferson, Thomas
    as author of Declaration of In-
        dependence, 73, 108
    as Democratic-Republican, 102
    in election of 1796, 105
    in election of 1800, 107, 108
    Louisiana Purchase and,
        109–111
    second term of, 112–113
    as secretary of state, 99, 100
    slavery and, 153–154
Jews, 49, 213
    employment of, 214
    Holocaust and, 323–324.
    See also Anti-Semitism
Jim Crow laws, 234
Job Corps, 367
Johnson, Andrew, 191
    impeachment of, 194–195
    Reconstruction and, 191–192,
        193–194
Johnson, Hiram, 251, 281
Johnson, Lyndon, 364, 365
    Great Society under, 366–367
    Vietnam War and, 368–369
Joint-stock companies, 27, 29
Joseph, Chief, 229
Journalism, 54–55
    muckrakers and, 248
    Spanish-American War and,
        265
Judicial review, 91, 109
Judiciary Act (1789), 99, 109

Kalb, Baron de, 76
Kansas-Nebraska Act (1854),
    171–172
Karzai, Hamid, 406
Kellogg-Briand Pact (1928),
    312–313
Kelly, William, 204
Kennan, George, 337–338
Kennedy, John F., 362–363
    administration of, 363–365
    assassination of, 365
    Vietnam War and, 368
Kentucky, 123, 124
    as border state, 181
    settlement of, 123, 124
Kentucky Resolution, 106
Kerouac, Jack, 373
Kerry, John, in election of 2004,
    404
Key, Francis Scott, 114
Khrushchev, Nikita, 345–346
King, Martin Luther, Jr., 357,
    364, 365, 374–375
King, Rufus, 116
King Philip's War, 43
King's Mountain, Battle of, 78

Kissinger, Henry, 378
Knights of Labor, 210, 211
Know-Nothings, 134
Knox, Henry, 99, 100
Korean War, 341–345
Kosciusko, Thaddeus, 77
Kosovo, 401
Ku Klux Klan, 197, 235, 294, 310
Kuwait, 390

Labor unions, 150–151, 255, 293
    problems of, 209–212
    under Roosevelt, Franklin D., 302, 304–305
    under Truman, 352–353
    post-World War I, 292.
    See also specific
Lafayette, Marquis de, 76
La Follette, Robert, 251, 281
La Follette Seamen's Act (1915), 257
La Salle, Robert Cavelier de, 23
Latin America
    Alliance for Progress in, 363
    Cold War and, 346
    Dollar Diplomacy and, 254, 257
    Good Neighbor Policy toward, 313
    Monroe Doctrine and, 117
    Roosevelt Corollary and, 252
League of Nations, 280–282
    debate on U.S. membership in, 281, 287
    in 1930s, 314
Lease, Mary Elizabeth, 246
Lebanon, 388, 389
    Israeli conflict with, 388, 409
Lee, Richard Henry, 73
Lee, Robert E., 183, 189, 190
Leisler's Rebellion, 52
Lend-Lease Act (1941), 318
Lewis, John L., 304
Lewis and Clark expedition, 110, 111, 223
Lexington, Battle of, 71, 72
Leyte Gulf, Battle of, 325
Liberia, 154
Liberty League, 302
Liberty party, 154
Libraries, 55, 218
Lieberman, Joseph, 403–404
Liliuokalani, Queen, 264–265
Lincoln, Abraham, 175
    assassination of, 191
    Civil War and, 181–184
    debate with Douglas, 173–174
    Emancipation Proclamation of, 187
    Gettysburg Address of, 190
    Reconstruction plan of, 191
Lindbergh, Charles, 296
Literacy tests, 234
Little Bighorn, Battle of, 230
Livingston, Robert, 110
Lloyd George, David, 279
Lobbies, 149
Lodge, Henry Cabot, 281
Long, Huey P., 302
Louisiana, 23, 104, 413
    in Civil War, 174, 183
    Reconstruction in, 191

Louisiana Purchase, 109–111, 116, 170
Louis XIV, King of France, 23
Lowell, Francis, 128
Loyalists, 70
Lusitania, 275
Lutherans, 48
Luxembourg, 318
Lyon, Mary, 152

MacArthur, Douglas, 299
    in Korean War, 342, 349–351
    in World War II, 324, 325
Madison, James, 88, 93
    as Democratic-Republican, 102
    election as president, 113
Magellan, Ferdinand, 19
Magna Carta, 49
Mahan, Alfred Thayer, 263–264
Mail-order companies, 208
Maine explosion, 265
Maliki, Nuri Kamal al-, 407
Manhattan Project, 325–326
Manifest destiny, 161
Mann, Horace, 151
Mann-Elkins Act (1910), 254
Marbury v. *Madison,* 109
Marconi, Guglielmo, 204
Marshall, George, 338
Marshall, John, 109, 145
Marshall Plan, 338, 339
Martí, José, 284–285
Maryland, 33, 35
    as border state, 181
    Catholic Church in, 33, 35, 48
Massachusetts Bay Colony, 29–30, 31
Massasoit, 29
Mayflower Compact, 29
McCarran Act (1950), 354–355
McCarthyism, 354–355, 356, 361
McClellan, George B., 183, 184
McCord, James, 380
McCormick Harvester Company, 210
McGovern, George, 369
McKay, Claude, 294
McKinley, William, 242, 243
    administration of, 237, 265, 267, 285–286
    assassination of, 251, 293
Meat Inspection Act (1906), 253
Medicine, 360
    health insurance and, 398, 416
    Medicare and, 398
    prescription drugs and, 412
Mellon, Andrew, 288, 289
Mennonites, 48
Mentally ill, care of, 148
Mercantilism, 26, 64
Mergers, 206–207
Methodists, 150
Mexican Cession, 163, 170
Mexico, 162
    revolution in, 257, 270
    U.S. war with, 163–164, 182
    World War I and, 276
Middle Colonies, 31–33
    commerce in, 47–48
    farming in, 44
    homes in, 55

Middle East, conflict in, 344–345, 384–385, 388, 402–403, 408, 409
Midway Island, 265, 324
Militia, colonial, 51, 70
Milosevic, Slobodan, 401
Minutemen, 70, 71
Miranda v. *Arizona,* 357
Mississippi, 123, 124
    in Civil War, 174, 183
Missouri, 181
Missouri Compromise, 170, 171–172, 173
Mitchell, Maria, 152
Mondale, Walter, 383, 386
Monitor vs. *Merrimac,* 183
Monroe, James, 116
    administration of, 116–117
    Louisiana Purchase and, 110
Monroe Doctrine, 117
    Roosevelt Corollary to, 252, 270
Montana, 223, 230
Montgomery, Bernard L., 321–322
Montreal, 23, 63
Morgan, J. Pierpont, 208
Mormons, 149, 165–166
Morrill Act (1862), 218
Morrill Tariff, 185
Morse, Samuel F.B., 132
Morton, "Jelly Roll," 295
Moseley-Braun, Carol, 398
Mott, Lucretia, 153
Mound Builders, 8
Mountain men, 134
Muckrakers, 248
Munn v. *Illinois,* 238
Mussolini, Benito, 315, 322

Nagasaki, Japan, 326
Napoleon, 110
Nasser, Gamal Abdel, 344
National Aeronautics and Space Administration (NASA), 360–361
National American Woman Suffrage Association, 249
National Association for the Advancement of Colored People (NAACP), 250, 356–357
National banks, 100–101, 129, 145–146
National Conservation Commission, 253
National Industrial Recovery Act (1933), 301
National Labor Relations Board (NLRB), 302
National Recovery Administration (NRA), 301, 303
National Republicans, 143, 146–147
National Road, 131
National Security Agency (NSA), 405
National Trades Union, 151
National Urban League, 250
Native Americans, 1–5
    in California, 12
    in Civil War, 228

colonists and, 27, 28, 29, 33, 43, 51–52
Dawes Act and, 230, 307
in Eastern Woodlands, 9–10
farming by, 3–4, 7, 8
French policy toward, 24
frontier settlements and, 104, 112–113
in Great Basin, 12
impact of diseases on, 21
impact of horse, 11
Jackson and, 117, 123, 145
languages of, 5
missions for, 22, 24, 162
New Deal and, 307
in Northwest Coast, 12–14
in Plains, 10–12
religion of, 9–10, 11–12, 13–14, 230
reservations for, 228–231
in Southeast, 8–9
in Southwest, 5–8
Western settlement and, 123, 126–127, 228–231
women, 12
Nativism, 134, 214
Navigation Acts, 64
Nazism, 315, 323–324
Netherlands
as colonial power, 24–25, 53
in Revolutionary War, 76
slave trade and, 22, 28
in World War II, 318, 323
Nevada, 223
New Amsterdam, 24, 25, 53
New Deal, 300–308
legacy of, 306–308.
See also Great Depression
New Deal coalition, 307, 386
New England
colonies in, 29–31
commerce in, 47
factories in, 128
farming in, 44
homes in, 55
town meetings in, 50–51.
See also specific colonies and states
New France, 23–24
New Jersey, 32, 52
in Revolutionary War, 74–75
New Jersey Plan, 88
Newlands Act (1902), 253
New Mexico, 22, 163
New Nationalism, 255
New Netherland, 24, 25, 31–32, 33, 53
New Orleans, 183
destruction of, in Hurricane Katrina, 413
Pinckney Treaty and, 104
New Sweden, 33
New York, 52. *See also* New Netherland
colonial assembly in, 66
in Revolutionary War, 72, 74–75, 76
settlement of, 31–32
New York City
antidraft riots in, 186
as first capital, 99
growth of, 131, 150

Henry Street Settlement in, 217
immigrants in, 212
skyscrapers in, 291
transportation in, 216
Tweed Ring in, 216–217
unions in, 151
Nez Percé, 229
Niagara Movement, 249, 261
Nicaragua
civil war in, 387–388, 389
U.S. troops in, 270, 313
Nineteenth Amendment, 257
Ninth Amendment, 93
Nixon, Richard M., 362–363
administration of, 377–382
in election of 1968, 369
Vietnam War and, 369, 371
Watergate crisis and, 380–382
No Child Left Behind Act (2002), 412
Nominating convention, 143
Non-Intercourse Act (1809), 112
North America, 1
European settlers in, 18–35
native cultures of, 1–14, 16–17
after Treaty of Paris (1763), 63–64
after Treaty of Paris (1783), 79
North American Free Trade Agreement (NAFTA), 401, 415
North Atlantic Treaty Organization (NATO), 340, 363, 401
North Carolina, 35, 358
in Revolutionary War, 78
secession of, 181
North Korea, 341–342
nuclear proliferation and, 408
Northwest Ordinance (1787), 86, 124, 154
Northwest passage, 22, 25–26
Northwest Territory, 17, 86, 124–126
banning of slavery in, 154
British and, 85, 104
Norway, 318
Nuclear proliferation, 365, 408
Nullification, 106, 144–145
Nuremberg Trials, 335

Office of Economic Opportunity, 366–367, 380
Oglethorpe, James, 35
Ohio, 65, 69
growth of cities in, 214
reform in, 250
Oil, 204–205, 380, 383
Okinawa, Battle of, 325
Old Southwest, 123, 124
Oliver, Joe "King," 295
Open Door Policy, 268, 312, 314
Open range, 226
Ordinance of 1785, 86, 124, 125
Ordinance of 1787, 124
Oregon, 136–137, 162
Organization of American States (OAS), 346
Organization of Petroleum Exporting Countries (OPEC), 380

Oswald, Lee Harvey, 365
Otis, James, 65

Pacifists, 293
Pahlevi, Shah Mohammed Reza, 385
Paine, Thomas, 73
Palestine Liberation Organization (PLO), 402–403, 408–409
Palmer, A. Mitchell, 293–294
Panama Canal, 271–273
construction of, 251–252
Panama Canal Treaties (1977), 384
Paris, Treaty of (1763), 63–64
Paris, Treaty of (1783), 79, 86, 104
Paris Peace Conference (1918), 279
Parks, Rosa, 357
Patriot Act (2001), 405
Patriots, 70
Payne-Aldrich Tariff (1909), 252
Peace Corps, 363
Pendleton Act (1883), 236
Penitentiaries, 148
Penn, William, 32–33, 53
Pennsylvania, 32–33
Civil War in, 189–190
labor disputes in, 211
Perkins, Frances, 300
Perot, H. Ross, 397–398, 400
Perry, Matthew C., 268–269
Pershing, John J., 258, 277
Persian Gulf Wars, 390, 406
Pet banks, 146, 147
Philadelphia, 150
Constitutional Convention in, 87–89
First Continental Congress in, 69–70
library in, 55
in Revolutionary War, 75
settlement of, 32–33
as temporary capital, 100
unions in, 151
Philip, King, 43
Philip II, King of Spain, 25
Philippines
interest in independence, 267–268
Spanish-American War in, 266, 267
in World War II, 324, 325
Phillips, David Graham, 248
Pickett, George E., 189
Pike, Zebulon, 111
Pilgrims, 29
Pinchot, Gifford, 253, 254–255
Pinckney, Charles, 45, 105
Pinckney, Eliza Lucas, 45
Pinckney, Thomas, 45, 104
Pinckney Treaty, 104
Pitt, William, 62–63, 66, 70
Platt Amendment, 269, 313
Plessy v. *Ferguson,* 234, 356–357
Plymouth, Massachusetts, 29
Pocahontas, 28
Poland, 280
Solidarity in, 390
as Soviet satellite, 337
in World War II, 316, 317–318, 323–324

Political machines, 216–217
Political parties
first, 102–103
in Jacksonian era, 142–143
in late 1800s, 232–233.
See also specific
Polk, James K., 161
Poll taxes, 234
Ponce de León, Juan, 20
Pontiac's Rebellion, 65
Pony Express, 224
Pools, 207
Popular sovereignty, 170, 174
Populist movement, 239–241
Populist party, 240–241
in election of 1896, 242–243
Portsmouth, Treaty of, 252, 269
Portugal, 18, 19
slave trade and, 21–22
Potlatch, 14
Potsdam Conference (1945), 334
Presbyterians, 149
Presidents
in Constitution, 90–91.
See also specific
Princeton, Battle of, 75
Privateers, 77
Proclamation of 1763, 65
Proclamation of Neutrality
(1793), 103
Progressive Era, 248–258
city and state reforms in,
250–251
presidents in, 251–258
reformers in, 248–250
Progressive party, 255
Prohibition, 149, 257, 295
Promontory Point, Utah, 225
Prophet, the, 113
Protectionism, 145, 236–237. *See
also* Tariffs
Puerto Rico, 266–267, 269
Pulaski, Casimir, 77
Pulitzer, Joseph, 265
Pullman strike, 212
Pure Food and Drug Act (1906),
253
Puritans, 26, 29, 48, 53, 56
Putin, Vladimir, 402

Qaddafi, Muammar, 408
Quakers, 48, 155
in Pennsylvania, 32–33
Quartering Act, 65–66
Quebec, 23, 63
Quebec Act, 69

Rabin, Yitzhak, 402
Race riots, 186, 250, 294
Racial discrimination, 233–235,
356–357
Radical Republicans, 192, 197
Rahman, Sheik Omar Abdel, 403
Railroads, 132, 172, 207
cattle ranching and, 226
Grange and, 238–239
improvements to, 203
reforms for, 252–253
strikes on, 210, 211
transcontinental, 224–225
Raleigh, Sir Walter, 26–27
Randolph, Edmund, 99, 100

Reagan, Ronald, 385–388, 395
Recall, 251
Reconstruction, 190–192,
196–197
Congress and, 192–195, 232
end of, 197–198, 233
Reconstruction Acts, 194
Reconstruction Finance Corpora-
tion (RFC), 298
Red Scare, 293–294
Referendums, 251
Reformatories, 148
Religion. *See also specific*
in Colonial America, 48–49
in early 1800s, 149–150
freedom of, 29–30
Native-American, 9–10, 11–12,
13–14
as reason for colonization, 26
Reparations, 279
Representative assemblies, 49–51
Republican party, 171–172
in Civil War, 185
in late 1800s, 232–233
in Reconstruction, 192–195
tariffs and, 237.
See also specific Elections
Revels, Hiram R., 196
Revere, Paul, 71
Revolutionary War, 70–79
battles in, 71, 72–75, 77
end of, 77–79
foreign aid in, 76–77
women in, 71
Rhode Island, 30–31
Richmond, Virginia, 182, 183,
184
Riis, Jacob, 217
Robinson, Jackie, 362
Rochambeau, Count, 79
Rockefeller, John D., 207
Rockefeller, Nelson A., 382
Roe v. *Wade,* 379
Rolfe, John, 28
Romania, 280
as Soviet satellite, 337
in World War II, 318
Rome-Berlin Axis, 316
Rommel, Erwin, 321, 322
Roosevelt, Eleanor, 300
Roosevelt, Franklin D., 299–308
death of, 325
foreign policy of, 313
Supreme Court and, 303–304
in World War II, 319, 324,331,
333–334, 336
Roosevelt, Theodore
in election of 1904, 251
in election of 1912, 255
Panama Canal and, 251–252,
271–272
as Rough Rider, 266
Russo-Japanese War peace ne-
gotiations and, 269
Square Deal under, 251–254,
269
Roosevelt Corollary, 252, 270
Rosenberg, Ethel and Julius, 354
Rotation in office, 144
Rush-Bagot Agreement (1817),
115
Russia, 136

Bolshevik revolution in, 276,
293, 313
nonaggression pact with Germany, 316
under Putin, 402
in World War I, 273, 274, 276.
See also Soviet Union
Russo-Japanese War
(1904–1905), 269
Rutledge, John, 88
Rwanda, 403

Sabin, Albert, 360
Sacagawea, 111
Sacco and Vanzetti, 294
Sadat, Anwar, 384, 385
St. Augustine, Florida, 22
St. Leger, 75
Salk, Jonas, 360
Salutary neglect, 64
Samoan Islands, 265
Sandinistas, 387–388
San Jacinto, Battle of, 135
Santa Anna, Antonio de, 135–136
Santa Fe, New Mexico, 22, 134
Saratoga, Battle of, 75, 76
Savannah, Georgia, 35
in Civil War, 189
Revolutionary War in, 77, 78
Savings and loan institutions
(S&Ls), 387
Scalawags, 196
Scott, Dred, 173
Seattle, Washington, 293
Secession of states, 174–175
Second Amendment, 93
Second Bank of the United
States, 129, 145–146
Second Continental Congress, 71,
72, 73
Secret ballot, 251
Sectionalism, 167–180
Segregation, 234, 306–307,
356–357
Seminoles, 9, 117, 126
Senate, U.S., 88, 90, 232
direct election of, 257
Separation of church and state,
29–30
Separation of powers, in Consti-
tution, 90
Separatists, 26, 29
September 11, 2001 terrorist at-
tacks, 397, 404–405, 406
Serbia, 273, 401
Serra, Junípero, 162
Seven Days' Battles, 183
Seventeenth Amendment, 91, 257
Seventh Amendment, 93
Seven Years' War, 61
Seward, William H., 170, 263
Shakers, 150
Shays' Rebellion, 87
Sherman, William T., 188–189
Sherman Antitrust Act (1890),
239, 256
Sherman Silver Purchase Act
(1890), 241
Sinclair, Upton, 253, 261, 292
Sino-Japanese War (1894–1895),
269
Sioux, 11, 229–230

Sirica, John, 380
Sitdown strikes, 305
Sit-ins, 358, 365
Sitting Bull, 230
Six-Day War, 384
Sixteenth Amendment, 254, 256
Sixth Amendment, 93
Skyscrapers, 215, 291
Slater, Samuel, 128
Slavery, 21, 43, 55, 167–175
    abolition of, 172, 192
    crusade against, 153–155
    politics of, 169–175, 179
    Three-Fifths Compromise and,
    89
Slaves
    emancipation of, 187
    lives of, 43, 55, 167–168,
    178–179
    price of, 167
    runaway, 117
    uprisings of, 110, 169
Slidell, John, 163
Smith, Alfred E., 289, 302
Smith, Bessie, 295
Smith, John, 27, 165–166
Smith, Joseph, 149
Socialists, 292
Social Security, 302, 304, 333,
    399, 411–412
Social work, 217–218
Solidarity, 390
Somalia, 403
Sons of Liberty, 66, 68
South, 33, 35, 48
    Civil War in, 181–190
    economic development in, 233
    farming in, 43, 44–45
    racial discrimination in,
    233–235
    Reconstruction in, 190–192,
    196–197
    Revolution in, 73, 77–79
    secession in, 174, 181
South Carolina, 35
    Civil War in, 189
    Reconstruction in, 196
    Revolution in, 73, 77
    secession of, 174
    settlement of, 35
South Carolina Exposition and
    Protest, 144–145
South Korea, 341–342
Soviet Union
    under Gorbachev, 388, 390–391
    space achievements of,
    360–361
    U.S. diplomatic relations with,
    313, 345–346, 378, 388
    in World War II, 316, 318, 321.
    See also Russia
Space, achievements in, 360–361
Spain
    colonies of, 21–22
    control of Florida and, 116
    exploration by, 18–21, 20–21
    missions of, 22, 24, 162
    Pinckney Treaty and, 104
    territorial disputes and, 11,
    85
Spanish-American War, 265–267,
    269

Spanish Armada, 25
Spanish Civil War, 316
Spargo, John, 248
Specie Circular, 147
Spoils system, 144, 232
Square Deal, 251–254
Stagflation, 379
Stalin, Joseph, 316
Stamp Act, 66
Stanton, Edwin, 195
Stanton, Elizabeth Cady, 153
Starr, Kenneth, 400
"The Star-Spangled Banner," 114
States' rights, 145
States' Rights party, 353
Steamboats, 132
Steel industry, 204, 206
Steffens, Lincoln, 248
Stephens, Alexander, 175, 192
Steuben, Baron von, 76–77
Stevens, Thaddeus, 192
Stock market crash, 296–300
Stowe, Harriet Beecher, 171
Strategic Arms Limitation Talks
    (SALT), 378
Strategic Defense Initiative,
    387
Strikes, 210, 211, 212, 253, 293
    sitdown, 305
Submarines
    nuclear-powered, 360
    in World War I, 275, 276
Subsidiaries, 208
Sudan, civil wars in, 407
Suez Canal conflict, 344–345
Sugar Act, 65
Sullivan, Louis H., 215
Sumner, Charles, 192
Supply-side economics, 386
Supreme Court, U.S., 90, 173, 238
    under Burger, 379
    creation of first, 99
    under Marshall, 109, 145
    Roosevelt and, 303–304
    under Warren, 356–357
Syria, 409
Szilard, Leo, 359–360

Taft, William Howard, 254–255
    in election of 1912, 255
    as governor of the Philippines,
    268
Taft-Hartley Act (1947), 352–353
Taiwan, Nationalist regime on,
    378
Taliban, 404, 405–406
Tammany Hall, 289
Tarbell, Ida, 248
Tariffs, 101, 129, 144, 145,
    236–237
Taylor, Zachary, 163
Tea Act, 68
Teapot Dome scandal, 288
Tecumseh, 113
Tehran Conference (1943), 334
Telegraph, 132, 204, 224
Telephone, 204
Television, 361, 362
Teller, Edward, 360
Tenements, 214–215
Tennessee, 123, 124
    Reconstruction in, 191

secession of, 181
Tennessee Valley Authority
    (TVA), 301, 356
Tenth Amendment, 93
Tenure of Office Act (1867),
    194–195
Texas
    annexation of, 161–162
    Reconstruction in, 192
    Republic of, 134–136
    secession of, 174
Textile industry, 128, 185
Thailand, 324
Third Amendment, 93
Thirteen Amendment, 192
Thoreau, Henry David, 179
Three-Fifths Compromise, 89
Thurmond, Strom, 353
Ticonderoga, Battle of, 72
Tilden, Samuel J., 197
Time zones, 203–204
Tippecanoe, Battle of, 113, 126,
    147
Toleration Act, 35
Tonkin Gulf Resolution, 368, 369
Town meetings, 50–51
Townsend, Francis E., 302
Townshend Acts, 66–67
Trail of Tears, 127, 145, 228
Transcontinental railroads,
    224–225, 227
Transportation, improvements in,
    130–132, 215–216, 224–225.
    See also specific
Travis, William, 135
Trenton, Battle of, 75
Triangular trade, 47, 48
Truman, Harry S, 325
    administration of, 352–353
    Korean War and, 342
Truman Doctrine, 338
Trusts, 207–208
Truth, Sojourner, 154
Tubman, Harriet, 155, 187
Turkey, 338
Turner, Nat, 169
Tweed, William M., 216–217
Twelfth Amendment, 107
Twentieth Amendment, 300
Twenty-First Amendment, 295
Twenty-Second Amendment, 353
Tyler, John
    annexation of Texas and,
    161–162
    as president, 147–148

U-2 incident, 346
Underground Railroad, 154–155
Underwood Tariff (1913), 256
Unemployment, 209, 299
Unions. See Labor unions
Unitarians, 150
United Auto Workers (UAW), 305
United Mine Workers (UMW),
    304
United Nations, 335–336
    Israeli-Arab conflict and, 385
    Korean War and, 342
    Persian Gulf War and, 390
    recognition of China, 378–379
    Suez Canal conflict and, 345
Utah, 165–166

Valley Forge, 75, 77
Van Buren, Martin, 147
Vanderbilt, Cornelius, 206–207
Venezuela
 under Chávez, 407–408
 U.S. involvement in, 269, 270
Verrazano, Giovanni da, 22–23
Versailles, Treaty of, 279–280
 German resentment of,
  315–316
 ratification of, 281, 287
Vertical integration, 206
Vespucci, Amerigo, 19
Veto, 90–91
Vicksburg, Battle of, 188
Vietnam War, 367–371
 background on, 367–368
 cease-fire and withdrawal
  from, 371, 382
 opposition to, 368–369
Vikings, 18
Villa, Pancho, 258
Virginia, 27–28, 51–52, 174
 Civil War in, 182–184, 189–190
 House of Burgesses in, 28, 66
 Reconstruction in, 191
 in Revolutionary War, 78
 secession of, 181
Virginia Resolution, 106
Voting rights, 50, 142
 for African Americans, 233,
  234, 235
 property qualifications for, 142
 reforms in, 250–251
 for women, 249, 257

Wabash Railroad case, 238
Wagner Act (1935), 302, 303, 304
Waksman, Selman, 360
Wald, Lillian, 217
Walker, Mary Edwards, 187
Wallace, George, 369
Wallace, Henry A., 300, 353
War Hawks, 112
War of 1812, 113–115
 causes of, 112–113
 Jackson in, 142
War on Poverty, 366–367
Warren, Earl, 356–357
Warsaw Pact, 340, 391
Washington, Booker T., 249, 253
Washington, D.C., 100, 108
 abolition of slavery in, 172
 War of 1812 and, 114
Washington, George, 61–62
 as commander of Continental
  Army, 71, 72–73, 74–75, 79,
  83

as delegate to Constitutional
 Convention, 88
domestic developments under,
 99–103
as Federalist, 102–103
foreign affairs under, 103–104
Shays' Rebellion and, 87
slavery and, 153–154
Washington Naval Conference,
 312
Watergate crisis, 380–382, 394
Wayne, Anthony, 84, 112–113
Weapons of mass destruction
 (WMDs), 406
Weaver, James B., 241
Webster, Daniel, 145, 146
Welfare, 307, 416
Western settlements, 123–127
 cattle ranchers in, 225–226
 expansionism and, 112–113,
  126–127, 161–166
 exploration in, 161–166
 farmers in, 226–228
 mining in, 223–224
 Native Americans in, 127, 145,
  228–231
 transportation and communi-
  cation in, 224–225, 227
West Virginia, 181
Whaling, 46
Wheeler-Howard Act (1934), 307
Wheelwright, John, 31
Whigs, 161
 decline of, 99
 origin of, 146–147
Whiskey Rebellion, 101
Whitney, Eli, 128, 129, 130, 169
Wilderness Road, 123
Willard, Emma, 152
Williams, Roger, 30, 150
Wilson, Woodrow, 256–258
 in election of 1912, 255
 in election of 1916, 273
 Fourteen Points of, 279
 League of Nations and,
  280–282
 at Paris Peace Conference, 279
Wilson-Gorman Tariff, 237
Winthrop, John, 29
Woman's Christian Temperance
 Union, 149
Women
 in Civil War, 187–188
 colonist, 28
 education of, 152
 in humanitarian movements,
  148
 in labor unions, 210

Native-American, 12
new freedoms for, 295–296
in Revolutionary War, 71
rights of, 152–153, 249, 257
in temperance movement, 148
in workplace, 151, 152, 248
in World War I, 276
in World War II, 320.
 See also specific
Woolworth, F.W., 208
Worchester v. *Georgia,* 145
Workers' compensation, 255
Works Progress Administration
 (WPA), 302
World War I, 273–278
 airplanes in, 290
 American neutrality and, 275
 Europe after, 280
 home front in, 276–277
 outbreak of, 273–275
 peace conference following,
  279–281
 Western Front in, 277–278
World War II, 317–326
 African Americans in, 319
 allied victory in Europe and
  Africa, 321–324
 causes of, 314–316
 costs of, 333
 Pacific front in, 324–326
 postwar conferences and,
  333–336
 start of, 317–318
 U.S. home front in, 319–321
 U.S. neutrality in, 318–319
 Western Europe in, 318
 women in, 320
Wounded Knee, Battle of, 230
Wright brothers, 290
Writs of assistance, 65, 66
Wyoming, 249

XYZ Affair, 105–106

Yalta Conference (1945), 334, 350
Yeltsin, Boris, 391
Yorktown, Battle of, 78, 79
Young, Brigham, 166
Yugoslavia, 280
 Communist government in,
  337
 ethnic violence in, 391, 401
 in World War II, 318

Zenger, John Peter, 54–55
Zimmermann, Arthur, 276

PHOTO ACKNOWLEDGMENTS

We gratefully acknowledge the permission of the following persons and organizations to reproduce the prints and photographs in this book. Each bold number refers to the page number where the image appears in this book.

Cover photo: Gettysburg Battlefield, from Veer, Inc.

7: National Archives **10:** North Wind Picture Archives **13:** Boyer/Roger-Viollet/The Image Works **24:** Library of Congress **27, 31,** and **40:** North Wind **43:** Library of Congress **44:** North Wind **50:** Library of Congress **51:** North Wind **53:** New York Public Library **62:** *The American Revolution: A Pictorial Sourcebook*, by John Grafton (NY: Dover Publications, 1975) **67:** Corbis **69:** Library of Congress **71:** Library of Congress **74** and **87:** North Wind **88:** Virginia Museum of Fine Arts, Gift of Col. and Mrs. Garbisch **100:** Library of Congress **102** and **105:** The Granger Collection **108:** Library of Congress; **108 (inset):** Maryland Historical Society **111:** Corbis **115:** Library of Congress **127:** Woolaroc Museum, Bartlesville, Oklahoma **129** and **131:** North Wind **144:** Library of Congress **146** and **149:** Granger Collection **150:** North Wind **154:** Library of Congress **163** and **166:** North Wind **173:** Library of Congress **175:** New-York Historical Society **187:** Corbis **188:** Library of Congress **196:** North Wind **205:** National Archives **207, 211, 215,** and **217:** Library of Congress **224:** North Wind **225** and **229:** Library of Congress **235:** North Wind **238:** Culver Pictures **242:** Corbis **249** and **252:** Library of Congress **272:** North Wind **275:** Library of Congress **278:** The Granger Collection **290:** Topham Picturepoint/The Image Works **295 (both):** AP/Wide Word Photos **303:** Fred O. Seibel Editorial Cartoonist's Research Collection, MSS 2531, Special Collections, University of Virginia Library **305:** National Archives **319** and **320:** Library of Congress **335:** United Nations Photo **341:** National Archives **358:** Corbis **360** and **364:** National Archives **379, 384, 390,** and **391:** AP/Wide World Photos **399:** The White House **402:** Corbis **405:** AP/Wide World.